The United States
and the Philippines

STUDIES IN POLITICAL ECONOMY

General Editor: Bruce J. Berman

The United States and the Philippines

A STUDY OF NEOCOLONIALISM

Stephen Rosskamm Shalom

ISHI

A Publication of the
Institute for the Study of Human Issues
Philadelphia

Manufactured in the United States of America

Library of Congress Cataloging in Publication Data

Shalom, Stephen Rosskamm, 1948–
   The United States and the Philippines.

   (Studies in political economy)
   Bibliography: p.
   Includes index.
   1. United States—Foreign relations—Philippine
Islands. 2. Philippine Islands—Foreign relations—
United States. 3. Philippine Islands—Politics and
government. 4. Philippine Islands—Economic
conditions. I. Title. II. Series: Studies in political
economy (Philadelphia).
E183.8.P5S5   327.730599   80-29357
ISBN 0-89727-014-2   AACR1

For information, write:

Director of Publications
ISHI
3401 Science Center
Philadelphia, Pennsylvania 19104

To my parents,
Sarina and Albert

═ CONTENTS ═

= MAPS =

═ PREFACE ═

The rebirth of political economy over the past twenty years has deeply influenced the practice of historians and social scientists. Shaped equally by increasing social tension and turmoil in the Third World and the growing domestic crises of capitalist metropoles, political economy has been refreshed and reforged by a variety of perspectives, including dependency and underdevelopment theory and various schools of Marxism and neo-Marxism. From an era dominated by a liberal social science so secure in its hegemony that "capitalism," "class," and the "state" had all but disappeared from the vocabulary, we have moved to one in which these concepts and the problems they denote stand once again at the top of the agenda.

In the study of the periphery of the world capitalist system in Asia, Africa, and Latin America, attention has shifted—after a devastating critique of liberal theories of "modernization"—to the need for a theoretically rigorous understanding of the social forces at work and their interaction with external forces, particularly those of international capital and the advanced capitalist states. The prospectus of topics for both research and action is already vast and is still growing: agrarian crisis and the decay of peasant societies, processes of class formation and struggle, the growth of multinational corporate capital, technological innovation and transfer, the development of increasingly authoritarian and repressive states—to name a few. Behind them all lies a recognition that the last decades of the twentieth century are fraught with danger and opportunity: the danger of a descent into staggering inequality and exploitation, unprecedented totalitarian control and repression, or the final irrationality of a nuclear holocaust; and the opportunity to begin finally to move toward the humane, equitable, and democratic global society that has been often promised and never achieved.

To act against the dangers and for the opportunities requires understanding of both the universal social forces that sweep around the world and the particular forms of their local expression. *Studies in Political Economy* is a series that seeks to contribute to such an understanding through rigorous studies of the historical and contemporary development of capitalism. We hope that the series will range widely, and yet focus on the identification of the central forces and contradictions that determine patterns of crisis, struggle, and change. Without in any way seeking to promote a single "line" of analysis, the series will encourage efforts that give due weight to both structural determination and human agency, avoiding the alternative dangers of rigid determinism and naive voluntarism. This plan reflects a conviction that successful enquiry and effective action must be based on a proper balance between the two poles. We also believe that endeavours of this kind should be accompanied by the most open and active debate possible. For this reason suggestions are invited for the future development of the series, with a view to promoting a continuing dialogue on the vital issues with which it is concerned.

We are pleased to present as the first volume in the series *The United States and the Philippines: A Study of Neocolonialism* by Stephen Rosskamm Shalom. The most important former colony of the United States, the Philippines has been overshadowed in public and academic consciousness by the enormous scale and violence of American involvement elsewhere in Southeast Asia. However, as Shalom lucidly demonstrates, the Philippines has served in many ways as the testing ground for the economic, political, and military instruments of American imperialism in the Third World. Indeed, the early success in crushing and co-opting popular political forces and diverting reform into innocuous channels in the Philippines may well have encouraged the American counterinsurgency strategies that were later to fail so spectacularly in Vietnam and Cambodia.

Making full use of presidential, congressional, State Department, and military papers, Shalom reveals the remarkable degree to which American neocolonialism in the Philippines has been conscious and programmatic. Laid out before us we find not only the unequivocal evidence of conspiracy and covert action, but also the shared premises of ideology and interest that motivated American policymakers. Equally important, and of great theoretical interest, Shalom provides us with an outstanding case study of the process of class collaboration that is the cornerstone of neocolonialism, demonstrating how the United States politically and economically built up a local dominant class that would protect American interests. He shows as well how members of this class manipulated the relationship to their own profit, and even in many instances were able to move from collaboration with the United States to wartime collaboration with the Japanese and back again; and how the United States, having helped to create this class, has had to sustain it in its excesses. The consequences of this alliance of American and Philippine capital—growing profits for the few and increasingly desperate misery for the mass of the population—are sharply delineated. Finally, Shalom discloses how these processes culminated in the protracted cycle of widening violence and repression that marked Philippine politics in the recent period of "martial law." In so doing he contributes to our understanding of the pervasive crises of state and society throughout the Third World.

Bruce J. Berman

═══ ACKNOWLEDGMENTS ═══

I have incurred many debts in the course of writing this book and I would like to acknowledge them—however briefly—in the few paragraphs that follow.

David C. Forbes kindly granted me permission to quote from the papers and journals of W. Cameron Forbes. Thomas B. Buell generously allowed me to examine and quote from his papers on deposit at the Naval War College in Newport, Rhode Island. Numerous librarians and archivists gave of their time and expertise in helping me to locate materials. In this regard I would like to thank the staffs of the Truman, Eisenhower, MacArthur, and Kennedy Libraries, the National Archives, the Library of Congress, the Naval War College, Harvard, Princeton, and Boston Universities, and William Paterson College of New Jersey.

I am grateful to many individuals who assisted me in so many different ways. Howard Zinn, Arnold Offner, Boone Schirmer, Robert C. Rosen, Ben Kerkvliet, and Martin Weinstein read and commented on portions of the manuscript at its various stages. From my friends on the staff of the *Philippines Information Bulletin*—Marjorie Bakken, Barbara Cort, and Boone Schirmer—I learned a great deal. They also helped me in obtaining materials, as did Chibu Lagman, Vivian Rosskamm, and Edward Tawil. Cindy Ardolino and Evelyn Rosskamm Shalom gave me much practical assistance. My editors at ISHI, Doug Gordon and Peggy Gordon, have helped to sharpen the work and bring it from manuscript to book; it has been a pleasure working with them. None of these people bear responsibility for any errors in these pages, nor do they necessarily agree with any of my interpretations or conclusions. They deserve to share credit, however, for whatever merit the book may possess.

Evelyn, Jessica, and Alexander Rosskamm Shalom gave me the emotional sustenance without which this project would never have reached completion. I hope that I shall be able to reciprocate their patience and support.

Stephen Rosskamm Shalom

=== INTRODUCTION ===

In July 1969, President Richard M. Nixon spoke to newspeople on the island of Guam. "Whether we like it or not," he said,

> geography makes us a Pacific power. And when we consider, for example, that Indonesia at its closest point is only 14 miles from the Philippines, when we consider that Guam, where we are presently standing, of course, is in the heart of Asia, when we consider the interests of the whole Pacific as they relate to Alaska and Hawaii, we can all realize this.[1]

What is particularly interesting about this statement is that the Philippines, unlike Guam, Alaska, or Hawaii, was an independent nation. It had been independent since 1946, and the Philippine flag flew over its territory—or over most of it anyway. Yet apparently no reporter saw fit to challenge Nixon's assumption that the Philippines was part of the United States.[2] One suspects the press might have responded quite differently had China declared itself an African power by virtue of the fact that Kenya bordered on Tanzania, or had the Soviet Union declared itself a Latin American power because Haiti was so near Cuba.

Nixon's remarks were no doubt inadvertent, but they suggest that formal independence need not indicate a decisive break with the colonial past. As Nixon spoke, a Philippine Civic Action Group was aiding the U.S. war effort in Vietnam, U.S. bases on Philippine soil were providing the main logistical support for that war, and Philippine law granted investment privileges to U.S. capital. If at the same time the United States had exercised formal political sovereignty over the Philippines, one would have no trouble identifying the existence of a colonial relationship, but when strategic and economic domination coexist with legal independence, the relationship is not so easily recognized. It is this latter relationship which will be referred to here as neocolonialism.

It might seem that neocolonialism is an internally incoherent concept. With colonialism it is plain what is meant by one country ruling another, but where both parties are independent, one country dominates another only with the other's consent—in which case, it is not domination but sovereign choice. Neocolonialism, said British Foreign Secretary Alec Douglas-Home in 1964, "has no place in Britain's political dictionary. We quite simply do not know its meaning."[3] This confusion results from a misunderstanding about colonialism.

Colonialism is traditionally regarded as the rule of one country over another. But when defined in this way, strictly in terms of nation-states, the concept becomes hopelessly narrow. What does it mean to say that Britain ruled Jordan or India? Surely not that all the citizens of Britain ruled over all the citizens of these colonies. The factory workers of Manchester and Liverpool not only did not rule over the Hashemite monarch or the Indian rajahs, they lived under incomparably worse conditions. Nor is substituting "British government" or "British ruling classes" for "Britain" a sufficient emendation. In 1907, in areas of India encompassing 17.5 million people, there were only twenty-one British civil servants and twelve police officers.[4] This was possible only because the British had the cooperation of the Indian elite. The latter collaborated with the British—as junior partners to be sure, but as partners nonetheless—in ruling over the mass of the Indian population. The alliance was a symbiotic one. The Indian elite was able to maintain its position of local dominance, and the British elite acquired its greatest outlet for trade and investment. The interests of the two elites were not identical, but they were close enough to permit the mutually beneficial relationship to last for ninety years. Colonialism, then, must be viewed in class terms as well as in national terms.

Neocolonialism follows the same pattern. It shall be defined here as an alliance between the leading class or classes of two independent nations which facilitates their ability to maintain a dominant position over the rest of the population of the weaker of the two nations. This definition resolves the seeming contradiction between domination and consent, because the group being dominated is not the group giving the consent—a distinction that is lost if one views nations as homogeneous entities rather than as conglomerates of conflicting classes.

My aim in this book is to show that the relationship between the United States and the Philippines since 1946 has been a neocolonial one. I will try to describe how the relationship came about, what the mutual interests of the U.S. and the Philippine elites have been, what mechanisms have served these interests, and what impact neo-colonialism has had on the lives of most Filipinos.

The neocolonial relationship between the United States and the Philippines had its roots in the four decades of formal colonial rule.[5] From the beginning, U.S. policymakers sought to groom a Philippine governing class that would administer the islands while preserving American strategic and economic interests. Power was gradually transferred from American colonial officials to the Filipino elite. The latter were corrupt, reactionary, undemocratic, and unrepresentative, but what mattered to U.S. officials was that they were willing to cooperate with the United States. Nationalist public opinion prevented the elite from openly acknowledging its collaboration in the furtherance of U.S. aims, but American officials could separate the patriotic grandstanding from the private views of Philippine leaders, whose commitment to the United States and to the status quo was never doubted.[6]

And just to cement this commitment, the U.S. government provided the Philippine elite with preferential access to the American market for their export crops. This was a huge bonanza to the large landowners and their supporters in the government, but, as even U.S. officials acknowledged, little of this tremendous wealth filtered down to the majority of Filipinos.[7]

As Washington's "colonial experiment" went forward in the western Pacific, a potentially more important experiment was being conducted closer to home. Cuba, like the Philippines, had been a prize of the Spanish-American War, but unlike the Philippines, which was annexed by the United States, Cuba was granted its independence. It is significant, however, that U.S. interests did not suffer on this account. The Platt Amendment—which established the terms of independence—and periodic visits by the U.S. Marines were able as well as any colonial arrangement to protect U.S. capital and the American military base at Guantánamo. Indeed, from Washington's point of view the Cuban model—the neocolonial model—was more effective than traditional colonialism, for it avoided the necessity of a brutal war of conquest, which in the Philippines had cost over 4,000 American lives.

The suggestion to "treat the Philippines like Cuba" was made by some U.S. policymakers almost from the beginning,[8] but it was not until the Great Depression—which made the economic and social costs of empire too burdensome—that Washington was willing to set a date for Philippine independence.[9] The Tydings-McDuffie Act of 1934 provided for the establishment of a Philippine Commonwealth, to be followed by independence ten years later. The Japanese invasion of the islands intervened before the end of the Commonwealth period, but following the American reconquest independence was granted on schedule.

The years surrounding the achieving of independence are crucial for any nation. It is in this embryonic state that the patterns and possibilities for the future are largely determined. This was especially true in the case of the Philippines, where the interruption of World War II provided an unprecedented opportunity for the restructuring or redirecting of Philippine society on the one hand, or a restoration of the prewar status quo on the other. The first two chapters of this book examine the critical years immediately following the end of World War II. Chapter One shows how the policies of U.S. officials in the Philippines restored the prewar elite to power. Chapter Two examines the legislation drawn up in Washington to define the terms of Philippine independence and demonstrates how U.S. economic and strategic interests were preserved. Together these chapters describe the genesis of the neocolonial relationship between the United States and the Philippines.

In the early 1950s, the stability of the regime in Manila plummeted to an all-time low, and the entire neocolonial structure threatened to come undone. Chapters Three and Four deal with the accelerated levels of U.S. intervention in Philippine affairs in response to this crisis. They describe the activities of covert operatives and military advisers and the programs of economic and military assistance emanating from Washington. It was a major vindication of the neocolonial approach that relative calm could be restored without committing U.S. troops.

As the crisis receded, the instruments of neocolonial control were cut back but not withdrawn. Chapter Five examines the various continuing military and economic aid programs by·which Washington has attempted to further its own interests and those of its allies among the Philippine elite. These aid programs have not been unique to the U.S.-Philippine relationship; rather, they have been the standard tools by which the United States has sought to maintain its neocolonial empire in much of Latin America and Asia.

Understanding—no less evaluating—neocolonialism in the Philippines requires an examination of its impact upon the lives of most Filipinos. Chapter Six documents the staggering poverty and, what is more tragic, the negligible improvement over time in the well-being of the majority of the population, who are the victims of the alliance between the American and Philippine elites.

In September 1972 martial law was declared in the Philippines. While the martial law period marked in certain respects the end of an era, it has been characterized by a large measure of continuity. Chapter Seven discusses the origins of martial law and demonstrates that the neocolonial relationship, though modified, remains intact. Moreover, the chapter shows that the living standards of the Philippine people have been stagnating if not declining.

In the pages that follow, then, it will be argued that the concept of neocolonialism is appropriate for describing the relationship between the United States and the Philippines. Like all concepts, neocolonialism is an abstraction, but it has had very real consequences for the people of the Philippines.

Major Cities of the Philippines

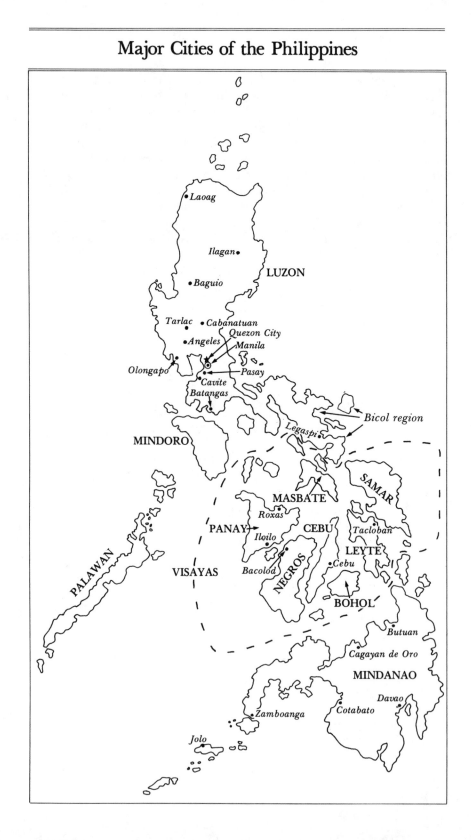

CHAPTER ONE

The Restoration, 1944–1946

For three years during World War II, Japan replaced the United States as the colonial master of the Philippines. Japanese authorities attempted to enlist the support of the Filipino elite in administering the archipelago, just as Washington had successfully done during its four decades of colonial rule.

The Filipino elite accepted the Japanese occupation with alacrity. Four months before the surrender of the last American and Filipino forces at Bataan, leading Philippine politicians were organized by the Japanese into a Provisional Council of State. In October 1943 the Japanese established a nominally independent "Philippine Republic," again with the cooperation of the elite. The last secretary of justice, Jose P. Laurel, served as president. Another 6 of the 11 members of the prewar cabinet, 10 of 24 senators, and about one-third of the 98 representatives served in key posts under the Japanese. The members of the Supreme Court and the Court of Appeals were basically the same during the occupation as during the Commonwealth, and some 80 percent of the officers of the Philippine Army held positions in the Japanese-sponsored Philippine Constabulary. Sixteen of the 46 provincial governors in 1943–1944 had been governors of the same province in 1940.

The collaboration of the Filipino elite with the Japanese took an economic form as well. Many Filipinos became buy-and-sell agents—middlepeople who provided the Japanese with war materials and other needed goods. Some new fortunes were made in this manner, but previous wealth provided one with a good start in this line of

1

work. Perhaps the most prominent economic collaborator was Vicente Madrigal. A close personal friend of the Philippine president, he had become one of the richest people in the islands during World War I by supplying German raiders with fuel and food. He had been affiliated with the Japanese Mitsubishi interests and was elected to the Senate in 1941. During the Japanese occupation he protected and enhanced his economic fortune by selling goods to the Japanese. "He will change to whatever side seems to be winning," reported an American intelligence agent.[1]

The Philippine collaboration issue has been debated heatedly for many years and will not be analyzed in depth here, but the following brief remarks are in order. Contrary to what some U.S. officials maintained, the Philippine elite did not undergo a sudden conversion to treason. What was involved was rather a continuation of the policy that the elite had been following for at least four decades, namely, collaborating with the colonial power in return for political office and other rewards. An elite which had placed its interests and the interests of a foreign country above those of its own people had no trouble when the Japanese replaced the Americans. The name of whom they were collaborating with changed, but the basic policy did not.

Under the assumption—not unreasonable in early 1942—that the war would end in some kind of compromise settlement in the Pacific, the surest way for the elite to guarantee itself political and economic influence in the postwar Philippines was by cooperating with the Japanese. As the tide of war shifted in favor of the United States, however, the elite began to hedge its bets by establishing contacts with some guerrilla groups and American intelligence networks and giving them some assistance.[2]

It was the desire to maintain power that motivated elite collaboration. In general, duress was not a factor.[3] Nor was the later collaborationist claim that they were only concerned with the welfare of the population particularly convincing. Consider the collaborators' own prime example of their altruism. In September 1944 the Japanese-sponsored Philippine Republic declared war on the United States and Great Britain. The collaborators have contended that here they performed their greatest service to the Philippine people because they were able to prevent the Japanese from conscripting Filipinos into the military. In fact, however, the evidence clearly indicates that the Japanese did not intend to draft Filipinos. The Japanese did not have sufficient logistic support to supply even their own troops in the Philippines, and, more important, they did not wish to provide weapons to unreliable Filipino troops who might give them to the guerrillas or even turn the arms against the Japanese. Indeed, one American guerrilla officer has stated that he tried to get Laurel to convince the Japanese to arm Philippine troops, for he knew that the weapons would be used against the Japanese.[4] Japanese fears of arming the population after less than three years of controlling the islands were not at all surprising. Some U.S. officials had been apprehensive about arming Filipinos as late as the mid-1930s, after more than three decades of U.S. rule. And, as a Japanese official reminded a prominent Filipino collaborator in 1943, although Japan had controlled Korea for over thirty years, there was still no conscription there.[5]

While much of the elite was collaborating with the Japanese, a large number of Filipinos joined guerrilla groups. Many of these groups were recognized by the U.S. Army Forces in the Far East and they became known as USAFFE guerrillas. These units were led in part by American officers who had eluded the Japanese after the surrenders at Bataan and Corregidor, but principally by members of the Filipino elite, who had been the only people able to afford military schools and Reserve Officers' Training Corps (ROTC) programs before the war. Tomas Confesor, Alfredo Montelibano, and Ruperto Kangleon were prominent examples of elite guerrilla leaders. A large component of the USAFFE rank-and-file was made up of men from the prewar Philippine Constabulary and Philippine Scouts.[6]

One of the largest autonomous guerrilla organizations was that formed by the dissident peasants of Central Luzon, the area of the country with the highest rate of land tenancy. In the last years before the outbreak of the war, class conflict in the Central Luzon countryside had become increasingly intense. Militant peasants had been organized into left-wing unions, while the landlords and the pro-landlord politicians had employed escalating force against them. The Constabulary was used as one tool of repression; groups of strike-breakers were organized as another. Governor Sotero Baluyot set up the Cawal ng Kapayapaan (Knights of Peace) as one such group in the province of Pampanga. In 1940 socialist leader Pedro Abad Santos ran against Baluyot for governor. Though more than 50 percent of his followers were illiterate and thus disqualified from voting, and though the province was placed under the equivalent of martial law immediately prior to and during the election, Abad Santos polled 45 percent of the votes. In eight of the twenty-one towns of the province, socialists were elected as mayors.[7]

In March 1942, after the Japanese invasion, left-wing labor and peasant leaders and intellectuals established a People's Anti-Japanese Army, the Hukbalahap (Huks for short). The prewar peasant unions provided the mass base for the guerrilla force. On paper, the Hukbalahap was controlled by the Communist Party of the Philippines (PKP), but the reality was quite different. For example, when the PKP called for a policy of "retreat for defense," many in the Huks, including some PKP peasant leaders, refused to go along.[8]

At the beginning of the war, the Huks were denied arms by General Douglas MacArthur. They contacted the head USAFFE officer in Central Luzon, Colonel Thorpe, and offered to cooperate with him, but Thorpe took the attitude that unless the Huks would submit entirely to him he would not work with them.[9] The Huks refused; gathering weapons from American soldiers before they surrendered, from deserters, and from the dead of both sides, they forged an effective anti-Japanese fighting force. Estimates of Huk strength vary, but 10,000 is a reasonable approximation of their number in most of 1943 and in 1944.[10] Their base of support was many times larger.

In addition to armed attacks on the Japanese, a key element of Huk strategy was denying to the Japanese access to the rice harvest of Central Luzon. Within Huk-controlled territory, village elections were held in which everyone eighteen years old and over could vote, and in many cases a jury system for administering justice was set up, a practice that had not been part of the Philippine court system.[11]

It was perhaps inevitable that the war could not submerge the previous animosities in Central Luzon. Clashes between USAFFE guerrillas and Huks occurred frequently. The USAFFEs charged that the Huks were doing communistic political organizing, and the Huks accused the USAFFEs of backing the landed gentry and of mistreating the peasants. The encounters between the Huks and the USAFFEs became increasingly bitter. At times the latter gave active assistance to the Japanese in unsuccessful efforts to eliminate the Huks.[12]

As the defeat of the Japanese became more obvious in 1944, many collaborating officials began to make contacts with USAFFE leaders. This was a way both to side with the winner and to get allies for any postwar conflicts with the Huks. Many people, including a large number who had been part of the Japanese-controlled Constabulary, joined or formed USAFFE units in the last months of the war in order to get on the right side. Even after the Japanese surrender in August 1945, guerrilla units were still being organized. There were so many of these eleventh-hour guerrillas that one out of nine Luzon residents later claimed to have been a guerrilla. "Even the pickpockets," observed one American counterintelligence agent, "were organized into a guerrilla force."[13]

In October 1944 U.S. troops landed on the Philippine island of

Leyte. "I have returned," proclaimed General Douglas MacArthur. "By the grace of Almighty God, our forces stand again on Philippine soil."[14] MacArthur's return was not simply a wartime reconquest; he and his staff were returning to their prewar home, where they had been members of or associated with Manila's elite. MacArthur himself was the son of Arthur MacArthur, a veteran officer of the Philippine campaign some forty years before in charge of suppressing Philippine nationalism. Douglas had served in the islands as a second lieutenant in 1903–1904, as a brigadier general commanding the Philippine Division from 1922 to 1925, and as a major general and commanding officer of the Philippine Department from 1928 to 1930. In 1930 he had returned to Washington to serve as chief of staff of the Army, where he achieved considerable notoriety when he took charge of the dispersal of protesting veterans. In 1935 he became military adviser to Commonwealth President Manuel L. Quezon. In the latter post he was given the specially created title of field marshal in the Philippine Army and a salary which, together with his army pay, was higher than that of either Philippine President Quezon or the American high commissioner.[15]

During his years in the islands, MacArthur developed close personal ties with upper-class Filipinos. Unlike many Americans living in Manila, MacArthur was willing to associate with and befriend Filipinos, but very few nonelite Filipinos were included among his friends. He became particularly close to Quezon, who in 1938 served as godfather to his son. When Quezon became seriously ill in April 1944, he wrote to MacArthur giving him—rather than Vice-President Sergio Osmeña—full power and authority to act in his behalf on all matters affecting the government of the Philippines. Other close prewar friends of MacArthur included prominent politico Manuel Roxas, influential newspaper editor Carlos P. Romulo, and the extremely wealthy Joaquin "Mike" Elizalde. He had also been friendly with Jose P. Laurel, who became president of the wartime Philippine Republic.[16] In addition, MacArthur had economic interests in the Philippines; he had been an officer and stockholder of the Manila Hotel Company and probably owned shares of stock in Andres Soriano's mining firms.[17]

Soriano was a member of MacArthur's wartime staff and one of the richest people in the islands. As a Spanish citizen, he had been a leader of the Spanish Falangist movement in the Philippines and had contributed in his first gift alone half a million pesos to the Franco cause. Before Franco's victory, he had acted as the Falangist consul in Manila until Washington warned him that he was violating the Espionage Act. When the United States recognized Franco's government in 1938, Soriano reassumed the title "Representative of the Spanish State." During these years, according to U.S. government sources, he "enjoyed high social standing in Manila" and was "favored with attentions and considerations by a number of U.S. Army officers . . . even during the period of his more intense Falange activities."[18] Soriano had ties to the Philippine elite as well; he was, for example, a generous financial backer of Quezon and a friend and business associate of Manuel Roxas.[19]

In 1941 Soriano had put his devotion to Franco second to his own fortune; it was unclear whether the United States was going to freeze the accounts of Spaniards as Axis nationals, so Soriano acquired Philippine citizenship. When the Japanese invaded, Soriano escaped to the United States and served as secretary of finance for the government-in-exile. While in the States, he laid private plans for postwar economic activities in the Philippines in association with some American businesspeople. In late 1943 he foresaw the imminent American return to the islands and was anxious to be one of the first back, so that he might further his financial interests. He got Quezon to ask MacArthur if he might serve on the general's staff, and MacArthur was glad to comply. Secretary of the Interior Harold Ickes opposed permitting Soriano to return to active duty, where he could influence the character of the Philippine government, but the War Department overruled Ickes. Later, in 1945, Soriano switched to U.S. citizenship, with MacArthur as one of his sponsoring witnesses. In October 1945 MacArthur awarded Soriano a Silver Star for gallantry in action three and a half years earlier.[20]

MacArthur's chief of staff was Richard Sutherland. Termed "a natural-born autocrat" by MacArthur, Sutherland favored instituting a dictatorship in the United States during wartime. Chief of intelligence was Charles Willoughby, a friend of Soriano who shared his high regard for Franco.[21] And Courtney Whitney was in charge of civil affairs in the Philippines. Later to become the general's confidant, chief spokesperson, and biographer, Whitney had been a prominent lawyer in Manila before the war and had considerable investments in the islands. He was, Quezon confided in 1943, "well-known among the Filipinos as reactionary and imperialistic."[22]

The ties between U.S. military officials and the Philippine elite had been firmly cemented on embattled Corregidor in February 1942. Quezon, with Roxas as a witness and with Washington's knowledge, secretly transferred $640,000 in Commonwealth funds to the accounts of MacArthur ($500,000), Sutherland ($75,000), and two other American officers.[23]

On June 29, 1944, Franklin Roosevelt had declared with regard to the Philippines: "Those who have collaborated with the enemy must be removed from authority and influence over the political and economic life of the country; and the democratic form of government guaranteed in the Constitution of the Philippines must be restored for the benefit of the people of the islands."[24] MacArthur, Soriano, Sutherland, Willoughby, Whitney: these were among the people charged with the mission of eliminating collaborators and restoring democracy. That instead they would restore the elite to power should not be surprising.

With MacArthur when he waded ashore on the beach of Leyte was Sergio Osmeña. As vice-president, Osmeña had been evacuated from the Philippines in early 1942, along with Commonwealth President Quezon, after a U.S. official had advised Washington that Quezon might reach an accommodation with Japan.[25] In the United States, Quezon and Osmeña constituted a Commonwealth government-in-exile, and when the former died in August 1944 Osmeña had succeeded to the presidency.

Three days after the Leyte invasion, the Commonwealth government was officially reestablished. Throughout the next months, as territory was cleared of Japanese troops, MacArthur formally turned it over to Osmeña. The U.S. Army's Philippine Civil Affairs Units (PCAUs), however, continued to function in these areas. A month after the February 27, 1945, ceremonies in Manila, at which MacArthur restored full constitutional government to the Filipinos, the U.S. consul general in Manila reported: "General MacArthur made it very clear that up to the present time practically all important decisions with respect to the local government had been made by the Army; although great care had been taken to ensure that the nominal authority for enforcement was given to the Commonwealth Government." On August 22, 1945, MacArthur announced that all participation by the U.S. Army in the civil administration of the Philippines would be discontinued by September 1.[26]

There were many tensions between MacArthur and Osmeña, but there was at least one thing they did agree on: the government they were reestablishing was that which had existed before the war. On October 23, 1944, MacArthur announced that all the laws and regulations of the Commonwealth were in full force and legally binding on all persons in areas of the Philippines free from Japanese control.[27]

Even prior to the Leyte landing this view had been made clear when a high U.S. military official wrote to the Hukbalahap that "any organization which fails to cooperate will be regarded by incoming troops as unlawful armed bands" and that the "United States Army does not recognize any political aims or ambitions, and it is the position that in time of war, the only political activity which is legal is political activity aimed at the maintenance of the loyalty of the masses to the established and legal existing government."[28]

The Huks had been the most effective anti-Japanese guerrilla group on the island of Luzon, and in the campaign to rid the island of Japanese forces the Huks made a major military contribution.[29] Despite the dire warnings in military intelligence reports that the Huks would attack U.S. troops, they eagerly welcomed the Americans. In January 1945, when the Huks liberated the towns of Cabiao and Tarlac (in the provinces of Nueva Ecija and Tarlac, respectively), they hoisted U.S. flags along with those of the Philippines.[30] Nevertheless, when the U.S. Army entered villages or municipalities in which the Huks had established local governments, American and Commonwealth officials refused to recognize them. The Huk governments were replaced—with the support of American arms—by people selected by the PCAUs, often USAFFE guerrilla leaders. In Talavera, Nueva Ecija, for example, the United States appointed Carlos Nocum, a USAFFE leader who had been expelled from the Huks for allegedly stealing from peasants and whom the Huks suspected of having ties to Filipinos in the Japanese-sponsored government. The PCAU-selected officials were soon replaced with Osmeña's own choices: old-line politicians with mixed war records.[31]

The elite was to have over two years to firmly entrench itself in local politics, because until November 1947 all municipal offices were filled by appointment from Manila. For example, in September 1945 the Huks and others denounced the appointment of Jose Robles, Jr., as governor of Nueva Ecija—a position he held during the occupation. He had been a prewar politician from a wealthy, landed family. When he finally left office to face charges of criminal acts committed while collaborating with the Japanese, he was replaced by Juan Chioco, who had served under Robles during the war and was implicated in the same crimes. In November 1945 Chioco too was replaced, but again by someone who had served under the Japanese. Under each appointee, the peasants charged there were abuses and repression.[32]

In addition to dismantling the local Huk governments, the U.S. Army, along with the USAFFE units which were under U.S. jurisdiction, proceeded to disarm Huk squadrons at gunpoint and to imprison their leaders. The Hukbalahaps, according to the official explanation, were not bona fide guerrillas but armed civilians. One Huk commander, Silvestre Liwanag, had joined with U.S. and USAFFE troops in mopping up western Pampanga and Bataan. At the conclusion of the fighting, he and his unit were disarmed and taken into custody. Wartime clashes between Huks and USAFFEs were continuing, exacerbated by the presence in USAFFE ranks of numerous eleventh-hour guerrillas eager to absolve themselves in the eyes of the Americans for their service in the Japanese-sponsored Constabulary by an excessive display of anticommunism. On February 7, 1945, over one hundred Huks were massacred by USAFFE guerrillas.[33]

Although some Huks were disarmed, MacArthur was not eager to enforce a total collection of all unauthorized weapons. He considered this to be a Commonwealth matter, and he feared that he might provoke "most violent reactions." "If it becomes the white man against the Filipino we will have another insurrection with all Filipinos finally crystalizing against us." However, in MacArthur's view, the guerrillas posed "absolutely no menace to our armed forces"—which was quite true.[34] In mid-July 1945 Major General J. A. Lester of the U.S. Military Police Command stated that no action would be taken "at this time to carry out a general program of disarming guerrillas by armed forces" since there were still Japanese stragglers.[35]

In mid-March 1945 two high-ranking Huk leaders, Luis Taruc and Casto Alejandrino, were released from prison after mass demonstrations. American and Filipino officials had apparently hoped that these freed leaders would persuade their followers to turn in their weapons, for when this did not happen they were rearrested in early April. In the words of a Philippine Army officer instrumental in the later anti-Huk campaign. "The people of Pampanga then petitioned General MacArthur and President Osmeña to recognize the civil officials and the local government set up by the Communists [i.e., the Huks]. As expected, the petition was ignored."[36]

In the meantime, Osmeña was setting up his national-level government. Some of his appointees had been guerrilla leaders during the war, the most prominent being Tomas Confesor, who was named secretary of the interior in February 1945, and Alfredo Montelibano, who was given the post of secretary of national defense in July. But though the two had been part of the guerrilla movement during the war, they were not men of the people. Confesor, as prewar governor of Iloilo province, had used terror and strikebreakers against striking sugarcane workers.[37] And Montelibano was a millionaire sugar baron. Within a month of his appointment as defense secretary he confiscated for himself 12,000 piculs (800 tons) of sugar as partial repayment for sugar he lost to the Japanese[38]—as though no one else had suffered any losses during the war.

Other Osmeña appointees had collaborated with the Japanese. Osmeña himself, of course, had been in the United States for the duration of the war, but the collaborators were his friends and the allies he would need if he was to retain control of the government. Also, the fact that his sons were accused of being economic collaborators must have lessened any inclination Osmeña might have had to deal harshly with collaborators.

One of the first actions taken by the American forces upon landing in the Philippines had been the rounding up of those who had collaborated with the Japanese. On December 30, 1944, MacArthur issued a proclamation stating his policy with regard to these people:

> Whereas, evidence is before me that certain Citizens of the Philippines voluntarily have given aid, comfort and sustenance to the enemy in violation of allegiance due the Governments of the United States and the Commonwealth of the Philippines ... Now therefore I, Douglas MacArthur ... hereby do publish and declare it to be my purpose to remove such persons, when apprehended, from any position of political and economic influence in the Philippines and hold them in restraint for the duration of the war; whereafter I shall release them to the Philippine Government for its judgment upon their respective cases.[39]

This statement had two important implications. First, as the U.S. Central Intelligence Agency later noted, MacArthur's action "in effect established a policy of leaving prosecution of those charged with collaboration entirely to the Philippine Government." Second, the proclamation protected the collaborators from popular wrath while passions had a chance to subside. Resistance leaders were clamoring for the punishment of those who had aided the Japanese; if the alleged collaborators had not been incarcerated by the United States, they might well have met the same fate as, for example, officials of the Vichy collaborationist government. One contemporary observed that, since MacArthur's proclamation protected collaborators from immediate reprisal "it will not be surprising to see many of them— including members of Jose Laurel's puppet cabinet—seeking sanctuary behind the American lines as soon as they can elude their Japanese masters."[40]

This remark proved prescient. In April 1945 a number of cabinet officers of the Japanese-sponsored Republic made their way to American-held territory near Baguio. The *Manila Free Philippines*, printed by the Office of War Information under strict military censorship, reported that MacArthur had announced the *capture* of four cabinet members but the *rescue* of Manuel Roxas. This was a peculiar distinction, for Roxas had been a minister without portfolio in the Laurel cabinet. The *Free Philippines* article provided some background on Roxas but omitted all mention of this and other posts he had held under the Japanese.[41]

Roxas had been, after Quezon and Osmeña, the most prominent politician in the Commonwealth government. He had married into the extremely wealthy de Leon family and had been the senior member in the law firm that represented most of the Soriano interests.[42] His personal friendships with MacArthur and Soriano have already been noted. When the war broke out, MacArthur appointed Roxas as an officer in the U.S. Army to serve as his liaison with Quezon. Roxas fought at Bataan and Corregidor and then aided the guerrillas on the southern island of Mindanao until he was captured by the Japanese. Released shortly afterward, he remained in his home until the middle of 1943, when he helped draft the constitution for the Japanese-sponsored republic and was one of twenty signers of the document. In April 1944 Roxas became chairperson of the Economic Planning Board and, on April 14, assumed the concurrent position of chairperson of the board of directors of the government rice collection agency. On August 25, 1944, President of the Republic Laurel assigned Roxas the rank of minister-without-portfolio in his cabinet.[43] In September 1944 Roxas advised Laurel that if the Japanese asked for a declaration of war against the United States he should comply.[44] While holding these various positions, Roxas was also in contact with a number of guerrilla leaders and U.S. and Filipino intelligence agents.[45] The Japanese were apparently aware of these activities but felt that it was nevertheless useful to keep Roxas in the government; his national reputation enhanced the prestige of the collaborationist regime, and his death would only provide the resistance movement with its most widely known martyr. In 1942 the Japanese had distributed an appeal under Roxas's name, calling on guerrillas to surrender. Roxas claimed after the war that this was done without his permission, but the fact that he later accepted posts in the Japanese-sponsored government surely lent authority to the appeal.[46]

In short, Roxas had played both sides during the war, as had many members of the elite. However, his strategy for maintaining political influence in the postwar period involved a mix of collaboration with the Japanese and the Americans that was different from that used by, for example, Laurel. By 1941 it had been evident that Quezon had chosen Roxas as his political heir. Laurel, if he wanted to be able to challenge Quezon or Roxas for the postwar presidency, had to choose the risky course of accepting the top position under the Japanese; this would have worked out well had the war ended in some sort of Pacific compromise, but a U.S. victory turned it into a losing strategy. Roxas had in fact been offered the presidency by the Japanese, but he turned it down, recommending Laurel in his place.[47] With a proper balance of support for both sides, Roxas could avoid committing himself before the outcome of the war was certain and thus maximize his chances of postbellum influence. It is quite likely that had Japan won the war Roxas would have had a good shot at becoming president.

In any event, in 1945 Roxas was not treated like other high officials in the Japanese-sponsored government who had engaged in similar contacts with guerrillas and U.S. intelligence agents. While these people were all arrested, Roxas was flown by special plane to MacArthur, who greeted him with a bear hug. Roxas was then assigned to active duty in the intelligence section of MacArthur's general staff.[48]

What accounted for this differential treatment? MacArthur's headquarters stated that Roxas, unlike the others, had held a commission in the U.S. Army, making him an American officer rather than a Philippine collaborator. But this was not very convincing, for General Guillermo Francisco was arrested even though he too had a commission in the U.S. Army.[49] And the various intelligence reports that labeled Roxas as a "reluctant" collaborator and loyal to the U.S. did not provide a basis for treating him differently, for some of those arrested had been reported similarly loyal by intelligence agents.[50]

What Roxas did have in his favor was his close friendship with MacArthur and his staff. Roxas had been a party to the transfer of money to MacArthur and Sutherland. According to State Department officials, Roxas was said to be especially popular with officers of the U.S. Army who had financial interests in the Philippines, such as Whitney and Soriano; Soriano was reported to be one of Roxas "closest associates." At the end of March 1945 it was Soriano and MacArthur's military secretary, Brigadier General Bonner Fellers, who had prepared a memorandum on, among other things, Roxas's loyalty to the U.S.; it is not surprising that the evidence they looked at pictured Roxas as "completely loyal."[51]

United States military officials appreciated Roxas's administrative ability and were eager to see him obtain a powerful position in the Philippine government. His one real challenger for power, Osmeña, though having a long history of serving U.S. interests, was

aging and felt to be lacking in vigor; in addition, he had crossed
MacArthur by opposing the latter's plans for the military defense of
the Philippines back in 1936.[52]

The special treatment accorded Roxas had two important consequences. First, it thoroughly obfuscated the issue of collaboration,
for if Roxas was not a collaborator than were not Laurel and the
others innocent as well? Second, the unilateral exoneration of Roxas
provided the collaborators as a whole with an influential champion.[53]

Whether MacArthur had foreseen this is impossible to know,
but even if he had not, it is clear that his action was the result of the
natural affinity between U.S. officials and the Philippine elite. It was
not accidental that the special treatment was given to a person of
wealth and power, for such were the people that the American authorities had been collaborating with for years.

In early April 1945 Harry Truman had succeeded to the presidency upon the death of Roosevelt. Osmeña was in Washington at the
time, and Truman assured him that independence would be granted
to the Philippines as soon as practicable. During the war the U.S.
Congress had passed a bill allowing the American president to advance the date of Philippine independence. This legislation had considerable propaganda use; it was a reason to trust and rally to the
United States, as Filipinos were told during the U.S. reconquest of the
islands.[54] But it had no practical effect, for, in the words of Secretary
of War Henry L. Stimson, the United States was determined

> that certain relations between the two nations should be settled before
> they severed their relationship. It was much easier to negotiate in the
> flush of the good relations of the war and the victory. If we waited
> until after they were separate, then we should have the delays and
> formalities of diplomatic procedure.

In particular, said Stimson, the rights of Americans in the Philippines ought to be adjusted before independence. By mid-June 1945
the press reported that the plan to push forward Philippine independence had been virtually abandoned.[55]

But though independence was not going to be advanced, neither
was it going to be postponed past July 4, 1946, the date specified by
the Tydings-McDuffie Act of 1934. Despite the pleas by some U.S.
business interests in the islands to put off independence for five or
ten years, the United States and Truman were committed to ending
colonialism. There was concern, the U.S. Office of Strategic Services
(OSS) noted, that any deviation from the independence goal, however

slight, "may be seized upon by other colonial powers as an excuse for maintaining the colonial status in the Far East."[56] The kind of independence planned, however, was in the neocolonial pattern. Truman's goal, as recorded in his memoirs, was to make the Philippines "as free as we had made Cuba." In September 1945 Truman appointed Paul McNutt high commissioner to the Philippines. In addition to having tried to promote a "re-examination" of Philippine independence while high commissioner before the war, McNutt had publicly recommended the postponement of Philippine independence in late March 1945.[57] He was certainly the appropriate choice for making the Philippines as free as Cuba.

In the meantime, events had been progressing in the Philippines. In June 1945, at MacArthur's urging, Osmeña called the Philippine Congress into session. Those who had been elected to the legislature back in 1941 who were not dead or being detained by the U.S. Army for collaboration came to Manila to take their seats.[58] Not all who had held positions under the Japanese were in U.S. custody, however, for at least 8 of the 14 available senators and 19 of the 67 available representatives had served in some post during the occupation.[59] At least two senators had been released by the army in order to allow them to attend the sessions of Congress.[60]

At the first meeting, Roxas was elected president of the Senate. To the senators, Roxas was the obvious choice to be their leader. Aside from his prewar prominence, it was clear that he would not take a hard line against collaborators. On the first day of the Senate session he declared that only those who had remained in the Philippines during the war could be aware that "everyone fought back." He knew no one in the legislature, he stated some days later, who could justly be charged with collaboration. Indeed, a Roxas newspaper was soon to claim that collaboration was "nothing but a myth."[61]

In late August 1945 MacArthur began turning over to the Commonwealth the alleged collaborators that he was holding, including seven senators and seven representatives. Under pressure from the Congress, Osmeña allowed those who could afford it to be released on bail, thus enabling them to influence Philippine politics again.[62]

Whatever their war records, however, all the legislators were members of the elite and had the same disregard for the well-being of the population that had characterized the Filipino elite in the prewar years. This was most convincingly demonstrated when they passed a bill giving to each legislator 31,600 pesos back pay for the period January 1942 to February 1945, when the Congress was unable to meet. Twenty members of Congress had served in the Japanese-sponsored Assembly, but the bill did not prevent them from collecting back pay as well. Lesser government officials and personnel, however, were to receive only up to three months back pay, provided they had not served the Japanese. Osmeña scolded Congress for passing this legislation, but he did not veto it.[63] A rally called to protest the back-pay bill was denied a permit.[64]

In August, Representative Manuel V. Gallego, head of the Ways and Means Committee, proposed a bill to give various tax benefits to landowners. "Those who suffered most during this war," he declared, "are precisely the owners of big landed estates. . . ." To those who had a grudge against the landed class he said, "Who is supporting this government . . . the have-nots class or the capitalists class?"[65] Gallego did not mention that he was reported to have engaged in buying and selling rice on the black market during the war; since before the war, he apparently had not dared return to the province he represented in the Congress, because of the hostility of the people toward him.[66]

As president of the Senate, Roxas was ex officio chairperson of the powerful Joint Commission on Appointments. All those whom Osmeña wished to appoint to office had to be approved by this body. Dominated as it was by those tainted with collaboration, the legislative branch was able to deny high office to staunch anticollaborationists. The first test came in late June. Two Osmeña cabinet officers, Tomas Confesor and Tomas Cabili, had been vocal critics of collaboration and of Roxas in particular and had to be confirmed by the joint commission. But just before it could act on them, Osmeña backed down and withdrew their names. In mid-July, Osmeña nominated eleven judges to the Supreme Court. The commission confirmed the three who had held office during the occupation and rejected the others.[67]

It may seem that the situation was simply one of a collaborationist Congress stymieing a weak anticollaborationist president, but things were more complicated. Roxas had told his supporters, even before the Congress was convened, to launch his campaign for the presidency.[68] The Filipino elite was engaging in its traditional struggle for office, and the collaboration issue was an instrument of this struggle. Thus, when Osmeña nominated as his secretary of commerce and agriculture a man who had held office in the Laurel government, the Commission on Appointments temporarily blocked the appointment. The reason for both the nomination and the obstruction was that the man was known to be a devoted Osmeña follower. (Once in office, he also came to be known as a crook when he sold government property to the black market.[69]) And while it was true that the Commission on Appointments selectively confirmed justices for the high court, it was also true that the three approved collaborators had been chosen by Osmeña.

Another indication of the role played by the struggle for office was the case of Tomas Cabili. Realizing that his political fortunes would be greatly enhanced if the collaborators were discredited, he sharply attacked Roxas, although some months earlier he had publicly declared that Roxas's "patriotism and love of country cannot be questioned."[70]

Osmeña revealed his true position when Congress ended its session. Now he would no longer need legislative confirmation for his appointees, and he proceeded to remove Roxas supporters and replace them with his own followers. Not infrequently this involved replacing noncollaborators with collaborators.[71] By March 1946, 5 of 11 Supreme Court justices—all Osmeña appointees—had held judicial positions under the Japanese and 16 of 47 governors that Osmeña selected had collaborated, while only 8 had had a clear connection with the underground movement.[72]

Osmeña's campaign strategy involved a number of components. First, he wished to avoid an open break with Roxas, for Osmeña was still head of the Nacionalista party, to which they both belonged. This was the motive behind his capitulation on Confesor and Cabili and behind attempts on his part to get Roxas to agree to be his vice-president.[73] Second, in the event of a formal split, Osmeña wanted to maximize his backing among the elite and place as many of his supporters as possible in positions of influence. Third, he wanted to keep alive the collaboration issue enough to weaken Roxas. And fourth, he was eager to curry favor in Washington. United States economic aid would give an Osmeña candidacy a valuable boost.

Roxas's strategy was aimed at gaining the support of the bulk of the Nacionalista machine, which had collaborated, by assuring them lenient treatment, and at the same time not alienating the United States. Thus, Roxas declared that he would deal firmly with collaborators but that most of the elite who worked for the Japanese had not been collaborators.

The majority of the elite collaborators supported Roxas, for he offered them the best chance of avoiding punishment. A substantial portion of them, however, supported Osmeña out of personal loyalty, and a number supported him on the grounds that because of his advanced age—he was sixty-seven in 1945—Osmeña might decree an amnesty out of magnanimity, while Roxas, young and politically ambitious, might fear the threat from rehabilitated elites to his continued power.[74]

In September 1945 Roxas supporters in the Congress passed a bill establishing a People's Court to try collaboration cases. Lorenzo Tañada, who was to be the chief prosecutor of the court, called the bill "weak and rotten" and charged that some of its provisions were "intended to protect certain influential members of Congress" who might be brought to trial. Osmeña vetoed the bill. United States Secretary of the Interior Harold Ickes provided Osmeña with a weapon to use against the Roxas forces when he sent him a telegram indicating that the United States might well be reluctant to give aid to the Philippines if the Commonwealth government did not deal sternly with collaborators. Osmeña, however, pushed for only a mild compromise, agreeing with Congress on a People's Court bill which provided that there would be only fifteen judges, twenty-five prosecutors, and a strict six-month time limit for filing indictments against the 5,600 people turned over by the U.S. Army. This placed an almost insurmountable practical obstacle in the way of preparing cases against the collaborators.[75]

On September 23 a mass rally of over 30,000 persons was held in Manila calling for the release of Hukbalahap leaders; placards in the crowd denounced the "traitor Congress." According to the *Manila Times* account, the secretary of national defense "was observed trying to extricate himself from such questions as to why Hukbalahaps in Tarlac are being thrown in jail." Two days later a bill was introduced in the Congress to investigate the subversive role of "aliens" (i.e., Chinese) in the demonstration. "They must be subversive," said the bill's sponsor, since they had been "demanding the release of Taruc, Alejandrino and all Hukbalahaps." One representative asked whether it wouldn't be better for the good name of the Congress to have the solicitor general investigate each member of the House. He was cut off, as recorded in the *Congressional Record:* "The House: No, no, no, no." Accordingly, a special House committee was formed to investigate the subversive aliens.[76]

While the civilian organs of the Philippine government were becoming dominated by the elite who had served the Japanese, much the same was happening in the army. On March 17, 1945, with U.S. approval, Secretary of National Defense Cabili had issued General Order No. 20, which barred collaborators from the Philippine Army unless they had ceased collaborating and joined the guerrillas prior to September 30, 1944. Enforcement of this order, however, was left up to the army hierarchy, and the order was ignored, evaded, and sabotaged. After Osmeña removed Cabili from the defense portfolio on June 29, the order was revised to make anyone who had ever aided the guerrillas in any capacity innocent of collaboration regardless of their services to the Japanese. In August the U.S. consul general in Manila reported that no officers had yet been removed from the army, although 80 percent of them were thought to have collaborated. The first court martial trial proved, in the words of a special U.S. Justice Department investigator, to be "a fiasco." The officers in charge of judging collaboration were often collaborators themselves.[77] By May 1946 the Philippine Army had not convicted a single officer or enlisted man.[78]

The collaborators also made an effort to assure their continued domination of the economic life of the country, but here they ran into difficulty, for they were competing with U.S. business interests. Before the economy of the islands could be restored, some determination had to be made as to the validity of the debts paid off in Japanese military notes during the occupation. This currency had begun as the equivalent of the peso, but excessive inflation in 1943 and 1944 greatly reduced its real value. Numerous wealthy Filipinos, especially buy-and-sell merchants who were the most likely to acquire large amounts of Japanese notes, paid back their prewar loans in this inflated currency. The creditor was often forced to accept payment in Japanese scrip or was absent or in prison during the transaction; this was particularly true of American and British banks and business interests, since the Japanese treated them as enemy aliens during the war. United States High Commissioner Paul McNutt, his financial adviser who worked for the Bank of America, and Osmeña's special bank adviser who worked for the Chase National Bank proposed that prewar debts paid in the Japanese currency be deemed only partially cleared, according to a formula that converted the Japanese notes to their peso value for different time periods during the occupation. Osmeña agreed to support such a scheme, but the Congress, led by Roxas, passed a bill that instead validated debt payments at their face value, and Osmeña signed it.[79] Among the Philippine politicians who would benefit financially from this were Roxas and Osmeña.[80]

Before the bill could become law, however, it had to be approved by Truman since, under the Tydings-McDuffie Act, legislation dealing with currency required the U.S. president's concurrence. McNutt called for a veto, and on February 7, 1946, Truman did veto the legislation, on the announced grounds that it "would work to the benefit of persons who did business with and under the Japanese to the prejudice of those who were loyal. . . ." The National City Bank of New York and several British banks had urged the veto.[81] The Philippine Congress would have to wait until independence to try again to validate their wartime transactions. In the meantime, they were in a position to make sure that no serious war profits tax could be imposed, so their buy-and-sell fortunes remained intact.[82]

Throughout the second half of 1945 and early 1946, American officials grappled with the problem of what do about collaboration in the Philippines. It is important to keep in mind that, to Washington, collaboration was a matter not of betraying the Philippine people but of being disloyal to the United States—the disloyalty of siding with Japanese colonialism instead of American colonialism.

Two considerations argued for a U.S. policy of forcefully insisting upon the purging of collaborators. First, there was always the danger that someone who collaborated with the Japanese was not simply an opportunist willing to work for the highest bidder but genuinely anti-American. At least one State Department official in Washington was concerned that this might be the case with Roxas.[83] If so, it would further U.S. interests to eliminate such people from positions of political and economic influence. This consideration, however, lost much of its force in that the two highest U.S. officials in the Philippines, MacArthur and McNutt, as well as many army officers and McNutt's assistant, were friends of Roxas, supported him, and were able to work with him. And McNutt had been entrusted by Truman with much more authority over Philippine affairs than any previous high commissioner.[84]

Of course, MacArthur and McNutt were right in one sense: regardless of their war records, Roxas and many of the other collaborators *were* willing to cooperate now with the United States. By the spring of 1946, U.S. officials in Manila were reporting increased anti-Americanism from the Osmeña camp while Roxas was maintaining a "moderate" tone.[85] Thus, though Roxas's followers included the majority of the collaborators, they did not appear to be hostile to U.S. interests. Indeed, their fear that they might be subject to an American-ordered purge may well have increased their desire to serve the United States.

The second consideration that called for a strong U.S. response with regard to collaboration was American public opinion. News from the Philippines did not really get through to the United States until September 1945, when MacArthur lifted his wartime censorship,[86] and there was a wide public outcry against collaborators in the Philippine government. Only at this point did the Truman administration move on the question—but it moved in such a way as to diffuse criticism.

On September 10, Acting Secretary of State Dean Acheson told the U.S. consul general in Manila to advise Osmeña that the failure to deal promptly and effectively with the collaboration problem had created an unfavorable impression in the United States.[87] On October 25 Truman publicly ordered the attorney general to send an investigator to the Philippines to report on the collaboration situation. This, in the words of one official, "served to make inappropriate any action" by the U.S. government regarding collaboration for the duration of the investigation.[88] The study was not completed until more than three months later, giving public opinion a chance to cool down.

In late February 1946 High Commissioner McNutt announced that the United States would give aid to the Philippines regardless of whom it elected president. Three weeks later, Truman declared that the United States would let the Commonwealth government settle the issue of collaboration on its own. Truman explained that he believed the Philippine authorities were pursuing "an earnest and well-directed effort" to deal with the collaborators and that he had "every confidence in the determination of the Philippine people" to "punish those who served the enemy." This explanation was rather disingenuous, however. The Justice Department's special investigator had warned in the strongest terms that without prompt U.S. action it was extremely likely that the collaborators would escape punishment. Earlier the consul general in Manila had expressed similar doubts, and a few days after Truman's announcement the special assistant to the high commissioner repeated the prediction.[89] There were, however, more compelling arguments favoring a lenient attitude toward collaboration.

One U.S. official felt that the Filipinos had untapped human resources to use if the collaborators were eliminated from public life, but others were not so sanguine. A strict removal from the Philippine Army of those who served the Japanese, according to a high MacArthur aide, would result in the loss of "valuable" officers and men, comprising about 90 percent of the army's total personnel. Accordingly, he recommended a less stringent policy on collaboration. And an assistant to McNutt recalls that the attitude in the high commissioner's office was that the collaborators included the most promising leaders in the Philippines.[90]

Pushing the collaboration issue also had the disadvantage of polarizing Philippine society—collaborators versus guerrillas—a situation U.S. officials wished to avoid. Even Harold Ickes, the Truman administration's most adamant opponent of collaboration, warned that a political struggle was developing between guerrillas and collaborators and that there was reason "to fear" that Osmeña's "moderate program will be superseded by either a collaborationist or an extreme 'purge' group of political leaders."[91] The identity of this "purge group" was not mentioned, but it is clear that the left-wing Hukbalahap was at least part of it. The Huks were among the most uncompromising anticollaborationists, as U.S. officials knew,[92] and would be prominent in any government that excluded collaborators. As one American scholar, influential in policymaking circles, has explained, if the United States "had pressed the collaboration issue with the threat of withholding financial help unless all collaborators were tried and punished, the Communists would have ridden to power."[93] With the Axis defeated, collaboration seemed to U.S. officials to be an issue less important than one's attitude toward communism, and the collaborators were staunch opponents of the left. In fact, Osmeña had struck McNutt as only halfhearted in his efforts to crush the Huks in the summer of 1945.[94] For the elite to split—or be split—over the question of collaboration would weaken Washington's main counterweight to the left.

Two final considerations of a practical nature also militated against a U.S. policy of pressuring the Commonwealth government to remove collaborators from office. First was the problem of precisely defining collaboration: there were so many gradations of cooperation with the Japanese that drawing the line would have been quite difficult.[95] Second was the adverse reaction, both in the Philippines and in Asia in general, that would result from U.S. intervention in an internal Philippine affair. Numerous U.S. officials raised this issue in their deliberations.[96] There was a real practical difficulty for the United States in attempting to impose a purge of collaborators; as Quezon had privately warned back in 1943, for the United States to try to do so would cause the deepest bitterness, especially among the elite. One American official even foresaw the possibility of "non-cooperation" on the part of the elite.[97] But it is important to realize that this was not a question of deciding whether or not to leave collaboration to be judged by the Philippine people free of outside intervention; rather, what was involved was whether or not to leave the disposition of the collaborators up to the Filipino elite, a large part of which had itself collaborated and which had been reinstalled and maintained in power with the help of the United States. Whatever else this was, it had little to do with self-determination.

The first step in the American-sponsored restoration of the elite has already been described: the dismantling of the Hukbalahap local governments and the turning over of jurisdiction to Osmeña—an old elite leader whose power rested on the elite, including some of those who had collaborated. It was not, as McNutt claimed, American "inattention" that had allowed collaborators to come into control of the Congress;[98] it was the quite intentional U.S. policy of restoring the prewar oligarchy to power.

The second step was providing the elite with the means to assure its dominance over the radical peasantry of Central Luzon. Not that the Hukbalahap was attempting to overthrow the government in 1945 or 1946. On the contrary, the Huks somewhat naively depended upon parliamentary tactics to secure their ends.[99] They joined in a coalition of liberal and left-wing resistance forces called the Democratic Alliance and with it planned to contest the upcoming congressional elections. The Huks organized meetings and legal, peaceful, unarmed parades in an effort to win supporters. A U.S. military intelligence report on the Huks in Nueva Ecija found them generally law-abiding.[100] At the same time, they built a peasant union to fight for improved conditions for peasants. During the war many landlords had fled to the relative safety of Manila, and the peasantry, having become "conscious of greater powers, freedom, and better conditions"—in the words of another military intelligence report—were "reluctant to return to the feudal conditions and extreme poverty of prewar tenancy."[101] The Filipino elite, however, was determined to reassert its control: to permit no autonomous peasant movement to exist which would challenge the absolute power of the landlords to decide working conditions, crop division, wages, and justice in the rural areas.[102] Accordingly, the elite acted forcibly to crush the Huks and their affiliated peasant union.

In the spring and early summer of 1945, in many parts of Central Luzon, the USAFFE guerrillas, which were formally under U.S. jurisdiction, had conducted a reign of terror against the Huks. In the words of a U.S. Army historian, "brutality, looting, and excesses of other kinds became the lot of anyone suspected of even a remote connection with the Hukbalahap." The municipal officials appointed by Osmeña enacted laws which added the bludgeon of legal authority to that of USAFFE terrorism. In Concepcion, Tarlac, ordinance nos. 1 and 7 required that a permit be obtained from the mayor for any public meeting or demonstration, with a penalty of six months in jail plus a fine for violators. The Philippine Lawyers Guild charged that under the guise of safeguarding peace the mayor had refused to grant permits. Ordinance no. 4 provided a six-month jail sentence and a fine for persons found within the town without legitimate business or visible means of support, and no. 6 threatened the same penalty for any householder who failed to promptly report any nonresident who entered his or her dwelling for shelter or accommodation. This last ordinance, the Lawyers Guild asserted, was nothing more than the neighborhood system that had been set up by the Japanese to help them combat guerrillas.[103]

In October 1945, with World War II over, units of the Philippine Army were ordered demobilized, including the USAFFE guerrilla units. The elite now needed alternative instruments for enforcing its rule. The Philippine Constabulary, a onetime prop of landlord power, was thoroughly discredited at the end of the war. It had, in MacArthur's words, been employed as "a notorious instrument of Japanese oppression" during the occupation.[104] This rendered it quite unsuitable as an instrument for maintaining law and order because it was likely to create more unrest than it could put down. One of MacArthur's aides observed that "tenants, workers and organizations which have always opposed constituted authority" posed a threat for which the "establishment of an efficient national police system is essential." He transmitted to MacArthur a report recommending the reactivation of the Philippine Constabulary under a different name and under the temporary control of the U.S. Military Police Command.[105] In November 1945 MacArthur advised the War Department that instead of reestablishing the Constabulary it would be desirable to substitute a Military Police Command of the Philippine Army to perform substantially the same functions. Truman was somewhat concerned that giving the military peacetime jurisdiction over internal law and order might cause adverse public reaction in the United States and the Philippines, but he went along with the suggestion.[106]

The United States trained this force, and it was at first under the direct control and supervision of the U.S. Army. Gradually operational control was turned over to the Commonwealth government. At the beginning of January, four and a half months after the end of the war, the responsibility for the Central Luzon provinces was transferred to Commonwealth authority; by February 1, all the provinces had been turned over, and on March 1 the Manila Police were turned over as well. Only after this latter date did U.S. Military Police cease to have jurisdiction over Filipino civilians. The United States, however, continued to provide arms, advisers, and full financial support for the Philippine Military Police (MP) until July 1.[107] In addition, ultimate authority over the entire Philippine Armed Forces rested with the United States until July 1, just before independence.

The Huks claimed that 80 percent of the MP force being used in Central Luzon in May 1946 had served in the Japanese-sponsored Constabulary. A U.S. official reported that this figure was unduly high but acknowledged that no serious effort had ever been made to eliminate "disloyal elements" from the Philippine Army of which the

MP units were a part. According to the *Manila Times*, Secretary of National Defense Montelibano stated that most MPs in these areas were ex-USAFFE guerrillas with grudges against the Huks dating back to the Japanese occupation.[108]

The MPs continued the reign of terror against the Hukbalahap that the USAFFEs had begun. At the beginning of January, a U.S. official in the Philippines reported that the Huks had legitimate complaints but that the "most direct answer which they have received thus far has come from the Secretary of National Defense who has issued 10,000 submachine guns to his MPs and has announced that 'Peace will be maintained at any price.'" The submachine guns, it should be noted, came from the U.S. Army. A week later the same official filed the following account:

> It is reported that on 10 January the MPs went into action in three different places in Central Luzon.
>
> In barrio Santo Nino, Concepcion, Tarlac, a meeting which had been called to select delegates to the Democratic Alliance provincial convention was raided by MPs, and one man was wounded. All those attending the meeting were released after questioning.
>
> In barrio Sierra, La Paz, Tarlac, a similar meeting which was being held in a private house was broken up, and 49 of those attending were lodged in jail under a charge of illegal association. In barrio San Nicolas, Bongabong, Nueva Ecija, MPs opened fire on a group of people who were celebrating the end of the rice harvest, reportedly killing 5 and wounding 11. Their explanation of this action, which possibly is true, is that they heard a shot which they believed came from this group.[109]

And the next month he reported that a Democratic Alliance meeting with a proper permit was broken up by a large group of Philippine Army MPs by the "simple expedient of drowning out the speakers with the sirens of the two tanks which they had brought with them."[110]

Not content with having only the MPs on their side, the landlords of Central Luzon organized their own units of civilian guards. Generally led by the sons of the landed proprietors, civilian guards were composed to a large extent of former USAFFE guerrillas and former guards for large landowners prior to the occupation. Their arms were provided both by the landlords and by the provincial governors, and they participated with the MPs in joint operations against the peasants. At first the MP commander had denied this, saying that the armed civilians accompanying his troops were merely hitchhikers on tanks or guides, but the cooperative operations were

Central Luzon

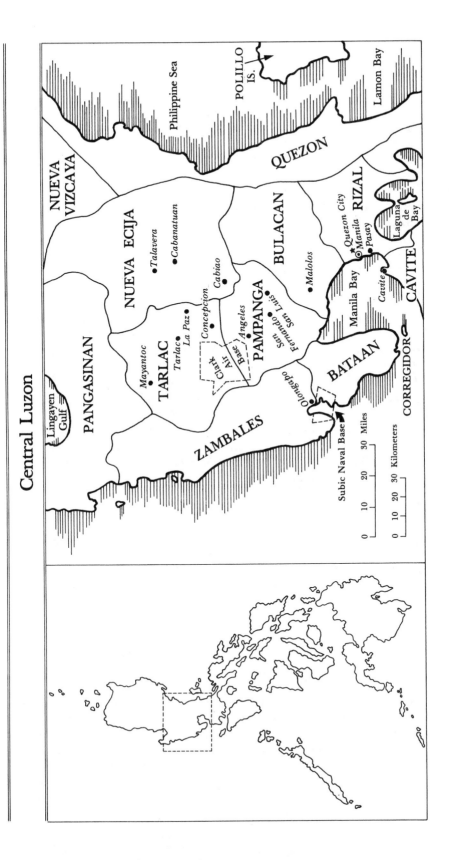

later acknowledged. The civilian guards, a Philippine official later recalled, were among the most undisciplined groups imaginable. Many of the crimes that were attributed to the Huks, a U.S. intelligence report acknowledged, were in fact committed by the MPs and the civilian guards, "the most serious offenders."[111]

While the MPs and civilian guards were helping the landlords dominate the radical peasantry, the elite also had a backup line of defense in the quarter of a million U.S. troops still stationed in the islands. With the end of the Pacific war, American officials were reluctant to employ U.S. soldiers against Filipinos. Even the conservative former colonial official, W. Cameron Forbes, felt that the United States should not deviate from its longtime practice of using Filipinos against Filipinos.[112] But Washington was not willing to withdraw the troops until it was sure the Philippine government—which is to say, the elite—could adequately handle the Huks.

In December 1945 and January 1946, more than four months after V-J day, the GIs in the Philippines organized demonstrations demanding their return home. According to the Associated Press, Lieutenant General W. D. Styer, commander of the U.S. Army Forces in the Western Pacific, told the troops that "the changing international situation" made it impossible to send all eligible men home at once. The next day, according to United Press, Truman "explained that 'critical need for troops overseas' still exists and told protesting GIs and others that demobilization cannot be speeded up if the United States is to do her share toward keeping world peace."[113] A few days later, Army Chief of Staff Dwight D. Eisenhower elaborated:

> There is no effective Philippine agency now in existence to maintain law and order. As a result of the war the Philippines were left without an effective police force and the splendid Philippine Scout organizations were practically destroyed. Now armed bands of guerrillas roam the hills, bent on pilferage which only our active presence controls. We are now engaged in recruiting a force of 50,000 Filipinos to replace a comparable number of our men in the Philippines and elsewhere in the Pacific, but it will be many months before this force becomes effective enough to accept the responsibility of policing the islands. It is our clear obligation to assist until that time arrives.[114]

When Cameron Forbes returned from a trip to the Philippines and warned Eisenhower of the Huk menace, he found the general "very sympathetic and very well informed."[115]

In the first week of January, a U.S. Army newspaper ran a story quoting an officer of the 86th Infantry Division in the Philippines, saying that the unit was to be put on battle status to cope with possible unrest in the islands. Pentagon spokespeople denied this report, but when Secretary of War Robert Patterson was asked if U.S. troops in the Philippines might be utilized in the event of internal disorders, he replied that he could not comment because he had not been apprised of the local situation. More than three months later, on April 30, Eisenhower announced that the United States was gradually reducing its force in the Philippines and would maintain only a garrison force after the Philippine government had the internal situation well in hand.[116]

In the meantime, the final rupture between Roxas and Osmeña was taking place. Osmeña had been anxious to postpone elections as long as possible, both because he thought his chances would be better later and because he would be president until the elections. Under U.S. pressure, he agreed to schedule elections for the presidency and Congress for April 23, 1946. On December 22, 1945, Roxas formally opened his campaign headquarters. The Nacionalista party convention nominated Osmeña for president and Eulogio Rodriguez for vice-president, while the Roxas forces held their convention under the name Liberal Wing of the Nacionalista party. This soon became shortened to simply "Liberal party." There was nothing particularly liberal about this faction, but then again there had never been anything particularly nationalistic about the Nacionalistas either. The Liberal party chose as its standard-bearers Roxas and Elpidio Quirino.[117]

The platforms of the two parties were virtually indistinguishable, a fact that accurately reflected their identical social base; they were both parties of the elite, divided on the basis of personal loyalties rather than principles.[118] Both publicly favored independence (though privately, both were less than eager).[119] Both advocated loyalty to the United States and welcomed the investment of U.S. capital. Both parties drew on the support of collaborators, although the majority backed the Roxas candidacy. The Osmeña senatorial ticket included one person who had held a fairly important post in Laurel's government, two who had held minor positions under the Japanese, and a fourth of "uncertain reputation." There was an unconfirmed report that Osmeña's campaign manager tried to pressure the solicitor general of the People's Court to rush through an acquittal of a high-ranking collaborator so that he might serve as Osmeña's vice-president. Of the Liberal party's senatorial candidates, ten out of sixteen had held positions in the Japanese-sponsored governments, and three others were accused of making money off the war.[120]

Both parties were also corrupt. For example, a pro-Osmeña

newspaper editorial conceded that high officials of Osmeña's administration had used the distribution of relief goods for their personal gain; and it was only some newspaper publicity that prevented Roxas from having one of his private homes rebuilt at governmental expense.[121]

The Democratic Alliance was enamored of neither candidate but disliked Roxas more because of his war record and the fact that his was the party to which the bulk of the collaborators adhered. The Democratic Alliance agreed to back Osmeña for president in return for its own congressional candidates in Central Luzon being accepted on the Nacionalista ticket. This arrangement did not indicate that Osmeña had become a supporter of the left; it was for him merely a campaign tactic. In fact, Roxas himself had tried unsuccessfully to court the Hukbalahap.[122] Relations between the Democratic Alliance and Osmeña were far from harmonious. The attacks against the Huks and their peasant union continued unabated. The MPs and the civilian guards, it is true, had stronger ties to local elites than to the national government, but Osmeña was not inclined to restrain them, for he wanted to avoid alienating his elite supporters or offending his elite sensibilities. Between September 1945 and the beginning of May, a conservative estimate placed the number of Huks killed in Central Luzon at 660, while the MP death toll was about 60. Nevertheless, Osmeña's alliance with the Democratic Alliance scared many of the elite, who sought safety in the Roxas camp. "I am fighting in this election," Roxas declared, "because we must save this country from chaos, corruption, and Communists."[123]

With an atmosphere of near civil war in Central Luzon, Roxas cabled McNutt, who was in Washington at the time, asserting that terrorism and intimidation were being used against his followers in these provinces. McNutt broke his announced policy of nonintervention and publicly cautioned Osmeña to maintain free and orderly elections.[124] McNutt was acting here not as a disinterested defender of unobstructed balloting but as a partisan opponent of the Huks. He told Osmeña that he had no firsthand knowledge of the veracity of Roxas's charges, yet when his assistant had reported MP terrorism against the Huks and the Democratic Alliance, he had issued no warning. When his assistant documented the falsity of Roxas's allegation that voter registration was inflated in Pampanga and showed that in fact voter registration in that province had declined since 1941, while in Roxas's home province of Capiz it had increased, McNutt made no comment.[125] McNutt's attitude toward the Hukbalahap was extremely antagonistic. The Huks opposed the U.S.-Philippine trade agreement that McNutt had been instrumental in drafting. But more generally they stood for fundamental social change. McNutt was a New Dealer, but he had not—as his secretary once assured an inquirer—"been identified with the group of extreme reformers." He had earned the epithet "Hoosier Hitler" from Norman Thomas for his prewar use of troops during strikes by Indiana workers. And his personal friend Douglas MacArthur appreciated "the conservative caution" of his liberalism.[126]

In October 1945 Truman had requested that McNutt conduct a study of agrarian unrest. This, like the instructions to the Justice Department to investigate the collaboration question issued the same day, was designed to allay public criticism of events in the Philippines. Three months later, McNutt announced that the United States was studying the problem, but was not interested in, and would not address itself to, "the political aspects of the so-called agrarian unrest." The United States, he said, was concerned only with the economics of the problem; "we will not be impressed by demonstrations or signs of disorder [nor will we] solicit petitions or declarations of political grievances." This was a peculiar way of studying agrarian unrest, but McNutt neglected to mention his efforts to get the FBI and the Department of Justice to investigate the Huks.[127]

As previously noted, part of Osmeña's campaign strategy was to remove many Roxas supporters from government posts and replace them with people loyal to himself. This, however, was the only privilege of being the incumbent that Osmeña enjoyed. Pork barrel was unavailable to him, for the Commonwealth had few funds or supplies of its own, and Washington was slow in providing rehabilitation funds, for reasons to be discussed in the next chapter. Poll watchers had traditionally played a role in Philippine politics equivalent to ward captains in the United States, but in December 1945 the Roxas forces in Congress had forced Osmeña to agree that each faction would get an equal number of poll inspectors in the event of a split in the Nacionalista party.[128]

On the other hand, in Roxas's favor was the fact that he had the support of many of the largest financial interests in the islands. Some, like Vicente Madrigal, wanted to back the candidate they thought most likely to clear them of collaboration charges. Others, frightened by Osmeña's having accepted the support of the Democratic Alliance, were drawn to Roxas by his vow to crush the Huks within sixty days of his election. The prewar Falangists contributed heavily to Roxas's campaign.[129]

Out of a population of 18 million, 3 million people were qualified and registered to vote in the election. On April 23, 2.5 million people cast ballots, 54 percent of them for Roxas.[130] The conduct of the elections will be discussed in the next chapter, but the result was that the elite—particularly that portion of it which had collaborated with the Japanese—confirmed its hold on the political life of the country. Six of Roxas's ten cabinet officers either had served in one of the Japanese-sponsored governments or had been implicated in the buy-and-sell rackets. Numerous other high-level advisers and executive officers in the Roxas administration had collaborated as well. Even those who had not, however, had all been part of the economic and political elite.[131]

Any lingering doubts Washington may have had about Roxas were laid to rest by intelligence reports that assured that Roxas's election would not hurt relations with the United States and might even lead to closer ties. Roxas was viewed as much more competent than Osmeña, and he had "repeatedly affirmed his resolution to work closely with the United States and to 'make America's Far East policy effective through whatever machinery the United States needs.' "[132]

Shortly after his election, Roxas denied that he intended to grant amnesty to alleged collaborators, but as U.S. military intelligence knew, it was simply a matter of time.[133] In August 1946, a Philippine senator argued against disqualifying those judges on the Supreme Court who had been appointed by Laurel during the war from judging Laurel's alleged treason. To do so, he said, would encourage people to "distrust our justices." Starting in October, bills were introduced in the Congress calling for amnesty for collaborators. The solicitor general in charge of the prosecutions, Lorenzo Tañada, complained repeatedly of the lack of witnesses, lack of investigators, postponement of trials, excessive restrictions on the admissibility of evidence, and illegal influencing of witnesses. Finally, Tañada resigned after he discovered that some of Roxas's key advisers were actually involved in the defense preparations of the leading alleged collaborators.[134] By January 1948, of the approximately 5,600 cases heard by the courts, there were only 156 convictions, and most of these involved some criminal act besides treason. Only one prominent political collaborator had been convicted; although sentenced to life imprisonment plus disqualification from public office, in January 1948 he was out on bail pending appeal and holding a minor government position. The trials of most ranking officeholders under the Japanese were still pending. At the end of the month, Roxas declared a general amnesty for anyone accused of political or economic collaboration.[135] In the words of later American political commentators who placed a high value upon ending the polarization in Philippine society, the amnesty proclamation was "the only wise and statesmanlike thing to do" and "the sensible as well as the humane thing."[136]

Meanwhile, Roxas's electoral victory had resulted in a sharp escalation of the level of violence in Central Luzon, for Roxas was determined to make good his pledge to restore "law and order." At the beginning of May 1946 there were nineteen companies of MPs in Central Luzon; two months later there were thirty-five. In April, May, and June, eight hundred Huks were reported killed in Nueva Ecija alone, according to Military Police headquarters. Armed encounters between MPs and peasants were reported almost daily.[137]

In mid-May, news stories in Manila asserted that Roxas and McNutt—who were in Washington together on a mission—were discussing U.S. Army assistance in suppressing the Huks. McNutt issued a public denial, stating that neither he nor Roxas had discussed the agrarian situation in the Philippines, "except as an economic problem." Later, however, McNutt acknowledged that while in the United States Roxas had arranged for American military aid. As will be seen in the next chapter, the internal security purpose for the military assistance was fully appreciated in Washington. On June 30, 1946, the U.S. Army gave to the Philippine Army $100 million worth of arms, equipment and supplies.[138]

When the Philippines became independent on July 4, 1946, little changed in Central Luzon. What a U.S. official termed almost a "small-scale civil war" continued to rage. In late August, the biggest battle ever fought between Huks and MPs took place. For the MPs and the civilian guards, all suspected Huks and peasant union members were fair game. Barrios thought to harbor Huks were shelled indiscriminately; villagers were tortured and forcibly evacuated, their homes looted and burned.[139] Roxas was determined to restore law and order—but it was to be the law and order of the elite. Thus, for example, at the same time that the government was attempting to forcibly disarm the Huks, a Roxas supporter was announcing on the floor of the Congress that he personally had five thousand armed followers.[140]

United States officials publicly commended Roxas for his announced policy of combining reforms with firmness, but the nature of the reforms was revealed in a confidential report to Washington by McNutt's assistant, who doubled as an adviser to Roxas. Roxas, he said, had launched a "psychological offensive" by explaining that he supported agrarian reform; the explanation was designed "for dispersal especially in Hukbalahap concentrations preceding attacks by the Military Police Command."[141] Roxas had legislation passed that supposedly guaranteed tenant farmers on rice lands 70 percent of the crop, and U.S. officials publicly accepted this claim at face value. In fact, however, the law stated that the peasant received 70 percent of the harvest only if he or she provided all the supplies, farm implements, and work animals and bore the cost of planting and cultivating.[142] There was no improvement in the condition of the tenant farmer from this legislation.

Serious reform was never contemplated by the elite. The wealthy landlord whom Roxas had appointed as governor of Pampanga province to carry out his hard-line policy declared, "There's really no agrarian problem in central Luzon."[143] To him, and to the elite in general, it was a problem solely of lawlessness, which could be solved by organizing even more civilian guards.

After July 4, the United States continued to do its share in maintaining the elite in power. United States Army intelligence prepared dossiers on "communist leaders" in the Philippines and made them available to "interested agencies" of the Philippine government.[144] And, as will be documented in the next chapter, U.S. military aid continued to flow.

The United States had chosen to support the elite over the militant peasantry. Many of the elite had collaborated with the Japanese, and many of the elite were corrupt, but, as MacArthur said of Kuomintang officials, they might be venal but they should be supported because "they are on our side."[145] In the Philippine context, being "on our side" meant supporting the postwar economic and military plans that the United States had for the islands. This the elite was happy to do.

===CHAPTER TWO===

Independence Legislation

Rehabilitation

Rehabilitation was a pressing need for the Philippines. The war had left in its wake terrible destruction throughout the islands. Manila was, after Warsaw, the most completely devastated capital city anywhere in the world.[1] Many U.S. officials felt that the United States had an obligation to assist the Philippines in repairing the ravages caused by the war. This obligation had two sources. First, as a means of bolstering Filipino morale during the fighting, U.S. leaders had repeatedly pledged in public that there would be American aid for rehabilitation at the war's end.[2] Second, much of the physical destruction in the Philippines had been caused by the U.S. military during the American reconquest of the islands. As one U.S. official explained, in order to "save as many American lives as possible," the U.S. Air Force had "blasted" military targets in "areas of heavy population."[3]

In order to fulfill this obligation to the Philippines, the U.S. House Committee on Insular Affairs conducted hearings on rehabilitation assistance. But humanitarian concern for Filipinos was by no means the only motive of U.S. policymakers. Senator Millard E. Tydings, the sponsor of the rehabilitation legislation, stated that the Philippines had been the sixth largest customer for U.S. goods before the war and that American jobs depended upon the rehabilitation of the Philippine economy. "We must now think of the Philippines," Tydings said, "as a great staging area for trade."[4] A few months before becoming high commissioner to the Philippines, Paul McNutt expressed a similar view. A high-ranking officer on General MacArthur's staff reported McNutt as saying that he wanted the United States to go

> "whole hog" on rehabilitating the PI because of their future importance to us. That it was imperative for U.S. business to dominate in the Pacific; that the PI should be the Asiatic springboard for Asiatic trade dominance; that the PI could not achieve stability, provide an outlet and example for U.S. trade unless we did everything necessary to rehabilitate the PI.[5]

To Washington, rehabilitation of the Philippines would also serve the purpose of strengthening a political ally in Asia. It was known in the executive branch in mid-1945, for example, that the Philippine delegation to the United Nations had been instructed to follow the lead of the United States as far as possible without injuring its position as a small power. Over the next few years, U.S. officials repeatedly emphasized that the Philippines had "thrown its lot with the United States," and that the Roxas administration had "attempted to play down nationalistic feeling and to work closely with the United States on basic matters of policy" and was "bent on maintaining the strongest ties" with the United States.[6] But the stability of such a pro-American regime was dependent upon rehabilitation funds; without "some concrete steps" to rehabilitate the Philippine economy, warned a State Department official, "there is danger of the agrarian unrest now existing in Central Luzon sweeping over the entire country with the most drastic results."[7]

United States military strategy necessitated Philippine rehabilitation as well. The War Department's key objective in the Philippines was the utilization by the United States of military bases in the islands. This objective would be furthered, the military asserted, by "maintaining Filipino friendship for the U.S., which is currently a valuable military asset" and by maintaining a stable government in the Philippines, based upon a reasonably prosperous economy.[8] In the words of Senator Tydings, "politically, economically, and strategically the Philippines are a great outpost of this Nation."[9] Rehabilitation funds to the Philippines would strengthen this American outpost.

There were also other considerations in the minds of U.S. policymakers that helped to shape the character of the rehabilitation legislation. An important concern was assuring Philippine dependence upon free enterprise. During the hearings, the issue was raised as to whether the Philippine *government* should receive funds beyond those necessary to restore prewar governmental projects. Committee chairperson Jasper Bell waxed eloquent:

> Individually, personally, I am not willing by way of one comma to encourage anything that even borders on communism or social-ism . . . . I think we have to draw the line somewhere in the world today whether we stand for the American type of government or whether we stand for communism. I think right here is where we have to draw the line. . . . We are giving them [the Filipinos] out of our own pockets the property and money to restore their own government projects, those they already had. But when we go further and say, "You can use this to set up businesses in competition with private industry," I think we are giving the kiss of approval to Socialists and Communists.[10]

The rest of the committee—although not nearly as impassioned as their chairperson—agreed that "under no circumstances can it be interpreted that the American Government has gone into this in competition with private industry."[11]

The legislation resulting from these hearings provided $120 million to the Philippine government for the repair of roads, port and harbor facilities, and other public property, and $100 million worth of surplus U.S. property (of "no real value to us," said Tyd-ings) in order to aid "existing governmental units."[12]

The remainder of the money that the Rehabilitation Act pro-vided was to be allocated to individuals for the restoration of their private property. This meant that, rather than use the destruction of the war as an opportunity to reconstruct Philippine society on a more egalitarian basis, those who were economically dominant in the prewar period were to be maintained in their preeminent position.[13] At least one-quarter of the value of war damage claims exceeding $50,000 were submitted by U.S. citizens, reflecting the significant American role in the prewar Philippine economy. Among the indi-vidual Filipinos who received benefits under the Rehabilitation Act were some whose wartime loyalty to the United States was "at least in question."[14] This both reflected and served to encourage the con-tinued influence of those members of the Philippine elite who had collaborated with the Japanese. There is a considerable irony here in that one of the main arguments advanced in favor of rehabilitation legislation was that the Filipinos deserved U.S. aid because of their loyalty to the American cause during the war.

The policy of favoring private enterprise was being followed as well by local U.S. officials in the Philippines. The head of the Foreign

Economic Administration established in Manila in June 1945 stated, "The basic policy of the United States Government is to encourage private trade, and no government agent, either United States or Commonwealth, should go into business." One of the first companies to benefit from this "basic policy" was the Luzon Stevedoring Company, owned by Charles Parsons of MacArthur's staff. As High Commissioner McNutt explained, "Stevedoring, which had first been carried on by the Army, was soon turned over to prewar firms, chiefly the Luzon Stevedoring Co. This was the first step in the gradual but continuous program designed to turn shipping back to private hands."[15] Emergency relief supplies being given out by the U.S. Army in the islands were distributed through "established wholesalers and retailers," and U.S. government surplus property was sold to private persons who were usually able to resell it at great profit.[16]

The cost of food in Manila in 1945 was about eight times higher than in 1941. The incidence of beriberi, a disease caused by malnutrition, was up sharply over 1940. Unskilled workers did not reach their prewar real wages until 1948, and skilled workers not until the end of 1949. Businesspeople, however, were thriving. They were able to turn the scarcity of consumer goods to their advantage and were little disposed to share their profits. For example, after a strike in early 1946 by Manila dockworkers, six thousand of them were fired by Luzon Stevedoring.[17] The prewar elite was being handed back the reins of the economy by U.S. agencies in the Philippines and being rehabilitated by the legislation in Washington.

The Rehabilitation Act provided a total of $400 million for payment to private individuals. A Philippine War Damage Commission, consisting of two Americans and one Filipino, was established to determine the validity of claims. Representative Walter Judd explained to the House Insular Affairs Committee that if the Filipino member were "appointed by the President of the Philippines I, of course, would not want him there. But he is appointed by our President."[18]

On March 26, 1951, the three commissioners sent a letter to President Truman stating that they had completed their task. "Although the funds authorized and appropriated were inadequate fully to repair the ravages of war in the Philippines, they were of tremendous assistance," they wrote. "Much rehabilitation," they noted, "remains to be done."[19] The lack of sufficient aid to completely cover the war damage was no oversight. It had been a conscious element of American policy to leave as much of the job of rehabilitation as possible to private capital, in particular to U.S. capital. "The half billion dollars provided in the War Damage Act," said

McNutt, "can pay for only half of the actual war damage, perhaps even less. For the rest, the Philippines must depend on private capital." As a companion piece to the Rehabilitation Act, Jasper Bell drew up legislation which established trade relations between the United States and the Philippines and gave incentives to American investment in the islands. "Apparently," Bell stated,

> there are two ways in which the Philippines can be rehabilitated so they can stand on their own feet as a nation among nations . . . . One is for the United States of America to open up the Treasury of the United States and pour millions of dollars in money into rebuilding their plants, rebuilding their structures that have been torn down and destroyed.
> The other way is for us to give them the kind of trade relief which will make it possible for them and for the citizens of this great country to enter into private industry over in the Philippines. . . .
> One of the purposes of this bill . . . is to see that American capital has an opportunity to go down and invest on the basis that they will be safe in their investment.[20]

The Rehabilitation Act provided an obvious source of leverage for use in getting the Philippines to accept the trade legislation. U.S. officials differed, however, on how to employ this leverage. As head of the House Committee on Insular Affairs, Bell held up consideration of the rehabilitation bill so as not to have it passed too much before his trade bill. McNutt went a step further and proposed title six of the Rehabilitation Act, which provided that no payments in excess of five hundred dollars would be made under the bill until the Philippines accepted the trade legislation. "Very frankly, gentlemen," McNutt testified, "this is an effort to tie this bill" to the Philippine Trade Act. Title six was adopted by the committee without objection.[21] The Interior and Commerce Departments had no objection to this provision, but the State Department prevailed upon Truman to issue a statement when he signed the two bills, calling the tie-in "unfortunate." For all practical purposes, Truman said, "this provision is surplusage, as the benefits which will flow under the enactment of the two bills are so great as to ensure" Philippine acceptance. The State Department was aware that the United States was being charged with practicing imperialism, and in the department's view nothing would be gained by the "surplusage" provision.[22] A week later, Representative Harold Knutson introduced a bill calling for the repeal of title six on the grounds that Congress "did not realize, because of the haste and urgency of the situation, that we were coercing the Philippines into signing a trade agreement." Such coercion, he declared, "was the farthest thing from our minds." The Knutson bill died in Bell's Committee on Insular Affairs, apparently ignored by Truman.[23]

Trade Relations

Many of the same considerations that U.S. policymakers took into account in formulating the Rehabilitation Act for the Philippines were also involved in the drawing up of legislation regarding U.S.-Philippine trade relations, considerations such as the desire to build up a political and military ally. But the crucial issue here was the relationship between any U.S.-Philippine trade agreement and overall American strategy as to foreign economic policy. On this question policymakers were seriously divided. For the Department of State the key concern was providing foreign markets for U.S. goods. As Assistant Secretary of State Dean Acheson testified in 1944, the United States had to have foreign markets if it was to achieve full employment and prosperity. With an alternative kind of economic system, Acheson acknowledged, it might be possible for the United States to use its entire production internally, but as presently constituted the United States had to sell goods abroad.[24]

The Department of State took the broad view with regard to promoting markets abroad. It favored a world economic system in which all discriminatory barriers to trade would be eliminated. The United States had emerged from World War II with undisputed economic primacy, and it did not need trade preferences of its own in order to secure foreign markets; but it did need to remove the obstacles to trade imposed by other nations. This was not a uniquely American approach. During the period of its economic ascendancy in the nineteenth century, Britain had been an advocate of universal free trade. It was only after its preeminent position was challenged that it erected a tariff wall against non-Empire trade, and put its trade with the Empire on a preferential basis. Like Britain in the era of its hegemony, the United States—in the view of the State Department—should forgo the small advantages to be gained from special arrangements with *its* empire in return for securing nondiscriminatory access to the rest of the world's markets.

To facilitate the promotion of such a policy, there was established within the executive branch an Executive Committee on Economic Foreign Policy (ECEFP). In March 1945 ECEFP met to discuss the issue of trade relations with the Philippines and how this would fit in with the broad objectives of foreign economic policy.

The committee noted that before the war the United States had sent 3 percent of its exports to the Philippines, compared to 40 percent to the British Empire, and getting the removal of Empire preferences was thus of greater importance than any advantages the United States might obtain in Philippine trade. "Any move now which would seem to give new life to the regime of U.S.-Philippine preferences would inevitably weaken our chances of getting satisfactory commitments on preferences from the British and others."[25]

It might be asked why the State Department opposed preferences, since bilateral tariff reductions between the United States and the Philippines would seem to be a step in the direction of removing trade barriers.[26] But as ECEFP explained, tariff preferences

> are discriminatory against third countries, they operate to divert trade from its natural courses and they tend to create international ill will. They are inconsistent with our objective of promoting the expansion of world trade on a multilateral, nondiscriminatory basis. In particular they are inconsistent with the fourth point of the Atlantic Charter (to which the Philippines have adhered) calling for the enjoyment by all states of access, on equal terms, to the trade and to the raw materials of the world which are needed for their economic prosperity and with the provisions of Article VII of our mutual aid agreements with the United Kingdom and other countries which look toward agreed action for the reduction of tariffs and other trade barriers and the elimination of all forms of discriminatory trade treatment.[27]

This approach to foreign economic policy was not, however, shared by all departments and branches of the U.S. government. This difference reflected the differing interests represented by the various segments of officialdom. When Jasper Bell testified on the Philippine trade bill before the House Ways and Means Committee, he declared, "Every man here, of course, has contacts with business."[28] But the business interests represented in Congress were not the major exporters with worldwide markets who traditionally worked through the Departments of State and Commerce and who concurred in the need to eliminate trade barriers. Rather, Congress spoke for a wide variety of parochial and often conflicting interests: industries eager for tariff protection, and importers and exporters with particular markets. As the representatives of such constituents, members of Congress were frequently willing to subordinate general principles to narrow interests.

Consider the case of Senator Robert Taft. Although he made a career out of opposing foreign aid legislation, he had been a strong advocate of rehabilitation funds for the Philippines and had in fact sponsored an earlier version of the Rehabilitation Act. Taft was reported to have filed this bill, according to a knowledgeable source, "at the request of Senator Taft's personal friend and political backer, Judge John W. Haussermann, 'gold king of the Philippines.' " Haussermann had a formidable economic interest both in Philippine rehabilitation and in trade preferences. He had been an ardent reexaminationist of Philippine independence, and one U.S. official remarked that Haussermann "will remain a Nineteenth Century American." He had also been a prewar financial supporter of Paul McNutt.[29] While the State Department feared that trade preferences with the Philippines would hurt chances to eliminate the British Empire preferences, Taft did not think the British should abandon these preferences. He did "not see why nations should not have a special relation as to customs matters." Taft went on:

> We are going to have military bases in the Philippines; we are going to have Americans established in Manila for many years to come. I do not see why we should not recognize in the economic field a permanent relationship, just as much as we recognize it in the political field . . . .
> . . . the Philippines should always be an American outpost in the Pacific. The fact that they have a completely independent, autonomous government is, I think, a good thing. . . . But certainly we shall always be a big brother, if you please, to the Philippine Islands.[30]

During the hearings on the trade bill, the Departments of State and Commerce repeatedly raised objections to provisions discriminating against third nations. The following exchange between Representative Harold Knutson, a Republican from Minnesota, and Winthrop G. Brown, Chief of the Division of Commercial Policy of the Department of State, typified the contending views:

> Mr. Knutson: In other words, you are afraid American citizens might get some benefits that all the rest of the world would not have?
> Mr. Brown: Well—
> Mr. Knutson: Yes or no?
> Mr. Brown: In this particular case, yes.
> Mr. Knutson: Well, that is what I thought. Of course, it would be a crime to give American citizens any better treatment.[31]

It is important to keep in mind that Congress did not have a unified foreign economic policy to counterpose to the policy of the State Department. What Congress agreed on was their unwillingness to allow general commercial policy to override particular interests.

The Department of the Interior also did not support the State Department's efforts to construct a world economic system. As the department in charge of the Philippines—with no responsibility for any other foreign market—Interior dealt with and received input from those with economic interests specifically in the Philippines and did not have to concern itself with the consequences that a Philippine trade agreement might have on U.S. commerce as a whole; to the Interior Department's constituents it was of little import whether Malaya or India was opened to U.S. trade. In addition, Americans with an economic interest in the Philippines were willing to have concessions in the U.S. market given to the Filipino elite. Such concessions would pay back the Philippine elite for preferential treatment of Americans without hurting these Americans, though they might well come into conflict with other U.S. interests, such as domestic agricultural producers.

The American vegetable oils and fats industry, which processed the Philippine raw material, called for a minimum of twenty-five years of preferential trade relations. The American Chamber of Commerce in Manila urged that there be twenty years of free trade between the United States and the Philippines. Philippine government officials, speaking for the economic elite of the islands, also advocated twenty years of free trade.[32] Both U.S. and Filipino businesspeople in the Philippines had feared independence and had supported various reexaminationist schemes. But when Jasper Bell—with the backing of the Department of the Interior—introduced a trade bill incorporating free trade, the State Department's intelligence division reported, "Big business interests in the Philippines . . . may no longer oppose the granting of Philippine independence since their interests are safe-guarded."[33]

The State Department strongly opposed this bill, but the alternative they supported provided not for the immediate removal of preferences but for their gradual elimination. This, the department felt, would be acceptable to the British, and in any case it was clear that any British abandonment of preferences would also be gradual. Twenty years of free trade, however, was unacceptable to the State Department.[34]

A structure of declining preferences might seem to be a reasonable way to avoid the economic dislocation of sudden measures, but in the postwar Philippines there was little economy to dislocate. The sugar industry—the backbone of the colonial economy—had been largely destroyed during the war as a result both of military activity and of the conscious policy of the Japanese to shift the islands from sugar production to cotton and other crops. At the end of 1945, the

Commonwealth government was called upon by sugar planters to *import* 50,000 tons of Cuban sugar to alleviate the shortage, and some U.S. sugar was also sent to the Philippines.[35] ECEFP was aware of this situation: "The war has created an unprecedented opportunity to reconstruct the Philippine economy on a sound basis." The "immediate postwar period will be a favorable time to adapt Philippine trade to a non-preferential position. Enemy occupation and the resulting lack of access to American markets have already resulted in a significant contraction of industries which depend on preferential treatment." While "recognizing the weight of these points," however, ECEFP "nevertheless" recommended a period of approximately twenty years of declining preferences. The only explanation given was that this was consistent with the 1938 suggestions of a joint U.S.-Philippine committee.[36]

It seems likely that there were other considerations here, beyond some 1938 suggestions rendered obsolete by the war. The rebuilding of the sugar centrals, which even a declining preference would encourage, would entrench in power the sugar barons who had been such valuable allies of the United States throughout the colonial period. When Osmeña came to the United States in 1945 asking for trade preferences, the administrations of both Franklin Roosevelt and his successor, Truman, promised that full duties would not be imposed. At the same time, Osmeña made it abundantly clear that he would be cooperative in serving U.S. political and military policy. Not only did Osmeña approve of the United States holding bases in the postwar Philippines, but he went so far as to "definitely and specifically" state that whatever suggestions the United States "wished to make relative to United States postwar bases would be agreeable to him."[37] Here was an ally worth having.

This is not to suggest a conspiratorial payoff. State Department officials anticipated Philippine cooperation on the military bases and recommended against suggesting a *quid pro quo* (though "this could be utilized later if any serious opposition should arise on the part of Philippine officials").[38] What was involved was not a conspiracy but the recognition that each side needed the other.

It is important to keep in mind that Osmeña did not represent some abstract Philippine nation; he spoke for and was part of the Filipino elite. Representative Roy Woodruff of Michigan declared on the floor of the U.S. Congress:

> It is generally contended that the lowest standards of living [in the Philippines] are found among those producing sugar for export to the United States. Wage rates and other conditions are considered the

very lowest to be found almost anywhere. In other words, other branches of agriculture, even in the Philippines, are much more conducive to high living standards, good health, and so forth.

Woodruff, of course, was anxious to prevent competition to his own state's sugar industry, but it is significant that no one rose to dispute his remarks.[39] In 1950, after four years of trade preferences, a U.S. economic survey mission reported that both "industry and agriculture have been very prosperous in the Philippines since the end of the war, but little of this prosperity has seeped through to the working force." Outside of Manila, real wages were found to be "generally lower than the inadequate prewar level."[40] Commercial preferences then— whether declining or free trade—were a windfall to the Filipino elite, not to the country as a whole.

Another reason that the State Department was not pushing for an immediate termination of trade preferences was that the War Department advised that in the interests of U.S. military strategy the Philippine economy should not be allowed to become complementary to the economies of either Japan or the Soviet Union. Military dependency is furthered by economic dependency, cautioned the War Department, and the first five or ten years of postwar recovery would establish the orientation of the Philippine economy.[41]

The split in the U.S. government on Philippine trade policy was finally resolved in November 1945. At a White House conference, Bell, Tydings, McNutt, and representatives of the Departments of State and Interior agreed to a compromise. Bell would redraft his bill to provide for eight years of free trade to be followed by twenty-five years of gradually declining preferences.[42]

The details of the legislation were still a matter of dispute, however, as each of the different lobbies represented in Congress rushed to advance its interests. As ultimately formulated, the bill—the Bell Trade Act—specified that U.S. exports were to be admitted into the Philippines free of duty, with no limitation on quantity, for a period of eight years. The tariff would then be incrementally increased over the next quarter century until at the end the full duty was being paid. This arrangement gave U.S. goods an advantage in the Philippines over the goods of other nations. In some cases, such as cigarettes, there would have been no appreciable market for the U.S. product if full duties had to be paid. Adherents of the bill emphasized that the Bell Act would reestablish the Philippines as one of the best customers for U.S. goods. Moreover, the Philippines could become a "great gateway" to trade with "the teeming millions of the Orient."[43]

Philippine exports to the United States were to follow the same pattern with the following significant exceptions: absolute quotas were placed on the entry of Philippine sugar, cordage, rice, cigars, scrap tobacco, coconut oil, and buttons of pearl. This list included most of the major exports of the islands. Absolute quotas are not just limitations on the quantity of a product that can be admitted duty-free, but an absolute limitation whether at full duty or not. The motives for the quotas were quite clear. As one member of the Ways and Means Committee explained, "I am telling you we know we are going to have the quotas because that is the kind of protection our domestic producers will want and will get." High Commissioner McNutt was more specific; with regard to the coconut oil provision he stated, "The reason for that, of course, is obvious. It is an effort to protect the dairy interests of this country." Harold Knutson of Minnesota pointed out that he had "no desire to close the door on Philippine oil . . . provided it is rendered unfit for human consumption." The tobacco quota, McNutt explained, had been "increased . . . on information . . . that the United States cigar manufacturers need an additional quantity." Knutson probably spoke for the entire Ways and Means Committee when he said:

> We have interests to look after, too. . . . It is not that we do not desire to be helpful to the Philippine people. God knows, I would give them the shirt off my back, if I had another one to replace it. In other words, I would give them half. But we have certain obligations here and we can't let our hearts run away with us altogether.[44]

It was a curious rendering of the phrase "give them half" for the richest nation in the world to insist on unrestricted free entry of its exports into a war-torn and backward colony while placing absolute quotas on the latter's exports.

United States officials were not always so candid. McNutt told the Philippine Bar Association in May 1946, "The only selfish advantage, if you call it a selfish advantage, which the United States hopes to derive from its activities in the Philippines is the respect and friendship of the peoples of the Orient"; he later wrote, "There was at no time any inquiry into the exact reciprocal benefits which the United States might derive" from the Bell Act.[45]

The Departments of State and Commerce objected strongly to the absolute quotas. Warned by dispatches from London that absolute quotas would weaken the U.S. negotiating position with the British on trade matters, the departments told the congressional committees considering the bill that absolute quotas were, "without doubt, one of the most vicious of trade restrictions." They explained that enacting these provisions "would seriously limit what this Government could do in obtaining commitments from other governments to abandon the use of quotas against American exports."[46] But the committee members remained unconvinced.

Some claimed that the absolute quotas did not limit trade but rather limited the extent of the tariff concession the United States was giving to the Philippines.[47] This would have been true if the quotas had been "tariff quotas," whereby the entry of a product above a certain quantity was not prohibited but charged the full duty. With regard to absolute quotas, the claim was simply false. Others asserted that absolute quotas would "tend to prevent an uneconomic expansion of Philippine industry dependent upon preferences."[48] One might ask why give tariff preferences in the first place if the goal was to avoid uneconomic development. As both U.S. and Philippine officials acknowledged, the preferences would restore the Philippine economy to its prewar situation.[49] But equally significant is the fact that another provision of the trade act discouraged diversification of the economy. Title V, section 504(a) stated that should the U.S. president feel that any other Philippine product, in addition to those placed under absolute quota, was "coming, or likely to come, into substantial competition" with U.S. products, the president could set a quota on it. The State Department had complained in committee that this one-sided provision was solely "for the protection of the United States interests." One senator had replied, "We have got to do some thinking about what disrupts the United States, or else we will not have any United States to do any good with."[50]

The trade act specified that the absolute quotas were to be allocated to Philippine exporters on the basis of their share of prewar production. The force of the provision was to maintain the dominance of those who had controlled the economic life of the islands— the Filipino elite and foreign investors. The cordage industry had consisted of three firms before the Japanese invasion; two of them, accounting for about 90 percent of total production, were owned by the Elizalde family, and the remaining 10 percent by a San Francisco–based company. The two largest tobacco export firms were American and Spanish. Together with one Filipino company, they made up 90 percent of the prewar production. The two most important coconut oil firms were subsidiaries of U.S.-based Procter and Gamble (the largest Philippine manufacturing enterprise) and Britain's Lever Brothers. The sugar industry was about one-half Filipino-owned, one-third American, and the rest Spanish.[51]

An American economist has claimed that the impact of this quota allocation provision of the trade act was nil:

> If allocation of the export quotas on the basis of prewar production had not been specified and if competitive forces had been permitted to determine the conditions of production, there is no reason to assume that those firms and producers which were competitive in the prewar period would not have been competitive in the postwar period.[52]

The first point to be made about this claim is that the concept of "competitive forces" is inappropriate in analyzing industries in which a few firms control the market. Second, the internal quota allotments prevented the Philippine government from taking measures to increase competition—if it had wanted to. And third, while it is certainly true that the prewar producers were economically powerful, giving them a monopoly on exports at this time could not but increase their power. In particular, the internal quotas alone on sugar were soon found to be worth more than the value of the sugar. Quotas could be bought, sold, or transferred, just like land. In effect, the prewar producers were given a fully negotiable U.S. government subsidy.[53]

The Departments of State and Commerce had numerous objections to the internal quota allotment section of the trade act. The provision, the Commerce Department claimed, would benefit business interests "which collaborated with the occupying forces" during the war, was "inconsistent with sovereignty and independence," and would legislate benefits to non-American nationals, namely, Filipinos and Spaniards. Acting Secretary of State Acheson objected to the internal quota allotments, in part because the "virtual monopoly" given prewar producers would prevent new American enterprises from investing in the export industries. Supporters of the bill in Congress replied that the provision was necessary in order to encourage war-damaged U.S. firms to rebuild.[54] The truth of this proposition is debatable, but in any case it presupposes an approach to rehabilitation based on private enterprise.

Another provision of the trade act prohibited the Philippines from imposing export taxes. This would benefit those Americans in the export sector of the Philippine economy as well as prevent the Philippine government from redistributing—if it had so desired—the windfall profits resulting from preferential access to the U.S. market. The Philippine government, of course, had no such intention, but this legislation made doubly sure. Under the guise of reciprocity, the Bell Act also prohibited the United States from imposing export taxes—something it was already prohibited from doing by the U.S. Constitution.

Another section of the trade legislation stated:

> The value of Philippine currency in relation to the United States dollar shall not be changed, the convertibility of pesos into dollars shall not be suspended, and no restrictions shall be imposed on the transfer of funds from the Philippines to the United States, except by agreement with the President of the United States.

Following World War II, the peso was highly overvalued relative to the dollar, and thus the pegging of the peso to U.S. currency especially benefited the Manila Americans and U.S. exporters. But the wider significance of the first part of this provision lay in the fact that from now on all sectors of the American business class were to have a say, through the U.S. president, in determining the value of the peso. The second part of this section of the trade act—assuring the convertibility and transferability of funds—was of benefit to all Americans doing business in or with the Philippines, currently or potentially.

The State and Treasury Departments registered their dissent from all the currency provisions. They proposed that the pegging of the peso to the dollar be eliminated and that the imposition of exchange restrictions require only consultation with the U.S. president rather than approval. This alternative, they suggested, would protect U.S. interests just as well, but without infringing as blatantly on Philippine sovereignty. They noted that the prospective establishment of an International Monetary Fund, in which the United States was to play the dominant role, would adequately safeguard U.S. interests from the risk of independent monetary policies on the part of any nation that was tied to the capitalist world system. The slightest such independence would invite the retaliation of the international financial community—an intolerable prospect for any nation committed to capitalist development. In addition the Departments of State and Treasury pointed out that consultation with the U.S. president would "certainly be more than a mere formality," given the relative power of the United States and the Philippines, the special trade relations, and past political ties. It would be unlikely, they contended, that U.S. views would be lightly disregarded.[55] Again the Congress was unmoved by the criticism and the bill remained unchanged.

A section of the Bell Trade Act that provoked widespread criticism among Filipinos was the so-called "parity" clause. The Philippine constitution, ratified during the Commonwealth period with U.S. approval, specified that operation of public utilities and ownership or use of natural resources be restricted to firms that were at least 60 percent Filipino-owned. The "parity" provision, however, declared that American citizens and business enterprises were to be given full and equal rights with Filipinos in these areas. To accept the trade act, then, the Philippines would have to amend its constitution.

Supporters of the "parity" provision defended it on the grounds that it was the only way to attract capital to the Philippines for badly needed rehabilitation, or at least the only way without draining the U.S. Treasury. This bill, said Representative John D. Dingell, "is the only formula which will lure the only available capital into the Philippines. It will incidentally give American capital a chance and an inducement to assist in the rehabilitation of these islands."[56] The word "incidentally" suggests that U.S. officials devised a plan for rehabilitating the Philippines and then noticed that —wonder of wonders!—their plan just happened to involve a major role for U.S. investors. That this was not just a happy coincidence can be seen from some alternative methods of achieving Philippine rehabilitation that were not even broached by U.S. legislators. For example, U.S. investors could have been heavily taxed to finance an equitable program of reconstruction in the islands. Even within a private-enterprise framework, if Philippine rehabilitation alone had been the goal there would have been no need to force the Filipinos to accept "parity." Presumably, the Filipinos as rational people (for had they not had over four decades of U.S. rule?) would have been willing to provide incentives to American investors without any prodding from the United States, if they found that this was necessary in order to get the economy back on its feet. It seems quite clear then that, despite the rationalizations, the primary motive behind the "parity" provision was the protection of U.S. capital.

The case of Paul McNutt is interesting in this regard. As one of the foremost proponents of "parity," McNutt had been very careful to point out that he had "no financial interest in the future of the Philippines."[57] However, after retiring as U.S. ambassador to the Philippines, McNutt took on numerous lucrative business positions, including the chairpersonship of the board of both the Philippine-American Finance and Development Company (a firm engaged in the exploitation and development of Philippine natural resources) and the Philippine-American Life Insurance Company. In 1950 McNutt told a U.S. congressional committee that he had "accepted no employment in any matter having to do with his public service."[58] It is not being suggested that all U.S. officials had business interests in the Philippines, though in the absence of financial disclosure this cannot be precluded. The point, however, is that no U.S. policy-maker saw anything wrong with foreign investment; it was taken as axiomatic that U.S. capital should be protected and promoted wherever possible. Foreign investment not only was viewed as natural, but was considered to be synonymous with the "American way."

The Departments of State and Commerce shared this view of foreign investment but felt that "parity" was not the way to advance the interests of U.S. capital. Since "parity" gave Americans investment rights in the Philippines that were not given to citizens of other countries, the United States would find it difficult to convince Britain and others to remove the preferential treatment accorded these powers in their own colonies. World opinion would not see much difference between "parity" and similar rights obtained by Japanese investors during the war—and not without good reason. Already, the secretary of state warned Truman, the Soviet press was using the "parity" clause as evidence of the reactionary turn in U.S. policy towards the Philippines.[59] The State Department recommended that in place of "parity" the United States negotiate with the Philippines the standard Treaty of Friendship, Commerce, and Navigation (FCN), which would protect U.S. business without discriminating against the nationals of other nations.[60] Such an approach, the department suggested, would be consistent with overall U.S. foreign economic policy and at the same time eliminate grist from the Soviet propaganda mill.

Another objection to the "parity" provision raised by the Departments of State and Commerce was that it was not reciprocal, that is, that Filipino investors were not permitted to utilize American natural resources on an equal basis with U.S. citizens. In fact, of course, reciprocity was not terribly meaningful; witness the following exchange between General Carlos P. Romulo, Philippine resident commissioner in Washington, and Walter Lynch, Democrat of New York:

General Romulo: We would expect the same treatment here that we would give to Americans there.
Mr. Lynch: Well, that does not mean much, in view of the fact you have not any capital to come into this country.
General Romulo: Not much; but, in all treaties, it is customary to have reciprocal rights. . . . [61]

To the Department of State, appearances were important. One of their earliest recommendations concerning the trade act had been that, because of "the present efforts of the United States to obtain a reduction of preferences abroad, it would seem desirable to remove from the bill a few words and clauses which, without adding anything as to substance, place an undesirable emphasis on the preferential nature of trade relations with the Philippines."[62] In this same spirit, the State Department pushed for a gratuitous reciprocity clause with regard to "parity." The congressional committees, however, refused to budge.

Another provision of the Bell Trade Act gave the U.S. president the right to suspend all or part of the act if he or she should find that the Philippines was "in any manner" discriminating against U.S. citizens or business enterprises, but the act did not specify what constituted discrimination. Did it mean that the United States was to be granted "national treatment" (that is, having the same rights as Filipinos) or "most-favored-nation treatment" (that is, no worse than the treatment accorded a citizen of the most-favored third country)? The Philippine government accepted the latter interpretation. Technically, the provision could even be used to assure Americans voting rights in the Philippines.

In mid-1947 the State Department took the position that it would not recommend that the president suspend all or part of the trade agreement unless the Philippines failed to grant U.S. citizens most-favored-nation treatment in general and national treatment in areas customarily so treated in more recent FCN treaties and in areas where Filipinos were similarly granted national treatment in the United States. Such a policy, the State Department contended, would avoid charges of imperialism and the difficulties of litigating what did or did not constitute discrimination. The policy, however, was kept confidential and not made known to the Philippine government, so as not to weaken U.S. bargaining power.[63] Although this provision of the trade act was never invoked, the ever-present threat it held over the Philippine government helped to protect U.S. interests in the islands.[64] In an effort to obtain national treatment with respect to all commercial, financial, and professional activities, the State Department opened talks on an FCN treaty with Manila in 1947. No agreement could be reached, however; the Filipinos refused to grant such rights, and Washington was unwilling to give Philippine citizens equal rights with Americans in mining and other uses of natural resources.[65]

This, then, was the Bell Trade Act. The House Ways and Means Committee reported the bill unanimously, indicating that it provided a little bit for each of the special interests represented. As Paul McNutt explained:

50

We used every contact, every strategem, every trading point we could through those long weeks of negotiations, deliberation, committee hearings, legislative drafting and redrafting of that trade bill. We buttonholed senators and congressmen in their offices, at their homes, at social gatherings . . . . We had, perhaps, the most active and persistent lobby any bill has ever attracted.[66]

In defending the bill on the floor of Congress, Representative Dingell remarked, "It has been charged that the bill is one-sided, lopsided, and even monopolistic—but there is no other way out. Capital will not go back into a devastated country without some assurance. . . . " And Carlos P. Romulo, Manila's resident commissioner in Washington, advocated the bill's passage, noting that in "the best of all possible worlds," the "parity" provision would not be in the bill, for the Philippines would voluntarily amend its constitution to give U.S. citizens "parity" without being required to do so.[67]

The trade act passed both houses of Congress and, together with the Rehabilitation Act, was sent to the president for his signature. On April 30, 1946, Truman signed them both but remarked, at the urging of the Departments of State and Commerce, that he had some reservations regarding some of the provisions and that these might at a later date need reconsideration. Furthermore, he stated that though preferential trade relations were alien to his administration, he was approving the trade legislation because it was in substance a rehabilitation act whose "sole purpose and guiding philosophy is to furnish a formula for the rehabilitation of the Philippine national economy through the encouragement of private enterprise and private initiative."[68]

How a Bill Becomes a Law

More than Truman's signature was necessary for the trade and rehabilitation acts to take effect. The Philippines, with formal independence scheduled for July 4, had to approve the trade act and, as already noted, the rehabilitation funds were partially tied to this act. Approval required ratification of the trade bill by the Philippine Congress, the signing of an Executive Trade Agreement by the U.S. and Philippine presidents incorporating the provisions of the Bell Act, passage by the Philippine Congress of an amendment to the constitution incorporating "parity," and, finally, acceptance of the amendment by the Philippine population voting in a national plebiscite.

Manuel Roxas, as the newly elected president of the Philippines and representative of the interests of the elite, undertook to guide the trade act over each of these hurdles. The first difficulty involved the matter of timing. Truman and the State Department insisted that the Executive Agreement be signed after the Philippines achieved formal independence, both to dispel any doubts as to the validity of the agreement in international law and to avoid the charges of American imperialism that would result from the establishment of trade relations while the Philippines was still a colony. Roxas, however, had another worry. The Philippine Supreme Court might construe an executive agreement reached after July 4 as a treaty, requiring a two-thirds vote in the Senate; before July 4 the agreement could not be considered a treaty (there not being two sovereign nations involved), and a majority of Congress would suffice. The majority Roxas was confident of; the two-thirds vote would be more precarious. After frantic telephone conversations between Manila and Washington, it was decided that Roxas would get congressional passage of the trade act prior to July 4 and that the Executive Agreement would be signed on July 4 itself, right after the independence ceremonies. The Philippine congressional committee considering the legislation held sessions lasting until four in the morning in order to assure that it could be voted on before July 4.[69]

On July 2, the Philippine Senate and House approved the Bell Trade Act. Some of the arguments made in favor of passage, however, reveal that an affirmative vote did not invariably indicate enthusiasm. The majority floor manager of the bill in the House observed that it was not a perfect act but that it would assure war damage payments and give "fair prospects of negotiating a loan" from the United States. "Between two evils, I choose the lesser so I vote yes," said another representative. "I vote yes because we are flat broke, hungry, homeless, and destitute." And one member of the House noted that if, as the critics of the act charged, vested interests controlled the U.S. Congress, then any wavering on accepting the Bell Act would lead to a U.S. denial of a loan to the Philippines.[70]

It should be pointed out that the alleged connection between cooperating with U.S. policies and having a loan request accepted was not imaginary. For example, in June 1946 McNutt cabled Washington urging favorable consideration of Roxas's application for a loan. "Roxas has indicated by word and deed," said McNutt, "his desire to follow American pattern of government and retain closest ties with us in all matters. . . ."[71]

Getting the Philippine Congress to pass the "parity" amendment, however, was not to be as simple. In this case it was indisputable that a three-fourths majority was necessary, and, as a U.S.

official noted, "it is evident that the opposition can block acceptance of this measure if it remains unified . . . ."[72] Accordingly, Roxas and his supporters in the Congress had to resort to more drastic measures: the ousting of some of their opponents from the legislature.

On the opening day of the new congressional session, May 25, 1946, Jose Topacio Nueño, a member of Roxas's majority Liberal party, introduced a resolution to bar the seating of nine representatives on the grounds that there had been fraud and terror in Central Luzon. The nine consisted of six members of the Democratic Alliance, two Nacionalistas, and one Liberal, Jose Roy. In the previous few days, both the Democratic Alliance and the Nacionalista party had gone on record against the Bell Trade Act, the latter in opposition to the titular head of the party, Osmeña. Roy had been a buy-and-sell lawyer in Manila during the war and was elected from the first district of Tarlac (in Central Luzon).[73] Said Nueño in defense of his resolution:

> Just to show that this matter is not brought up because of partisan motives, one of the members of the Liberal Wing is included in this resolution—Representative Roy from Tarlac. If this were brought up because of partisan impulses or vindictive motives, I would not have included my distinguished friend, one who belongs to our party.[74]

Of course, Liberal party strategists might well have decided to sacrifice a single affirmative vote in order to eliminate eight negative ones, but in any case Nueño's motivation became clear four days later, when after conferring with Roxas he amended his resolution to permit Roy to be seated.[75]

Nueño had justified his original resolution by reference to the report of the Commission on Elections which, he said, spoke of irregularities in the four Central Luzon provinces without distinction as to congressional district. Upon introducing his amendment he stated that he had satisfied himself that there had been no terrorism in Roy's first district of Tarlac, since the only Tarlac towns specifically mentioned in the report of the Commission on Elections were from the second district. But, as the House minority leader remarked, these Tarlac towns were mentioned only in connection with Democratic Alliance complaints regarding polling procedures, so this was hardly a compelling justification for unseating the Democratic Alliance representative from Tarlac's second district. Nor did Nueño explain why Vicente F. Gustilo, a Nacionalista elected from Negros Occidental, was included among those to be denied their seats because of alleged terror in Central Luzon.[76]

Nueño's amended resolution was then sent to committee, and the chair ruled that until the matter was voted on by the House as a whole the eight would be prohibited from taking their seats; that is, they were to be deemed guilty until proven innocent. The House did not display equal caution, however, when it decided to allow the seating of three representatives under indictment for wartime collaboration.[77]

Some members of the House challenged the right of the Liberal party's Tomas B. Morato to hold a seat, on the grounds that he had been born in Spain and that the constitution specifically required members of Congress to be "natural-born" citizens. In defense of Morato, one representative argued that the "Constitution provides that the Electoral Tribunal of this house shall be the sole judge of contests relating to the elections, qualifications and returns of Members of this Body." This was an accurate rendering of the constitution, but it applied as well to the eight disbarred representatives: the House Electoral Tribunal had not yet been formed and so, naturally, had taken action against no one.[78]

Morato, Roy, and three representatives under indictment for treason were all permitted to vote on the "parity" question. The excluded eight were not even allowed to participate in House debate; in fact, they were not permitted to have their speeches inserted into the record either as the comments of private citizens or as part of the remarks of another (seated) member of the House. The two disbarred Nacionalistas were given back their seats, but only twelve days after the "parity" vote was taken.[79]

In the Senate, the Roxas forces assured their two-thirds majority by similar shenanigans. When the Nacionalista minority temporarily walked out over a procedural dispute, a resolution was passed in their absence suspending three of their number on the ground that if votes from Central Luzon—where fraud and terror had been alleged—were discounted they would not have been elected. As in the House, the Senate Electoral Tribunal that was to decide such matters had not yet been formed. At the same time, three senators under indictment for treason were permitted to retain their seats. When the ouster of two other senators who had forfeited their seats by accepting judicial positions was suggested, "quiet was restored," as the Manila Times pithily reported. All save the three suspended Nacionalistas were permitted to vote on the "parity" issue.[80]

The events in Central Luzon on or immediately preceding election day lent little justification for the action of the Roxas forces in Congress. As described in the previous chapter, there *was* a small-scale civil war raging in the area; private landlord armies and military police were conducting a reign of terror against the peasants and their organizations. That there was much violence in Central Luzon, then, was undeniable, but this is very different from the charge that the Democratic Alliance stole the election through use of terror. That candidates of the Democratic Alliance won handily in some races is not in itself evidence that they were the perpetrators of fraud and terror, since they had the sympathies of a large proportion of the Central Luzon population. Socialists had done well in local elections in the area before the war. United States military intelligence in late 1945 had reported that a Huk leader would be a strong candidate for governor of Nueva Ecija (Central Luzon). "Outlaw bands," stated another intelligence report referring chiefly to the Huks, "have the backing of the majority in many cases." And the Philippine government's Agrarian Commission had indicated that by the end of the war about 90 percent of the farm workers in Central Luzon were members of the left-wing National Peasants' Union, which was a major component of the Democratic Alliance.[81] *Prima facie,* it was just as likely that Roxas supporters would use terror to minimize Osmeña's majority from Central Luzon as that the Democratic Alliance would resort to terror to ensure the victory of its local candidates. For example, the commander of an anti-Huk guerrilla unit privately wrote to Roxas in February 1946:

> The leaders and candidates of Osmeña [cannot] go out to the barrios [for] they are afraid of the 103rd Regiment, especially of the men under my command. . . . My men are authorized to confiscate arms and to shoot bandits and Huks. We are out always to shoot the Huks, and the more my men shoot Huks and chase Huks the more votes my men shoot and chase for General Roxas.[82]

The Commission on Elections reported that it had received no official reports of acts of violence on election day. It was advised by its representatives in Nueva Ecija that ballot boxes were stolen by armed bands in four municipalities; these incidents were still under investigation by the Military Police Command. Newspapers, the commission continued, gave accounts of acts of violence and intimidation, as did the report by the provost marshal general and other reports which "reached this Commission." In light of this, the commission said, the election in Central Luzon "did not reflect the true and free expression of the popular will. It should be stated, however, that the Commission is without jurisdiction, to determine whether or not the votes cast in the said provinces which, according to these reports have been cast under the influence of threats or violence, are valid or invalid." Nowhere in the commission's summary of these unsubstantiated reports was there any attribution of blame for the irregularities.

One of the three election commissioners (all of whom had been appointed by Osmeña and confirmed by Roxas's Commission on Appointments) submitted a minority report. He specifically named anti-Roxas elements, including the Huks, as being responsible for terrorism, but the only substantiation he provided was a report by the assistant chief of intelligence for the Military Police to the provost marshal.[83] Since the MPs throughout this period were involved in open warfare with the radical peasantry of Central Luzon, this is hardly an unbiased source.

A few days after the election, a U.S. official filed a confidential report that discussed, among other things, the conduct of the balloting. His only remarks on events in Central Luzon during or just prior to the voting were as follows:

> In the period immediately preceding the election Edilberto Joven, the head of the Democratic Alliance in Pampanga [Central Luzon], and his son, were forced out of their car by a group of armed men and killed. . . .
>
> Ballot boxes were stolen by armed gangs in the barrios of San Gregorio and San Mariano in Nueva Ecija; and military police were charged with intimidating voters in various different localities.[84]

Stolen ballot boxes in Nueva Ecija were mentioned by many sources, but usually without attribution of blame. The relatively objective *Manila Times,* however, reported that Governor Mariano Santa Romana of Nueva Ecija registered an official complaint with the secretary of the interior on the day after the election, charging that a guerrilla organization supporting Roxas was responsible for carrying off eight ballot boxes from areas that were voting heavily for Osmeña. No counterclaims were reported.[85]

The *Manila Times* accounts of the election in Central Luzon included descriptions of incidents and irregularities implicating the supporters of both sides and the Military Police. Other evidence for evaluating the events in Central Luzon is the later testimony of participants. Luis Taruc was a leader of the Huks until the mid-1950s after which time he broke with the organization and became extremely critical of his previous activities. Nevertheless, in 1967 he continued to assert that the Huks initiated no terror during the 1946 election. Another participant, Roxas's executive secretary Emilio Abello, conceded twenty-five years after the fact that the Democratic Alliance had been denied its seats for political reasons. Realizing how many votes had to be eliminated in order to assure the passage of "parity," he recalled, "We just had to count heads." And Judge Antonio Quirino, brother and political confidant of Roxas's vice-president, admitted that the opposition members of Congress had been unseated "in order to assure the necessary two-thirds vote." A U.S. Army historian has provided this summary of the conduct of the election: "[In Central Luzon] Osmeña and the DA [Democratic Alliance] had emerged victorious, despite a campaign of terror and intimidation Roxas supporters conducted, sometimes running into counterterror and counterintimidation on the part of ex-Hukbalahap forces."[86] Again, these are hardly ideal conditions for an election, but they do not show a one-sided theft of the election by the Democratic Alliance. The real thievery had taken place in Congress, where opponents of "parity" had been denied their seats.

On September 16, 1946, two days before the "parity" vote, McNutt cabled Washington that Roxas was "devoting every effort secure requisite majority both houses for equal rights amendment Constitution" and that the Philippine president was "seriously concerned as sufficient votes not definitely pledged as of last night." Roxas's "every effort" involved not just moral suasion; pork-barrel funds were widely distributed to win over opponents of the amendment. And at least one member of the Congress hoped to trade an affirmative vote on "parity" for lenient treatment in his trial for wartime collaboration.[87]

The "parity" amendment came to a vote on September 18. Again, the public statements of some of the supporters of the amendment were not indicative of overwhelming enthusiasm:

> I want to make it appear on the Record of the Congress that if the representatives of the United States who were responsible for the inclusion of this onerous condition . . . think or believe that they have fulfilled with honor the obligation and the promises of the United States, and that we Filipinos are very satisfied, happy and grateful to the United States, they are very much mistaken.[88]

In the Senate, the amendment received 16 ayes and 5 nays; in the House, 68 ayes and 18 nays. The Roxas forces announced that this was precisely enough for passage, because the necessary three-quarters should be computed on the basis of 21 senators and 90 representatives, that is, exclusive of the 3 senators and 8 representatives who had been ousted. The constitution, however, required that an amendment receive the affirmative vote of three-quarters of *all* the members of each house. The minority insisted that this meant three-quarters of 24 senators and 98 representatives, in which case the amendment would have failed.

The issue went to the Supreme Court, where an object lesson in the subservience of the judiciary was provided. The court voted 8 to 3 to deny the challenge to the "parity" amendment. Of the 8, 4 justices held that the court lacked jurisdiction and that enrollment of the amendment made it irreversible; two justices found that the court had appropriate jurisdiction, but agreed that enrollment and publication in legislative journals made an amendment irreversible; and two denied that the members of Congress who were denied their seats would have voted against "parity." Yet the previous July in the House, the minority leader had asked to make it a matter of record that the eight ousted representatives would have voted "no" on the Bell Act if they had been allowed to vote. The chair had refused to "accept or to put on record such observations."[89]

With the "parity" amendment past Congress, the Roxas forces had one final task: to secure the acceptance of the amendment in a nationwide plebiscite. Roxas himself then made "one of the most intensive campaign tours of the entire island network ever undertaken" by a member of the Philippine government, as one U.S. official put it. Another reported that Roxas was a "tireless" campaigner as a "flaming" advocate of "parity"; cabinet members made "tours of their own in support of this proposition and it may be said that the entire government machine has been fully mobilized."[90]

The plebiscite was scheduled for March 1947. The ballots were printed only in Spanish and English, schoolteachers were prohibited from serving as poll watchers on the grounds that they were biased against "parity," and polling places were moved out of rural areas in order to minimize the Democratic Alliance vote. A U.S. official cabled to Washington:

> There is some question as to how honest the ballot count will be. This, of course, is nothing new in Philippine politics. It would be most revolutionary if an honest count were made. There are no suggestions that the election will be "stolen" except by the most rabid of anti-Roxas spokesmen. It is merely accepted that the size of the majority will be greatly increased with all able-bodied voters being counted whether they vote or not. . . .
>
> The opponents of parity . . . are finding it virtually impossible to raise funds. Businessmen are fearful of retribution by the Philippine National Bank, National Development Company and other government institutions.[91]

On the day of the plebiscite, a large majority of the less than two-thirds of registered voters who cast ballots backed the "parity" clause. To the *New York Times*, Filipinos had "given evidence of political maturity." The U.S. head of the Philippine War Damage Commission hailed the vote as a "victory for the Philippine people." And Jasper Bell remarked:

> To me, as an American, it was refreshing to witness the act of the Filipino people in supporting by such an overwhelming majority what is essentially a program of free enterprise. I am sure that as time goes by, not only will the ties of friendship between Filipinos and Americans be broadened and strengthened by the effects of this trade act, but the very foundation of democracy both here and in the Orient will be given new life and vitality by a rich and ever-growing flood of commerce, based not upon totalitarian state controls, but upon private enterprise thriving in free democracy.

In the "parity" plebiscite, Bell added, Roxas emerged victorious in "a battle in which a small minority received inspiration from totalitarian sources abroad."[92] No doubt to Bell only a totalitarian could possibly have any objection to the "parity" amendment or to the trade agreement which bore his name.

The Military Dimension

In the same month as the "parity" plebiscite, March 1947, Manila and Washington concluded a pair of agreements formalizing military relations between the two countries. The first of these granted the United States naval and air bases on the islands.

The position of the executive branch of the U.S. government regarding military bases in an independent Philippines had fluctuated a great deal before World War II: Would such bases be a military asset or a military liability?[93] By 1943, however, the ambivalence of American officials came to an end. That the United States would emerge from the war as the foremost economic and military power was obvious, and a global network of bases was necessary for the dominant role that the United States was determined to play in world affairs. In September 1943 Secretary of War Stimson told Senator Millard Tydings that the United States would need bases in the Philippines. At the end of the year President Roosevelt's chief aide, Harry Hopkins, told Allied representatives at the Teheran conference that the United States would likely maintain naval and air bases in the Philippines. Philippine leader Manuel Quezon, who had vacillated with the winds of public opinion on this question before the war, wrote MacArthur in October 1943 that he would propose that the United States retain military bases in the islands.[94]

In June 1944 the U.S. Congress passed a resolution authorizing the American president, after negotiations with the Philippine president, to acquire military bases in the Philippines. Quezon and Osmeña enthusiastically supported the resolution. Some members of Congress had proposed deleting the requirement for negotiations, but Stimson—a former high commissioner in Manila—dissuaded them; he confided that while the requirement "to us is meaningless," since the United States has the authority to retain whatever bases it chooses, to the Filipino negotiation is a great source of face and courtesy.[95]

To some, overseas bases were part of an American Manifest Destiny reminiscent of an earlier era. Tydings, for example, declared on the floor of the Senate in 1945: "We should give up no base, whether previously a mandated island or not, which has been won by the blood of our gallant soldiers, sailors, and airmen. . . . Therefore, whether we want it or not, we must do it if it is to be done."[96] Other U.S. officials thought in more hardheaded terms. A high-level memorandum from the U.S. Office of Strategic Services stated that the United States should attempt to

> secure and strengthen our position in the Pacific Islands. The vital importance of the Philippines in controlling the sea-lanes from the North to the rich resources of the East Indies is now more obvious than ever. In the interest of the Philippine Republic as well as in our own, the future relationship of the islands to the United States should be reconsidered, and if possible full provision should be made for adequate American sea and air bases.[97]

The economic potential of the western Pacific was well appreciated in Washington. "The major portions of the world supply of certain important strategic materials," stated a secret 1945 War Department study, "are located within this area, each of which is of utmost importance to the industrial and commercial interests of the U.S." Japan's forced withdrawal from the region, together with the development of China and possibly the East Indies, "will expand this area to one of the future great world markets." In addition, the region "offers great possibilities for investment and development. . . ."[98]

The role that Philippine bases could play in the western Pacific was spelled out in a top-secret report by the Joint Chiefs of Staff: "The United States bases in the Philippines should be considered, not merely as outposts, but as springboards from which the United States armed forces may be projected."[99] The army should be prepared to use its Philippine bases, said the War Department, "to conduct punitive operations against Japan, and possibly other nations in the Far East."[100] Paul McNutt made much the same point publicly in July 1946:

> They are not designed merely for the protection of the Philippines, nor even for the defense of the United States. These bases are expected to be secondary, supporting installations for supply, repair and staging activities for all our armed forces in the Far East . . . . Committed as we are to a long-time occupation of Japan, to a strong policy in Asia, the Philippines are designed to play a major role in our diplomacy in the Orient.[101]

How did this jibe with Philippine independence? McNutt quite frankly conceded that foreign military bases were inconsistent with the traditional notion of independence. But, he argued, in the new era of global wars the fate of the United States and the Philippines was inextricably linked and the old definition of independence was obsolete. Even a year and a half after formal independence, top State Department strategist George F. Kennan wrote to Secretary of State George Marshall that the U.S. objective should be to "permit Philippine independence, but in such a way as to assure the archipelago remained a bulwark of American security in the Pacific region."[102]

In April 1945 President Osmeña assured the American secretary of state that he would be agreeable to whatever suggestions Washington wished to make regarding postwar bases. On May 14 Osmeña and Truman signed a secret preliminary statement of general principles pertaining to U.S. bases in the Philippines, incorporating all the provisions of a draft drawn up in the U.S. War Department. One provision specified that no other nation was to be permitted to establish or use any bases in the islands without the approval of both Washington and Manila.[103] In July 1945 the Philippine Congress—at this point consisting entirely of those elected before the war—unanimously passed a resolution authorizing the Philippine president to grant military bases to the United States after negotiations with the American chief executive. In the election campaign of 1946, both Roxas and Osmeña publicly favored giving the United States bases, and after he became president, Roxas assured U.S. officials that they could write their own ticket as to the size and location of military bases.[104]

The Philippine elite was willing to be accommodating on the bases, for they realized that this was the way to tie the interests of Washington to their own. When a member of Congress from Pennsylvania complained about the free-trade relations which the Philippine elite cared so much about, Resident Commissioner Carlos P. Romulo replied, "America will have air and naval bases in the Philippines. Certainly America would not want to have the Philippines on an unstable economy."[105]

The negotiations on the specific base rights that Washington would have in the Philippines ran into difficulties because of the rather extraordinary demands made by the U.S. military. All the executive departments of the U.S. government were agreed that the United States should have exclusive criminal jurisdiction over all offenses committed on the bases, unless *both* parties were Philippine citizens. This would give the United States greater authority than it was to have in base agreements with any of the NATO countries. The War and Navy Departments, however, were eager to have U.S. jurisdiction extend to offenses committed by American personnel off the bases. The State Department warned that the Philippine government would be politically unable to grant this and that it would be regarded by Asians as a revival of extraterritoriality; it would "hurt us in terms of good will without commensurate advantage to this country."[106] The War and Navy Departments deferred to the State Department on this matter. The bases agreement gave the United States jurisdiction over all offenses committed on base, except where both parties were Philippine citizens, and over offenses committed off the bases by one member of the U.S. armed forces against another. In addition, the United States was given jurisdiction over U.S. military personnel off base if the offense was committed during the performance of a specific military duty or if there was a period of national emergency or war.[107]

Another area of discord was the insistence by the Navy that all real property located within the naval reservations should belong to the United States after the expiration of the bases agreement. The State Department felt this was a negligible concern and that it would endanger approval of the bases agreement by the Philippine legislature. As a way out of the impasse, the State Department suggested that title rights to property not be mentioned in the agreement, that instead an exchange of notes would provide for subsequent negotiations regarding these rights. The text of the notes was not to be made public before debate and passage of the agreement by the Philippine Congress.[108]

A final area of disagreement was less easy to resolve. The War Department wanted to retain the McKinley-Nichols Field area, a large prewar military installation located within metropolitan Manila. In light of the numerous frictions being reported daily between American armed forces personnel and Filipinos, the prostitution and related activities that invariably surrounded U.S. bases overseas, and the fact that the base was in a natural expansion area of Manila, it was clear that retention of McKinley-Nichols Field was unacceptable to even the most cooperative Philippine leader. "Gentlemen," Roxas is reported to have said, "you can have what you want. You can have as many as you like. Just keep away from populated centers."[109]

Washington considered Philippine objections to U.S. troops in the Manila area "understandable" and realized that army bases were not particularly useful if opposed by the Philippine government. However, building new army facilities elsewhere in the Philippines would require a considerable expenditure, which the War Department felt it could ill afford. In addition, U.S. plans to station occupation forces in Japan and Korea as well as in Europe would take all the War Department's resources, especially personnel. It would be a waste of strength, wrote the secretary of war, to maintain "a force of any considerable size in the Philippines."[110]

Accordingly, the War Department reconsidered the strategic importance of Army and Army Air Force bases in the Philippines. It decided, with Truman's approval, to withdraw the bulk of Army personnel from the islands, leaving a token force of one composite Air Force group with a small ground detachment. The Navy reduced its base requirements so as not to need Army troops to defend its facilities.[111]

Despite these reductions, however, the March 1947 Military Bases Agreement granted the United States military installations of staggering proportions. The 130,000-acre Clark Air Base was just the largest of the numerous air and naval bases given to the United States on a ninety-nine–year lease. Under the terms of the agreement, the Philippine government was prohibited from granting "any bases or any rights, power, or authority whatsoever, in or relating to bases" to any other nation without U.S. consent. The United States was permitted to recruit, on a voluntary basis, Philippine citizens for service in the American military. The agreement made the Philippine city of Olongapo, in the words of a 1959 account in *Time* magazine, "the only foreign city run lock, stock and barrel by the U.S. Navy . . . . 4,500 Americans pour $20,000 a month into a city that has no industry of its own but boasts more than its share of pimps, peddlers, and 2,000 registered prostitutes that the Navy euphemistically calls 'hostesses.' " The Navy commander had the right to tax, distribute light and power, hand out business licenses, search without a warrant, and deport undesirables. And the Air Force bases provided some unique opportunities for Filipinos: "The privilege of the Clark Air Base dump and other concessions, including the right to retrieve lost golf balls from the Base course water holes, was granted by General MacArthur to the Negritos tribe. About 1,000 members of this tribe live on the base pursuing the opportunities created by these privileges."[112]

The following year, 1948, the secretary of the army privately recommended to the secretary of defense that consideration be given to completely abandoning the bases in the Philippines because of repeated incidents between Filipinos and U.S. military personnel. The Joint Chiefs of Staff strongly rejected this recommendation, for a number of reasons.[113]

First, U.S. observers and high officials in Manila had stated that the presence of U.S. armed forces in the Philippines exerted "a stabilizing influence" on the population and that this would be the case for some time to come. The U.S. forces at Clark Field in Central Luzon, where the population was "particularly unpredictable," were considered an especially effective symbol of law and order.[114]

Second, in the view of the Joint Chiefs, as long as the U.S. Navy or Air Force was going to operate in the western Pacific, a requirement for bases in the Philippines would exist. The Philippines was not considered strategically vital, but Pentagon planners nevertheless saw bases there as useful for protecting air and sea lines of communication, for staging limited air operations, and for exerting "a decisive strategic influence on the course of events in Asia and the islands of the Southwest Pacific." And events in China led State and Defense Department officials to anticipate the increasing strategic importance of Philippine bases.[115]

Finally, the Joint Chiefs noted that withdrawal from the Philippines might cause Manila to turn to another country for military assistance and support, a circumstance which Washington was unwilling to tolerate.[116]

The second component of the U.S.-Philippine military relationship was formalized in the Military Assistance Agreement of 1947, signed just one week after the bases accord. Despite the public denials of U.S. officials, the military assistance was viewed in Washington and Manila at least in part as payment for the bases. The State Department consciously delayed concluding the aid agreement pending the outcome of the bases negotiations. And Roxas at first refused to sign the bases pact until the aid agreement was finalized; it was only after McNutt gave the Philippine president his word that the military assistance pact would be signed that Roxas agreed to approve the bases treaty.[117]

Securing base rights was not, however, the only purpose of the military aid. The Military Assistance Agreement was intended to help the Philippine government maintain internal security, which is to say maintain itself in power, maintain the status quo by force of arms, and reduce the need for U.S. forces to garrison the bases. The agreement was retroactively effective to the date of independence, July 4, 1946. Surplus military supplies were being given to Manila both prior to and after this date, so the signing of the agreement merely formalized what was already policy.

"For at least a year following the granting of independence," the Pentagon's Joint Staff Planners wrote, the Philippine government would need a military force capable of functioning as a national police force. In June 1946 the congressional sponsor of the military aid legislation declared:

> If this Government does not enact the legislation provided in this bill, on July 4 and after that date the Philippine Islands will be left without any protection at all and . . . there are between three and four hundred thousand guerrillas, well armed, over there. We armed them because they were our guerrillas during the war. They are pillaging the whole country. There is no other situation on the face of the earth that is comparable with the situation in the Philippine Islands and that which will obtain after July 4.

And in late 1947, when the Philippine Constabulary was reorganized separate from the Philippine Armed Forces, the Joint Chiefs of Staff approved allocating part of the U.S. military aid to this police force: "Since one of the principal purposes of military assistance to the Philippines is the maintenance of internal law and order, the United States should support the organizations performing this function even though they are not members of the armed forces of the Philippines."[118]

There was one final purpose of the military aid given to Manila. It was not to enable the Philippines to repel an external aggressor, for U.S. officials unanimously agreed that no such threat existed.[119] Rather, military aid was viewed in Washington as a means to support the political orientation of the Philippines toward the United States and to strengthen its morale.[120]

U.S. military assistance did not consist just of equipment. The aid agreement also established a Joint U.S. Military Advisory Group, JUSMAG. (The word "Joint" did not indicate U.S.-Filipino cooperation; rather it signified the involvement of all the branches of the U.S. military.) The mission of JUSMAG was spelled out in a War Department directive:

a. Primarily, to advise the Military Forces of the Republic of the Philippines on training, organization, tactics, strategy, planning, service, supply, procurement, administration, and other related military subjects.
b. To increase the efficiency of the Military Forces of the Republic of the Philippines by advising in the training of their personnel in the military doctrine of the Military Forces of the United States.
c. To promote the standardization of military equipment and encourage the use of material of United States manufacture and design.
d. To foster friendly relations and strengthen the ties of United States–Philippine solidarity.
e. To occupy the field of military cooperation in the Philippines to the exclusion insofar as possible of all other-than-United States participation and influence.
f. To function as a Liaison Group between [U.S. and Philippine military forces] with reference to joint plans and joint operations of these forces.
g. To advise the Commander-in-Chief, U.S. Army Forces, Pacific on all important matters pertaining to the Military Forces of the Republic of the Philippines.
h. To carry out such other duties, consistent with its primary mission as may be directed by the Commander-in-Chief, U.S. Army Forces, Pacific.[121]

Items (c) and (e) were facilitated by a provision of the military aid agreement prohibiting the Philippines from accepting military equipment or advice from any government other than the United States without U.S. approval.

JUSMAG officers "closely associated themselves with their Filipino counterparts," drew up plans for the organization of a national police force, and made staff studies on the coordination of Philippine intelligence agencies. "Most of the major reforms recommended by the [U.S. advisory] Group were accepted by President Roxas," JUSMAG reported to Washington in 1948. Roxas's successor, Elpidio Quirino, "stated that he will rely heavily upon the advice of the Chief of JUSMAG prior to making any major decision affecting the national military policies and has consulted him on the few occasions when important military matters have required his attention." Quirino accepted the JUSMAG recommendation for Philippine chief of staff, who in turn "volunteered full cooperation" with JUSMAG.[122]

As formal sovereignty changed hands in the Philippines, U.S. strategic and economic interests remained intact. The United States had bases from which to pursue its "strong policy in Asia" and special investment rights. The Philippine elite, for its part, had continued preferential access to the American market for sugar and other exports and received military assistance with which to assure its elite position.

In mid-1947, the French minister in Siam, Pierre-Eugene Gilbert, told the American ambassador there that the goal of French policy in Laos and Cambodia was to "grant them [the] same measure [of] independence granted [to the] Philippines with orientation in economic and political matters toward France." Washington cabled the U.S. ambassador to tell Gilbert that the Philippines was totally independent and that any special arrangements were based on the free decision of the Filipino people through plebiscite or their elected representatives.

The French were not alone, however, in their failure to appreciate this point. The *Washington Post* noted editorially that the "basic fact to remember is that independence for the Philippines will not take them out of the orbit of our close and immediate interests any more than the independence of Cuba broke the intimate ties between that country and our own." American political scientist David N. Rowe remarked a few months after formal Philippine independence that, both economically and militarily, "the United States is actually in a stronger position in the Philippines although the islands are independent now." And a U.S. military analyst wrote in October 1946; "In spite of their independence the Philippines are of course extremely dependent on us militarily, economically and politically. At the moment their independence consists principally of face. . . . "[123]

===== CHAPTER THREE =====

The Crisis of the Early 1950s

Had the Philippine government been only somewhat less venal and repressive, or Asia only moderately less important to U.S. policy-makers at mid-century, the relationship between the United States and the Philippines might well have continued roughly as described in the previous two chapters. But Philippine leaders were so thoroughly corrupt, and their efforts to restore the old relations of domination in the countryside so arrantly brutal, that the Philippines was soon on the brink of disaster. And given events in China, Indochina, and Korea, Washington was unwilling to tolerate a disaster in the Philippines.

Between 1946 and 1948 the Philippine government and landlords continued their reign of terror against the peasantry of Central Luzon. The Hukbalahap had no intention at this time of trying to overthrow the government, but they were increasingly forced to take up weapons to defend themselves. They were, in the words of one scholar, "reluctant rebels"; Huk leaders later recalled that they adopted a generally defensive posture, avoiding encounters and fighting only when attacked or when victims of persecution asked for their protection.[1] In March 1948 Roxas declared the Huks and their affiliated National Peasants' Union to be illegal organizations, an action used as justification for further indiscriminate terror against the rural population. In at least two cases, barrio inhabitants were massacred by Constabulary troops and civilian guards.[2]

Roxas died the next month and was succeeded in office by his vice-president, Elpidio Quirino. Quirino tried to negotiate an amnesty with the Huks, but the efforts were deliberately sabotaged by the landlords in his administration. Some anti-Huk military operations were undertaken during the period of the amnesty, and the U.S. Embassy doubted that the Constabulary was sincerely cooperating with the amnesty program. On a more basic level, the amnesty offer failed because—in the words of a Philippine counterinsurgency specialist—it was "not accompanied by tangible efforts of the government to rid itself of graft and corruption, nor was it accompanied by positive steps towards removing discontentment among the masses," nor was the government able to "counter the Huk accusation of bad faith on the part of the administration." The chief of JUSMAG, however, thought Quirino had gone too far in making concessions to the Huks and that the time had come for a showdown. By September, Quirino reverted to the mailed-fist approach.[3]

The Constabulary made armored sweeps during which areas suspected of containing Huks were sprayed with machine gun and artillery fire. White phosphorus shells were used to burn areas to flush out Huks. "Civilians within the vicinity of operations always suffer more than the dissidents," a Philippine military intelligence report stated. The Philippine Constabulary seized food without paying for it, employed torture, abused women, and mistreated the peasants. In marked contrast, the Huks obtained food from local residents without coercion and generally "increased their popular support by correct behavior."[4]

In the meantime, the Philippine elite continued to use political power for its personal aggrandizement. In 1946 Congress amended the tax laws to make the rates more regressive. In October 1946 the war profits tax was altered to exclude a major part of the buy-and-sell trade from the coverage of the law; in any case, by April 30, 1947, of the estimated 30,000 individuals and corporations liable to file war profits tax returns, only 1,920 had done so, and of these 1,440 claimed no tax liability. Veterans' benefits paid by the U.S. Army to Filipinos who had served under the American flag during World War II often ended up in the hands of corrupt officials, as did the proceeds from the illicit sale of surplus war material that the United States had turned over to the Philippine government.[5]

At war's end the Philippines had been in an excellent balance-of-payments position because of U.S. military spending, rehabilitation funds, and other payments, but these were rapidly dissipated by the conspicuous consumption of luxuries and nonessentials by the rich. By 1950 the United States had provided the Philippines with $1.4 billion in aid of one sort or another, but, in Dean Acheson's words, there was not "a great deal to show for it." Mismanagement and corruption, observed Acheson, were threatening to turn the

U.S. effort in the Philippines into a "shambles." This view was shared by American business interests who considered the situation in the Philippines too unstable to justify increased investments.[6]

The last straw came in the Philippine presidential election of 1949. It was a three-way contest between the incumbent, Quirino, Senate president Jose Avelino (a member of Quirino's party), and Jose P. Laurel, the man who had served as president of the Philippine Republic under the Japanese. Quirino had Avelino ousted from his Senate post for fraud and for advocating tolerance of graft and corruption. Avelino was alleged by Quirino to have said, "If you cannot permit abuses you must at least tolerate them. What are we in power for? We are not hypocrites. Why should we pretend to be saints when in reality we are not?"[7] Quirino's own commitment to government probity, however, was revealed after he won the balloting when he had Avelino reinstated as Senate president in exchange for the support of Avelino's faction in proclaiming Quirino's election.[8]

In Washington, Quirino was thought to be the least of three evils. Though thoroughly corrupt, Quirino "at least is basically friendly to us, and is willing that our two countries continue their present special relationships." Laurel, on the other hand, was viewed as anti-American, and the U.S. Central Intelligence Agency warned of his "extreme nationalism and anti-foreignism." U.S. businesspeople in Manila feared his victory. They recommended that while there be no public U.S. denunciation of Laurel (lest this encourage a nationalist backlash—a view concurred in by Washington) means be found by which they could translate their support of Quirino into action. Apparently, these business interests contributed to Quirino's campaign fund.[9]

The Philippine off-year election of 1947 had been described at the time as the "bloodiest in Philippine history," and official Philippine sources estimated that 12 percent of the ballots were fraudulent.[10] But even by this dubious standard, the presidential election of 1949 was a landmark of dishonesty. Official records estimated that more than one-fifth of the ballots were spurious. The *New York Times* called it the "costliest, most violent" national election in Philippine annals. A contributor to *Reader's Digest* observed, "Every device known to fraudulent elections was used. . . . Filipinos sadly wisecracked that even the birds and the bees voted in some precincts."[11]

In response to the election, Laurel supporters in his home province of Batangas led a minor armed rebellion that was swiftly crushed by government forces. More significant, the Huks, finding parliamentary struggle useless, called for the overthrow of the government. Gaining the backing of a disillusioned peasant population,

Huk strength soon reached 12,000 to 15,000 armed supporters with a mass base of from 1.5 to 2 million. The very continuity of the Philippine state was in question. Quirino kept a motor launch moored to the presidential palace to evacuate him and his family should the guerrillas enter Manila. And U.S. officials saw the possibility of the country being reduced to chaos and the Huks coming to power.[12]

Before getting to this point, the U.S. government had taken a number of steps to buttress the Philippine situation, but the efforts had had little effect. In early 1947 a joint U.S.-Philippine Finance Commission, set up at Washington's urging, had advanced numerous recommendations for improving the financial position of the Philippine government: tax reform, establishment of a Central Bank, imposition of import controls[13]—in short, measures that would allow the Philippine government to support itself rather than depend on grants or loans from the United States. Three years later, however, a U.S. Treasury Department official noted that there had been "no progress whatsoever" in enforcing revenue laws, and negligible tax reform. A Central Bank had been established, but it had failed to institute a program of domestic borrowing; and import controls, instituted in January 1949, were being "corruptly and ineffectively managed," with foreign exchange reserves declining 40 percent during the year.[14]

These events, of course, were not taking place in a vacuum. Developments in Asia were causing serious reconsiderations of policy by U.S. officials. Just the month before Quirino's 1949 election victory, the Chinese Communists had proclaimed their government in Peking.

At the close of World War II, U.S. strategy in Asia had been based on China. A strong and friendly China was to have been the bastion of American power in the western Pacific. Japan, defeated in war, was to have been demilitarized under the control of a U.S. occupation force. Over the next few years, however, the situation had changed drastically. Corrupt, reactionary, and without a significant base of popular support, the Kuomintang rapidly lost ground to the Communists, despite considerable U.S. assistance. This profoundly altered the strategic balance for U.S. policymakers. A revitalized Japan was now to be brought into the American alliance. From mid-1949 on, U.S. policy was to be based on the "assumption," as Secretary of State Dean Acheson put it, "that the United States does not intend to permit further extension of Communist domination on the continent of Asia or in the southeast Asia area." In late

1949 the National Security Council (NSC) secretly stated that the Asian offshore island chain—Japan, the Ryukyus, and the Philippines—represented "our first line of defense and in addition, our first line of offense from which we may seek to reduce the area of Communist control. . . ." Since the United States might "lose" Formosa, "every effort [should be made to] strengthen the over-all U.S. position with respect to the Philippines, the Ryukyus, and Japan." [15]

Officials in Washington all agreed that developments in China made the U.S. position in the Philippines much more important than before. The dilemma for U.S. policy, however, was that the Philippines did not appear capable of filling its more important role. As one news report that was entered into the *Congressional Record* put it, the Philippines was "perhaps the weakest link in our defensive structures in the western Pacific and southeast Asia." The danger was not external attack, Dean Acheson assured, but internal "disintegration." [16]

The Philippines was also of strategic value to the United States in other than a military sense. In an age of nationalism, the National Security Council concluded, intervention by a Western power in Asia was likely to be counterproductive. The United States must work with, and even strengthen, a moderate nationalism as a means for opposing communism. The United States, the NSC noted, "should refrain from taking the lead in movements which must of necessity be of Asian origin." An American propaganda official made the same point: "We must present American ideas dressed in Asian clothes, coming from Asian mouths, if we are to succeed." The United States "should help from behind the scenes—and stop trying to play the leading part on the stage."[17] There was no more perfect Asian clothing for American policy than the Philippines. As President Roxas had said in a speech in the United States in 1946, "We are not of the Orient except by geography. We are part of the Western world by reason of culture, religion, ideology, economics. . . . We expect to remain part of the West, possibly as the ideological bridge between the Occident and the Orient."[18]

Practical examples of this attitude were not difficult to find. Carlos P. Romulo, the Philippine delegate to the United Nations, declined to support the radical nationalist movements in Indochina or North Africa, "since the major battle was against Communism." And the Philippine government had allowed the United States to set up a Voice of America relay transmitter in Manila capable of reaching China, Indochina, and Korea. Philippine foreign policy, said Roxas, was "committed to the cause and international program of the United States of America." And just before his death in 1948,

Roxas offered the United States a pledge of loyalty that the State Department found "so strong as to be unusual in international relations."[19]

"We should endeavor to induce the Philippines," the secretary of state had told the NSC in 1949,

> to assume an active and constructive role in developing a counter-force to communism in SEA [Southeast Asia] and otherwise to further spontaneously our major objectives in Asia. We should encourage the Filipinos to take the initiative publicly in many projects which they, as Asians can advance more effectively than we, but always to come to us for confidential and friendly guidance.[20]

There was also an economic motive for U.S. concern with the stability of the Philippines. As one member of Congress put it,

> it is to our own self-interest to stabilize the economy of the Philippines, they will buy our goods. Southeast Asia represents the greatest potential market in the world for American goods. . . . here is a country that, once its economy is stabilized, will want durable goods and want them in great quantities.
>   It has things that we need and it would provide a potential market for these exchanges.[21]

Another reason the Philippines was important to U.S. policymakers was that it provided a test case of the benefits that might accrue to countries from having close friendships with the United States. "It is a laboratory sample of the choice which exists between our kind of world and the kind of world on the other side of the iron curtain," noted Assistant Secretary of State Dean Rusk. Another official remarked, "Our standing in the Orient, our brand of democracy and way of doing business depend on how the Philippine example turns out." The failure of the Philippine "experiment" would be a great propaganda defeat for the United States in the cold war.[22]

All these factors led U.S. policymakers to take steps to prevent the collapse of the Philippines. In December 1949 Manila imposed foreign exchange controls after getting the permission of the U.S. president, as required by the Bell Trade Act. Though in the short run detrimental to U.S. economic interests, "there appeared no other means of retarding the drastic decline of dollar reserves." Unchecked, this decline could cause the total bankruptcy of the islands, rendering all U.S. investments there worthless. According to a Philippine official, however, the U.S. Embassy in Manila did warn the Philippine government that Truman might withdraw his approval of the controls if they were applied in a discriminatory manner against American firms.[23]

In February 1950, when Quirino came to the United States, the State and Treasury Departments recommended that Truman "firmly advise President Quirino that no further American aid could be considered unless and until there is tangible evidence that the Philippines has taken steps to put its house in order and that it would then need and be in a position to effectively use additional aid." Specifically, Truman was to propose to Quirino that a U.S. economic survey mission be sent to the Philippines. Quirino agreed, but over the next four months he wavered, suggesting that the mission be a joint Philippine-American team rather than a purely American one. United States officials remained insistent, feeling that Quirino's appointees would whitewash Philippine corruption and mismanagement, and in early June, Quirino finally accepted. On June 29 Truman announced that an economic survey mission was being sent to Manila, headed by Daniel W. Bell, president of the American Security and Trust Company and a former undersecretary of the treasury.[24]

In 1947–1948 U.S. officials had decided to provide only minimal military aid to the Philippines. A request by Manila for additional assistance had been turned down on the grounds that it was not needed. Military aid was continued at low levels for the next two years; for fiscal 1950 (approved in early 1949) less than $6 million in military assistance was programmed for the islands, which placed the Philippines "in the lowest considered priority" for military aid.[25] In the spring of 1950 deliveries of scheduled U.S. military supplies were speeded up. Then, with the outbreak of fighting in Korea, Truman was able to obtain congressional approval for a massive supplemental military aid appropriation. For the Philippines, the fiscal 1951 appropriation came to more than three times the previous year's allotment. And both JUSMAG and the U.S. security forces at the Philippine bases were brought back up to strength.[26]

Though Truman had justified his military aid request to Congress by referring to "the increased jeopardy to the Pacific area caused by the Communist aggression in Korea," the threat to the Philippines was wholly internal. There was no evidence of any significant outside aid to the Huks, and, indeed, the State Department was actually surprised at how little the Soviet Union had been doing for the Huks. Washington had explicitly decided, however, that it would not permit the Philippines to succumb to external attack *or* internal subversion. Communism, "however Filipinized it might appear, will be considered as aggression."[27]

United States officials, in particular the officers of JUSMAG, repeatedly advised the Philippine government that a sound military policy "justifies maximum emphasis and expenditures upon forces required for the maintenance of internal security and minimum expenditure upon forces contributing largely to national prestige or to forces and reserves designed for defense against external invaders." In late 1949, JUSMAG persuaded the Philippine government to alter its defense budget by reducing the air force and navy allocations in favor of the more directly counterinsurgency-oriented army. Even the Korean War did not change JUSMAG's view of the Philippine Armed Forces' primary mission; when Quirino offered to send 5,000 Filipino troops to Korea, JUSMAG advised him that he would not be able to maintain internal security in the Philippines. It was decided that Manila would contribute one combat infantry battalion of 1,275 men—just enough to give the Korean action an international image—with its supplies to be provided by the United States. Nor did the U.S.-Philippine Mutual Defense Treaty of 1951 signify any U.S. fear of external aggression. Washington signed this treaty strictly to get the Philippines to agree to the Japanese peace treaty. United States officials were happy to humor the Philippine government by signing the Mutual Defense Treaty, so long as they did not have to exchange military information with Manila or disturb "our present military arrangements in the Philippines which are particularly advantageous to the United States."[28]

JUSMAG drew up recommendations that were accepted by Philippine officials for a thoroughgoing reorganization of the antidissident campaign. Responsibility for combating Huks had rested with the Philippine Constabulary. Because the Constabulary was under the authority of the Department of the Interior, it was easily influenced by local politics; in addition, JUSMAG felt that Constabulary units were too small, with poor discipline, training, and leadership. Therefore, the United States "insisted" that the Constabulary be combined with the Armed Forces of the Philippines, under the office of the secretary of national defense, and that these merged armed forces be given the task of fighting Huks. JUSMAG further advised that instead of anti-Huk units of about 90 men, as the Constabulary had had, battalion combat teams be organized: contingents of 1,170 soldiers, with artillery, which could engage in major offensive actions instead of police-minded static defense. In the spring of 1950, Philippine officials implemented the JUSMAG recommendations. Recruiting to augment the Philippine Army was undertaken "throughout all areas, except Central Luzon where dissidents are concentrated."[29]

Also in early 1950, at the request of the Philippine chief of staff, JUSMAG prepared a study proposing a complete reorganization of the intelligence agencies of the Philippine government, and the JUSMAG recommendations were carried out.[30] And in August 1950, CIA operative Edward G. Lansdale was ordered to Manila to advise the Philippine government on counterinsurgency.[31]

In the summer of 1950, U.S. officials in the Philippines moved to get their choice appointed as secretary of national defense. The head of JUSMAG and the American ambassador, Myron M. Cowen, strongly urged Quirino to select Ramon Magsaysay for the post. (Just a short time before, Cowen had replied to a Philippine senator's complaint that the head of JUSMAG had recommended for the job another high Philippine official—the one convicted of collaboration with the Japanese: "It is not the policy or practice of this Embassy to make any recommendations whatsoever to the Philippine Government as to what officials it should appoint.") In any case, Quirino was not in a strong bargaining position—being dependent on the United States for military aid—and on September 1, 1950, Magsaysay was appointed to the cabinet position.[32]

Later mythology was to portray Magsaysay as having come from humble origins, a "man of the masses." In fact, his family was the most well-to-do in their barrio and one of the wealthiest in the town. They owned a general merchandise shop and various farms, including one of over a thousand acres, and they employed tenant labor. Magsaysay first worked as a mechanic at a bus line owned by a relative. He was soon made a shop superintendent and later a branch manager. His salary at the time, 1939, was higher than the average wage made by nonself-employed agricultural workers by about a factor of 35. In 1940 the employees under his authority went on strike because of his harsh methods, such as arbitrary suspensions and dismissals. Magsaysay tried to organize strikebreakers and ultimately broke the strike by getting a court to rule that the strike leaders were attempting to sabotage American military preparations by hindering transportation.[33]

During the war, Magsaysay headed a USAFFE guerrilla unit. He was appointed military governor of Zambales province by the U.S. Army when it returned to the islands. In 1946, he was elected to Congress on a platform pledging to obtain benefits from the United States for USAFFE guerrillas and other war veterans. He was a loyal member of the Liberal party; for example, he praised Quirino as a modern "Sir Galahad, a knight in shining armor in search of the Holy Grail of clean and honest government." He was made head of the House Defense Committee, a position which involved him in a great deal of contact with JUSMAG. In 1948 he made a trip to the United States to obtain veterans' benefits legislation, at which time he also established good contacts in the Pentagon. And in March 1950 he traveled to the United States to request additional military aid, meeting again with top American officials. Upon his return he delivered his first and only privileged speech in his four years in Congress, a speech defending the United States against its critics.[34]

As secretary of national defense, Magsaysay was able to obtain for himself a free hand in running the armed forces: he was able to contact the Pentagon to put pressure on Quirino, using the leverage of U.S. military aid, to get his enemies removed from office.[35] But this does not mean that Magsaysay was going to lead the anti-Huk campaign alone. He leaned heavily for advice on Major General Leland S. Hobbs, the head of JUSMAG. A few years later Hobbs would write to President Dwight Eisenhower, "I think I know [Magsaysay] and his innermost desires as do few Americans." In early 1951 JUSMAG secretly reported that the United States was "fortunate" in having as the Philippine secretary of national defense a person "with a genuine admiration and faith in the United States, [whose cooperation with JUSMAG] has been outstanding, and its advise and assistance is constantly sought and utilized by him." And another Defense Department official was "particularly impressed" with Magsaysay's "determination and pro-American attitude."[36]

A week after Magsaysay's appointment, the CIA's Edward Lansdale arrived in Manila. In the early postwar years, when Lansdale had been chief of army intelligence for the western Pacific, stationed in the Philippines, he had befriended Magsaysay among others. Now he set up a desk in Magsaysay's defense office and had Magsaysay share his bedroom in the JUSMAG compound, and the two worked closely together on the problems of counterinsurgency. Lansdale, the U.S. ambassador reported to Washington, was "the right hand" of Magsaysay.[37]

Under the guidance of Lansdale, Hobbs, and some of their staff officers, Magsaysay was able to revitalize the armed forces. Corrupt officers were removed and, though Magsaysay himself used his office to dispense patronage and pork-barrel,[38] it was no longer at a level that prevented the military from functioning. Magsaysay also increased troop morale. As two of his biographers have said, "Magsaysay was winning army loyalty with the human touch. Soldiers who killed Huks earned a stripe and a personal letter of praise from him." Magsaysay initiated a policy of giving liberal "cash incentives" for Huk bodies as well as for information, citing movies of the

American wild West for his model. The first such reward paid out was for 5,000 pesos—about ten times the annual wage of agricultural laborers in the Philippines. For top Huk leaders, one could make as much as 100,000 pesos.[39]

An Office of Psychological Warfare was set up directly under Magsaysay. It was soon renamed the Civil Affairs Office (CAO), though its function remained unchanged. At its head was Jose Crisol, who, as Lansdale confided, operated "mostly under my direction." The CAO undertook a massive propaganda effort against the Huks. Within two years more than 13 million leaflets and other literature had been distributed, and over 6,000 meetings were held, reaching 1.5 million people. Literature and films were provided by the U.S. Information Service (USIS). The USIS set up a Regional Production Center in Manila in 1950 to reproduce propaganda materials for use by American personnel throughout Asia, and it prepared leaflets, posters, and pamphlets in local Philippine dialects for use against the Huks. JUSMAG helped in the selection of targets for air drops of propaganda leaflets.[40]

The CAO organized anticommunist forums in universities, patriotic writing contests were set up for high school and college students, and propaganda materials were distributed in the grammar schools. The downtown headquarters of the National Student Movement was secretly subsidized by the CAO. Yabut, a disc jockey ("a sort of Arthur Godfrey of the Philippines"), was put on the CAO payroll. Members of the press were given food, transportation, entertainment, gifts, and even salaries. Lansdale and others forged Huk documents and spread false information through the media. Magsaysay was especially cooperative with journalists who invented news stories about his exploits.[41]

What is quite remarkable about this propaganda barrage is that it was all in addition to the usual subordination of the Philippine media to U.S. interests. In the early 1950s, three major Manila newspapers were American-owned. Advertising in Manila dailies by American manufacturers apparently contributed a major share of newspaper revenues. News of the world outside the Philippines was largely filtered through American-owned wire services, and newspapers that could not afford wire services used a USIS press service. Of the forty-one Philippine radio stations, twelve were owned by the Voice of America. Sixty percent of the films shown in the Philippines were imported from the United States. (Not all American films were suitable, however; *Viva Zapata* was banned outside Manila.)[42]

Some of the psychological warfare operations involved actions as well as words. Lansdale relates the example of a psywar operation designed to get the Huks to leave a particular hill. Stories were circulated among Huk sympathizers of an *asuang* (vampire) that lived on the hill:

> The psywar squad set up an ambush along a trail used by the Huks. When a Huk patrol came along the trail, the ambushers silently snatched the last man of the patrol, their move unseen in the dark night. They punctured his neck with two holes, vampire-fashion, held the body up by the heels, drained it of blood, and put the corpse back on the trail. When the Huks returned to look for the missing man and found their bloodless comrade, every member of the patrol believed that the *asuang* had got him and that one of them would be next if they remained on that hill. When daylight came, the whole Huk squadron moved out of the vicinity.

Another technique of the psychological warfare campaign was the exploiting of ethnic differences among Filipinos. As Lansdale described it, a Huk commander in Laguna

> requested, and had, a private rendezvous with Magsaysay to discuss amnesty for Laguna Huks. Magsaysay gave him a counter proposal: let the Laguna Huks surrender, join the Armed Forces in hunting down the Pampanga Huks whom they dislike so, and they can thus earn a pardon and will be resettled in Mindanao. . . . Even if negotiations are not resumed, Magsaysay has planted a seed of sectionalism which can grow.[43]

The CAO also undertook a campaign of covertly fomenting mass demonstrations against the Huks. In San Luis, Pampanga, the hometown of Huk leader Luis Taruc, Taruc's birthday was celebrated by burning him in effigy, "supposedly as a spontaneous public action"—to use the words of a secret JUSMAG report.[44]

Lansdale has recently written, presumably with a straight face, "The martyred Philippine hero Jose Rizal once said 'A man retains his freedom so long as he preserves his independence of thought.' In these days of Pavlovian behavioral controls subtly created by skilled propagandists, as in Rizal's day of colonial repression, we need to hold fast to such truth."[45]

The most successful psychological warfare technique was the Economic Development Corps (EDCOR). Essentially, the Army took as its own the Huk slogan "Land for the Landless" and promised to resettle any recanting Huks on their own plots of land. When the project was completed, fewer than 1,000 families had been resettled—this in a country with over 600,000 tenant farm families—and only 246 of these were ex-Huks (some, in fact, were members of Magsaysay's armed forces added as a stabilizing influence). "Actually," an American land settlement adviser reported, "this project contributed little to the rehabilitation of dissidents." The lack of substantive reform, however, was more than made up for by the thorough propaganda effort: films, posters, pamphlets, and leaflets were distributed throughout the Philippines extolling the EDCOR project. As the Huks themselves acknowledged, EDCOR helped to deplete the mass base of the insurgency.[46]

Another program in which the propaganda value far exceeded the actual reforms was the Philippine Army's offer of free legal services to poor farmers. One U.S. official later explained it in this way:

> [Magsaysay had] made a big publicity binge, that all you've got to do is walk into any post office in any village in the Philippines and send a collect telegram to me, Magsaysay, and within twenty-four hours I will have a team of lawyers there to take care of your grievance. And as Magsaysay says, if they'd really challenged him on it, he didn't have that many lawyers. But a few people did do this, and he went down there—you know, peasants who had land problems—he got the lawyers to them within twenty-four hours. And the word got around, and they began to believe him. He wasn't able to accomplish the social reforms, but they believed that he would. And that defeated the Hukbalahaps.[47]

In October 1950 the anti-Huk campaign made a major breakthrough when, in what a U.S. Army historian called "a great stroke of luck," an informer provided information leading to the capture of the entire Communist politburo in Manila. JUSMAG assisted Philippine officials in preparing evidence for use in the trial and subsequent conviction of the politburo members. There had been no need to worry about the friendliness of the judge, for the Philippine secretary of justice had assured the U.S. embassy that the secretary had been responsible for the judge's recent appointment.[48]

Magsaysay and JUSMAG used the Manila roundup as the opportunity to get Quirino to suspend the writ of habeas corpus. When the writ was restored two years later, more than a thousand people were being held in prison without having been charged with a crime or having received public hearings. For these people and for all the others jailed for insurrection and the like, imprisonment was a grim experience; until mid-1952, according to the same U.S. Army historian, beatings were the normal procedure for extracting information from prisoners.[49]

In the meantime, the military operations continued. JUSMAG had recommended that the Philippines "increase ground forces as rapidly as possible." In the latter half of 1950, the Army was increased from ten to sixteen battalion combat teams "upon direct JUSMAG advice." And in the first half of 1951 ten new teams were added. Total strength of the Armed Forces of the Philippines (AFP) rose from 32,000 at the beginning of 1950, to 40,000 at the start of 1951, to 56,000 in late 1952.[50]

Washington had a policy of not providing direct financial support for the pay or maintenance of foreign armed forces. But the unlimited U.S. determination to prevent the "loss" of the Philippines led the Joint Chiefs of Staff to approve in mid-1951 a onetime payment of $10 million to the AFP. So that it would not become a precedent, this decision was kept top secret, and confidential funds were used.[51]

On JUSMAG's recommendation, further organizational reforms were implemented in the AFP and in the Philippine military intelligence agencies. JUSMAG wrote some "standing operating procedure" directives for the AFP and assisted in the preparation of others. JUSMAG considered a particular directive it wrote to be "one of the most important steps taken by the Army during the past several months to strengthen military striking power." Philippine officials set up an intelligence school, which used mostly American materials and whose lectures were rehearsed in front of a JUSMAG representative before delivery.[52]

In the summer of 1950, JUSMAG had advised Philippine military intelligence to compile an alphabetical list of all known Huks and then to initiate broad searching and screening campaigns over cordoned areas suspected of harboring Huks. In the first six months of 1951, 15,000 people were arrested under this program.[53] Also in the summer of 1950, JUSMAG began a policy of inspecting AFP tactical units, training installations, and supply agencies. Some time later JUSMAG officers received official sanction to accompany Philippine troops on major operations as unarmed combat observers. Ambassador Cowen sent a cable to Washington suggesting that U.S. influence over the AFP should be increased, since Magsaysay would not retain his post indefinitely. The Joint Chiefs of Staff also considered having JUSMAG officers serve as advisers to Philippine combat battalions, but JUSMAG insistence that this was unnecessary, plus the excessive costs such a policy would involve, led the Joint Chiefs to defer the matter.[54]

The Huks were fought from the air as well. The Philippine Air Force, which was of negligible value against an invader using modern jet aircraft, had as its primary mission the "support of army troops in anti-dissident operations." Between August 1, 1950, and June 30, 1952, the Philippine Air Force flew 2,600 bombing and strafing sorties, expending over 1 million rounds of .50 caliber ammunition and 250,000 pounds of explosives on Huk targets.[55] (These are small figures by the later standard of the Vietnam War, but this was the *Philippine* Air Force, not the American, and the Huks did not use tunnels.) As early as November 1949, Philippine officials had asked the United States for napalm. The request was held up for a while because the State Department feared that napalm created more Communists than it destroyed. The Philippine Air Force tried a locally fabricated napalm imitation, developed with some JUSMAG assistance, but, as JUSMAG noted, it "did not give the desired effect because of inferior burning qualities." Finally, at the end of 1951, U.S.-provided napalm arrived in the Philippines and was used against suspected Huk concentrations.[56] Incendiary raids against Huk agriculture were also conducted, at times with clandestine support from the U.S. Air Force.[57]

In early 1952 a proposal was aired in the Philippine Congress to attempt an amnesty with the Huks. The Philippine military reacted with public alarm, while privately the papal nuncio and JUSMAG indicated their firm opposition.[58] Nothing came of the proposal.

Although the Huks did not formally concede defeat until the mid-1950s, when they announced their retreat from armed to parliamentary struggle, they were essentially beaten militarily and psychologically in the first few years of the decade. And significantly, from Washington's point of view, advisers and military aid had sufficed to crush the Huk insurgency. United States policymakers had been willing to use American troops directly in the Philippines if necessary, but they welcomed not having to do so. "Much of the stigma of colonialism can be removed," stated a high-level State and Defense Department mission to Southeast Asia, "if, where necessary, yellow men will be killed by yellow men rather than by white men alone."[59]

Keeping the Philippine government afloat required more than defeating the Huks, however. The economic disintegration of the country also had to be checked. In October 1950 the U.S. Economic Survey Mission headed by Daniel W. Bell delivered its report to Truman. Shortly thereafter the report was released to the public. The Philippine economy, declared the Bell Report, was on the brink of collapse. The mission concluded that the Philippines would become totally useless to American strategic and economic interests if the disastrous state of the economy were not immediately rectified.

"If the situation is allowed to drift," the report warned, "there is no certainty that moderate remedies will suffice."

To correct this situation, the report recommended that the Philippine government increase tax receipts, establish a tax on the sale of foreign exchange, enact a minimum wage law, undertake land reform, and improve and reorganize public administration. It further called upon the U.S. government to provide the Philippines with $250 million in loans and grants over a five-year period, on the condition that the Philippine government enact the recommended reforms.[60]

However, control of all such aid funds—even those funds allocated by the Philippine government to match U.S. aid—was to be in the hands of the United States. In Washington's view, unless aid was under rigid U.S. control it would be dissipated. This was the key lesson that the defeat of Chiang Kai-shek had taught U.S. officials: aid given to or through the governments of "free Asia" would be simply wasted because of the corruption of those governments. Daniel Bell and Secretary of Defense George Marshall told Truman that there ought to be a U.S. mission to Manila of 150 to 200 people "which would in effect have to assume direction of most of the Philippine Government activities."[61]

In November 1950, William C. Foster, head of the Economic Cooperation Administration, went to Manila and concluded an agreement with President Quirino. Quirino, for his part, agreed to formulate a legislative program involving tax reform, an agricultural minimum wage law, and a general statement expressing Congress' accelerated concern for implementing the social and economic measures recommended by the Bell mission. In addition, Quirino agreed to accept American advisers. In return, the Truman administration pledged to ask the U.S. Congress for $250 million in aid over several years. This aid, a U.S. official privately acknowledged, was a bribe to get Manila to agree to reforms and to U.S. supervision and advice. Acheson explained to a closed congressional committee hearing that the Philippines "will accept American advisers throughout their Government. We will come up to Congress with an aid program which will be modest in dimensions but which lays the foundation for American technicians and American advisers all through their Government."[62]

In August 1951 Quirino signed a minimum wage law, drafted largely in the U.S. Department of Labor, and that same day Washington announced the release of the first $15 million in U.S. aid. Four months later the *New York Times* reported that U.S. officials found that "evasion of the law is prevalent, enforcement machinery is insufficient, and there are too many loopholes in the law itself."[63] This probably was not what the United States intended, for Washington was committed to a strategy of eliminating the conditions breeding insurgency, though with two important limitations.

First, the reforms must not too seriously challenge the power of the Philippine elite, for U.S. economic and military interests depended upon the alliance between Washington and this Filipino elite. The best illustration of this is land reform, a recommendation of the Bell Report but not specifically included in the Quirino-Foster agreement. The Bell Report had noted that the land situation in 1950 "remains the same or worse than four years ago." The minor agrarian reform program that did exist had simply enriched Quirino's friends, apparently including the secretary of justice and Quirino's brother.[64] Clearly no land reform would be voluntarily initiated by Philippine officials, but neither were U.S. officials anxious to push too hard on this point. The assistant director of the Mutual Security Administration (MSA) reported from Manila in 1952 that the United States would have to use all its influence simply to assure free elections in 1953, and that he "would hate to see us use up our ammunition in what would probably be a futile attempt to get an adequate land reform program at this time." (U.S. influence was substantial. At its peak in 1952, American aid accounted for almost 11 percent of total Philippine government revenues.) Moreover, the MSA official noted, to have Quirino promise to carry out a land reform without being serious about implementing it would inflame the peasantry even more.[65]

In 1952 Robert Hardie, an overzealous MSA land reform adviser in the Philippines, submitted a report calling for a redistribution of land. He suggested that the Philippine government purchase land from landlords with bonds paying 4 percent interest and maturing over twenty-five years, and resell small plots to tenants who would pay off their purchase over thirty years with interest. The administration of the program was to "at all times be guided by the principle of . . . private rather than state, individual rather than collective ownership of land." The existing land tenure system, Hardie warned,

> fosters the growth of communism and harms the United States position. Unless corrected, it is easy to conceive of the situation worsening to a point where the United States would be forced to take direct, expensive, and arbitrary steps to insure against loss of the Philippines to the Communist block [sic] in Asia—and would still be faced with finding a solution to the underlying problem.[66]

But when Hardie's report was made public, he was denounced by the speaker of the Philippine House of Representatives as a Communist. He was recalled from Manila in August 1953.[67]

The second self-imposed limitation on the U.S. strategy of eliminating the conditions fostering unrest in the Philippines was that American economic interests were not to be harmed in any substantial way. Thus, for example, the Bell Report did not recommend freezing the prices of U.S. products or requiring U.S. firms to distribute their profits to their employees—both measures that could conceivably have reduced popular unrest. The tax on foreign exchange, recommended by the Bell Report and approved by the U.S. president, was viewed by U.S. officials as a temporary measure, thought to be preferable to the alternative of devaluing the peso. The foreign aid urged by the Bell Report was not antithetical to the interests of U.S. investors; on the contrary, they favored it as a means for stabilizing their investment market.[68] And one Bell Report recommendation called upon the Philippines to liquidate its governmental corporations. Said the Bell Report, the "extent to which the Government intends to retain and increase its activities directly in the field of commerce has been a source of much concern to the business community." Moreover, the report recommended that "in the development of Philippine resources preference should be given to private industry (if necessary, with government financing in the form of preference shares), and that the government withdraw from trading activities on export products, from agriculture, and from other activities that are now in competition with private industry."[69] United States investors, of course, could well appreciate reforms of this sort.

In the first few years of the 1950s, the Philippine economy substantially recovered from its desperate straits of 1949–1950. There were a number of factors accounting for this. The Korean War had caused an international boom in commodity prices which greatly benefited Philippine exporters. Various U.S. loans and U.S. grant aid combined with the instituting by the Philippine Congress of various tax measures (as called for in the Quirino-Foster agreement) had ended the government's budget deficits. Exchange and import controls were able to prevent a dissipation of the country's foreign currency reserves. And finally, the defeat of the Huks restored business confidence in the Philippine economy.[70]

Militarily and economically the crisis in the Philippines was averted in the early 1950s. It remained for U.S. policy to maintain the political credibility of the Philippine government.

=== CHAPTER FOUR ===

"America's Boy"

Preserving the political stability of the Philippines involved three tasks. First, a repetition of the corrupt 1949 elections had to be avoided; another stolen election would surely reduce the legitimacy of the Philippine government to disastrous levels. Second, a replacement had to be found for Quirino, whose corruption made popular support for the government impossible. And third, the trade and military bases agreements between Washington and Manila had to be revised in order to eliminate the affronts to Philippine sovereignty that had fueled nationalist agitation. United States officials, and those Filipinos who worked closely with them, took steps to deal with each of these problems.

Before the 1951 off-year elections, a "good government" organization called NAMFREL—National Movement for Free Elections—was set up with the help of CIA funds and officials, as well as private American money.[1] NAMFREL members conducted a mass publicity campaign urging clean elections. United States materials, including voters' guides and pamphlets, were distributed through NAMFREL, though without attribution of U.S. authorship. The Civil Affairs Office of the Philippine Armed Forces distributed leaflets exhorting the cynical population to vote. And Magsaysay used the Army and ROTC students to police the balloting and supervise an honest count.[2] The election turned out to be one of the bloodiest in Philippine history—twenty-one killings on election day itself, and at least thirty election-related deaths in the weeks before.[3] Nevertheless, since the opposition Nacionalista party Senate slate swept the elections, the votes were generally thought to have been tallied honestly, and this served to undercut the Huk slogan of "Bullets Not

Ballots." The real test was yet to come, however, in the more important presidential election of 1953.

As early as the summer of 1951, the U.S. ambassador in Manila
warned Washington that Quirino would be a candidate in 1953 and
would inevitably win the election. This was a depressing prospect to
U.S. policymakers, for their opinion of Quirino was unreservedly
negative. In private, U.S. officials referred to the Philippine president as "an opportunist of the first order . . . whose political reliabil-
ity and trustworthiness cannot be counted upon very strongly," a
man with a "constitutional inability to preserve confidences," "over-
weening vanity and arrogance," "pettiness and vindictiveness," who
would rather see his country ruined than "compromise with his insa-
tiable ego or accept outside assistance on any terms except his own,"
and who was ignorant, morally irresponsible, and heading an administration that was weak in all respects save in talents for keeping itself
in office by dishonest means. And Quirino's offer to withdraw the
name of Vicente Madrigal as his ambassador to Washington if the
United States paid off Madrigal's war damage claim further es-
tranged U.S. policymakers.[4]

"If there is one lesson to be learned from the China debacle,"
Secretary of State Acheson told Truman, "it is that if we are con-
fronted with an inadequate vehicle it should be discarded or immo-
bilized in favor of a more propitious one." In 1950 the United States
had tried private approaches to Quirino's colleagues to get them to
force the Philippine president from office but to no avail.[5] The alternative was to groom a challenger to Quirino for the 1953 election.
The obvious choice was Ramon Magsaysay, who was relatively honest
and thoroughly pro-American, though without the wide reputation
and political connections necessary for a presidential bid. United
States officials endeavored to provide the defense secretary with both
of these.

Lansdale introduced Magsaysay to foreign correspondents in
Manila and to visiting journalists, some of whom worked for the
CIA. Articles praising Magsaysay appeared in almost every major
American periodical.[6] Roy Q. Howard reported from Manila that
"the achievements of the defense minister were taken more or less in
a stride by the local press until they began to attract the attention of
American correspondents whose press dispatches, special articles
and magazine stories soon began to glamorize the courageous but
not overly colorful Magsaysay."[7] In the course of glamorizing the
defense secretary, there was little concern for factual accuracy. Typical in this regard was the false portrayal of Magsaysay as having
come from humble origins.[8]

The CIA wrote Magsaysay's speeches, and the Philippine armed forces also contributed to the Magsaysay public relations effort. With Magsaysay's knowledge, safe conduct passes with his picture on them were dropped in areas where there were known to be no Huks. A more elaborate scheme was having Magsaysay's own troops disguise themselves as Huks and set upon some village, so that these "guerrillas" could be repulsed by troops under the command of Magsaysay—thus enhancing the defense secretary's image as a fearless Huk-fighter.[9]

The next stage of Magsaysay's as yet unannounced campaign was engineered by Lansdale and Manuel J. ("Dindo") Gonzalez. Gonzalez was a wealthy advertising and business executive, with a reputation as a "kingmaker"; he was president of the Manila Lions Club and a confidant of President Quirino, being the brother-in-law of Quirino's only daughter. He was, however, a Magsaysay supporter and, with Lansdale, he convinced the president of Lions International that Magsaysay ought to be the keynote speaker at the group's convention in June 1952 in Mexico City. This would be a further boost to the defense secretary's reputation.

Magsaysay and Lansdale first went to the United States. Quirino had insisted that the publicity given Magsaysay be minimal, but nevertheless Magsaysay was honored in New York City with a nineteen-gun salute, a troop review, and an elaborate reception arranged by Leland Hobbs, who had recently completed his tour as JUSMAG commander. Jesuit contacts in the Philippines arranged to have Magsaysay receive an honorary degree from Fordham University in New York. In Washington, D.C., Magsaysay held closed-door meetings with Truman, Acheson, Defense Secretary Robert Lovett, and top Pentagon officials.[10] He was given $500,000 in clandestine funds—for which he would not have to account—for use against the Huks. The original source of this money is unclear, but both JUSMAG and a high-level mission that had earlier visited the Philippines had recommended that the CIA provide funds for covert anti-Huk activities.[11] This money, together with a "peace fund" of 1 million pesos raised by Vice-President Fernando Lopez in the Philippines, financed rewards for informers and other unconventional military operations. In Mexico City, Lansdale and Gonzalez saw to it that after Magsaysay had finished his keynote address the Lions gave him a couple of million dollars' worth of agricultural equipment for his resettlement projects.[12]

Once Magsaysay decided to run for the presidency, according to one of his biographers, "which party would sponsor him was of secondary importance." On November 20, 1952, he met privately with Nacionalista party leaders Jose P. Laurel and Claro M. Recto and signed a secret pact whereby Laurel and Recto agreed to support a Magsaysay presidental bid on their party ticket. Lansdale and U.S. Ambassador Raymond Spruance hid the document for safe-keeping. It was arranged that Magsaysay would continue as secretary of defense in Quirino's cabinet until shortly before the Nacionalista convention in April 1953, so that he might prolong his control over the armed forces. In January, Magsaysay privately signed a Nacionalista party affiliation card; in February he resigned his cabinet post.[13]

Liberal party politicians got word of the secret pact and charged that U.S. Embassy vaults harbored the document. Spruance was challenged to deny this and other accusations of U.S. interference in Philippine politics. He told the press:

> I wish to state now that the United States Embassy will observe strict neutrality in the course of the coming campaign and election. For this reason I don't propose to comment upon, to confirm or deny, charges of the sort that appeared in the public press recently, since to do so would be tantamount to intervention in Philippine politics.[14]

The American Embassy was also called upon to deny Magsaysay's frequent statements to the effect that the U.S. government had lost confidence in Quirino and that American aid would be cut off if Quirino were reelected. Again the embassy replied that to comment on the charges would constitute interference in Philippine internal affairs. It should be noted that when in 1946 Osmeña had claimed that only he could get U.S. financial aid, High Commissioner McNutt had issued a press statement declaring that the United States would carry out its aid pledge regardless of who won the election. McNutt also had denied charges that Roxas was his candidate, and in 1949 the U.S. ambassador in Manila had stated that U.S. aid would be forthcoming no matter who was elected.[15]

On April 12 Magsaysay was nominated by Laurel and became the Nacionalista party's presidential candidate. Public relations efforts in his behalf picked up steam. Most of the Manila press—in particular the three major American-owned papers—boosted Magsaysay, and U.S. journalists continued to write glowing articles about him. Roy Q. Howard of the United Press observed, "the Magsaysay boom bears definite 'Made in America' markings." Howard asserted that these were journalistic markings "without design or premeditation," but Philippine ambassador to Washington Carlos Romulo wrote privately to ex-Ambassador Cowen, "It looks as though the build-up you started for Magsaysay is giving results." "As a practical matter," wrote Joseph Alsop in an article that ran in the *Manila Daily Bulletin* as well as in the United States, "Magsaysay is the American candidate."[16]

The head of the Civil Affairs Office of the armed forces, Jose Crisol, resigned from the Army to begin a student organization for Magsaysay which soon developed into a large Magsaysay-for-President Movement. NAMFREL, though theoretically nonpartisan, secretly worked for Magsaysay's election, and a new nonpartisan organization, Citizens Committee for Good Government, covertly gathered political intelligence for Magsaysay.[17]

In June 1953 the "sugar bloc" bolted from Quirino's Liberal party and formed a third party, the Democrata, with Carlos Romulo as their standard-bearer. Romulo was a sincere friend of the United States, and the CIA apparently had been able to blackmail Vice-President Fernando Lopez into running on the Democrata ticket, thus effectively splitting the Liberal party.[18]

The sugar barons pledged to match one peso for every dollar Romulo was able to raise from supporters in the United States. Romulo wrote to U.S. Ambassador Myron Cowen to try to get (illegal) contributions from U.S. firms with interests in the Philippines, and he even proposed code names for use in future communications regarding fund-raising. Romulo soon learned, however, that American money was backing Magsaysay and was not willing to divide the anti-Quirino forces by bankrolling him. This convinced the Democratas, in August, to give up their third-party effort by merging with the Nacionalistas. The Nacionalistas agreed to support the sugar bloc's choices for Senate president, three senators, thirty representatives, and half the cabinet. Romulo became Magsaysay's campaign manager, announcing that in the event of victory he would "ask nothing, expect nothing, accept nothing" in the way of enrichment, patronage, high office, or appointment. It is not clear whether he asked for or expected anything, but after a discreet interval he accepted positions representing the Philippines at the United Nations and elsewhere.[19]

Traditionally, in Philippine politics, the incumbent party has the financial advantage. But once the sugar bloc joined the Nacionalistas, the Magsaysay campaign raised more money than did Quirino's. Moreover, the Nacionalista sweep in the Senate in 1951 allowed them to block the expenditure of government funds by Quirino for political purposes. Illegal contributions from U.S. business interests swelled the Nacionalista campaign chest, but the American money was particularly important before the Democrata-Nacionalista merger, when the Magsaysay forces were desperately short of funds. Almost every American businessperson was for Magsaysay, but there were two problems with getting their contributions to the former defense secretary: (1) the difficulty of getting the funds from the United States into the Philippines and (2) preserving the anonymity of local managers of U.S. firms who wanted to give Magsaysay money but feared retaliation by Quirino. In June 1953 Lansdale confided that he could solve both these problems.[20] Whether this turned out to be the conduit for private U.S. funds is not clear— Lansdale has recently denied it—but American money did flow to Magsaysay. As *Time* magazine reported, "in spite of a Filipino law which forbids foreigners to contribute to election campaigns, U.S. business interests in the islands anted up some $250,000 at a time when Magsaysay's Nationalist Party was seriously short of funds." Informed Filipino politicians agree that the figure for total U.S. contributions to Magsaysay was considerably higher.[21]

Lansdale also had CIA money to give out. In a recent interview, Lansdale stated that he had $1 million to use in the Philippines but only spent $50,000 or $60,000. Whether this is true, and how much additional money was disbursed by Lansdale's Manila superior, Brigadier General Ralph B. Lovett—who controlled the distribution of all CIA funds in the Philippines—is not known.[22] The CIA response to a Freedom of Information Act request on this matter has been to claim national security exemption from the provisions of the act; the issue was appealed, and although the law requires a response within thirty days, two years later the CIA replied that they would not even confirm the existence of relevant records.

President Eisenhower and Secretary of State John Foster Dulles were generally familiar with the situation. The administration publicly declared its "absolute impartiality," though it also expressed its concern that the balloting be kept honest—an implicit warning to Quirino. United States officials were convinced that if the election was fair Magsaysay would win.[23] To help in this regard, Lansdale burnt a warehouse in which Quirino supporters had stored bogus ballots. But other CIA activities were not so nonpartisan: CIA operatives infiltrated the Liberal party and doped the drinks of Quirino speechmakers. The head of JUSMAG later recalled that the CIA was "furnishing money, furnishing political advice and in some cases I think a little strong arm."[24]

Magsaysay was the first major Philippine politician to do a great deal of campaigning in the rural barrios, thus furthering his image as a "man of the masses." The truthfulness of his campaign rhetoric, however, was quite typical of Philippine politics, as when he told Muslims in Mindanao that if elected he would make available navy ships for pilgrimages to Mecca. Both the Nacionalistas and the Liberals spent large sums of money on buying votes—another standard practice of Philippine politics.[25]

A few days before the election, a U.S. naval flotilla paid a visit to Manila Bay. The *New York Times* reported, without attribution, that the "naval visit was purely routine." Nacionalista Senator Jose Laurel, however, confided a year later that the presence of the U.S. warships was not entirely accidental.[26]

On election day, the JUSMAG commander deployed a couple dozen of his officers to observe Filipino army personnel as the latter watched the polls. The CIA also made sure that American and foreign reporters were on hand to oversee the balloting. The election was one of the most peaceful in Philippine history—depending on the count, ten or twenty people were killed on election day. Major fraud did not take place, and Magsaysay won an overwhelming victory, capturing more than two-thirds of the votes cast.[27]

Eisenhower sent his congratulations to the CIA station in Manila, and *Time* magazine remarked it was "no secret that Ramon Magsaysay was America's boy." And once in office, Magsaysay indeed performed as "America's boy." In January 1954, in his first State of the Union message, he declared:

> Private capital, from sources both at home and abroad, will be preferred to direct government financing whenever possible . . . . I hope that our own people will go into new ventures and take full advantage of the incentives now and to be provided by our Government. . . . We also welcome foreign capital, assuring it fair treatment. In the past it was perhaps discouraged by the uncertainty of our attitude, and I propose that we mark out clearly a stable basis on which foreign investors can put their capital to work in this country.[28]

This was precisely what the Bell Report had earlier recommended. In 1955 the U.S. Department of Commerce was able to assure American investors that the Philippine government's "general adherence to principles of private enterprise and welcome to foreign capital makes the likelihood of expropriation seem remote."[29]

But it was in the field of foreign policy that Magsaysay most convincingly demonstrated that he was "America's boy." Thus, Magsaysay wrote in the influential journal, *Foreign Affairs*, "We have learned from our own Communist Hukbalahap revolution that Communism is not just some distorted nationalist ambition, like Hitler's, to be satisfied with land or riches, but an unremitting universal campaign to rule the earth, to eradicate individual liberty, to destroy God and the souls of men."[30] A constant theme of Magsaysay's foreign policy was that "neutralism is anti-Filipino," that the Philippines had "no need for fence-sitters in the struggle to preserve our way of life." When Claro Recto suggested that he might run for the presidency in 1957 on a platform opposing neutralism yet recognizing the need for peaceful coexistence, Magsaysay thundered, "He can run as the candidate of Mao Tse-tung and I will run as an enemy of Communism and a friend of the United States, and we will let the Filipino people decide whether they want a party-liner or one who is firmly and unequivocally and unconditionally against godless communism."[31]

That Magsaysay's foreign policy so closely followed that of Washington was by no means coincidental. One former CIA agent has written that all important Philippine decisions in the foreign affairs field were made between Magsaysay and his CIA station contacts.[32] When the United States wanted a conference convened to found the Southeast Asia Treaty Organization (SEATO), the Philippine government called and hosted it. During the Formosa crisis of 1955, Magsaysay stood "squarely behind the U.S.," and in July 1955 Manila recognized the American-created South Vietnam.[33]

In 1954 a high-level U.S. committee secretly reported that American policy in Southeast Asia was "most effectively represented in the Philippines and in Thailand from which countries—outside of Indo-China—any expanded program of Western influence may best be launched." One such program was the Freedom Company of the Philippines, purportedly a public service organization (with Magsaysay as honorary president) but actually "a mechanism to permit the deployment of Filipino personnel in other Asian countries, for unconventional operations" covertly supported by the United States. Through this mechanism, Lansdale and the CIA were able to get Filipinos to help write a constitution for South Vietnam and train Diem's presidential guard battalion.[34]

With Magsaysay in the presidency, there remained a final task for U.S. policymakers: to alter the 1946 U.S.-Philippine Trade Agreement and the 1947 Military Bases Agreement to better fit the changed circumstances of the 1950s. The Bell Economic Survey Mission had examined the workings of the Trade Agreement and had noted that provisions of the Agreement "which limit Philippine sovereign perogatives, i.e., the 'parity provision,' . . . and the limitations on the Philippine Government in allocating quotas established for certain products, do not in practice provide the proper type and degree of protection for American interests." Repeating the arguments of the Departments of State and Commerce during the original debate on the Trade Agreement in 1946, the Bell Report asserted that "some provisions of the Trade Agreement, such as the absolute quotas (except in the case of sugar) and the internal tax preference given Philippine coconut oil, are prejudicial to the attainment of the objectives of United States commercial policy on a multilateral basis." The provision of the Trade Agreement pegging the peso to the dollar was

> not necessary to safeguard the interests of the United States. As a member of the International Monetary Fund, the Philippine Government cannot change the par value of the peso until it has consulted with the Fund, and for any change in excess of 10 percent of the present par value, unless it has concurrence of the Fund. This provision for considering any proposal for a change in the par value of the peso by an international organization provides adequate protection for the interests of the United States in the stability of the Philippine currency.[35]

These provisions of the Trade Agreement, which gave no benefit to U.S. interests, were an affront to Philippine sovereignty and thus lent fuel to anti-American sentiment in the islands.

Accordingly, the Bell Report had recommended that, at the earliest practicable date, the United States and the Philippines sign a Treaty of Friendship, Commerce, and Navigation which would establish reciprocal rights and a clearly defined long-term legal basis for commercial relations and would "serve to define the climate for private investment by giving definite assurance of equitable treatment and security for American investors." In the Quirino-Foster agreement, the two parties agreed to undertake negotiations for such a treaty and to reexamine the provisions of the 1946 Bell Trade Act.[36]

As 1954 approached, there was added pressure for amending the Trade Agreement. According to the agreement's provisions, the duty-free entry of Philippine products into the United States would come to an end on July 4, 1954, and a gradually increasing fraction of the full duty would be imposed. Philippine exporters, in particular the sugar interests, were eager to have these tariffs reduced as much as possible. In mid-1953, the Philippine government, speaking for these exporters, sent a note to the United States proposing that the peso be no longer pegged to the dollar, that "parity" be made reciprocal, and that U.S.-Philippine trade be at full duties except for specified duty-free commodities, namely, all the islands' main exports—sugar, copra, coconut oil, cordage rope, embroideries, lumber, pineapples, cigars, and scrap and filler tobacco.[37] United States domestic producers of these items would never agree to such terms, but when Magsaysay became president, with the support of the sugar bloc, Washington was eager to reward the Philippine elite for its loyalty to the United States.

In 1954 negotiations on a new trade agreement began, and in June, Manila requested that free trade be extended for eighteen months while the talks were going on. Legislation to this effect was drawn up in the American Congress, and it was endorsed by the Departments of State, Commerce, Treasury, and Agriculture. The importance of the bill, supporters said, was not economic but political, and the State Department in particular urged passage "in light of the present situation in the Far East."[38]

The North Carolina delegation in the Congress, however, declared that they would block the bill unless the Philippine government removed its restrictions against American leaf tobacco. Carlos Romulo gave his personal assurances that the restrictions would be lifted, and the tobacco bloc dropped its objection. On July 7 free trade was extended until December 31, 1955. The National Congress of the Philippine Sugar Industry passed a resolution expressing their gratitude to the U.S. president and Congress.[39]

The negotiations on revising the trade agreement faced some rough going. A Filipino participant has claimed that he secured U.S. agreement to elimination of the provision pegging the peso to the dollar only by threatening to walk out of the talks. And when the U.S. Congress was considering the Laurel-Langley Agreement—as the revised trade agreement was called after the chief negotiators for Manila and Washington, respectively—some Filipino leaders threatened to trade with China if the Congress voted it down.[40] But the difficulties were ironed out and the agreement was signed on September 5, 1955.

The first article of the Laurel-Langley pact altered the tariff schedule contained in the 1946 Trade Act. The graduated tariffs on U.S. exports to the Philippines were to be applied at an accelerated rate, and the tariffs on Philippine exports to the United States were to be applied at a decreased rate, although both would still reach 100 percent of the full duties by 1974. The Filipino negotiators had argued that nonessential American goods had harmed the Philippine economy, and they had proposed free trade until 1970 for all Philippine products and all U.S. essentials and full duties on other U.S. products. The American team had rejected this proposal, but the final agreement still represented a significant concession to the Philippine elite. Philippine manufacturers were given some tariff protection, and Philippine exporters were provided with the bonanza of greater access to the high-priced U.S. market. This was not without some benefit to Americans, as Langley noted:

> Some of those benefits which may seem there to be primarily Philippine benefits, for instance, the deceleration of the tariff they pay here, do have an American angle, too, because three of the industries which will suffer most quickly as the loss of Philippine preferences here occurs are industries in which this country has a considerable investment. The pineapple and pineapple juice industry, for example, employs some 2,000 people, and is entirely an American capitalized industry . . . . Another industry which these terms help, and in which the capital is all American, is the so-called embroidery industry . . . . [41]

Notice that Langley used the phrase "industries in which this country has a considerable investment." Of course, these were industries in which *particular* Americans had investments, not the country. But it has been a common official assumption that the interests of the few and of the country are the same. Much the same was true on the Philippine side. Contrary to the rhetoric, the beneficiaries of the added access to the American market were Philippine exporters, not the Philippines as a whole. For example, in 1956, after ten years of free trade, sugarcane workers in Negros Occidental were paid an average wage of 1.94 pesos—less than $1—a day, even though the minimum wage was 2.50 pesos. Six years later, the daily wage was still less than the minimum wage.[42]

In return for the tariff modifications, the U.S. negotiators insisted upon and obtained Philippine agreement to the elimination of the existing tax on foreign exchange sales and its replacement by a special import levy which would be reduced by 10 percent a year. As one U.S. scholar has noted,

> [the] interest of the United States business community in the Philippines in this change should be obvious. To the extent that foreign exchange is allocated for remission for profits and disinvestment and repatriation of capital, repeal of the Special Tax on Sales of Exchange establishes a more favorable rate for such transactions and thereby increases the relative profitability of United States enterprises.

Carlos Romulo considered the new provision to be a benefit to the Philippines because it provided an incentive to foreign capital.[43]

The tie-in of the peso to the dollar in the Bell Trade Act was eliminated in the Laurel-Langley Agreement, as the State Department had recommended in 1946. This served to mollify nationalist critics somewhat, but it made little practical difference. Philippine currency changes still required International Monetary Fund approval, and U.S. pressure was sufficient to reverse any devaluation opposed by the American business community.[44]

Article II of the Laurel-Langley Agreement eliminated the absolute quotas on all Philippine exports except sugar and cordage and replaced them with declining tariff quotas (again as the State Department had urged in 1946). The absolute quotas had been of little economic significance, since Philippine exports of these commodities had been far under the quotas. Only the quotas on sugar and cordage had actually restricted Philippine exports, and these were retained.[45]

Article III allowed each country to impose restrictions on imports of products that harmed domestic producers. United States interests favored this provision because it clearly specified—in ways the 1946 Bell Trade Act did not—the conditions under which and to what extent such restrictions could be imposed. Had there been such a provision in the 1946 Trade Act, observed advocates of the Laurel-Langley Agreement, "the Philippines would not have been free to adopt drastic limitations on imports of American tobacco." Thus this article "is considered by the United States delegation as an important improvement in the agreement from the standpoint of the United States."[46]

The provision of the 1946 Trade Act that had evoked the greatest amount of Filipino hostility was the "parity" clause. The Laurel-Langley Agreement undercut much of this hostility by establishing a meticulously formal reciprocity of parity rights. The reciprocity, of course, was only a legal construct; Filipinos were hardly likely to invest in the United States with the same vigor that American nationals invested in the Philippines. Nevertheless, the Magsaysay administration played up the reciprocity as a great triumph for nationalism; and U.S. Senator Herbert Lehman declared that the fears of American exploitation expressed back in 1946 (though "never realized") would finally be laid to rest by the Laurel-Langley Agreement's "formal equality and reciprocity." In fact, however, the substantive change in "parity" was not its being made reciprocal but its extension to cover all business activity—not just the development of natural resources and public utilities. Langley explained that what constituted business discrimination had been vague under the old agreement and that the only recourse had been to void the whole agreement. In the new pact, on the other hand, U.S. business was given explicit protection in all fields of activity. Americans in Manila had pushed strongly for this revision.[47]

The Laurel-Langley Agreement had the approval of the U.S. Departments of State, Treasury, Defense, Agriculture, Commerce, Labor, and Interior. In the Senate, Herbert Lehman remarked that, although he gathered the pact was "not without commercial advantage for us," the main reason to back it was that it was a means of paying back the Philippines for supporting the United States in World War II, in Korea, and elsewhere. John McCormack explained in the House that he favored the bill because he wanted to help Magsaysay, who was "the first man in Asia to defeat communism." Others offered similar arguments.[48]

In sum, the Laurel-Langley Agreement was partly a means of furthering U.S. economic interests, partly a way of appeasing Philippine nationalism without substantive change, and partly a concession to the Philippine elite in the form of tariff modifications in recognition of their commitment to the American cause.

By the early 1970s, according to Department of Commerce figures, U.S. investment in the Philippines had a book value of $700 million; the market value was estimated to be on the order of $2 billion. During the thirteen years from 1957 to 1969, Department of Commerce data give the average annual rate of return on U.S. equity in the Philippines as 11.8 percent before U.S. taxes. Taking a high estimate of U.S. taxes as 10 percent of earnings yields an after-tax profit rate of 10.6 percent, compared to an overall return on U.S. investment for this period of 7.2 percent.[49] Other studies give higher figures for profits in the Philippines,[50] and there is evidence that profit rates are understated due to transfer-pricing and the exclusion of royalty payments.[51] From another perspective, one-third of the Philippine industrial sector was owned by foreigners in 1970, and of this one-third, Americans held about 80 percent.[52]

Starting under the Magsaysay administration and continuing through the mid-1960s, the 1947 Military Bases Agreement was also revised. Despite all the revisions, however, the essence of the agreement remained the same; only the form was changed to pacify Philippine nationalism. The essence of the bases agreement was to provide the United States with bases from which its "strong policy in Asia" might be pursued, and this central function has never been altered. From these bases Dien Bien Phu was sent supplies, arms were airlifted to rebels in Indonesia, and forces were deployed in the Quemoy-Matsu area.[53] In 1962 a Defense Department official called the Philippine bases the "cornerstones of any U.S. staging of military operations to the west or southwest." In 1964 the bases were considered "of great strategic importance because of their geographical position relative to the Chinese mainland and their potential use as U.S.-SEATO staging areas for operations in southeast Asia." In 1966 Assistant Secretary of State William P. Bundy stated that the bases "today fulfill a vital role in the logistic support of the free world's effort in Vietnam." A year later, Defense Secretary Robert McNamara testified, "as the Vietnam conflict progresses, we have relied increasingly on U.S. bases and facilities in the Philippines."[54] The Philippine bases have provided the principal logistical support for the U.S. Air Force in Indochina and the chief supply and repair depot for the Seventh Fleet. The Philippines also has served as the major hub for military communications for the Air Force and Navy in the western Pacific, with, for example, an undersea cable to Vietnam. And, according to at least one source, the United States has stocked nuclear weapons in the Philippines.[55]

The alleged function of the bases as a means for defending the Philippines has rarely been taken seriously by U.S. officials. In 1959 the Pacific naval commander testified that he could not "visualize the Philippines being attacked in any situation short of a general war situation. The Philippines are pretty far removed from the threat. The threat in the Philippines today is subversion." A decade later, another admiral asserted that the principal external threat to the Philippines was China but that it was currently a "very small" threat. A year later, it was said that that Philippines was "not threatened by conventional, external attack." And in 1972 there was "no identifiable conventional force that is likely or capable of invading the Philippines."[56]

Many of the provisions of the Military Bases Agreement were, however, not necessary to the central mission of the bases. The United States had tremendous tracts of territory—including a city— on a ninety-nine year lease. Clark Air Field was so large that when a U.S. ambassador wanted to attend air exercises there, he flew to the main base and then transshipped to a DC-3 and continued flying for fifteen minutes within the base. That all this land was not needed for the primary mission of the bases was indicated by the fact that, unknown to air force authorities, some 50,000 squatters had moved onto the base area. "I think we over-did that vastly in requirements," confided General George Marshall. And the criminal jurisdiction arrangements were highly unfavorable to the Philippines. For example, between 1947 and June 1969 thirty-five Filipinos were killed on U.S. bases, and none of the alleged killers was tried in a Philippine court.[57]

It was precisely these kinds of issues—size of the bases and jurisdiction—that most inflamed vocal Philippine nationalists. Therefore, starting in 1956 the United States took steps to modify the bases agreement so as to mute nationalist objections. In 1956 Magsaysay and U.S. Vice-President Richard Nixon issued a joint statement declaring that Washington always acknowledged and now reaffirmed

The Setting of the Philippines, 1967

Adapted from *Area Handbook for the Philippines, 1976* (Washington, D.C.:
U.S. Government Printing Office, 1976).

full Philippine sovereignty over the bases. This was felt to be necessary because a few years earlier the U.S. attorney general had asserted precisely the opposite. Carlos Romulo called this statement "the most effective refutation of all the Communist prattle that the United States has mercenary motives or aggressive designs," but he also revealed that it took twenty-nine conferences and twenty-five drafts before the United States consented to the statement.[58]

Among the future refinements, in 1959 some base areas and the city of Olongapo were returned to the Philippines. The United States also agreed to consult with the Philippine government before using the bases for combat operations, but this did not give the Philippines a veto over base operations, and logistic or staging activities were not included within the meaning of the term "combat operations." Moreover, U.S. naval forces operating directly from the Philippines were not considered covered by this agreement either. The prior consultation provision, a U.S. official testified in 1969, "has not degraded the effectiveness of military operations with respect to Vietnam."[59]

In 1965 the United States revised the criminal jurisdiction provisions of the bases agreement to conform to the NATO status-of-forces pattern. This revision was so long in coming because of the view in Congress that the NATO arrangement was "thoroughly un-American" and that jurisdictional disputes might best be resolved by sending in U.S. destroyers. And in 1966 the ninety-nine year lease on the bases was reduced to forty-four years.[60]

Other adjustments to the bases agreement turned over unneeded base lands to the Philippine government (sometimes in return for alternative base areas), provided access to base territory to Filipinos wishing to develop natural resources so long as they did not interfere with the military use of the bases, and established standards to govern the conditions of employment for the Filipinos working on the bases.[61]

None of the revisions in the bases agreement detracted from the primary mission of the U.S. bases. In September 1972, after sixteen years of amendments and adjustments, a U.S. Senate Foreign Relations Committee staff report could state that "U.S. authorities note that nowhere in the world are we able to use our military bases with less restrictions than we do in the Philippines."[62]

In the mid-1950s, U.S. policymakers looked upon the Philippines as a real American success story. True, the pace of reforms under the Magsaysay administration had slowed compared to 1950–1953,[63] but what mattered to Washington was that the Huks had been defeated, economic collapse averted, a staunch American ally placed in the presidency, and U.S. economic and strategic interests maintained while nationalist sentiment was placated. On their own terms, U.S. officials could compliment themselves on a job well done, at least for the time being.

CHAPTER FIVE

The Instruments of Neocolonialism

The crisis of the early 1950s was over, but the underlying problems of Philippine society remained. The unequal distribution of wealth and power had not been fundamentally modified by U.S. policies; in fact, it was precisely the massive U.S. intervention that had allowed the status quo to survive. So while the return of stability by 1954 permitted Washington to reduce its previously high level of activity in the Philippines, the mechanisms of neocolonial control could not be dispensed with. Covert activities and military and economic aid programs were continued, often with growing sophistication, throughout the 1950s and 1960s.

Covert Activities

In 1954 the National Security Council secretly called for the intensification of "covert and psychological actions to strengthen the orientation" of, among other Southeast Asian countries, the Philippines "toward the free world."[1] Most of the details on covert U.S. activities in the Philippines remain classified, and much has never even been committed to writing. A few pieces of evidence, however, should indicate the scope of such activities.

In 1954 the head of the CIA in Manila and the American ambassador discussed the possibility of assassinating Magsaysay's political rival, Claro M. Recto. Ultimately this option was rejected on pragmatic grounds, and the vial of poison that was to have been

103

used was tossed into Manila Bay.[2] When Recto ran for the presidency in 1957 on a third-party ticket, the CIA distributed defective condoms bearing his name. In the 1959 elections, CIA money flowed to favored candidates, and an agency operative played a key backstage role in determining the electoral alignments. Asked whether the CIA stayed out of the 1961 Philippine elections, Ambassador William E. Stevenson replied, "I would be surprised because they've got to do something with all that money and that staff, and what else have they got to do."[3]

There was no lack of other things to do, however. The CIA subsidized the Foreign Correspondents' Club in Manila, had an agency employee as the manager of the Manila Press Club, and had an investment in the *Manila Times*.[4] A "counter-subversion, counter-guerrilla and psychological warfare school" called the Security Training Center was set up on the outskirts of Manila. Publicly operated by the Philippine government, it was covertly sponsored by the CIA.[5] And numerous projects in the sensitive area of "rural development" have been used by the agency for intelligence-gathering purposes and for establishing contacts with strategically placed Filipinos. CIA funds were channeled to NAMFREL's community centers, the Philippine Rural Reconstruction Movement (PRRM), and a rural redevelopment project called COMPADRE through conduits such as the Catherwood Foundation and through the Committee for a Free Asia (CFA), later renamed the Asia Foundation. Ostensibly a private organization, the CFA was set up and at least partially funded by the CIA. CIA operative Gabriel Kaplan was instrumental in the setting up of the NAMFREL centers and directed the COMPADRE project.[6]

A few other CIA activities in the Philippines will be discussed below, but again it should be kept in mind that what is known is likely to be just a small part of the total picture.

Military Advisers

The U.S. military advisers of JUSMAG, who had played such an important part in helping the Armed Forces of the Philippines (AFP) defeat the Huks in the early 1950s, continued to provide counsel to the AFP. In 1954 an incident revealed that JUSMAG influence was so pervasive that it got to approve the reading material that could be distributed to Philippine troops. In 1959 the AFP chief of staff stated that since 1955 the Philippines had not been consulted in the programming of military aid from the United States. Ironically, the Philippine president in 1959, Carlos Garcia, had been the lone senator who had opposed U.S. military advisers back in 1946. "What I am afraid of," he had warned, "is the possibility of our army becoming a simple appendage to that of the United States since the authority that they will exercise as assistants, advisers and technical men might turn out to be a way of getting control over even the internal organization and function of the Philippine Army."[7]

During the next Philippine administration—that of Diosdado Macapagal—a U.S. military official testified that the JUSMAG chief "has been able to exercise considerable influence." In 1963 the AFP chief of staff and the head of JUSMAG signed a "Memorandum of Understanding" that specified the organizational structure and mission of units of the AFP. A few years later, a Philippine congressional committee charged that JUSMAG officers had issued orders "directly to subordinate commanders of the AFP." United States officials denied the charge before an American congressional committee, but their testimony left something to be desired. Roland Paul, the committee counsel, asked the U.S. deputy chief of mission in Manila, James M. Wilson, Jr., if he knew of any instances of direct JUSMAG orders to the AFP. Wilson replied that he knew of none, but in the printed committee hearings his response is followed by a security deletion.[8]

One of the major areas of JUSMAG advice to the AFP was "civic action." This was the term employed for the using of military troops on public works projects. The doctrine of civic action was born in the anti-Huk campaigns of the early 1950s and refined by U.S. policy-makers on the basis of worldwide experiences. As the JUSMAG chief in the mid-1950s explained, civic action allowed the Philippine government to maintain troops in newly pacified areas when demobilizing them was considered too dangerous due to the possibility of a resurgence of Huk activity. The mission of the civic action units, said the JUSMAG head, was similar to that of the U.S. Army units stationed at various posts throughout "Indian territory" during the opening of the American frontier. Another JUSMAG officer cited four functions of civic action: (1) it uses underutilized military forces in a socially productive way, (2) it improves relations between the military and the population, (3) it provides security to the population, and (4) it opens up sources of information to the military on Huk activity. Other U.S. officials considered civic action to be a valuable counterinsurgency measure because it provided a subtle means of placing troops in a strategic location. In an area where insurgency threatened, a battalion could be sent in and could devote at least part of its time to useful labor; it could secure needed intelligence and discourage potential insurgents without antagonizing the uncommitted.[9]

During the administration of President John Kennedy, civic action became an important component of Washington's foreign military assistance programs. Secretary of Defense Robert McNamara explained, "We supply the training, the project assistance and direction and formulation, and certainly the equipment." Beginning in 1962–1963, U.S. military advisers in the Philippines "started to give more direction and encouragement on civic action." A U.S. civic action team spent three months in early 1963 doing training in Central Luzon. In 1966 JUSMAG proposed, and the Philippine Army accepted, that a U.S. civic action training team come from Okinawa to conduct joint exercises with Philippine troops. Six such exercises were held in the Central Luzon plains between July 1966 and February 1969, and, in the year and a half beginning July 1971, seven civic action exercises were conducted.[10] Such exercises, of course, allowed U.S. as well as Philippine troops to be strategically placed for intelligence and counterinsurgency purposes.

Military Training

One form of military aid has been especially valued by U.S. officials: the training of foreign military personnel. There was a direct military purpose to such training—providing Washington's allies with improved military capabilities, including skills even in such areas as chemical and biological warfare.[11] But, as the secretary of the Army confided in 1959, the benefits of the training program "transcend the military field." Secretary of Defense McNamara testified:

> These students are hand-picked by their own countries to become instructors when they return home. They are the coming leaders of their countries, the men that will have the know-how and impart it to their own forces. I need not dwell upon the value of having in positions of leadership men who have first-hand knowledge of how Americans do things and know how they think. It is beyond price to us to make friends of such men.

Three years later, McNamara stated:

> I have said before, and I think it bears repeating, that in all probability the greatest return on any portion of our military assistance investment—dollar for dollar—comes from the training of selected officers and key specialists in U.S. schools and installations. These students are hand-picked and screened by U.S. military personnel; they are the coming leaders of their nations. It is of inestimable value to the United States to have the friendship of such men.[12]

Military training was undertaken on a vast scale. At the end of fiscal 1963, foreign military personnel numbering 180,000 had been trained in the United States and another 54,000 at U.S. installations such as Fort Gulick in the Canal Zone and Clark Air Base in the Philippines. Additional thousands received training in their own countries from U.S. teams and technical representatives. Boasted General Maxwell D. Taylor, head of the Joint Chiefs of Staff:

> As a result of the proliferation of this training and the wide dispersal of graduates who have received training in our schools, it is impossible to travel without being buttonholed by enthusiastic alumni. I never get off an airplane in a distant country without being saluted by one or more officers proudly wearing the badge of Fort Leavenworth, of Fort Sill, of Fort Benning, or of one of our other military institutions.[13]

General Lucius D. Clay, head of the President's Committee to Strengthen the Security of the Free World, testified in 1963 that, where there are U.S. military training programs, "we have found that the army officers remained oriented to the West and opposed to other influences moving in. . . ." Unfortunately, Clay went on, efforts to prevent outside influences from moving in have at times led to military takeovers. Although he did not like to see this occur, "I think perhaps in some instances where this has happened there was no other choice. . . ."[14]

This brings up a second meaning of McNamara's comment that the foreign military officers are "the coming leaders of their nations." They were not going to be just lecturers at military academies, or even just influential in the armed forces; rather, they would be playing an increased role in running their societies. "If whether we like it or not," said John F. Kennedy when he was still a senator, "the military groups are going to play a more dominant role [in Southeast Asia], training these people becomes terribly important." A secret memorandum on "Training Under the Mutual Security Program" advised, "One must reckon with the possibility—indeed probability—that the Officer Corps, as a unit, may accede to the reins of government as the only alternative to domestic chaos and leftist takeover." And a study prepared for the Senate Foreign Relations Committee recommended: "In view of the growing role of the military in public life, the United States should help wherever possible the officer corps of southeast Asian countries to acquire the administrative and managerial skills necessary in the new task that they are assuming as the guarantors of their country's stability." The U.S. military training program was designed to prepare foreign military officers for this new role. As one Pentagon official testified, "what these people get in the United States in the more senior ranks, while it is military training, it does give them a feel for Government operations."[15]

The military training program was a key part of U.S. military aid to the Philippines. Though the Philippines was formally a democracy, as far back as 1947 Washington foresaw the long-range possibility of a military coup to check the left.[16]

In 1957 the CIA's Edward Lansdale confided that most Philippine general staff officers and many of the unit commanders had been trained in the United States (some before 1946). Between 1950 and 1971, Philippine military personnel numbering 13,588 received training from the United States, including 8,729 within the continental United States. One hundred and fifty-three senior officers attended U.S. command and general staff schools. This is all in addition to those officers trained at the Security Training Center mentioned above and at the National Defense College, a kind of graduate school for generals founded in 1965 with the assistance of the Asia Foundation.[17]

The Purposes and Extent of Military Aid

The primary purpose of U.S. military aid to the Philippines throughout the 1950s and 1960s was to assist the Manila government in maintaining internal security.[18] As the head of JUSMAG testified in 1969,

> When you have to conduct an active counterinsurgency military operation you have to have armored personnel carriers. We provide them with 15. We have given them four UH-lH helicopters. . . . When you look at the items we have given them, we are not giving them anything which cannot be used primarily for the counterinsurgency problems.

Even some of the aircraft given to the Philippines served this counterinsurgency objective. "When something occurs in Mindanao or in the south where there is a problem in land resettlement," explained a Pentagon official, the Philippine government "has very little capability to airlift anybody down there" without U.S.-provided planes.

> We are trying to give them a few transport aircraft so they can carry their security forces along those 4,000 miles of archipelago and those

islands. We are trying to improve their mobility and provide light weapons.

We are not trying to provide the Philippines with a force that could be used elsewhere or a force that expects an invasion from some outside conventional power. Our concern in the Philippines is the security of our bases and the security of the people of the Philippines against insurgencies.[19]

Another objective of military aid to the Philippines, in the view of U.S. policymakers, was to allow the Philippine Armed Forces to send troops to other Asian countries. This goal, however, was always made secondary to internal security, and units were to be considered for external use only when the internal treat was minimal. Thus, while PHILCAG, a Philippine civic action unit, was in Vietnam, the Philippines had a *combat* battalion team that was earmarked as a SEATO contribution yet was deployed in Central Luzon.[20]

Military aid also has had a political function. The most dramatic example was the military aid package that was used to pay off Philippine president Ferdinand Marcos for sending the token civic action group to Vietnam,[21] but there are more basic applications. "As a general rule," noted the CIA in 1959, "the flow of improved military equipment helps to assure the loyalty of the armed forces to the regime which secures such equipment." This is especially likely to be true in a country like the Philippines where, to a considerable extent, the armed forces serve as a means of enriching the officer corps. For example, in 1960 the AFP had more than four times as many officers (commissioned and noncommissioned) as privates. The CIA also noted that to the extent that military aid helps keep regimes in power, it does so not so much because of its directly military uses but "as one of several manifestations of broad U.S. economic and political support for the recipient government." Thus, the Pentagon reported in 1971 that military aid to the Philippines "is also important in demonstrating the firmness of the U.S. support to the Philippines."[22] Notice is thereby served to all potential dissidents that the United States is committed to defending the existing government and that the United States will take the necessary measures to defeat any insurgency.

Total U.S. military aid to the Philippines—equipment and training—has been officially put at $631.7 million between fiscal years 1946 and 1971 inclusive. But there have been numerous other categories of military aid not accounted for in this figure. Military equipment and supplies in excess of the requirements of the United States were given other nations without being charged to the military assistance program. The excess defense articles given to the Philippines from fiscal 1946 to 1972 had an initial acquisition cost of $72.6 million and a legal cost at the time of transfer of one-third this amount. Such nonappropriated aid contributed to a General Accounting Office (GAO) finding that the "magnitude of U.S. military assistance to foreign countries is not readily apparent to anyone, including the appropriate committees of the Congress." The GAO also noted that, until 1969, JUSMAG had given the interest earned on U.S.-owned local currency to finance Philippine military construction, though legally it should have reverted to the U.S. Treasury.[23]

The GAO further found that "U.S. assistance to the Philippines has been augmented by the use of regular U.S. military personnel and equipment." During 1969 and 1970 five U.S. military teams were detailed to assist the Philippine Armed Forces in training, supply, maintenance, and equipment operation at an estimated cost of over $300,000. More significantly, though uncited by the GAO, U.S. officials at Clark Air Base made a number of contributions to Philippine counterinsurgency operations between December 1967 and September 1969. This included weapons, ammunition, equipment, aerial reconnaisance, and a helicopter with an American crew and air-to-ground communications.[24]

The official figures on U.S. military aid to the Philippines, then, seriously understate the actual levels of military assistance. In addition, however, under the heading of economic aid there is a great deal that is in fact military in nature.

The General Purpose of Economic Aid

A number of objectives have been served by the U.S. economic aid programs. It is significant, however, that the role of humanitarian considerations has been quite small. Washington's priorities were well revealed in a closed-session hearing with Secretary of State Dean Acheson in May 1950. Acheson and Senators Millard Tydings and Theodore Francis Green agreed that should starvation break out in mainland China the United States should give a little food aid—not enough to alleviate the starvation, but enough for a psychological warfare advantage.[25]

There is much other evidence of the relative unimportance of humanitarian concern as a motive for economic aid. Secretary of State John Foster Dulles publicly stated in 1955, with Senator J. William Fulbright concurring:

I would not want to say that there are not a few aspects of what we do abroad which are purely humanitarian.

There are provisions, as you know, for the relief in the case of floods, disasters, and so forth, where the American people assist out of their generosity to meet needs. But that is not the main purpose of the mutual security program [the name of the U.S. foreign aid program in the 1950s].

A high-level committee appointed to study the operation of the foreign aid program in 1957 took as part of its "first general assumption" that "aid is extended to foreign countries in support of a national policy, first, to halt the spread of communism, and second to bolster the internal strength [of U.S. allies]." A senior economist for the Rand Corporation, an Air Force funded "think tank," wrote in 1960 that "humanitarian objectives are not, nor do they appear likely to be, prominent among the continuing objectives of U.S. foreign aid." And in 1962 a senator remarked that foreign aid "should be used as a weapon. Any time a dollar is not spent as a weapon which produces direct results in the support of our position in the free world we are wasting it."[26]

Public Safety Program

The Public Safety Program has been funded by the U.S. economic aid agencies—first, the International Cooperation Administration and then its successor, the Agency for International Development (AID)—but its purpose has clearly been counterinsurgency. It was designed to provide U.S. training and assistance to the local police forces of countries friendly to the United States. AID explained in 1964:

> The police constitute the first line of defense against subversion and terrorism. . . . Moreover, the police are a most sensitive point of contact between government and people, close to the focal points of unrest, and more acceptable than the army as keepers of order over long periods of time. The police are frequently better trained and equipped than the military to deal with minor forms of violence, conspiracy, and subversion.

The public safety programs, AID continued, "place us in a close professional relationship with over a million police throughout the world." At the 1968 graduation ceremonies of AID's International

Police Academy—a training center for foreign police officers in Washington, D.C.—General Maxwell Taylor told those assembled that the lesson of Vietnam was that the United States had been too late in recognizing the extent of the insurgent threat. "We have learned the need for a strong police force and a strong police intelligence organization to assist in identifying early the symptoms of an incipient subversive situation."[27]

AID officials have asserted that the public safety programs are intended to enable police to maintain internal security "with a minimum use of physical force" and by "encouraging the development of responsible and humane police administration." This is a highly misleading formulation. The U.S. goal has been to defeat insurgency. Where this goal has been best served by "humane" police techniques, such techniques have been preferred. For example, in the post-Trujillo Dominican Republic police were taught "nonlethal riot control" so that when "Communist-instigated" riots were quelled "no martyrs were created" and "the Communists had nothing to exploit." On the other hand, when the U.S. goal has been best served by terror tactics, these have been favored. South Vietnam is the most extreme instance of U.S.-sponsored terror, but hardly the only case. With respect to Indonesia, for example, the State Department's Roger Hilsman has written: "We helped equip and train Mobile Police Brigades (Mobrigs), whom the Communist rioters came to fear."[28]

The public safety program in the Philippines began in fiscal 1957 with U.S. assistance to the National Bureau of Investigation (NBI), an agency which was "patterned after" the U.S. FBI "in organization, functions and objectives." Under U.S. guidance, the NBI provincial offices were reorganized, radio networks established, and the crime laboratory improved. In addition, a "limited training program was activated to serve local police in selected areas of the country."[29]

In 1966 AID undertook a "Survey of Philippine Law Enforcement" under the direction of Frank Walton. Walton was an ideal choice for the job, having been chief public safety adviser in South Vietnam. Later, Walton would deny any knowledge of "tiger cages" in Vietnam; in fact, he asserted that Con Son Prison was more "like a Boy Scout Recreational Camp." However, in 1963 he had signed a report stating:

In Con Son II, some of the hardcore communists keep preaching the "party" line, so these "Reds" are sent to the Tiger Cages in Con Son I where they are isolated from all others for months at a time. This confinement may also include rice without salt and water—the United

States prisons' equivalent of bread and water. It may include immobilization—the prisoner is bolted to the floor, handcuffed to a bar or rod, or legirons with the chain through an eyebolt, or around a bar or rod.[30]

AID has refused to declassify the report of the survey team. Its declassification, wrote an AID official, "would be prejudicial to the foreign policy interests of the United States."[31] There is, however, an unclassified summary version of the report upon which the following remarks are based.

The report observed that peace and order in the Philippines was "deteriorating at a serious rate." Crime and lawlessness, the report acknowledged, were attributable to deep-rooted social problems, but, nevertheless, only 2 of the 408 recommendations in the report dealt with correcting these problems. The remaining 406 urged the upgrading, consolidation, and centralization of the activities of the various law enforcement agencies of the Philippine government.[32]

In particular, the report stated that the number of Philippine government law enforcement officers programmed for training by the United States should "be substantially increased," including training at the International Police Academy in Washington, D.C. One recommendation suggested utilizing the Security Training Center for local police. As indicated above, this center was covertly CIA-sponsored.[33]

Those law enforcement officers already trained by the United States, said the report, should be utilized "to the maximum" in training other officers. Previously, some Philippine Constabulary personnel had received training under the Military Assistance Program. The report noted that there was too much emphasis on purely military material: the course work on counterinsurgency and psychological warfare "better qualifies" the trainees to "perform their peace-and-order mission," while the infantry officer course should not continue to be taught.[34]

Over the next few years, with the close advice of AID's Public Safety Division, the police forces of the Philippines were substantially revamped. A high-level Philippine Police Commission was established to oversee the reorganization. Named as one of the three police commissioners was a former director of the NBI who had been forced to resign amid charges that Filipino officials were passing secrets to the CIA. In mid-1967, a centralized riot-control and internal security force, METROCOM, was set up in Manila. METROCOM troopers were given training in crowd control techniques by U.S. instructors. In 1970 and 1971 METROCOM got the opportunity to show what it had learned. Massive demonstrations were held at the U.S. Embassy, the presidential palace, and other targets; more than a dozen demonstrators were killed by police gunfire, and countless others were brutally beaten. A classic photograph of Manila riot police, one swinging a huge club at students lying on the ground, ran in the American press—although the *Washington Post*'s front-page caption read "Filipino riot police stand over two student demonstrators. . . ."[35]

In 1969 the public safety program in the Philippines was renamed the Internal Security Project, and U.S. funding increased sharply. For fiscal years 1970–1972, the Philippines was the third largest recipient of public safety funds in the world, surpassed only by South Vietnam and Thailand.[36] In 1970 AID helped establish a police communications network. By 1971, U.S. advisers and the Philippine Police Commission had set up eight regional police training centers, and some 17,500 policemen were trained at them in "crowd control procedures" and other specialized courses. Instructors for these programs were trained at the International Police Academy in Washington, D.C., and at other overseas locations. In 1974 it was revealed that theses done by the "students" at the International Police Academy included such passages as: "During interrogations the judicious use of official severity or the use of threat and force to some extent . . . when other techniques have failed . . . is a practical necessity."[37]

Food for Peace

One aid program that seemingly has a substantial humanitarian component is Food for Peace (Public Law 480). In fact, however, the attitude of the U.S. government was well expressed by a National Security Council representative who said, "To give food aid to countries just because people are starving is a pretty weak reason."[38] Food for Peace director George McGovern explained the realpolitik aims of the program:

> [P.L. 480] helps the United States find constructive outlets for our surplus food production; it reduces our storage costs; it stimulates our shipping industry and our ports; it bolsters farm income; it develops future dollar markets overseas; it raises the purchasing power of other countries; and it strengthens U.S. foreign policy objectives.

These goals are not totally compatible. A *Washington Post* reporter noted that the State Department has pressed for massive shipments of food aid to Indochina in furtherance of foreign policy objectives, while the Department of Agriculture has urged that priority be given to Indonesia and South Korea as the most promising of potential future markets for U.S. agricultural products. Significantly, however, "in this debate, pleas for a bigger share for some 90 other poor countries that received little or no food aid have gone mainly unheeded."[39]

The specific provisions of P.L. 480 have undergone a number of revisions and relabelings. Following, however, are the essential features of the law. One section provides for the United States to sell surplus agricultural products to allied foreign nations, who pay for them in their local currencies. The sales proceeds, called "counterpart funds," are deposited in the local central bank as the property of the United States. Between 1954, when P.L. 480 began, and 1969 more than $11 billion was deposited worldwide. These funds then have two general uses: American uses and country uses. The former contribute toward the expenses of the some thirty-five United States agencies operating abroad, thus preventing a deterioration of the U.S. balance of payments position (though at the expense of the foreign country's balance of payments position). In addition, as part of the American uses, funds are spent on developing agricultural export markets. Between 1954 and 1969, counterpart funds amounting to $116 million have been spent on this purpose.

Country uses of counterpart funds fall into three categories. First, low-interest "Cooley" loans are made to American and other corporations operating overseas. Second, funds are granted or loaned to foreign governments for AID-approved economic development projects. And third, the funds are used for grants for the common defense—that is, military aid—which since 1964 explicitly includes internal security. This military aid does not usually appear in figures on U.S. military assistance, and Congress does not authorize the particular allocations. From fiscal 1955 to 1970, over $1.5 billion in local currency has been granted for the "common defense," and $693 million in the fiscal years 1965–1970.[40]

Another section of P.L. 480 provides government-to-government aid for famine and other urgent relief assistance. Most of these grants, however, have gone to "countries that have suffered unnatural disasters," as one critic has observed. Thus, in fiscal 1970 the three largest recipients of this disaster aid were Brazil, South Vietnam, and South Korea. Another provision of P.L. 480 grants commodities to U.S. voluntary agencies for their overseas programs.

These last two sections are generally considered to be the humanitarian side of P.L. 480. However, from 1954 to 1969 less than one-fifth of P.L. 480 shipments have been made under these two sections. And in 1967, one of the main voluntary agencies distributing Food for Peace commodities, Catholic Relief Services, was found to be providing surplus foodstuffs as pay to the South Vietnamese army.[41]

Another section of the Food for Peace program provides for the barter exchange of surplus U.S. commodities for strategic materials. This has become relatively unimportant since 1962. And a final provision of P.L. 480 establishes long-term food supply contracts in return for dollars or fully convertible local currencies. From 1954 to 1969 a total of $3.3 billion was spent on these two sections of P.L. 480.[42]

Under all the sections of the Food for Peace law, the U.S. government has purchased surplus commodities from American farmers. During the 1950s, P.L. 480 was primarily an instrument of domestic policy, a means of disposing of the overproduction of American farms relative to the dollar demand. From 1954 to 1959, 25 percent of total U.S. agricultural exports were shipped under P.L. 480, and another 8 percent under other aid programs. This is not to say that foreign policy objectives were ignored. As Hubert Humphrey, a sponsor of P.L. 480, remarked in 1957,

> I have heard . . . that people may become dependent on us for food. . . . To me that was good news, because before people can do anything they have got to eat. And if you are looking for a way to get people to lean on you and to be dependent on you, in terms of their cooperation with you, it seems to me that food dependence would be terrific. . . .

Nevertheless, in 1959 an influential official complained privately that P.L. 480 was based on domestic considerations "regardless of embarrassment to our international relations."[43] But, starting with the Kennedy administration, the emphasis shifted to foreign policy objectives. In 1974 a congressional staff report estimated that 45 percent of U.S. food aid was used for security purposes.[44]

Food for Peace shipments to the Philippines have totaled $228.7 million since the program's inception. The amount of $32.5 million was paid for in pesos and planned for country use. Of this, $5.4 million was expended on Cooley low-interest loans to American and Filipino corporations, and $9.4 million on the "common defense." The latter outlays included costs for naval and air bases, Philippine Constabulary facilities, and a communications system for the Philippine Armed Forces.[45]

Another $83.6 million in P.L. 480 shipments was paid for with dollars on credit. And just as peace was not the only goal of Food for Peace, so not all the commodities distributed were food. In 1970, for example, half the P.L. 480 sales to the Philippines went for cotton and half for tobacco—and this at a time when over 50 percent of the Philippine population under ten years of age was estimated to be malnourished, and, according to a Food for Peace official, 6 to 7 percent of children under four were "probably seriously retarded" due to malnutrition.[46]

The U.S. tobacco industry, it should be noted, has always taken a special interest in the health of Filipinos. When the Philippine government was considering placing a tariff on American tobacco, a Virginia senator wrote to Secretary of State Dulles that, since the cigarette industry was imperiled by the fact that "the rapid increase in lung cancer has cast a cloud upon cigarette smoking as a possible contributing, if not a major, factor in that dread disease," the State Department should try to prevent tariffs that would hurt the U.S. tobacco industry.[47]

Land Reform

One major area of American foreign aid to the Philippines was that of land reform. Washington's definition of the term "land reform" has always been extremely opportunistic. According to U.S. officials, "an adjustment of landholdings . . . may or may not have a part in a particular land-reform program." Land reform "does not always, or even usually, mean . . . a distribution of land. It often means just a better relationship" between the tenant and the landlord.[48] When the rural population of a country has been relatively passive and revolution has not been a serious threat, American agrarian reform assistance has taken the form of improving agricultural productivity. On the other hand, when rural conditions have been volatile and revolution a real possibility, the United States has pushed for programs of mild land redistribution.

By and large, U.S. efforts have been of the first sort. For example, in AID's proposed budget for fiscal 1968, $800 million was allocated to assist foreign agriculture, of which only $1.6 million—or one-fifth of 1 percent—was to go toward land reform. And most of the aid to agriculture did not go to benefit the poor peasants in ways other than land redistribution. One study showed that from 1962 to 1970, 52 percent of U.S. assistance to agriculture in Latin America benefited primarily the larger commercial farms, 19 percent benefited the poorer farmers, and 29 percent benefited both.[49]

In those cases where U.S. assistance has gone specifically to land redistribution, U.S. policy has been circumscribed by two considerations. First, the fundamental wealth and power of the elite which is allied with U.S. interests are not to be abridged. And second, the capitalist nature of the agricultural sector of a country must be preserved and remain tied into the world capitalist economy. So, for example, land might be redistributed, but the landlords would receive compensation and the peasants would have to pay for their plots of land over many years. Such an arrangement would maintain the relative positions of rich and poor and increase the commitment to private property and free enterprise among the rural population.

It is not being suggested that landlords welcomed land reform (though, as will be seen, there are times when they did). Many landlords possessed a feudal set of attitudes, attitudes contrary to the more capitalist presuppositions of American-sponsored land reform. Thus, for landlords to receive compensation for their land in high-interest bonds would require shifting to savings a portion of what had previously been spent on conspicuous consumption. Or for landlords to get stock certificates in industrial enterprises in exchange for their land might be more profitable but would be less prestigious in feudal terms.[50]

So, generally, U.S. pressure has been necessary for capitalist land reform, and the amount of pressure that the United States has been willing to exert has been a function of the threat of revolution on the one hand and the threat of alienating the elite on the other.

In Chapter Three, mention was made of the recommendations and subsequent ousting of Robert Hardie, the U.S. land reform adviser in the Philippines in the early 1950s. His recall from Manila came at a time when the Huk insurgency had been substantially defeated. To U.S. officials, land reform as a means of undercutting agrarian revolt was no longer necessary. Accordingly, the next American land reform adviser, John L. Cooper, had a much more callous attitude toward peasant unrest. He prepared a report asserting that minor reforms would keep rural discontent at manageable levels, so that thoroughgoing reform was unnecessary. Finding that unrest occurred only in provinces with tenancy rates of over 50 percent, he suggested that efforts should be confined to reducing all provincial tenancy rates to below 50 percent.[51]

On the basis of Cooper's report, the U.S. Embassy in Manila submitted recommendations to Washington which Secretary of State Dulles approved in May 1954. Cultivated land was to be redistributed only in areas where the situation was critical or where landlords violated the law. Otherwise, reforms were to be limited to administrative actions designed to expand the number of owner-operated farms and measures for improving tenant-landlord relations.[52]

United States advisers then helped the Magsaysay administration draft a land reform program. Magsaysay made no appeal to the peasantry to help get the necessary legislation passed, and the landlords in Congress emasculated the program.[53] The land reform bill that emerged provided for extremely high compensation to landlords, with the burden of the program falling almost entirely on the "beneficiary"—that is, the tenant farmer. Landlords could retain 300 hectares of contiguous land and as much as they wanted in noncontiguous land, unless a court ruled that "justified agrarian unrest" prevailed. The compensation was to be in certificates payable on demand, the equivalent of cash. It is not surprising that some landlords not only consented to sell their land but initiated the offers themselves because of the exceedingly high prices.[54]

Magsaysay signed the legislation amid great fanfare, but by 1958 the Land Tenure Administration had acquired only about 2 percent of the 2.4 million hectares of land it classified as "concentrated holdings," and less than half of these had been distributed to peasants. And the various cooperative institutions and the resettlement agency established as part of the land reform collapsed amidst corruption and mismanagement. By 1960 the tenancy rate in the country had *increased* from 37.3 percent in 1948 to 39.9 percent.[55]

With the Huk insurgency at a low ebb, Washington saw no need for pushing for further land reform. The director of the American foreign aid program announced in Manila that the United States would put no additional pressure on the Philippine government to bring about fundamental agrarian reform. An outgoing land tenure adviser suggested that, since landlord resistance blocked any redistribution of land, "a middle-of-the-road compromise" ought to be pursued, aiming at getting farmers to a 70-30 crop-sharing ratio or to leasehold tenancy (i.e., paying fixed rents for land).[56] In short, land reform of even the weakest sort was no longer on the agenda.

United States involvement with Philippine land reform was renewed in 1963 with the passage by the Philippine government of the Agricultural Land Reform Code. The code solemnly declared that share tenancy was "contrary to public policy and shall be abolished." To no one's surprise, however, this declaration did not suddenly end tenancy. Indeed, it could not do so since it explicitly excluded from its jurisdiction tenants on lands planted to sugar, coconut, and most other crops aside from rice and corn. Moreover, the code explicitly exempted plots of less than 75 hectares. The effect of these exclusions was to restrict land reform—even if everything went perfectly—to considerably less than one-sixth of the country's tenant farmers.[57]

The 1963 Land Reform Code had a number of objectives. One was to undercut rural insurrection. "I do not want a civil war to rend our dreams apart," wrote a Philippine land reform official. "We can keep our wealth and our heads if we realize the responsibility which wealth engenders. . . ."[58] Second, the code aimed to increase agricultural productivity. Philippine agriculture had among the lowest yields per acre of any in the world, and, as a 1962 World Bank report noted, this has been largely attributable to the land tenure system. In the words of one scholar, the 1963 legislation "bears the unmistakable imprint of a group of young economists and intellectuals who were primarily concerned with the failure of existing agricultural development programs to generate sufficiently rapid gains in agricultural productivity to match the rapid population growth rate. . . ." Thus, for example, the code provides that a landlord may require a lessee (a tenant paying a fixed rental) to adopt proven farm techniques. The lessee's failure to comply is grounds for being dispossessed.[59]

A third objective, explicitly stated in the code, was to "divert landlord capital in agricultural to industrial development." This was to be done not by dispossessing the landed gentry ("a myth," "absolutely untrue" says the Philippine land reform official) but by compensating landlords for their land in part with industrial assets. The compensation for a piece of land was to be established by a land reform court on the basis of the full market value, thus making the Philippine land reform program one of the few in the world to set the compensation so high. This sum was then to be paid 10 percent in cash and 90 percent in 6-percent twenty-five-year bonds, totally tax free, or a maximum of 30 percent in 6-percent preferred shares issued by the Land Bank. The shares would be immune from inflation, because their value would rise with the expansion of the Land Bank's operations. The bonds were to be negotiable at their face value as payment for (1) real property purchases from the government, (2) shares purchased in government-owned or controlled corporations, (3) reparations goods received from Japan, or (4) public lands suitable for large-scale farm operations, provided the land is put under "plantation management" rather than tenancy. To help landlords choose the most profitable investment opportunities, the Land Reform Code provided for a group of economic consultants to assist them, and AID gave $150,000 to the Philippine government for this purpose.[60]

Tenants were required to pay the purchase price (full market value) plus 6 percent for administration expenses, amortizable for a period of up to twenty-five years. But the law contained a number of loopholes that made it unlikely that a tenant would ever receive land. Owners of rice lands increasingly turned to mechanized farming and the use of hired labor as a way to avoid land reform. Many large landlords divided their holding into 75-hectare parcels—which were not subject to land reform—and distributed them to family members. Other landowners shifted from rice culture to sugarcane. In the first four years of the code, two thousand cases of alleged illegal eviction were filed with the Court of Agrarian Relations. In no case was a landlord convicted of or even prosecuted for unlawful eviction.[61]

Even more significant was the fact that the landlord-dominated Philippine government had no interest in following through on the land reform. By 1970, seven years after the code had passed, only 6,600 deeds of sale had been issued to tenant farmers—that is, considerably less than 1 percent of the nation's tenant farmers. When Marcos became president in 1966 he announced that 350,000 tenants would be converted into lessees by the end of 1969. Less than 10 percent of this goal was reached. A study conducted for AID in 1970 concluded that effective land reform had "yet to come" and that there had been "little basic change in the power relations of society."[62]

Actually, somewhat before 1970 AID had concluded that Philippine officials were not serious about land reform. During Marcos's first term of office (1966–1969) the Philippine land reform program had shifted to what AID called "political objectives," that is, furthering the election and patronage opportunities of Marcos. AID disassociated itself from the program and channeled its aid to Philippine agriculture into productivity projects.[63]

The Green Revolution

If the United States was unwilling to push for fundamental social change, agrarian unrest could still be forestalled by increasing productivity. By spreading "miracle" high-yield strains of rice and wheat throughout Asia, Washington hoped that agricultural output could be expanded and the well-being of the rural poor improved. The Green Revolution would hold back Red revolutions.

Unfortunately for U.S. officials, however, there are no such simple shortcuts. Instead of undercutting the need for social change, the Green Revolution worldwide has exacerbated inequalities, making change both more urgent and more difficult. High-yielding seeds require for their successful utilization credit, fertilizer, pesticides, and irrigation—inputs disproportionately available to wealthy farmers. Moreover, the miracle strains make farm mechanization more profitable, resulting in the eviction of human labor.[64]

The experience of the Green Revolution followed this general pattern. Miracle rice was initially introduced into areas of Central Luzon, and the first noticeable effects

> were rising land values, increased insecurity of tenants and share-croppers and, finally, a wave of evictions, since " . . . the high returns from the miracle rice create an incentive for the landlord to ease out his tenants and operate the farm himself with the help of hired workers." A survey of the Mayantoc [Tarlac] municipality between 1965 and 1967 revealed that the number of tenant farmers had decreased by 6 percent.[65]

And between May 1968 and May 1969 agricultural employment in the Philippines declined considerably.[66]

Instead of complementing land reform, the Green Revolution in the Philippines slowed down the already snail-paced progress toward converting tenant farmers into fixed rental lessees or into landowners. This was because the introduction of the high-yielding seed varieties increased the price of land, making tenants less able to afford alternative tenure arrangements and landlords less willing to accept them.[67]

The spread of miracle rice required massive inputs of fertilizer, pesticides, credit, and education or extension services, and officials of AID and the Manila government took the view that "all possible encouragement should be given to private enterprises" in supplying these needs. The AID chief in the Philippines testified in 1966:

> In all our efforts, we have worked closely with private enterprise. Our [miracle-rice] demonstrations have been in cooperation with fertilizer and pesticide industries and dealers.
>
> We have worked with and provided financial assistance to private seed producers in the Philippines, and we have encouraged participating farmers and agencies to depend upon private industry rather than government entities to provide—and distribute—the seeds, chemicals, and machinery.
>
> There are three fairly large fertilizer companies and one small one in the Philippines; there are several companies, notably Union Carbide, producing a broad range of modern sophisticated pesticides. . . .
>
> The Esso Co. has just completed a $30 million chemical fertilizer plant which is now producing at full capacity. Equally important, this company has established a distribution network throughout the entire archipelago with storage depots at strategic locations. . . .

Our technicians work closely with these firms in the production of instructions, exhibits, and the carrying out of experiments.[68]

The supplying of rural credit was also primarily left to private sources. Credit is a vital need for the Green Revolution since the cash costs of production increase tenfold over those for traditional seed varieties. Repeated attempts to set up government credit systems all ended in failure, and so the United States backed the establishment of a system of private rural banks. However, despite the fact that the rural banks received financial support and training assistance from both the Philippine and the American governments, their lending policies have not served the needs of the small farmer, as indicated by the fact that four-fifths of their loans were protected by real estate collateral. The only source of small farmer credit in the Philippines between 1966 and 1971 was the Agricultural Credit Administration, which provided only 1 percent of total agricultural production credit and one-half of 1 percent of agricultural marketing credit, thus forcing small farmers to resort to the village moneylender.[69]

President Marcos of the Philippines was an enthusiastic advocate of miracle rice. The propaganda victory of making the Philippines self-sufficient in rice would be a great boon to his reelection, and it did not involve any sacrifice on the part of his landlord friends. Accordingly, Marcos undertook the rapid introduction of high-yielding rice seeds, and from 1966 to 1969 miracle rice was planted on 30 percent of total Philippine rice lands.[70]

There is, however, a grave danger in using a single seed strain on large contiguous areas; plant disease may cause a crop failure of catastrophic proportions. (This is precisely what happened in Ireland in the nineteenth century with the potato.) The traditional rice strains were numerous and interspersed, thus providing built-in protection against such an occurrence.[71]

The dangers of widespread single-strain planting were well publicized at the beginning of the Green Revolution, but Marcos was quite willing to risk the public well-being for his own political aggrandizement. He got his propaganda victory in 1970 when, for the first year in recent times, the Philippines exported rice. But the next year a virus struck: production dropped and rice prices skyrocketed.[72]

Rural Development

Mention has already been made of the CIA role in various rural development projects in the Philippines, but the covert component was only one aspect of these projects, for they had as a central goal finding ways to improve the welfare of the rural population without the need for thoroughgoing reform.

The Philippine Rural Reconstruction Movement (PRRM) was a major effort in this regard. Headed by Y. C. James Yen, a veteran of similar projects in pre-Communist China and Taiwan, PRRM was established in 1952 with the backing of many prominent Americans and Filipinos. In addition to the CIA, funding sources included CARE Inc. and numerous Philippine and U.S. corporations.[73]

PRRM borrowed much of its rhetoric from the Communist movement ("Go to the people/Live among them/Learn from them/ Serve them," self-criticism sessions, etc.), but in fact it was a deeply conservative organization. Since its goal was to improve the condition of the peasant masses without any serious social change, its program emphasized supplemental means of adding to farmer income, such as improved rice culture, second-cropping, home-lot gardening, and poultry- and swine-raising. PRRM had a response to the charge that such measures are meaningless without substantial social reform: "PRRM has found that it is not necessary to wait idly until basic agrarian reforms are carried out by government. Farmers can be shown that new methods can bring them better yields and better incomes. . . . "[74] This is a revealing answer, for it indicates that PRRM assumed that there were but two options: waiting idly for the government or improving productivity. That social change can come about other than by a benevolent government bestowing favors upon a passive population did not occur to PRRM.

Consider the PRRM motto of living among the people. PRRM's Rural Reconstruction Workers (RRWs) were instructed to live as paying boarders with an "influential and respected" family whose "economic and social status" was "at least equal to the average" in the village. The house had to have a toilet, bathroom, or safe drinking water, or the RRW was to offer to pay part of the cost of installing these facilities. Some of the villages where PRRM worked were located within haciendas. In these cases, the RRWs stayed at the house of the overseer. Interviewed RRWs admitted that they were happy to work in the hacienda barrios because they could stay in better quarters. These RRWs were fearful that discussions of the real causes of poverty or finding fault with the landlords would be construed as too revolutionary an approach. Instead, they joined the overseer in privately blaming the peasants themselves for their poverty. This is especially ironic, given that the barrio residents are generally landless laborers for whom the PRRM self-help programs of second-cropping and home-lot gardens offered no opportunity for improvement.[75]

On hacienda barrios, the owners themselves have approached PRRM to send in RRWs. In other cases, the sending of RRWs to barrios has been sponsored by rich individuals or companies, such as Shell Oil. This has become very much a worldwide pattern: as the fears of confiscation, nationalization, and communism seized American business leaders in the early 1960s, corporations began setting up all sorts of community-development projects overseas. The biggest such venture was a $1 million operation funded by steel and oil companies in Venezuela.[76] There, as in the Philippines, the aim was to improve rural living standards without changing the structure of rural society.

On one hacienda barrio in the Philippines, PRRM organized a credit union, but the overseer and the PRRM team captain were the dominant figures in it. No wonder one study found that PRRM "in the course of its thirteen years of existence, was able to achieve only very limited success in the sphere of cooperative activity by the barrio people." Another study reported that after twenty years PRRM had organized forty-eight credit unions in the province of Nueva Ecija, but only ten remained active, and only two or three were truly viable. In another barrio, "in spite of about two years of PRRM involvement . . . the interest of the barrio people in self-government seemed to be marginal."[77]

In late 1954 the U.S. government decided to take a direct role in rural development projects. Between 1956 and 1965 the United States provided about 42 million pesos in counterpart funds and 2 million in dollar costs. In addition, nine U.S. rural development advisers and six consultants were detailed to the Philippines during this period.[78]

Two major projects resulted from the U.S. assistance. A group of Presidential Assistants in Community Development (PACD) was set up; this was essentially an official version of PRRM, with people sent into the barrios to organize self-help activities. Like PRRM, none of these activities threatened to alter the power structure of the countryside. In Mindoro Occidental, for example, the self-help activities were chemical control of pests and diseases, canal dredging for irrigation, hog raising, swine vaccination, road repair, and others of a similar nature. To Washington, the utilization of local volunteer labor on such things as the construction of roads made the U.S. foreign aid dollar go further. The rural poor, however, were not nearly as enthused. Those who were unemployed part of the time were disinclined to offer their labor for activities likely to bring relatively greater benefit to landowners in the form of unearned increment on the value of their land. Those without idle time were unable to participate in activities in the absence of payment, for they lived from hand to mouth.[79]

The second project resulting from U.S. assistance was the drafting of various laws giving power to decentralized barrio (village) units. Before 1955, barrio councils were appointed by the municipal government; the councils were completely powerless, with a few nominal duties. The Huks had derived considerable popular support from the fact that they established organs of self-rule in the barrios, and U.S. and Philippine officials decided that it was important to counter this appeal. In 1955, 1959, and 1963, laws were passed giving power to elective councils on the barrio level, including the right to levy certain taxes. Nevertheless, the powers of the barrio councils were still so circumscribed that all they could really do was undertake projects similar to those of PRRM and PACD.[80]

The barrio's exercise of the right to eminent domain had to be approved by the municipal government; ordinances had to be consistent with municipal ordinances; the secretary of finance was able to suspend, pending appeal, any barrio tax ordinances that he felt to be unjust, excessive, oppressive, or confiscatory. In any case, the taxing powers of the barrio could not exceed one-half of a similar tax already levied by the municipal government; it could only be raised from store licenses, billboards, cockfights, and a tax on real property at a maximum of one-fourth of one percent of assessed valuation. In 1962 a survey found that only 3 percent of the barrios had imposed this one-fourth of one percent tax.

The barrio laws also provided that 10 percent of all taxes on real property collected in the barrio should accrue to the barrio government regardless of the level of government at which the money was raised. In fact, however, barrios often had to beg the municipal governments for the release of these funds. In 1962 only half the municipalities had distributed the 10 percent to all the barrios in their jurisdiction. In any event, the tax on real property has been extremely low, and the owners of the property often live outside the barrio.[81]

Because the barrio councils did not have the power to institute land reform or other substantive social change, they have not been the focus of local political struggles. According to one study, those with higher education—hence, presumably, the rich—"seem to attach importance only to municipal, provincial, and national political positions." The parochial nature of barrio politics was revealed by one study of two barrio councils, which found them composed of "men and women interested in barrio work. They were all engaged in canvassing for the candidates for the municipal beauty contest." As the report of an AID-sponsored conference concluded, one must distinguish between the form and the substance of participation. Where most critical issues are national—such as land reform or allocation of national resources—small amounts of local participation may not be meaningful and, in fact, may actually divert popular pressures into low priority areas. In the Philippines, the report observed, the community development program has provided barrios many linkages into the power structure and "has likely prevented a greater distance being created between the ruling classes and the bulk of the population," but still "it has not been able to bring about a shift of national resources into the lagging agricultural sector, exert much influence on the major question of land reform, or to check the growing inequality in distribution of income."[82]

In 1966 the U.S. Congress added a provision known as Title IX to its Foreign Assistance Act. Title IX called upon AID to place emphasis on "assuring maximum participation in the task of economic development on the part of the people of the developing countries, through the encouragement of democratic private and local governmental institutions." The timing here is important. In 1966 much of the liberal community in the United States was becoming disenchanted with American foreign policy because of the war in Vietnam. Title IX was an attempt to restore liberal backing to Washington's overseas programs. This can be seen from the rhetoric used in describing Title IX: "The people of the less developed nations should participate more than they do in the decisions that affect their lives." It can also be seen from the recommendation of the AID-sponsored conference on Title IX opposing the transfer of Title IX programs to international agencies:

> Such a transfer might also be damaging to the U.S. image abroad, for it would put the humanitarian programs into the hands of others, leaving the U.S. with the *Realpolitik* programs that cannot be placed in multilateral agencies. The aid program in general would then risk the loss of the liberal constituency that is essential to sustaining the spirit of its personnel and its public support.[83]

But the U.S. concern with increasing popular participation went only as far as the rhetoric and the image-building; anything more has come into conflict with the fundamental goals of enhancing

American strategic and economic interests around the world. Thus, in countries where the United States has bases or other facilities, the AID-sponsored conference stated, the "interest of reliable access will usually be served by the persistence in power of the regime which originally granted these rights in the first place." If leaders both in and out of power support the U.S. bases, then Washington can encourage sociopolitical change. But if there are groups on the threshold of power "which are ideologically or for other reasons opposed to our continued presence, normally the United States should not encourage change."[84]

As part of Title IX, AID views part of its mission as encouraging foreign governments to pay increased attention to the "private sector." This concern for capitalist development may conflict with popular participation, but no matter: "Increased inequality of income is often a necessary concomitant of development . . . and therefore desirable. To prevent it would inhibit development. The short-run Title IX interest should not, perhaps, be weighed as equal to the longer-run growth interest." United States foreign investors have a role to play in Title IX, according to the AID-sponsored conference. They should seek "ways whereby employees can be brought to *feel* they have a significant stake in the enterprise" (emphasis added) and they should devote some of their attention to solving community problems. One way to increase popular participation, of course, might be to have local employees play a role in the management of U.S. corporations abroad. But Title IX's aim is the opposite: to be helpful in preserving U.S. investments and raw materials by reducing the chances of a political explosion against an oligarchic regime. And "the threat of nationalization will mean we cannot push very hard on behalf of Title IX objectives the regime itself does not want."[85]

The AID-sponsored conference suggested a number of other Title IX-type activities: civic action by the Department of Defense, and AID funding for some of the projects covertly supported by the CIA prior to the disclosures of the mid-1960s.[86]

Though these latter two programs were pursued, in general Title IX was ignored. Two years after the provision was passed, it had not "influenced the actions of AID in major ways. . . ." A year later, a member of Congress remarked that "the only things we have gotten from Title IX so far are conferences." And a year after that, the head of AID acknowledged that his agency was having trouble getting off the ground with Title IX.[87] This should not be surprising, given that when taken seriously the goal of increasing popular participation has been contrary to U.S. interests.

The Peace Corps

The Peace Corps was established in 1961 under the administration of John Kennedy. It was a program whereby young American volunteers could be sent to lend technical assistance to the less-developed nations.

Kennedy explained to the Peace Corps headquarters staff that the United States is viewed in many key parts of the world as a militaristic power. This, said Kennedy, has adverse effects, particularly on foreign intellectuals, students, and others who have disproportionate influence in their countries. "The Peace Corps, it seems to me, gives us an opportunity to emphasize a very different part of our American character. . . ."

There were other ways to dispel the image of being militaristic, such as by cutting back military programs and operations. Kennedy did not do this; instead he presided over what White House adviser Theodore Sorensen termed the "buildup of the most powerful military force in human history—the largest and swiftest buildup in this country's peacetime history." By means of the Peace Corps, Kennedy and his successors in the White House have attempted to give the United States a peaceful image while pursuing warlike policies. From 1962 to 1972, about 1 percent of U.S. foreign economic and military aid was spent on the Peace Corps—a rather small price to pay for such an effective cosmetic.[88]

The Peace Corps began by recruiting idealistic young people to serve as volunteers. Not all idealists, however, were considered suitable. "These people," testified Peace Corps Director R. Sargent Shriver, "have had more screening before they go abroad then any comparable group the United States has ever sent overseas." With the help of psychologists and psychiatrists, "there has been practically nobody that you would call a beatnik in the Peace Corps abroad." A prospective volunteer who had criticized the House Un-American Activities Committee was dismissed during the training period, and, in general, "there is no place in the Peace Corps for beatniks, kooks, draft dodgers or their ilk." According to the act establishing the Peace Corps, only one subject was specifically required for the training of volunteers: "instruction in the philosophy, strategy, tactics, and menace of communism."[89]

Despite the screening and training, however, by the mid-1960s Peace Corps volunteers were becoming increasingly disillusioned with U.S. foreign policy and their role in it. Many came to view their work as sugarcoating for brutal international policies. A volunteer in the Philippines wrote a letter to the *Manila Times* wondering whether the Peace Corps was a political gimmick to make Lyndon Johnson appear peaceful. In 1967 a volunteer was fired for publicly opposing the Vietnam War, and other volunteers received warnings. In early 1968 the staff of the official Peace Corps publication in the Philippines resigned in protest against what they claimed were U.S. Embassy orders to suppress an interview they did with a nationalist economist.[90]

The Peace Corps soon became less interested in recruiting idealists, and the idealists less interested in joining the Peace Corps. A Peace Corps ad in 1967 read:

> So you'll get to be President of U.S. Copper two years later. What's your hurry? You know everything you want to do will still be here to do in a couple of years. The only thing you don't know is what a couple of years in the Peace Corps will do for you. Maybe it'll help you get to be President of U.S. Copper faster. . . .

And a Peace Corps recruiter complained that he could not recruit blacks from city colleges because they were too radical. "One fellow offered to join the Peace Corps to form a revolutionary committee to drive the whites out of South Africa. Well, we couldn't have that."[91]

In 1970 the Peace Corps director sent a memorandum to seventeen Republican representatives. It was recalled within a few hours and reissued with two deletions. The deleted sections stated that the Peace Corps was going to try to alter the fact that most volunteers had strongly liberal views and that it was "well on the way toward eliminating public protests and changing the type of Volunteers who go overseas." Both versions of the document stated that the Peace Corps was attempting to better utilize "background investigations to weed out undesirable applicants."[92]

One not unintended consequence of the Peace Corps was that former volunteers provided a pool upon which the U.S. government could draw in staffing its various overseas agencies. "I can think of no more significant recruiting ground than the Peace Corps," Kennedy told a group of trainees, "for our future Foreign Service Officers, for those who represent our information services and aid agencies abroad." And Kennedy's hope was realized when AID found it was able to fill its personnel requirements for rural development projects in Vietnam in large measure from former Peace Corps volunteers.[93]

The projects the Peace Corps undertook overseas varied from country to country: public health, teaching, technical training, etc. The Philippines, from the very inception, had one of the largest

Peace Corps contingents in the world. The initial project in that country—approved by the U.S. State Department and by the Philippine government—was to provide teachers' aides to assist in the teaching of English. The rationale for the project has been stated as follows:

> The Peace Corps project is of considerable importance to the Philippines because in the Islands English is the only language of instruction in science, technology, commerce, and culture. In recent years, English has been corrupted by the influence of a variety of local dialects to the point where it is becoming incomprehensible to the outsider. It is hoped that the Peace Corps project will be the first step toward reversing this trend.[94]

Repairing the "corrupted" English of Filipinos was not a wholly selfless undertaking. United States businesspeople had an obvious interest in having Filipinos speak English, as did U.S. officials, given that in 1957 there was not a single American Foreign Service Officer who had even some proficiency in Tagalog or Visayan—the major Philippine dialects.[95] But even for those Peace Corps volunteers genuinely motivated by idealism and altruism—and there were many—their role has been to provide a public relations cover for U.S. foreign policy.

Safeguarding U.S. Investment

The Investment Guarantee Program provided U.S. government insurance to American corporations investing overseas when commercial insurers were unwilling to give coverage. Two purposes are served by the investment guarantees. First, a subsidy is provided to U.S. business; this can be assumed to be true since if it were expected that such insurance would be profitable then private insurance firms would have offered the same coverage. The second purpose of the investment guarantees is to make capital available for the development needs of foreign nations. Note that if the second objective were the only one, there would be other ways of accomplishing it. For example, American corporations could be taxed to raise funds for grants to needy countries; such grants could be used where they would be most useful rather than where profits could be maximized, and there would be no "repatriated earnings" to detract from the productive value of the capital.

At first, U.S. business interests were wary of investment guarantees, for with government programs comes the specter of government interference. But by the 1960s business had moved squarely behind the guarantee programs.[96]

A variety of risks have been covered by investment guarantees: (1) losses due to civil strife related to war, revolution, or insurrection—which are generally exempted from the coverage of commercial insurers; (2) losses due to restrictions placed on the convertibility of foreign currencies; and (3) losses due to expropriation by a foreign government. Notice that all these guarantees give the U.S. government—never sympathetic to insurrection—a direct financial stake in preventing such things from happening.

One additional type of risk that U.S. investment guarantees cover (up to 75 percent) is the "extended" or business risk. As an AID official testified, "if the business failed through, for example, failure of the market for its products to develop, we would pay" up to 75 percent of the loss to the investment. This covers essentially all losses except those due to "fraud or misconduct for which the investor is responsible or from normally insurable risks such as fire and theft."[97]

The whole notion of investment guarantees confused one senator: "The basis of capitalism, as I understand it, is risk capital. If you get a guarantee against risks, it is hard for me to understand that you could call it 'private' enterprise. . . . I am not critical, but want to be informed." An AID official replied that this was indeed a dilemma and that "we will always be, as it were, whiplashed between fiasco and windfall."[98]

United States corporations evidently felt that the investment guarantee programs leaned toward the windfall. In 1968 the government covered about one-third of total direct American overseas investment. And by and large it was not the small company that took advantage of the guarantees. Four-fifths of the insurance issued went to either the 500 largest corporations or the 50 largest banks in the United States.[99]

The United States provided guarantees only for investments made in countries which signed agreements with Washington. In 1952 the Philippines concluded convertibility and expropriation agreements with the United States, making it the first non-European nation to sign the former and the fourth nation worldwide to adhere to the latter. By the end of fiscal 1969, the U.S. government had issued $432 million worth of coverage against expropriation, restrictions on convertibility, and war, revolution, and insurrection in the Philippines to firms including Caltex, Castle & Cooke, General Electric, General Telephone and Electronics, B. F. Goodrich, Kimberly Clark, Phelps Dodge, Westinghouse, and subsidiaries of Brown

Brothers Harriman, Chemical Bank of New York, Chase Manhattan Bank, and Morgan Guaranty Trust.[100]

Investment guarantees have been only one way in which the interests of U.S. corporations have been safeguarded. Aid has also often been used as direct leverage to prevent expropriations or unwanted fiscal or economic policies on the part of a foreign government. In 1959 and 1963 Congress passed the "Hickenlooper Amendment," instructing the president to suspend aid to any country nationalizing U.S. investments without adequate compensation or repudiating contracts with U.S. citizens. In 1972 Richard Nixon announced that it was the policy of his administration to extend no new economic assistance to countries expropriating U.S. property without compensation.[101] Aid leverage has been used not just for expropriations. In one particularly striking instance, Lyndon Johnson cut off Food for Peace funds for India in 1965 until it, *inter alia*, provided easier terms for foreign private investment in fertilizer plants.[102]

Another instrument of aid leverage has been the sugar quota. Countries that held quota rights into the U.S. sugar market received a windfall in the usually substantial difference between the U.S.-protected price and the world price. For example, Philippine sugar producers in the period 1951 to 1969 received an estimated $1 billion premium by virtue of their sugar quota. Congress' method for allocating these quotas was explained by Senator Thruston Morton of the Finance Committee: "We went through the matter country by country. If we liked the country we voted yea; if we did not like the country we voted nay." In the early 1960s a provision was added to the legislation allocating sugar quotas to give the U.S. president the power to suspend or cut the quotas of nations expropriating U.S. property without compensation. But far lesser actions of foreign nations have also provoked threats of a quota cut. In 1969 the Philippines decided to purchase some new sugar mills in Japan. Despite the fact that U.S. construction companies had the contracts to erect the mills, the U.S. AID head in Manila was "boiling mad," and one member of Congress reminded his colleagues that the United States gives the Philippines a $67.5 million benefit annually by the sugar quota, and he expressed the hope that Philippine ingratitude would be remembered when future quotas were to be allocated.[103]

Labor Unions

The United States has provided financial assistance, training, and advisers for Philippine labor unions. This may seem a curious undertaking for a government committed to defending the interests of its corporations overseas. In fact, however, imperial powers have had a long history of aiding trade unions in the Philippines—for their own imperial purposes.[104]

In the post–World War II period, U.S. programs dealing with Philippine labor were of two kinds. One involved assisting in the drafting of labor legislation on a national level, the other consisted of educational programs aimed at union leaders and members.

Until 1953, labor relations in the Philippines were governed by compulsory arbitration rather than collective bargaining. Under this system, the secretary of labor had the arbitrary authority to decide which unions were legitimate. Quirino's labor secretary, Jose Figueras, who had been the vice-military governor of Manila during the Japanese occupation, used this power with a vengeance. In fiscal 1952 he suspended 391 unions on the grounds—generally false—that they were subversive. He set up a national company union, NACTU, subordinate to himself, whose conventions included both employers and labor leaders, with the latter often being labor contractors.[105]

There was nearly universal opposition to this state of affairs. American firms were wary of compulsory arbitration because they had to face Filipino unions in courts presided over by Filipino judges. American executives felt these judges to be too generous to their compatriots, a situation likely to get worse as nationalism increased. American employers were much more willing to engage in collective bargaining, confident that they had more power at their disposal than the unions. Most Filipino employers faced weak unions and were not opposed to bargaining. On the labor union side, the strong unions thought they could do better with bargaining, and all unions (especially the suspended ones) were anxious to eliminate the discretionary power of the secretary of labor.[106]

Accordingly, U.S. advisers wrote a draft of a new labor law which in 1953 became Republic Act No. 875, the so-called Magna Carta of Labor. The act established a framework for collective bargaining. Unions still had to be registered by the secretary of labor, but the secretary's opinion could be appealed. Unions with Communist officials were prohibited, although the law did not prevent company-dominated unions from becoming registered. Thus, there were collective bargaining contracts with sections like the following:

> All employees shall devote themselves diligently and faithfully to their assigned tasks. Management abhors laziness.

> All employees shall perform their duties in a competent manner.
> Management resents malfeasance.
> All employees must carry out the instructions of supervisors.
> Management detests disobedience.[107]

Employers proved to be right in their feeling that they would fare well under collective bargaining. Wages rose more slowly in Manila in the two and a half years after the 1953 act than in the two and a half years before. In 1962 the Philippine ambassador to the United States told an American audience that members of the Filipino labor force

> have, the 8-hour labor law notwithstanding, stood by their lathes and sat at their desks, to render overtime work and thus earn a few more pesos to add to their take-home pay, many a time at the risk of their lives and physical well-being. True, there are still vestiges of indolence among a few of our people, the vice against which our national hero, Dr. Jose Rizal wrote; but, by and large, we have an adequate, able, and cooperative labor force . . . .

By 1972, real wage rates of skilled laborers in industrial establishments in Manila and suburbs were 27 percent lower than in 1953; unskilled workers suffered a decline of 11 percent over the same period. The U.S. Department of Commerce was able to assure American investors that, despite high inflation, "labor costs in the Philippines continue to be moderate to low."[108] Clearly the "Magna Carta of Labor" did not revolutionize the position of labor in Philippine society.

The second component of the American labor program in the Philippines was "educating" trade union leaders and members. In 1954 a Labor Education Center was established with U.S. financial assistance and U.S. advisers. In 1958 the Philippine government absorbed the budget of the center, and the United States gave another grant, so that union personnel from other Asian countries might also receive training at the center, then renamed the Asian Labor Education Center. Between fiscal 1958 and 1970 the U.S. government gave about $930,000 to the center.[109]

Of the many nobly stated objectives of the center, the only ones taken seriously were the goals of industrial harmony and greater productivity. Trainees were shown films with titles like "Carelessness Costs You," "Motion Study Principles," "Productivity[:] Key to Plenty," and "Supervision [of] Women Workers." Filmstrips included such items as "Industrial Harmony Through LMC" (presumably, "Labor-Management Cooperation"). The center led the observance of Labor-Management Cooperation Day and contemplated a program for educating women union leaders because of the "urgent necessity of training Amazon labor leaders for soberizing purposes in case of disputes."[110]

Students had to be selected for the various training programs; among other things, they had to have "a background free of Communism, totalitarianism, and subversion or willing collaboration with such parties or movements" and a "demonstrated awareness of the mutual interests of labor and management."[111]

It is no wonder, then, that the Labor Education Center enjoyed wide support from employers. Some managers expressed in writing the benefits they derived from having the leaders of "their" unions receive training. The personnel manager of the Franklin Baker Company of the Philippines felt that the president of his employees' union "profited immensely from the course given him":

> Relation between the union and management has been more harmonious.
> Because of frequent seminars and bull sessions that he conducts among members where rules and regulations of the Company are taken up, there are less instances of violations of such rules and regulations. . . .
> By imparting to union officials what he learned, these same officials have become more responsible leaders, resulting in a more stable and respected union as a whole.

Another manager had "nothing but praise" for the trainee whose "coolness and tact in his approaches to the management" had resulted in "labor peace and harmonious labor management relations." He would, the manager noted, "do everything within his power to preserve the already existing labor peace." Another manager reported that his trainee "has shown his loyalty to the policies of management. He is dependable, courteous, and progressive. . . . As a labor leader, he can be classed with that group of labor leaders who look upon every problem not as a cause for misunderstanding between management and labor but a means in keeping their harmonious relations." And still another manager remarked that the attitude of his firm's trainee "towards the company has changed favorably and he is endeavoring to have the workers perform their duties more efficiently and with understanding which will lead to greater harmony amongst the workers and a healthier attitude towards management."[112]

An internal evaluation of the center reached a similar conclusion: "Labor-management relations have become more reasonable.

As one worker said, 'Management is not as unreasonable as it originally appeared to me; it has its own valid reasons for doing what it does.' "[113] For comparison, it should be noted that back in 1953 the U.S. Department of Commerce had considered it an obstacle to American investment that Philippine labor leaders believed "wage scales should be based on the employers' ability to pay."[114]

It is perhaps suggestive that in 1967, due to job insecurity and low pay, eight of the eleven foreign-aid funded employees of the center left for high-paying jobs at prestigious universities and at "well-established business firms."[115]

The training programs were undertaken on a large scale. Between fiscal 1956 and 1962, over 11,000 union leaders and members had received some form of training. This, said AID, "effectively influenced the direction and policies of the Philippine labor movement by emphasizing self-reliance, voluntarism, and a pragmatic approach to industrial relations." Much of the credit for the industrial stability in the Philippines, asserted a memorandum by the International Cooperation Administration (the AID forerunner), "is attributed to the influence of the Labor Education Center." In addition, by 1970 over 600 labor leaders from seventeen other Asian nations also had received training at the center.[116]

There have been other U.S. government programs affecting Philippine labor. AID has provided funds to the Associated Labor Union, an organization representing the employees of Atlas Consolidated Mining and Development Corporation. The union is a corrupt one, and its president frequently speaks out in favor of free enterprise. AID has provided money and advisers to the Asian Productivity Organization (APO) and to its Manila unit. APO works to increase industrial productivity, as well as to assist private investment and promote business cooperation. AID had contributed to the funding of the Asian Institute of Management (AIM), a Manila-based facility backed also by the Ford Foundation, Filipino educational institutions, and "unusually extensive financial support from the Philippine private business sector." With a Harvard Business School team, it trains students to take key positions in the corporate world. Thirty percent of AIM graduates work for U.S. firms, which helps American companies to reduce nationalist resentments by "Asianizing" their management personnel. One graduate, who took a position with the First National City Bank of New York in Manila, explained what he learned: "I now appreciate more fully the problems of my former bosses, why businessmen apparently behave ruthlessly, and how many more aspects of the 'morality' of business decisions have to be evaluated before they are judged."[117]

Peasant unions were often a potent left-wing and anti-American force in the Philippines. To counteract the influence of these unions, the CIA-linked Asia Foundation provided a subsidy of 2,000 pesos a month to the Federation of Free Farmers (FFF). The federation was an undemocratically structured organization led by religious leaders, lawyers, and members of landed families.[118] It included a number of genuine militants within its ranks, but on the whole it was committed more to anticommunism than to effecting social change.

A final U.S. program aimed at Philippine labor was the Asian-American Free Labor Institute (AAFLI). AAFLI was set up in 1968 by the AFL-CIO and AID. Its purpose was to permit American unions to give direct assistance to their Asian counterparts. Early officers of AAFLI included George Meany, Morris Paladino, and James A. Suffridge, the latter two having had links to the CIA or its labor programs. But regardless of CIA connections, AID knows that through AAFLI it is promoting contacts between Asian trade unions and one of the more conservative elements in American society, the AFL-CIO bureaucracy. As a study for the Senate Foreign Relations Committee explained, "The dominant philosophy of the American labor movement has been 'business unionism.' . . . Although the U.S. labor movement in recent years has frequently deviated from strict adherence to these principles, it is this philosophy which U.S. labor leadership has attempted to implant abroad."[119]

Back in 1961, Suffridge had recommended that a union-to-union program be introduced in the Philippines in order, among other things, to help labor leaders there deal with the "real threat of leftist infiltration in some unions." AAFLI programs in the Philippines have included assistance to the Federation of Free Farmers and to the Trade Union Congress of the Philippines (TUC), a recently merged trade union federation. At the TUC's merger convention in February 1970, a list of far-reaching demands on the government was issued, but perhaps more indicative of its position was the fact that Philippine President Marcos swore in the organization's officers.[120]

Multilateral Lending

Increasingly, U.S. development funds have been directed through multilateral lending organizations. Between 1963 and 1973, U.S. contributions to these organizations increased about 350 percent, while Washington's bilateral economic assistance over the same period declined about 16 percent. In March 1970 a high-level U.S.

Task Force on International Development recommended that "the international lending institutions become the major channel for development assistance." A few months later, President Richard Nixon delivered a foreign aid message to Congress incorporating this proposal.[121]

Aid through multilateral organizations has held a number of appeals to U.S. policymakers. First, aid programs would not be subject to the yearly scrutiny of Congress and public opinion. Second, aid could be used as leverage to force compliance by Third World nations without inviting the charges of intervention that often accompany bilateral assistance. Multilateral organizations, said the president of the prestigious Overseas Development Council, "have a greater potential for intervening effectively in the domestic affairs of a developing country."[122]

A third advantage of multilateral aid has been that international lending organizations are approaching the status of cartel institutions, that is, it is becoming increasingly difficult for Third World nations to seek out the "highest bidder" for development aid; they must instead accept the terms and conditions of the capital cartel. Multilateral aid also has had the advantage, from the U.S. point of view, of getting other industrialized nations to contribute toward Third World development needs. To Washington, Japan and Western Europe have been long overdue in picking up their share of foreign assistance. A final appeal of the multilateral institutions has been that they raise some of their funds in private capital markets. This "provides a means by which private capital can re-enter the foreign investment field with safety," as banker John J. McCloy put it in 1947. While some developing nations might nationalize a privately owned foreign investment, few would be willing to default on a loan from the World Bank; in fact, no nation has ever done so.[123]

It might seem that in return for these advantages multilateral aid suffers from the serious disadvantage (again from the point of view of Washington) of preventing the U.S. executive branch from having control of its aid money, since the funds are to be administered by an international body. This is not the case, however. The aid that the United States wishes to use for purposes it does not share with the other capital exporting nations it distributes on a bilateral basis. The money funneled through the international banks is utilized to achieve objectives that are common to the advanced capitalist nations: stable and conservative economic development, protection of foreign investments, and conservative fiscal policies. The developing nations are also members of the international banks, but voting power is roughly proportional to capital contributions.

Thus, in the World Bank, the United States has 25 percent of the votes, while all the developing countries together have only 35 percent. In the Asian Development Bank (ADB), as of December 31, 1972, developed nations held about 58 percent of the voting power. A U.S. official has testified that "the majority of the votes are from the capital exporting countries, which is very important. In other words, the borrowers can't run the Bank." When all paid up, the United States and Japan plus any other country can veto any major decision of the Asian Development Bank.[124]

But this considerably understates U.S. influence. By unwritten agreement, the president of the World Bank is always an American. The need of all the multilateral banks to raise funds in private capital markets means that the industrialized countries have added leverage. The World Bank has a policy of not lending to countries that default on private debts or expropriate private property without compensation. A U.S. official has explained:

> The Bank felt that it had a direct stake in the principle of repayment on international bonds in view of its heavy reliance on private capital markets as a source of its own funds. The Bank's policy has evolved to include—for similar underlying reasons—situations where expropriation of direct investments takes place.[125]

Decisions at the Asian Development Bank, as at the other international financial institutions, are not made by the casting of votes, member by member, for or against a proposed loan. As U.S. officials have acknowledged,

> Instead, the proposal is discussed in the Board meeting . . . , the directors make comments and may make minor changes in the proposal, and approval is reached by consensus. Occasionally consideration of a particular proposal by the Board may be delayed by the President at the request of one or more directors.
>   To prevent nation-to-nation confrontations in the Board meeting which might damage U.S. foreign relations and reduce the effectiveness of ADB . . . U.S. policy is to try to avoid opposing formally, or raising serious criticism of, a proposed loan in the Board meeting . . . . If the United States found some aspect of a loan proposal objectionable, the [U.S.] Director and his staff would discuss it with other directors and the Bank staff and would attempt to convince them of the desirability of modifying the proposal before it goes before the Board for approval. If there is not enough time to accomplish this before it is scheduled to go before the Board or if there has not been enough time to study a proposal, the Director may request that consideration of the proposal be delayed.[126]

140

One can be sure that in this kind of behind-the-scenes maneuvering U.S. influence is far more than its formal voting share.

Officials of the various multilateral banks insist that theirs are apolitical institutions, making loans strictly on the basis of technical criteria.[127] These claims are simply false. The World Bank, as already noted, refuses to make funds available to countries that nationalize foreign-owned assets without compensation. The Articles of Agreement of the World Bank state one of the purposes of the bank as being to "promote foreign private investment." Loans must satisfy "a developmental need rather than some notion of equity or other objectives, however laudable." Whatever else one may think of these criteria, they are not apolitical. At the Asian Development Bank's inaugural meeting, Cambodia, then under Sihanouk, urged long-term credits at low interest, while the United States countered with a call for the prudent management of funds. The American view, no less political than the Cambodian, prevailed.[128]

The United States is not oblivious to the political nature of international bank decisions. Of all Asian Development Bank members, only the United States and Japan require their directors to obtain instructions from their national governments on each loan proposal. In January 1972 Nixon announced that should any country nationalize U.S. property without adequate compensation the United States would vote against its loan requests before international lending institutions. And in March 1972 a congressional provision, the "Gonzalez Amendment," was passed to this effect.[129]

The specific policies of the various banks have been just as political as their general guidelines. The World Bank stopped making loans to Colombia during the period 1956 to 1958 under Rojas Pinilla, to Brazil under João Goulart until the military government took over, and to Bolivia for a period after the 1952 revolution. The Asian Development Bank made loans to Cambodia only after Lon Nol's coup. And loans from the World Bank or its cousin the International Monetary Fund (IMF) have often carried stringent conditions. Argentina had to fire 70,000 railroad employees, Bolivia had to eliminate its subsidy to government commissaries selling consumer goods to miners, and many nations have had cut back government spending, devalue currency, eliminate controls, or encourage foreign investment.[130]

Multilateral aid to the Philippines did not begin in earnest until 1962. In the twelve previous years, the total of all such assistance to the Philippines, including that from the United Nations, was $25.1 million. In the decade 1962–1972 the figure was about seventeen times as much.[131] To understand the activities of the international banks regarding the Philippines, it is necessary to go back to the foreign exchange crisis of 1949. At that time, the Philippine government with U.S. concurrence instituted import and exchange controls. The controls enabled the industrial sector of the Philippine economy to grow at its fastest rate in recent history, but they also spread corruption on a wide scale.

At some point during the 1950s, Washington concluded that American foreign investors were harmed more by exchange controls than by devaluations. It was of more benefit, it was decided, for investors to be able to take their profits out of a country at will than to assure a constant value to the capital invested there. In 1958, suffering from a foreign exchange crisis, Manila applied for a stabilization loan from the IMF as part of a plan involving the charging of a fee for the sale of foreign exchange. The U.S. State Department considered this to be a violation of the Laurel-Langley Agreement and so advised the IMF. The IMF then refused the Philippine loan request and called for devaluation instead. The Philippines, however, was able to obtain loans from some New York banks and went through with its plan.

There were in Philippine society powerful forces that concurred with the American preference for devaluation and decontrol. These were the export interests (principally sugar), and in 1959, building on the public revulsion at the corruption of controls, they were able to get a bill through the Philippine Congress providing for the gradual elimination of controls over a four-year period.

In November 1961 Diosdado Macapagal was elected to the presidency on a platform promising the elimination of corruption and controls. Upon taking office he secured $300 million worth of loans from the IMF, the U.S. government, and private American banks. He promptly instituted an immediate and total decontrol and a de facto devaluation. According to Macapagal, Secretary of State Dean Rusk had approved the government part of his loan request in less than five minutes and Kennedy had assured him that if this were not enough he could "count on the full support of the American Government . . . to make the decontrol measure successful."[132]

United States officials were soon speaking of "heartening progress" and "remarkable success," but the impact of the decontrol and devaluation was disastrous for all save the traditional Philippine exporters and foreign investors. Consumers bore the main burden, having to pay sharply higher prices for food.[133] Filipino manufacturers were unable to meet their foreign debts, which had been effectively doubled by the devaluation. At the end of 1964, Filoil, a Philippine company with a minority share owned by Gulf Oil, was forced to sell out entirely to Gulf. At the beginning of 1966, close to 1,500 firms were near a state of collapse.[134] Corruption in the granting of currency and import licenses ended, but it resurfaced in another form: smuggling to avoid tariffs.[135]

Manila's external debt rose from $174 million in 1960 to $490 million in 1965. By 1967 the Philippine government had to impose mild import and exchange restrictions. Then, in 1969, President Marcos precipitated a major foreign exchange crisis by his massive spending effort in buying his own reelection. The IMF demanded devaluation as a condition for credits, and a consortium of U.S. banks made the same demand as the price for rescheduling the debts they were owed. Marcos de facto devalued the peso, and most of the controls imposed since 1967 were repealed. According to a Philippine research organization, 81 percent of the population suffered hardship as a result. Real wage rates in industrial establishments in Manila and suburbs *declined* 19 percent for skilled workers and 13 percent for the unskilled between 1969 and 1972. There was particular irony here in that in the election campaign that caused the crisis, Marcos had promised that there would be no devaluation, because to do so would hurt low-income groups the most. At the end of it all, in June 1971, the Philippines was more dependent upon external sources of capital than ever: the external debt stood at over $2 billion—about two and a half times the 1969 figure.[136]

From the U.S. point of view, it was certainly preferable in terms of world opinion to protect American capital from controls and the like by IMF stipulations than by sending in the marines.

The Accomplishments of Aid

A staff report for the Senate Foreign Relations Committee in 1976 concluded that after thirty years and $1.7 billion of U.S. economic assistance, concrete development advances in the Philippines were "hard to identify."[137] Given the self-imposed constraints on Washington's aid programs, this result should not have been unexpected. AID officials speak of what they call the "development equation": resources divided by population equals well-being.[138] It follows from this equation that increasing resources such as through the Green Revolution, while holding population in check through the population-control programs that AID inaugurated in the Philippines in 1967, increases well-being. The problem with this approach is that the equation is a very incomplete model of reality; in fact, it ignores precisely those factors which only genuine social change can alter.

From the equation, a given level of resources and a given population will always yield a constant well-being. But this neglects the matter of distribution. In a society in which a significant fraction of resources is spent on luxuries for a rich minority, well-being will be lower than in a more egalitarian society. Similarly, if a country's resources are repatriated by foreign investors or deposited in Swiss banks or squandered on government boondoggles, well-being will be lower than otherwise. United States aid programs have invariably sought the easy and palatable route of trying to juggle the denominator or numerator of the "development equation" rather than attempting to redistribute wealth or restrict the repatriation of profits. That such a strategy might be unsuccessful for coping with the pressing development needs of the Third World should not be surprising.

But if Washington's foreign assistance programs in the Philippines failed to meet their development goals, they were by no means wholly unsuccessful. They helped to keep in power in Manila governments friendly to the United States, to U.S. capital, and to U.S. bases. They helped to undercut Philippine rural unrest and tame urban labor unions. They contributed to the protection of American investors and to the promotion of American agricultural exports. In short, they served as the instruments by which Washington was able to further its economic and strategic interests in the Philippines.

CHAPTER SIX

The Human Costs of Neocolonialism

Neocolonialism has not been simply an abstract concept for the Philippines. The living standards and the general welfare of the Philippine people are very real, and they are to a considerable extent the consequence of the neocolonial relationship. Washington has opposed and helped to defeat all efforts by Filipinos to fundamentally alter their society. And Washington—through its programs of military and economic aid, and through its military advisers and covert interventions—has supported the Philippine elite in maintaining their dominant position in that society.

To argue that the Philippine elite has been more responsible than the United States for conditions in the Philippines is to miss the point, for the Philippine elite has owed its very existence to the United States. Likewise, the attribution of blame to the United States is no cause for self-congratulation on the part of the Philippine elite, for it is not that they are blameless but rather that they are so tied to U.S interests that they cannot be viewed as a wholly autonomous force.

In turning now to an examination of what the lives of Filipinos were like in the first quarter century of formal independence—from 1946 to the declaration of martial law in 1972—we will be investigating the human costs of neocolonialism. In the next chapter, we will consider the situation in the martial law period.

There was considerable economic growth in the Philippines in the twenty-five years after World War II, but, as a study for the International Labour Office (ILO) commented, "satisfactory growth rates have been accompanied by more and more unacceptable outcomes in terms of employment and income distribution."[1] And a Filipino economist noted that the increases in real per capita gross national product of 2 to 3 percent per year "have not had a visible impact on the poorer half of the population."[2] Similar remarks were made by knowledgeable observers throughout the 1950s and 1960s. "The inequality in incomes, always very great in the Philippines, is now even greater than before the war," stated the chief economist for the U.S. Economic Survey Mission, headed by Daniel Bell, in 1950.[3] In the mid-1960s, the head of the U.S. Agency for International Development in Manila testified that "in the past 10 years, the rich have become richer and the poor have become poorer," and a Philippine Senate committee reported that "except for public health services, the level of living of the vast majority of our people has not substantially improved since 1955."[4]

In examining the statistical material that will be presented below, it is important to keep in mind that, though Philippine statistics are better than those of many Third World nations, they are still quite unreliable. Philippine data on income distribution and living standards contain many sources of possible bias; some of these will be indicated in the text. Moreover, the published presentations of the data contain numerous internal inconsistencies.[5]

Table 1, based on household surveys by the Philippine Bureau of the Census and Statistics, provides data on income distribution. As can be seen, between 1956–1957 and 1965 the share of income going to the lowest fifth and the lowest three-fifths of families declined, while the share going to upper-income groups increased. The top 5 percent of families throughout this decade reported more income than the bottom 60 percent.

These figures are likely to understate severely the gap between rich and poor, because the rich can more readily hide their income (profits being more easily disguised than wages). The Bureau of the Census and Statistics has acknowledged the possibility of respondents being reluctant to reveal their full incomes, "especially among families in the higher income brackets."[6] For example, the private moneylender is still believed to be the largest source of rural credit in the Philippines,[7] but it is doubtful that the interest—at usurious rates—is declared for tax purposes.

Some sense of the income that escapes these surveys can be had by looking at the problem of tax evasion. In 1954, only 18 percent of physicians, 9 percent of lawyers, 4 percent of dentists, and 36 percent of accountants filed income tax returns. The collector of internal revenue who published this information had the further audacity to

TABLE 1   *Before-Tax Family Income Distribution, Philippines, 1956–1957, 1961, 1965, 1970–1971*

	1956–57[a]	1961[b]	1965[b]	1970–71[c]
Percent of total family income going to:				
Lowest 20% of families by income	4.5	4.2	3.5	3.7
Lowest 60%	25.0	24.2	24.3	25.1
Top 20%	55.1	56.4	55.4	53.9
Top 10%	39.4	41.0	40.1	37.1
Top 5%	27.7	29.0	28.7	24.8
Ratio of income of top 5% to bottom 60%	1.11	1.20	1.18	0.99
Ratio of income of top 20% to bottom 20%	12.3	13.4	15.8	14.7
Gini ratio[d]	0.48	0.50	0.50	0.48

[a]Twelve months ending 28 February 1957.
[b]Calendar year.
[c]Twelve months ending 30 April 1971.
[d]Gini ratio ranges from 0.0 (absolute equality) to 1.0 (absolute inequality).
Note: Unless otherwise noted, all tables in this chapter based on the household surveys use the same time periods indicated above.
Source: All figures calculated from National Economic and Development Authority (NEDA), *Statistical Yearbook of the Philippines, 1975* (Manila, 1975), pp. 410–11, Table 13.2, "Share of Total Family Income."

try to collect delinquent taxes from a member of the House of Representatives. The next year, Congress abolished the collector's job by refusing to appropriate funds for his office. For the next few years data on filed returns by occupation were unavailable[8]—illustrating that those with wealth are able, through the power they wield, to hide their wealth. In 1962 a Joint Legislative-Executive Tax Commission reported that professionals and businesspeople were "among the poorest in tax compliance." In 1965 the commission noted that a law allowing bank deposits to go undetected permitted "ill-gotten wealth" to be "hidden well beyond the reach of effective criminal prosecution." And in 1970 the head of the tax commission observed that "evasion usually occurs among the bigger taxpayers."[9]

With tax evasion rife, the underreporting of income to government pollsters should not be surprising. In fact, the total personal income calculated from the household surveys is about one-third less than the national income accounts figures for personal income, as Table 2 demonstrates.

The data for 1970–1971 in Table 1 indicate an improvement in

TABLE 2 *Total Personal Income, Philippines, 1956–1957, 1961, 1965, 1970–1971*

	1956–57	1961	1965	1970–71
Personal income, national income accounts[a] (millions of pesos)	8,258[b]	12,110	18,457	35,100[c]
Personal income, survey of households (millions of pesos)	5,824	7,982	13,024	23,714
Ratio	0.705	0.659	0.706	0.676

[a]National income accounts data have been revised back to 1960, so 1956–1957 figure is not strictly comparable.
[b]Five-sixths of 1956 figure plus one-sixth of 1957 figure.
[c]Two-thirds of 1970 figure plus one-third of 1971 figure.
Sources: National income accounts figure for 1956–1957 from *Statistical Reporter*, 13, no. 2 (April–June 1969), p. 55; all other figures from NEDA, *Statistical Yearbook of the Philippines, 1975*, pp. 96–97, 410–11.

income distribution over 1965, though the bottom 20 percent are still shown to have a smaller share than in 1956–1957. However, the 1970–1971 figures are even more suspect than the rest. In a breakdown, one finds that the top 10 percent of urban families went from 41.7 percent of all urban income in 1965 to 33.4 percent in 1971, a drop of 20 percent. As the study for the ILO has noted, this is a wholly improbable result, attributable in all likelihood to gross underreporting by the urban rich.[10]

Two Philippine statisticians suggest that the apparent narrowing of the urban gap in 1971 might be due to the resettling of low-income squatter families from Manila to adjacent provinces in the late 1960s. But there are problems with this explanation. First, if there had been a substantial transfer of low-income people, one would expect the average family income of Metropolitan Manila to have risen more sharply than that of the adjacent provinces.[11] In fact, however, between 1965 and 1970–1971 Manila's reported average income increased (in current pesos) only 18 percent, while the income of Central Luzon grew 59 percent and Southern Luzon 43 percent.[12] Second, it would require the elimination of approximately the full bottom 20 percent of the urban population to achieve the reported decline in the urban gini ratio,[13] and no one suggests that squatter removal occurred on this scale. Third, many relocated squatters soon return to the urban center from which they have been removed, drawn by the same economic factors that led them to the city in the first place. Full data are obviously lacking, but in one resettlement community established in 1963 a study in 1968 found that 55 percent of the people had moved out; by 1969, 60 percent

TABLE 3   *Rural Before-Tax Family Income Distribution, Philippines,*
1956–1957, 1961, 1965, 1970–1971

	1956–57	1961	1965	1970–71
Percent of rural family income going to:				
Lowest 20% of families by income	7.0	5.9	5.0	4.4
Lowest 60%	32.8	31.2	29.8	27.2
Top 20%	46.1	46.9	47.2	51.0
Top 10%	300.1	31.1	30.0	34.4

Note: Definition of "rural" and "urban" changed somewhat in 1965 and 1970–1971: "rural" included 66% of all households in 1961, 70% in 1965, and 69% 1970–1971. See Republic of the Philippines, Bureau of the Census and Statistics, *BCS Survey of Households Bulletin: Family Income and Expenditures, 1971*, Series no. 34 (Manila, 1971), p. xiii.
Source: International Labour Office (ILO), *Sharing in Development: A Programme of Employment, Equity and Growth for the Philippines* (Geneva, 1974), p. 10.

were gone, and in 1971 it was reported that close to 75 percent of the original inhabitants had returned to Metropolitan Manila.[14]

It is true, however, that while the squatter population of Manila probably did not decline, squatters in 1971 were likely to be far more reluctant about being interviewed by the government than they were in 1965, for fear that the survey was related to a relocation program.

In general, the household surveys seem to underreport the number of low-income families. In 1965 there were about 98,000 squatters and slum-dwelling families in Metropolitan Manila, of whom at least 17.4 percent had annual incomes of less than 600 pesos. This constituted 3.7 percent of the total number of families in Metropolitan Manila. Nevertheless, according to the household survey for 1965 only 3.2 percent of the families in Metropolitan Manila had annual incomes of less than 1,000 pesos.[15]

It can be conservatively concluded, as the ILO study has done, that from 1965 to 1970–1971 rural inequality increased and urban inequality remained constant.[16] Table 3 documents the growing rural inequality.[17]

The data in Tables 1 and 3 represent *before-tax* income, but taxation probably worsens the income distribution. Table 4 shows the results of two studies of the effect of taxes on income distribution. It is important to note, however, that these studies were based not on what families actually paid but on what they should pay. ("Each tax was . . . assigned to the various households belonging to

TABLE 4   *Anticipated* Impact of Taxation on Income Distribution, Philippines, 1960 and 1971*

	1960		1971	
	Before Tax	After Tax	Before Tax	After Tax
Percent of total family income going to: Lowest 20% of families				
by income	4.2	4.6	4.2	3.2
Lowest 50%	17.3	17.9	17.8	17.1
Lowest 90%	57.8	59.7	63.1	64.8
Top 10%	42.2	40.3	36.9	35.2

*See text.

Sources: For 1960: Angel Q. Yoingco, "The Philippine Tax System: Progressive or Regressive?" *The Tax Monthly* (Manila), 11, no. 6 (December 1970), p. 5. For 1971: National Tax Research Center, "Initial Report on Taxation and Income Redistribution: A Study of Tax Burden by Income Class, 1971," *The Tax Monthly* (Manila), 15, no. 1 (January 1974), p. 3.

different income groups that would likely pay it.")[18] But, as already noted, tax evasion predominates among the rich. In addition, graft and corruption is concentrated in the collection of the direct taxes, which are mildly progressive, thereby making the whole tax burden more regressive.[19] In the late 1950s, for example, "the number of tax returns reporting sufficient income to be subject to the personal income tax [was] equivalent to less than one-third of 1 per cent of the population."[20]

Thus far the discussion has focused on the living standards of the poor as indicated by their share of total income. When one looks at absolute measures of well-being, two things can be clearly seen: the grimness of daily existence for the mass of the Filipino people and the myth of progress under neocolonialism.

Real per family (and per capita) income has increased somewhat in the Philippines from 1956–1957 to 1970–1971. But progress for low-income families has been negligible. As Table 5 shows, the real income of low-income groups grew exceedingly slowly over this period. If the same compound annual growth rates were to continue, the average real income of the bottom three-fifths of families would not reach the 1956–1957 average real income of the country until the year 2003; the bottom two-fifths would have to wait until 2040, and the bottom fifth until the year 2297. The growth rates, however,

TABLE 5   *Real Per Family Twelve-Month Income of Low-Income Groups, Philippines, 1956–1957, 1961, 1965, 1970–1971*

Family Income Group	Real Per Family Income (constant 1965 pesos)				Percent Increase 1956–57 to 1970–71	Percent Compound Annual Growth Rate
	1956–57[a]	1961	1965	1970–71[b]		
Lowest 20%	458.0	477.6	446.8	487.2	6	0.44
Lowest 40%	645.2	686.5	733.6	783.3	21	1.40
Lowest 60%	851.8	913.3	1,032.7	1,105.8	30	1.88

[a]Consumer price index for 1957 used.
[b]Average consumer price index May 1970–April 1971 used.
Note: Percents of families are cumulative, that is, "lowest 40%" includes the "lowest 20%," and "lowest 60%" includes both.
Sources: Calculated from NEDA, *Statistical Yearbook of the Philippines, 1975,* pp. 410–11 (Table 13.2, "Share of Total Family Income"), pp. 412–13 (number of families); *Statistical Reporter,* 15, no. 2 (April–June 1971), p. 63 (1970 monthly consumer price indices only, converted to 1965 = 100); Central Bank, *Statistical Bulletin,* 24 (December 1972), p. 372 (consumer price indices for 1957, 1961, 1965, and January–April 1971).

did not continue; they surely declined, given the 15.9 percent leap in prices that occurred between May 1971 and September 1972.[21]

Real family income in the rural areas of the Philippines increased 45 percent over the years 1956–1957 to 1970–1971. But, as Table 6 shows, the bottom two-fifths of rural families experienced only a 6 percent increase over this same period, and the bottom fifth actually suffered a 9 percent decline. The head of U.S. AID in the Philippines testified in the mid-1960s that the living standards of the average rice farmer in Central Luzon had "not changed appreciably in the last 50 years."[22] What is particularly tragic about this stagnation is how low the living standards of the rural poor were to begin with. In May 1967, 40.7 percent of rural households had no toilet facilities at all; of the rest, 29.3 percent used a closed pit, and another 21.2 percent used an open pit. Half of all rural families got their drinking water from open wells (27.4%), springs (16.1%), creeks, streams, or river irrigation (6.0%), or rainwater (1.2%).[23] A few years earlier a study of eight barrios in Laguna province found that 15 percent of all children born to farm families there had died; in 74 percent of families one or more deaths had occurred. Tuber-

TABLE 6   *Real Per Family Twelve-Month Income of Low-Income Groups,*
Rural Philippines, 1956–1957, 1961, 1965, 1970–1971

Rural Family Income Group	Real Per Family Income (constant 1965 pesos)				Percent Increase 1956–57 to 1970–71	Percent Compound Annual Growth Rate
	1956–57[a]	1961	1965	1970–71[b]		
Lowest 20%	485	446	439	441	−9	−0.68
Lowest 40%	627	669	636	666	+6	+0.432
Lowest 60%	757	786	872	908	+20	+1.31
All rural families	1,385	1,511	1,755	2,003	+45	+2.67

[a]Consumer price index for 1957 used.
[b]Average consumer price index May 1970–April 1971 used.
Note: Percents of families are cumulative (see note to Table 5). Definition of "rural" changed in 1965 and 1970–1971 (see note to Table 3).
Sources: Calculated from ILO, *Sharing in Development,* p. 10 (rural income shares); NEDA, *Statistical Yearbook of the Philippines, 1975,* pp. 414–15 (number of rural families), pp. 416–17 (rural income); *Statistical Reporter,* 15, no. 2 (April–June 1971), p. 64 (1970 monthly consumer price index for regions outside of Manila, converted to 1965 = 100); Central Bank, *Statistical Bulletin,* 24 (December 1972), p. 371 (consumer price index for regions outside of Manila, 1957, 1961, 1965, and January–April 1971).

culosis among women and malnutrition among children were prevalent. Only half the homes had something that could roughly be called a bedroom, and eating, sleeping, cooking, and washing were generally done on the floor.[24]

The total amount of food available in the Philippines over the twenty-year period 1953–1972 provided, on an average basis, only 87 percent of the caloric intake, 88 percent of the protein, 21 percent of the milk and milk products, and 49 percent of the eggs recommended by Philippine health officials as necessary for an adequate diet. From 1966 to 1969, less than one-fourth the recommended levels of vitamin-C rich foods were available for consumption.[25] These figures assume that everyone received the same amount of food, but of course this was not the case. Like most of the goods in Philippine society, nutrition is unequally distributed among the population. Table 7 gives data on per family annual expenditures for certain food categories in 1965 by income class. Although these data do not allow us to draw any precise conclusions—the relationship between the cost of food and its nutritive content is,

TABLE 7 *Per Family Annual Expenditures on Selected Food Categories by Income Class, 1965 (in current pesos)*

Income Class	Percent of Families	Milk and Dairy Products	Meat and Eggs	Fish and Other Seafoods	Roots, Vegetables, and Fruits
Under ₱500	11.6	₱ 15	₱ 53	₱126	₱ 76
₱500–999	17.7	15	81	178	100
₱1,000–1,499	16.7	29	120	232	118
₱1,500–1,999	13.5	36	143	242	134
₱2,000–2,499	9.9	57	171	301	147
₱2,500–2,999	7.6	63	179	301	152
₱3,000–3,999	8.9	83	267	350	173
₱4,000–4,999	4.6	105	293	384	179
₱5,000–5,999	2.8	126	373	466	230
₱6,000–7,999	2.5	166	478	485	239
₱8,000–9,999	1.5	212	606	472	315
₱10,000 and over	2.6	286	1,082	661	466
Average		55	187	268	144

Source: Calculated from "Family Income Distribution and Expenditure Patterns in the Philippines: 1965," *Journal of Philippine Statistics*, 19, no. 2 (April–June 1968), pp. xviii, xxviii–xxix.

after all, not linear—the gap between the rich and poor in terms of the availability of nutrients is clearly substantial. Beginning in the early 1970s, surveys were conducted to ascertain diet by income group. The 1971 survey showed that the highest one-sixth of income earners received some 40 percent more calories and 70 percent more protein than did the lowest third of earners.[26] The World Bank estimated that in 1971 about half of all rural families had incomes below that required to provide adequate nutrition and other essentials of life.[27]

In 1972 the infant mortality rate was officially given as 68 per 1,000 live births, but the World Bank thinks 80 per 1,000 is more accurate, and some put the figure at over 100 per 1,000. Mortality among children ages one to four is among the highest in the world. Five percent of all Filipino children under six years old suffer from third-degree malnutrition (they are three-fifths or less of the normal weight for their age), and 30 percent show symptoms of second-degree malnutrition (they are three-quarters or less of normal weight). Biochemical tests of sample populations in Luzon and the Visayas found inadequate mean levels of urinary thiamine, urinary riboflavin, and serum carotene. Of those examined, 25.5 percent were judged deficient in serum vitamin C, and 27.3 percent low; for serum vitamin A, 22.0 percent were deficient and 22.2 percent low.[28]

Poverty has had an impact as well on the highly touted Philippine educational system. The school dropout rate has been tremendously high, and this has been the case particularly in the rural areas. In 1950, 22.7 percent of children five to fourteen years old were not enrolled in school; in 1960 it was 46.2 percent, and in 1970 35.4 percent. In 1960, of every 100 children who began school, only 34 finished elementary school and only 12 finished high school. Twenty-eight percent of the entire population had never entered school. A study in 1970 found that two-fifths of the students stayed away from school for "economic" reasons. Young teenagers belonging to poor families, noted an ILO study, "are forced by economic necessity to leave school"; most become "unpaid family helpers in agricultural activities and work part time to augment low family income." The young drop out even from the government-sponsored out-of-school training projects: among the seven reasons given for this were (1) "the youths are often too poor to afford transportation fare to the training centre"; (2) "meals are generally not provided"; and (3) "most of the rural youths are forced to drop out to help in family work or when extra hands are needed during the planting or harvesting season."[29]

Farm families are somewhat cushioned against the hardships of rising prices by the fact that a substantial portion of their income is in the form of crops that they grow for their own use. (This is counted as income in the household surveys.) For the landless agricultural laborer, however, the situation is considerably more bleak. Real wage rates for agricultural workers apparently fell 10 percent between 1941 and 1949.[30] Table 8 suggests that the daily wage of sugarcane workers, in constant 1965 pesos, was worse in 1971–1972 than fifteen years earlier. Because sugar harvesting is seasonal work, these laborers are idle for about six months a year on the average.[31] Thus, their average yearly earnings came to less than 500 pesos, in 1965 pesos (which in 1965 was about $128). The human meaning of these figures was captured in an article by *New York Times* correspondent Philip Shabecoff in early 1970. It is worth quoting at some length.

For as long as he could remember, Openien Polaez worked at cutting sugar cane on the haciendas of Negros Island.

There has been little joy in his life. Every day except Sunday he rose at dawn and spent nine hours under the equatorial sun cutting

TABLE 8 *Daily Wages of Philippine Sugarcane Workers, 1956, 1960, 1961–1962, 1971–1972*

Year	Location	Comment	Daily Wage in Current Pesos	Daily Wage in Constant 1965 Pesos[a]
1956	Negros Occidental	Includes cost of meals and deductions	1.94	2.72
1960[b]	Negros Occidental	Does not include meals or housing when provided	2.43	3.21
1961–62[b]	Luzon	Does not include meals or housing when provided	2.67	3.35
1971–72	Philippines	Does not include meals; laborer must provide work animal; average for all jobs[c]	3.79	2.34

[a]Current pesos divided by consumer price index for regions outside Manila. Price index of 1957 used for 1956 (probably very close); 1961 for 1961–1962; and 1971 for 1971–1972.

[b]Average hourly wage multiplied by average hours worked.

[c]Rough weightings based on division of work given in Robert E. Huke, *Shadows on the Land: An Economic Geography of the Philippines* (Manila: Bookmark, 1963), pp. 304–308: 71% to harvesting, 6% to planting, 8% to plowing, 10% to weeding, and 5% to everything else (assumed to be equally divided).

Sources: For 1956 and 1960: Republic of the Philippines, Department of Labor, Labor Statistics Division, "Wages and Working Conditions in Our Sugar Cane Haciendas in Negros Occidental," *Philippine Labor* (Manila), May 1962, pp. 14, 17–18. For 1961–1962: Liwayway M. Calalang, "A Survey of Selected Conditions of Employment in the Sugar Industry in Mainland Luzon," *Philippine Labor* (Manila), June 1962, pp. 18–19. For 1971–1972: *Journal of Philippine Statistics*, 24, no. 1 (January–March 1973), p. 94. Consumer price index from Central Bank, *Statistical Bulletin*, 24 (December 1972), p. 371.

the dense cane with his bolo and loading it on wagons bound for the mill. . . .

His earnings enabled him to buy enough rice to provide his wife and 12 children with one meal a day. Once in a while he could even afford a piece of dried fish. He and his family never had enough to eat, but at least they did not starve.

Now, at 54 years of age, Openien can no longer work because he is ill. His stomach hurts all the time, his eyes are streaked with blood and his close-cropped hair is turning white.

The doctors told him he must have an operation right away. They knew he could not afford it so they gave him a note for his hacendero—the plantation owner—to sign, saying he would be willing to defray the cost.

But, Openien told a foreign visitor, the hacendero, Abelardo Bantug, who owns 500 acres of prime sugar land, refused to sign.

"I told him I would die and my children would starve if I did not have the operation," the ailing man related. "He answered, 'Openien, you should have died long ago anyway.' " . . .

An official in the local governmental labor office—he was exiled from Manila because of his liberal views—asserted: "The hacenderos do not distinguish between their human workers and their carabao. In fact, they take better care of their carabao because cattle are valuable property and there are always plenty of workers." . . .

It is not easy to visit the haciendas and talk with workers. The hacenderos do not like strangers meddling into their affairs and hire armed guards to keep outsiders off their property. . . .

Moreover, workers seen talking with strangers are often thrown off the haciendas, leaving them with no way to feed their families. . . .

Not one of the haciendas visited on a two-day tour paid their workers the legal minimum wage of 4 pesos—about a dollar—a day. Most of the planters were paying 60 cents or less. . . .

[One group of "sacadas"—migratory sugar workers—] said they were paid about 30 cents for each ton they cut and could net almost 60 cents on a good day. The contractor receives a commission of 5 cents for each ton and charges the workers about 30 cents a day for the meals of rice he provides. . . .

These sacadas live in typical quarters. Six families, ranging in size from 5 to 12 people, sleep in a wooden barracks about 15 feet by 40.

There is nothing but the walls and floor. There are no partitions for privacy. There is no toilet—the people simply go in the fields. One water tap several hundred feet away is used by all the workers. There is no school for the children.

On a nearby hacienda, a man, his pregnant wife and three children aged 10, 12 and 15 worked cutting cane in a small field. It was a special contract, with the man and woman getting 60 cents a day and the children 30 cents.

"It is not work for women and children, that is true," said the man, "but we must eat—I cannot earn enough by myself."...

The hacenderos are still discharging workers who join unions as well as threatening the lives of organizers and workers.[32]

Table 9 presents data on the real income of low-income urban families. As already noted, there is probably underreporting of squatters, and thus the figures are almost certainly too optimistic. Even if these figures are accurate, however, in money terms (current pesos) over half of urban families received less than 4,000 pesos in 1970–1971, the level set by the Catholic church back in *1950* as the minimum budget for an urban industrial family of five. In real terms (constant *1950* pesos) the median income for all urban families in 1970–1971 was about half the church's figure.[33] In June 1970 a law was passed in the Philippines raising the minimum wage to 8 pesos a day. At five days a week, fifty-two weeks a year, this comes to 2,080 pesos. But the average money income of the bottom 40 percent of

TABLE 9   *Real Per Family Twelve-Month Income of Low-Income Groups, Urban Philippines, 1956–1957, 1961, 1965, 1970–1971*

Urban Family Income Group	Real Per Family Income (constant 1965 pesos)				Percent Increase 1956–57 to 1970–71	Percent Compound Annual Growth Rate
	1956–57[a]	1961	1965	1970–71[b]		
Lowest 20%	745	700	837	955	28	1.79
Lowest 40%	1,034	1,041	1,300	1,453	41	2.46
Lowest 60%	1,363	1,461	1,747	1,896	39	2.39
All urban families	3,310	3,684	4,405	4,151	25	1.63

[a]Five-sixths of 1956 consumer price index plus one-sixth of 1957 index used.
[b]Average consumer price index May 1970–April 1971 used.
Note: Percents of families are cumulative (see note to Table 5). Definition of "urban" changed in 1965 and 1970–1971 (see note to Table 3).
Sources: Calculated from ILO, *Sharing in Development*, p. 10 (urban income shares); NEDA, *Statistical Yearbook of the Philippines, 1975*, pp. 414–415 (number of urban families), pp. 416–417 (urban income); *Statistical Reporter*, 15, no. 2 (April–June 1971), p. 64 (1970 monthly consumer price index for Manila and suburbs, converted to 1965 = 100); Central Bank, *Statistical Bulletin*, vol. 24 (December 1972), p. 353 (monthly consumer price index for Manila and suburbs 1956, 1957, 1961, 1965, and January–April 1971).

urban families was less than this in 1970–1971. The minimum-wage law does not apply to cottage industries, household service, small retail or service employees, or local government employees, but in addition it is well known that except for large firms (which are visible to the inspectors) employers simply ignore the law.[34]

Table 10 provides data on the real earnings of nonagricultural workers and indicates that these earnings have been declining; in

TABLE 10   *Indices of Real Nonagricultural Earnings, 1965 = 100*

Year	(1) Real Monthly Salaries, Selected Nonagricultural Industries[a,b]	(2) Real Monthly Wages, Selected Nonagricultural Industries[b]	(3) Real Wage Rate, Skilled Industrial Laborers, Manila and Suburbs	(4) Real Wage Rate, Unskilled Industrial Laborers, Manila and Suburbs
1941	—	—	128.0[c]	92.9[c]
1949	—	—	123.5	106.6
1952	—	—	112.6	103.2
1957	105.8	109.6	117.5	110.2
1958	108.2	107.3	117.7	107.2
1959	115.2	113.9	120.7	109.1
1960	116.2	114.9	115.7	104.8
1961	113.8	110.4	113.6	105.7
1962	113.7	108.6	108.7	102.9
1963	108.6	101.5	106.0	102.8
1964	102.1	97.4	99.7	95.8
1965	100.0	100.0	100.0	100.0
1966	100.3	105.3	99.6	101.8
1967	96.7	105.6	98.1	100.3
1968	99.3	103.9	103.6	109.1
1969	102.6	106.8	106.9	112.0
1970	93.5	100.0	99.3	108.5
1971	82.6	88.7	91.3	101.3
1972	81.7	90.5	86.8	97.4

[a]Includes executives and supervisors.
[b]Money wages and salaries deflated by consumer price index for the Philippines.
[c]Figures for 1941 calculated from Bell Report, p. 16 (see Sources, below).
Note: Columns 1 and 2 refer to actual earnings, including bonuses, overtime, etc. Columns 3 and 4 represent the rates stipulated for a given amount of work time.
Sources: For columns 1 and 2: Central Bank, *Statistical Bulletin*, 24 (December 1972), pp. 376–377 (earnings), p. 372 (consumer price index). For columns 3 and 4: ibid., p. 378. For 1941 figures: *Report to the President of the United States by the Economic Survey Mission to the Philippines*, Far Eastern Series 38, Department of State Publication No. 4010 (Washington, D.C.: 9 October 1950), p. 16.

1972 they were at a point lower than two decades earlier. The figures in columns 1 and 2 represent total monthly earnings, including bonuses and overtime. To obtain these diminished earnings, the typical Filipino has had to put in more hours; the average hours worked of employed persons outside of agriculture has increased more than 17 percent from 1956 to 1971.[35]

There are other indications of the hardships of urban life. United States officials noted in the mid-1960s that for "the first time since the Japanese occupation, women and children are seen scavenging garbage cans in public places." In 1967, 9,000 children fifteen years old and under were arrested in Manila, including 3,780 for "obstruction," 1,561 for "vagrancy," 1,137 for curfew violation, 289 for theft, 154 for gambling, and 135 for begging. A reporter checked with authorities and found that "obstruction" simply meant children peddling on the sidewalks, loitering, sleeping on the pavement, or scavenging.[36]

A biochemical survey of Metropolitan Manila in 1959 found 91% of the sample low or deficient in serum carotene, 72% in urinary riboflavin, 59% in urinary thiamine, 19% in serum vitamin A, 62% in serum vitamin C, 9% in serum protein, and 29% in hemoglobin. Among pregnant women the corresponding figures were 88%, 78%, 67%, 17%, 33%, 56%, and 78%. For nursing mothers, the figures were 94%, 74%, 53%, 17%, 85%, 0%, and 45% respectively. And for children one to six years old, low or deficient levels of carotene were found in 90% of the cases examined, of serum vitamin A in 51%, of serum vitamin C in 44%, of serum protein in 15%, and of hemoglobin in 57%.[37]

National figures on mortality rate by income level are unavailable, but one careful study in Cagayan de Oro, a medium-sized city, found the lowest-income groups to have some two and a half times the death rate of the highest-income groups during the years 1958–1962.[38]

Then, of course, there are the squatters and slum dwellers. Barely a quarter of these families have toilets, and garbage collection is almost nonexistent. More than half have to buy their water from peddlers. Respiratory and gastrointestinal diseases are prevalent in these areas; one study in the Tondo (Manila) slum found that 87 percent of children showed some clinical signs of malnutrition. The typical slum dwelling—a makeshift structure put together from discarded materials—is approximately six feet by nine feet and provides shelter for some nine people. The housing is so dilapidated and congested that a single fire in 1971 rendered 70,000 people homeless.[39]

Finally, mention must be made of the cultural impact of neocolonialism on the lives of Filipinos. Poverty in general is bad enough, but when at the same time advertisements on all the media proclaim the wonders of products that the poor cannot afford, the burden becomes that much more difficult to bear. And when the advertising shifts people's consumption patterns in ways that are detrimental to their health and well-being, the situation is nothing short of tragic.

There are more than one hundred advertising and public relations firms in the Philippines, including subsidiaries of the American giants, McCann-Erickson, Grant, and J. Walter Thompson. Those ad firms that are not U.S.-owned nevertheless reflect the sway of American technique. "Having been strongly influenced by the American way of advertising," a Philippine ad executive has written, "Philippine advertising uses the hard-sell appeal extensively."[40]

In September 1966, residents of Metropolitan Manila were asked which print media ads they recalled from a particular weekend. Pepsi-Cola ranked first, Lux second, Palmolive fourth, Lifebuoy sixth, Marlboro seventh, Tide tenth, and, though it had not appeared in print for the previous three months, Coca-Cola eighth.[41] What is more significant than the dominance of American brand names on this list is the relatively low social utility of these products.

Much of the advertising is aimed at the relatively wealthy, and in fact top U.S. advertisers in the Philippines use mostly English ads, English being the appropriate language for reaching the middle- and upper-income brackets.[42] But the impact is felt through all sectors of society. A study by the International Labour Office reported that the "effect of the mass media is to create new wants and new desires, particularly among the young for whom the rural environment cannot provide satisfaction, and to lead to a pronounced drift to the town."[43] One statistic, perhaps better than any other, reveals the human consequences of this drift to the town: in a study of a slum district of Manila, in which most of the population were immigrants from the provinces, only 32 percent of the adults fifteen years old and above were found to be gainfully employed; of these, almost one in five worked as a "hostess"—the euphemism for "prostitute."[44]

=CHAPTER SEVEN=

Martial Law

In September 1972 President Ferdinand E. Marcos of the Philippines declared martial law. After a brief quarter century, formal democracy in the Philippines came to an end. The neocolonial relationship, however, remained basically unchanged, with only minor adjustments to accommodate the new balance of power in the Pacific region.

By the late 1960s three factors converged within Philippine society, each one feeding the others: (1) an accelerating level of conflict among the different sectors of the Philippine elite, (2) an intensifying challenge by the Philippine masses to those in power, and (3) a growing uncertainty about the status of American investments.

The split in the Philippine elite was not due to any fundamental differences of principle. In part, it was simply a continuation of the seven-decade-long struggle for the spoils of political office. But it was increasingly fueled by the diversifying economic interests of the Philippine oligarchy. Though the industrial elite came by and large from the same families as the agricultural aristocracy, the rich could not agree on the best ways to serve their fortunes. Each sector of the elite attempted to maximize the subsidies and support it could get from the government.

The debate was not on the proper role of government; the oligarchy was unanimous that government existed to defend and promote the interests of the rich. Rather, the controversy centered on the issue of who *among the elite* was to benefit most from government-provided windfalls.

Decontrol and devaluation favored exporters over those who

produced for the local market. Government subsidies to one sector of the elite meant that there was that much less for other sectors. Government-provided credit and import licenses went to political favorites.[1] Within agriculture, the tobacco bloc advocated high tariffs against American competition, while the sugar interests opposed such tariffs (since the *U.S.* tobacco bloc had made it clear that expansion of the Philippine sugar quota in the United States depended upon easy entrance for American tobacco products into the Philippines).[2]

Intraelite conflict manifested itself in a number of ways. Philippine election campaigns—always violent—were becoming increasingly so throughout the 1960s. In 1969 there was a record death toll for a presidential election year, and in 1971 election-related killings reached the all-time high of 243.[3] Elite rivalry also expressed itself in the growth of private armies. By early 1971 there were reported to be eighty political warlords, including six senators and thirty-seven representatives.[4]

The highest-level manifestation of elite rivalry was the conflict between President Marcos and Vice-President Fernando Lopez. Each man headed a clan of immense wealth and power. Marcos had married into the extremely well-to-do Romualdez family and had used political office to enhance his fortune manyfold. In 1963–1964 he had reported paying average annual taxes of 8,600 pesos; by 1968 he was the nation's fifty-seventh largest taxpayer (188,209 pesos); and by 1972 he was among the top ten.[5] Knowledgeable observers have reported that Marcos regularly demanded to be cut in on the profits of local business and had important allies on the boards of the Philippine subsidiaries of such foreign giants as Castle & Cooke and Gulf Oil.[6]

The Lopez family controlled vast resources. Originally based on sugar, family assets by the late 1960s included public utilities as well as cement, insurance, and media interests. Suggestive of their wealth was Vice-President Lopez's fortieth wedding anniversary in 1968; he imported a top American society dance band, flew in a group of European nobles, and guaranteed his guests that three fountains would keep real French champagne flowing throughout the evening.[7]

The Lopezes had supported Marcos in 1965 and 1969, but by late 1970 their feud had come out in the open as both families struggled to control the Philippine oil industry. Marcos accused the Lopez family of having financed a strike by jeepney (taxi) drivers against oil price hikes; Fernando Lopez denied the charge and resigned his cabinet post as secretary of agriculture and natural resources.[8]

Another arena of intraelite conflict was the Constitutional Convention which convened in 1971. Concon, as it was called, was to rewrite the 1935 constitution, which provided, among other things, that the president was restricted to two terms in office. This was of particular concern to Marcos, who was approaching the end of his second term. In September 1971 Marcos's opponents were able to get a "ban Marcos" clause accepted (prohibiting him or a member of his family from holding the position of head of state or government under any form of government decided upon by the convention). Marcos, however, had more resources than his rivals. The following summer, with money and patronage, he was able to get Concon to reverse itself by a vote of 155 to 31; the earlier "ban Marcos" clause had had the support of 161 delegates.[9]

Concurrent with the intraelite conflict was an increasing opposition to the elite as a whole from the rest of Philippine society. Though elections were sharply contested, they offered nothing to the masses of the population (other than money from vote-buying)— and people were beginning to understand this. As countless observers have noted, Philippine elections have been virtually devoid of issues, the two major parties have been ideologically indistinguishable,[10] and politicians have regularly switched from one party to the other.[11] (There was an issue separating the candidates in 1965: Marcos ran on a pledge not to send PHILCAG to Vietnam, but since he violated his campaign promise as soon as he won the election, this is hardly a meaningful exception.[12]) Growing popular disillusionment with the political system was reflected in a poll in 1970 that showed 10 percent of Filipinos receptive to reform through violence. A Pulitzer Prize–winning reporter for the *Wall Street Journal* noted that "a thoroughly unscientific 1972 Manila newspaper poll [showing] elective politicians ranking twenty-seventh in public trust and respect, behind barbers, taxi drivers and night club performers [probably] captured fairly accurately the mood of a public that was strongly alienated from politicians and perhaps the state of the political system."[13] Indeed, one of the reasons for the escalating levels of election violence was that traditional paternalism and even vote-buying were proving unable to assure votes for candidates any more. ("They take money but vote for the man they think is qualified," remarked one politician.) Violence had become increasingly necessary to hold on to the mass electorate.[14]

Opposition to the elite in the late 1960s came from students, urban workers, the rural population, and the Muslims in the southern Philippines.

Higher education in the Philippines was, by 1960, no longer the monopoly of the ruling class. Between 1949–1950 and 1960–1961 the enrollment at private colleges and universities grew ninefold, while the population as a whole grew less than 50 percent. In 1960–1961, 10 percent of the college-age population was enrolled in private degree-granting institutions of higher education.[15] The size of the college population shows that the students were not drawn exclusively from the few families of great wealth. And higher education did not necessarily prepare its graduates for dominant positions in society. In 1961, UNESCO estimated that some 35,000 Philippine college graduates were unemployed. A 1970 study reported that a commercial employment service for temporary office workers had raised its minimum requirements for secretarial applicants in Manila to two completed years of college and was seriously considering raising standards again to require a four-year degree.[16]

In 1964 a radically oriented group, Nationalist Youth (KM), was formed, based on students and young working adults. Within a few years it had a membership conservatively estimated at several thousand, with many additional sympathizers.[17] The war in Vietnam, and Philippine participation in it, increased student activism. In 1968 a Maoist Communist Party of the Philippines was organized.[18] Student militance reached a peak in early 1970, when massive demonstrations were held in Manila. One journalist reported, "Besides the United States, just about everything else connected with the government and big business here has come under fire."[19] Some of the demonstrations resulted in huge clashes with police, and several protesters were killed.[20]

At the same time, strikes in the Philippines were occurring at a growing rate. From 1947 to 1955 there were an average of 34 strikes a year; from 1957 to 1961 there were 56 a year; and from 1964 to 1968 the figure had risen to 108 a year.[21] Radicalism among Philippine unions was increasing and activist students joined with workers in strikes and demonstrations. In 1970 striking tobacco workers and jeepney drivers joined and were supported by protesting students. Peasants calling for land reform also participated in the demonstrations.[22]

Peasant unrest manifested itself as well in increased levels of activity by groups popularly referred to as the Huks. By the late 1960s there were three rival groups of armed dissidents operating in Central Luzon. One, under Commander Sumulong, controlled the rackets in and around Angeles City (near Clark Air Base) and had negligible ideological commitment. A smaller group, the People's Army under Commander Diwa, had ties with the Moscow-oriented Communist Party of the Philippines. And the third and largest group, the New People's Army (NPA), was linked with the Maoist Communist Party.[23] By the early 1970s the NPA was in control of most of the municipalities of Isabela province (according to official government sources) and the government was responding with air strikes.[24]

On top of all this, the government faced a situation of growing disorder from the Muslim population in the southern Philippines. The roots of this conflict are exceedingly complex; suffice it to say here that the desire of the Muslim minority for cultural and sometimes political autonomy conflicted with the efforts of Christian politicians and businesspeople to exploit for their own benefit the resources of the south, and conflicted as well with the influx of Christian settlers to the less densely populated southern regions. Intercommunal warfare and clashes with the Philippine Constabulary raged intermittently.[25] In 1966 a U.S. AID survey found peace-and-order conditions on Jolo, the main island of the Sulu Archipelago, exhibiting "a retrogression to the pre-1914 period." In the first eight and a half months of the year, forty-four engagements were fought by the Constabulary there. In mid-1971, the governor of Cotabato claimed that 800 persons had been killed and 2,000 homes burned in his province since the previous November. And at the end of 1972 Marcos stated that about 3,000 people had been killed in Muslim-Christian violence in the past two years and that there were more than 500,000 refugees from the fighting.[26]

The widespread opposition to the elite was fed by the intraelite conflict. Some politicians tried to ride the crest of mass discontent, and some even lent assistance to dissidents, hoping to turn turmoil to their own advantage. Sugar interests are thought to have helped promote anti-Americanism as far back as 1958, so as to discourage U.S. policymakers from taking Philippine friendship for granted when considering revisions of the sugar quota.[27] Some industrialists are suspected of backing dissidents so as to encourage U.S. investors to sell their assets at bargain prices.[28] The government too contributed to the mass unrest: armed goons, dubbed "the Monkees," are generally assumed to have been set up by the Philippine Constabulary to murder Huks and their sympathizers, and in 1969 the government reportedly was tolerating the Sumulong Huks so as to have a buffer against the NPA.[29]

The third factor contributing to the Philippine crisis of the early 1970s was the growing uncertainty about the status of U.S. investments. The Laurel-Langley Agreement was due to expire in 1974, and with it the preferred position U.S. citizens enjoyed in the Philippines over all other foreign nationals.

Article VI of the Laurel-Langley Agreement gave Americans "parity" with Filipinos in exploiting Philippine natural resources and public utilities until 1974; article VII gave U.S. citizens equal treatment with Filipinos in all other business activities. The former was no longer of prime importance to U.S. policymakers. The ill feeling generated by having forced a prostrate Philippines to amend its constitution in order to receive full war damage compensation made article VI a serious liability to U.S. interests, and in any case most U.S. investments were no longer in the "parity" sectors of the Philippine economy but in manufacturing. Article VII gave more general protection to U.S. capital, though often in public discussion article VI alone was referred to as the "parity" provision.

In 1965 and 1966, U.S. officials stated publicly that they had no intention of asking for a renewal of "parity"—article VI; they did not specify their attitude toward article VII. They did, however, indicate that in their view rights acquired under article VI prior to 1974 would continue, that is, that natural resources acquired before 1974 could be owned after that date.[30] The concern here was primarily with the land upon which most U.S. enterprises stood. Philippine courts had been treating such holdings as "private agricultural land,"[31] and it was solely by virtue of "parity" that Americans were permitted to own more than 40 percent of such land.

In late 1967 a joint U.S.-Philippine panel met for the first round of talks regarding a replacement for the Laurel-Langley Agreement. The panel's report stated, in part, "With the exception of certain areas, such as natural resources, public utilities, and retail trade, where most favored nation treatment should be accorded, the two groups believe that a provision according national treatment can be worked out."[32] As Philippine Senator Lorenzo Tañada correctly observed, this represented an acceptance by the Filipino members of the panel of the U.S. position, namely, that article VI should be permitted to lapse, but not article VII.[33]

The Philippine negotiators were accommodating on this matter because they were hoping for a concession in turn from the United States: continued preferential access to the U.S. market for Philippine goods. The U.S. members of the panel, however, stated that they could not take a position on this at the time because U.S. trade policy with respect to the Third World as a whole was under comprehensive review.[34]

Some differences remained between the negotiators on the issue of U.S. investments. The Filipino members of the panel took the position that all U.S. ownership of private agricultural land would cease in 1974 (although leases would remain valid throughout their

166

term). The negotiators agreed that the issue required a legal resolution and suggested that a declaratory judgment be sought as soon as possible.[35] There was disagreement as well on the question of whether "national treatment" required nondiscrimination in extending tax incentives.[36]

Another point of contention—and this had been a cause of dispute for years—involved the definition of "retail trade." A 1954 law had provided that within ten years retail trade was to be "nationalized" (i.e., restricted to Filipinos). Various Philippine courts had ruled that, despite the Laurel-Langley Agreement, U.S. firms were included by the law and, moreover, that all end-use sales constituted retail trade. (For example, if an oil company sold fuel to a factory for its own use and not for resale, this was to be adjudged retail trade.) Higher courts had reversed both these interpretations, but the latter issue was not fully resolved, and U.S. firms were concerned about future judicial renderings of the term "retail trade."[37]

All these uncertainties were exacerbated by the other conflicts in Philippine society. Although student protests were hardly at the point of overthrowing the state, American businesspeople could not be encouraged by the frequent demonstrations and attacks upon the U.S. embassy. The incidence of strikes was significantly higher at foreign than Filipino firms. And though U.S. executives believed that "somehow, the Philippine authorities always come around to adopting a pragmatic approach,"[38] the lengths to which Philippine nationalist rhetoric went in public could not but be somewhat disconcerting. One American analysis, for example, expected the Constitutional Convention to advocate moderate treatment of foreign investment but nevertheless considered the outcome of Concon's deliberations to be "unpredictable," given the pressures that street demonstrations might exert on the convention.[39]

It is important to emphasize that U.S. investments in the Philippines remained extremely profitable. A representative of a U.S. bank had reported back in 1948 that American companies had planned their investments in such a way as to recoup their capital by 1974. United States Commerce Department figures are incomplete, but they show that from 1957 to 1972, $216 million was transferred from the United States as direct investments in the Philippines; over this same period, $470 million was repatriated to the United States as profits from direct investments in the Philippines—and this does not include royalties or the various types of transfer-pricing that are known to increase the levels of repatriated capital from the Philippines to the United States.[40] Moreover, a considerable number of U.S. companies did not view the end of the Laurel-Langley Agreement as a serious obstacle to their operations. In mid-1972 it was reported that a U.S. embassy survey of American firms accounting for over half the U.S. direct investment in the Philippines found that the firms had intended to invest over a quarter of a billion dollars in the Philippines from January 1971 to December 1973.[41] Even if the U.S. firms could not own land, they knew there were a variety of ways that they could continue to do business in the Philippines, with Philippine government approval; for example, they could transfer the title to their land to the company provident fund and then lease it back.[42] With a few exceptions, some of which might in fact reflect deceptive transfer-pricing, U.S. firms had growing sales and earnings in 1971 and the first half of 1972.[43]

Nevertheless, it is clear that the prevailing uncertainty lessened the appeal of the Philippines as a place for U.S. corporations to do business. Various surveys and business voices rated the Philippines as one of the least attractive countries in Southeast Asia in which to invest and as the worst place to establish a regional headquarters.[44] The Philippine government's decision in 1971 to deny oil exploration special investment incentives and Congress' refusal to pass an administration "Oil Exploration" bill did not help matters. Congress also blocked approval of a Treaty of Amity, Commerce, and Navigation with Japan, a prerequisite to stepped-up Japanese business activity in the Philippines.[45]

In the summer of 1971 a series of events took place that foreshadowed the declaration of martial law a year later. During a Liberal party (anti-Marcos) rally in Manila on August 21, two grenades were tossed at the speakers' platform. The eight Liberal party senatorial candidates were injured, nine other people were killed, and dozens more injured. Marcos promptly suspended the writ of habeas corpus and proceeded to arrest various left-wing figures. Thirty-six hours later, Marcos announced—for the first time—that he was suspending the writ. He blamed the bombing on "desperate forces of an alien ideology [whose] conception of God and religion, whose notion of individual rights and family relations, and whose political, social and economic precepts are based on the Marxist-Leninist-Maoist teachings and beliefs."[46] This was hardly a realistic attribution of blame, given that the Maoists had been criticized by the Moscow-oriented elements of the Left for giving too much support to the anti-Marcos Liberal party.[47] In any case, Marcos asserted that the perpetrators of the crime were in custody. However, forty days later the responsible party had not yet been found. And when five furloughed convicts were formally charged with the crime in 1972, no evidence was presented as to who was behind them, and observers criticized the legal proceedings, claiming that the defense counsel seemed to side with the prosecution.[48] Noteworthy was the attitude of the foreign business community to the suspension of the writ of habeas corpus: the consensus seemed to be that it hardly affected them at all. As the chief executive of one U.S. subsidiary explained, "We are not in the business of rebellion—so why should it affect us?"[49]

If in 1971, U.S. corporations thought they had reason to be indifferent to democratic forms, a year later they had cause for downright hostility. Two decisions were handed down by the Philippine Supreme Court in August 1972, both of them extremely harmful to U.S. economic interests. The first of these was the Quasha decision. William Quasha, an American lawyer resident in the Philippines who owned "private agricultural land," had asked the Philippine courts for a declaratory ruling on whether his ownership rights to the land would continue after 1974. A lower court had ruled in Quasha's favor—that is, that he could indeed retain title—and this was expected to be upheld by the Supreme Court.[50] In a surprise ruling, however, the high court held not only that ownership rights did not extend past 1974 but that U.S. ownership of private agricultural land between 1946 and 1974 also had been illegal.[51] American firms now had visions of their lands being confiscated by the Philippine government or repossessed by the former owners, visions that were not discouraged by the calls for confiscation coming from nationalist circles. In 1972, U.S. corporate landholdings in the Philippines amounted to 17,300 hectares (43,000 acres).[52]

The second Supreme Court ruling affecting U.S. investment was the Luzon Stevedoring Corporation case (Lusteveco). The court held that firms in sectors of the economy reserved to Filipinos could not have foreigners as directors or as top management personnel. Applicable to Americans after July 1974, this ruling would prevent U.S. firms from using a management contract as a way to control minority-held subsidiaries.[53]

Marcos promptly tried to reassure U.S. investors that there would be no confiscation without just compensation following the Supreme Court rulings,[54] but they were not so easily calmed. Marcos, however, had been building up for a decisive step, one that he hoped would in a single stroke end elite conflict, crush opposition to the elite, and reassure U.S. investors. In the preceding months, a number of bombings had taken place in Manila. Marcos charged that this was the work of communist subversives; the only apprehended suspects, however, were a Philippine Constabulary explosives expert and an ex-convict, who were allegedly trying to extort money from a department store.[55] Many knowledgeable sources suspected Marcos of having engineered most of the bombings himself.[56] On September 22 there was an unsuccessful assassination attempt against Secretary of National Defense Juan Ponce Enrile, and the next day Marcos declared martial law. All serious observers agree that the attack on Enrile was staged by Marcos, a view substantiated by the later revelation that the declaration of martial law had been signed on September 21.[57]

Marcos immediately moved to imprison his opponents. The ever-inventive Carlos P. Romulo, the Philippine foreign secretary, announced that persons were being held to protect them from possible harm from insurgents. In the first few weeks of martial law, some 30,000 people were arrested. In 1975 Marcos told Amnesty International that altogether 50,000 people had been arrested and detained up to that time. Many detainees were later released, although in May 1975, 6,000 still remained in detention, virtually all held without formal charge or trial.[58] The early arrests included, in addition to suspected leftists, prominent politicians and journalists who had opposed Marcos. Amnesty International reported that torture was "widespread, systematic and severe," and even a few deaths have been reported.[59]

Marcos drastically curtailed civil liberties. The Philippine press, often called the freest in the world, had in fact always been tightly controlled by members of the elite. But the dynamics of elite competition had permitted a wide range of views to be expressed. Now, under martial law, the media became the private preserve of one elite family and its loyal supporters. The media, acknowledged the U.S. State Department, are "essentially controlled."[60] Freedom of speech and assembly were proscribed, and the right to strike was suspended. "Rumor-mongering" was made a crime. In August 1973 a presidential decree established a compulsory registration system whereby all citizens were to have a reference number and national reference card.[61]

Marcos effectively abolished Congress,[62] rendered political parties inactive,[63] and demanded undated letters of resignation from members of the judiciary.[64] Various referendums were set up to allow the people to approve both martial law and a new constitution, written largely by Marcos.[65] In the first referendum, voting was by show of hands, and in all the referendums there were numerous reports by foreign correspondents of government intimidation and falsified results. A high-level defector from Manila testified before the U.S. Congress about his role in rigging the voting figures. In one referendum, according to Philippine military authorities, 85 percent of all prisoners confined in military detention centers voted yes.[66] It is not surprising that Marcos's continued martial law rule received overwhelming approval in such referendums. Provisions of the new constitution permitted Marcos to remain in power indefinitely and to remove at will government officials and judges.[67]

In his proclamation of martial law, Marcos explained that this was his only alternative to save the country from communist—specifically Maoist—subversion. As a British business source commented, "This argument deserves the chorus of skepticism it has met."[68] There was certainly widespread unrest (as reviewed above), but it was far from threatening the overthrow of the government. Marcos cited a Philippine Senate report of September 1971 to buttress his case about the strength of the New People's Army, but he did not quote the conclusion of the report, which stated that there existed "no clear and present danger of a Communist-inspired insurrection or rebellion."[69] Nor did he announce the estimate given by Philippine generals to the Philippine National Security Council just three days before martial law: that the internal security situation was no worse than it had been for years.[70]

Marcos's claim that Philippine communists were acting for some foreign power did not impress most observers.[71] His evidence was a shipload of arms allegedly found by the Philippine Constabulary off Isabela province. But even before the "find," Marcos's political rival, Senator Benigno Aquino, Jr., had charged that weapons had been secretly bought by Marcos to be later unearthed as a justification for declaring martial law.[72]

Martial law was moderately successful in suppressing the legal forms of popular discontent—the abolition of civil liberties accomplished this. But illegal dissent—in particular that of the NPA and the Muslims—was exacerbated rather than crushed. In part this was because opponents of the status quo no longer had any but extralegal means by which to register their opposition. In part it was because of declining living standards, which will be discussed below. And in part it was due to the increased levels of brutality that the government employed against dissidents and the population in general. For example, the Philippine Armed Forces forcibly relocated some 50,000 residents of Isabela province in order to isolate the 500 NPA members claimed to be operating there. (This maneuver began before martial law, but local politicians had been objecting; after martial law these local officials were found to be more cooperative.) Prior to martial law NPA activity was confined to Isabela province. Two years later they were active in Panay, Negros, Samar, Sorsogon, Quezon, Bicol, Nueva Ecija, and Mindanao. And this was not, as the Philippine

Islands and Provinces of the Philippines, 1967

Provinces

1. Batanes
2. Cagayan
3. Ilocos Norte
4. Abra
5. Kalinga-Apayao
6. Mountain
7. Ilocos Sur
8. La Union
9. Benguet
10. Ifugao
11. Isabela
12. Nueva Vizcaya
13. Pangasinan
14. Nueva Ecija
15. Quezon
16. Zambales
17. Tarlac
18. Bataan
19. Pampanga
20. Bulacan
21. Rizal
22. Cavite
23. Laguna
24. Batangas
25. Camarines Norte
26. Camarines Sur
27. Catanduanes
28. Mindoro
    Occidental
29. Mindoro
    Oriental
30. Marinduque
31. Albay
32. Sorsogon
33. Romblon
34. Masbate
35. Samar
    del Norte
36. Samar
    Occidental
37. Samar Oriental
38. Aklan
39. Capiz
40. Antique
41. Iloilo
42. Negros
    Occidental
43. Cebu
44. Leyte
45. Southern Leyte
46. Negros Oriental
47. Bohol
48. Surigao del Norte
49. Camiguin
50. Zamboanga
    del Norte

51. Misamis Occidental
52. Misamis Oriental
53. Agusan del Norte
54. Agusan del Sur
55. Surigao del Sur
56. Zamboanga del Sur
57. Lanao del Norte
58. Lanao del Sur

59. Bukidnon
60. Cotabato
61. Cotabato del Sur
62. Davao del Sur
63. Davao del Norte
64. Davao Oriental
65. Sulu
66. Palawan

Adapted from *Area Handbook for the Philippines, 1969*
(Washington, D.C.: U.S. Government Printing Office, 1969).

government claimed, the result of the NPA being routed from Isabela, for that province remained an NPA stronghold. Moreover, since little effort was made to ease the plight of those relocated from Isabela, one can assume that the NPA mass base grew considerably.[73]

In the southern Philippines, stepped up government military operations had much the same effect. In February 1974 the government unleashed massive firepower upon the town of Jolo in order to "free it" from the control of Muslim rebels. Hundreds were killed and tens of thousands rendered homeless. "We should have taught these people a lesson a long time ago," said Secretary of National Defense Enrile. "We have been too easy on them."[74] With this approach it was not surprising that although martial law was supposedly declared because some 3,000 people had died in southern violence in 1971 and 1972, more than this number were killed in the first year of martial law alone (according to government figures.)[75]

In addition to the need to combat subversion, Marcos gave a second reason for declaring martial law: the need to reform Philippine society, to establish what he called his "New Society." Given the fact that Marcos himself was a prime contributor to and beneficiary of the ills of society that he claimed needed reforming, there was considerable reason to doubt his reformist zeal. And the record of accomplishment of Marcos's "New Society" confirmed the *prima facie* doubts.

To begin with, many of the reforms were not reforms at all but manifestations of Marcos's victory in the intraelite struggle. Thus, when Marcos announced that he was going to curb the power of the "oligarchs," in practice this meant selectively attacking his political rivals; in particular, the Lopez economic empire was taken over (through extortion) by the Marcos economic empire. In general, the oligarchs remain, the "main body of the big rich operate as before."[76] The disbanding of the private armies meant that the instruments of coercive power were taken from Marcos's opponents while the largest army—the Armed Forces of the Philippines—remained under his personal control. Top leaders of the AFP were directly loyal to Marcos; at the head of the Constabulary was Fidel Ramos, a close relative.[77] By mid-1974 the size of the AFP was about two-thirds greater than before martial law; by early 1977 it was more than twice as large. In May 1973 Marcos decreed the first military draft in the Philippines' independent history. Moreover, the government took steps to merge all local police forces into a national force, further centralizing the means of coercion in Marcos's hands.[78]

In the early days of martial law, there was a noticeable decline in the crime rate. This was not surprising, given the curfews and the military patrols. But equally unsurprising, since the "New Society" did not deal with any of the root causes of criminality, the crime rate was soon reported to be up to its previous levels. The Philippine press, however, now reported crimes only after they were solved.[79]

Marcos claimed that under martial law corruption would be eliminated, and he ordered a widely publicized firing of some civil servants. However, since half of all appointive officials had been appointed by the Congress (as provided in a formal executive-legislative agreement), there is the suspicion that most of those fired by Marcos were the patronage appointees of his political adversaries. Marcos was clearly not opposed on principle to patronage and nepotism: among the many members of his family appointed to high positions was his wife, Imelda Romualdez Marcos, whom he made governor of the greater Manila area in 1975. Observers have reported that the corruption formerly associated with politicians has been taken over by Marcos's inner circle and the military.[80]

The one reform upon which Marcos declared his willingness to have his whole "New Society" judged was land reform. On paper his land reform program left much to be desired: compensation levels, especially for the larger landlords, were to be on the generous side,[81] and various exclusions severely restricted the number of potential beneficiaries. Only tenant farmers on rice or corn lands of more than seven hectares were to receive land, thus excluding landless laborers, tenants working other crops (more than 20 percent of tenant families), and those on smaller plots of land (estimated at 56 percent of tenants).[82] In actual practice, however, the land reform has not come close to its paper promise. A number of categories of landlords owning between seven and twenty-four hectares of tenanted land were exempted from the land transfer, reducing the number of tenants affected by almost half.[83] Moreover, landlords evicted tenants, switched crops, subdivided their holdings, mortgaged their lands to corporations not covered by land reform, or took advantage of innumerable administrative delays. Marcos repealed a law which prohibited foreigners from growing food crops, and the wage laborers on these new rice plantations were excluded from agrarian reform.[84]

Many of these difficulties might not have been insurmountable had the peasants possessed strong autonomous organizations with which to press their rights. But as part of the martial law "reforms," peasant organizations were purged of their independent elements, while the barrio associations that replaced them were, in the words of a study for the International Labour Office, "essentially an arm of the Government."[85]

The Department of Agrarian Reform claimed that at the end of 1975 land-transfer certificates had been printed in the name of 200,000 tenants out of the total 285,000 eligible under the redefined program. But the printing of a certificate does not mean that the tenant has received it—a U.S. land reform adviser estimated that less than half have actually reached the farmers—and, in any event, the certificate is not a deed or title to the land but merely verifies that the tenant is in fact tilling the land.[86] As of late 1977, only 4.6 percent of rice and corn tenants could be said to own their land. A seminar organized by the Rand Corporation and funded by AID concluded that "the agrarian reform program in the Philippines has not fulfilled its initial goals and, in fact, is a failing program."[87]

These, then, have been the reforms of the "New Society." Marcos has been determined, however, that what the reforms lack in accomplishment would be made up for by the public relations efforts of the government. To this end, the open propaganda budget of the Marcos administration went from 3 million pesos to 68 million pesos in the first eighteen months of martial law.[88]

In the first few years of martial law, there was considerable aggregate economic growth in the Philippines, but the general consensus has been that while the rich have been getting richer the poor have been staying poor. Although the prices of export crops rose sharply on the world market, the workers on sugar and other plantations experienced no improvement.[89] And in real terms, since there was a tremendous price inflation, the living standards of the average Filipino plummeted. Unskilled laborers in the Manila area suffered a decline in real wages from an index of 112.0 in 1969 (1965 = 100) to 90.4 in 1973 and to 72.5 in 1974. For skilled laborers, the corresponding figures were 106.9 in 1969 (again, 1965 = 100), 82.8 in 1973, and 67.2 in 1974. With strikes and demonstrations illegal, there were widespread reports of violations of the minimum wage laws and of workers being dismissed for union activities.[90] The World Bank reported a decline in the per capita availability of calories in 1973 and 1974 and a deterioration in the quality of the diet.[91] At the same time, however, the return on equity for the 1,000 largest Philippine corporations went from 12.9 percent in 1968–1972 to 18.3 percent in 1973–74.[92]

Manila's response to declining living standards was to widely advertise abroad the fact that "prevailing wages are much lower than those customary in neighbor-countries" and that "the restoration of social order has resulted in a new era of industrial peace." Marcos told a meeting of international bankers in Manila that the export sector of the economy would not be jeopardized by a too rapid rise in wages. Skilled labor in the Philippines, the government told foreign investors, "stands out as a tremendous bargain." And this was not idle boasting. In mid-1973 the earnings of a Philippine secretary were 15 percent lower than in the next-lowest-paying Southeast Asian country; accountants received 13 percent less, and mechanical engineers 50 percent less.[93]

In fact, it was toward foreign investors that the only real "New Society" reforms were directed. The Quasha and Lusteveco rulings were overturned, first by executive decree and then by the new constitution. American firms were given until May 1975 to submit divestment plans for their land, and the government explicitly ruled out confiscation proceedings against those firms that did not submit plans on time. With the final expiration of the Laurel-Langley Agreement, U.S. firms adjusted without major problems and were reported to be doing well in the new situation.[94] The oil exploration bill that had been stalled in Congress was passed by presidential decree in October 1972, and two months later an amendment was enacted in order "to provide more meaningful incentives." The legislation was "considerably more liberal than any Indonesian oil contract," and First National City Bank called the terms "the best possible package of incentives." This was not surprising given that Marcos had told U.S. oil executives, "We'll pass the laws you need—just tell us what you want."[95] (Following the oil embargo and OPEC price hikes of late 1973, the Philippine government took a role in the oil industry, but the "ownership structure of petroleum production . . . is still much dominated by multinationals."[96])

Laws were passed opening up commercial banks to foreign investment, guaranteeing repatriation of capital and profits, liberalizing remittances of royalties, reducing tax liabilities, easing entry and clearance requirements for multinational executives, and making Manila the most attractive Asian site for corporate headquarters. Marcos issued a decree defining retail trade in a manner favorable to foreign investors, promulgated a commercial treaty with Japan, and opened up a large number of new areas of the economy to 100 percent foreign investment.[97]

To enhance Manila's appeal to foreign businesspeople and tourists, a crash program of luxury hotel construction was undertaken with government funds, despite the desperate shortage of housing for Filipinos. Imelda Marcos initiated a "beautification" campaign that included the forcible dumping of urban squatters in the countryside so that the squalor of their settlements would not offend tourists. And government estimates put the number of prostitutes working in licensed establishments in Manila at 100,000, more than one out of every twenty-five female residents of the city.[98]

As might be expected, foreign investors were ecstatic with martial law. The American Chamber of Commerce in Manila sent a cable to Marcos wishing him "every success" in his endeavors.[99] Business sources were nearly unanimous in praising the improved investment climate; it had come full circle, remarked the head of Mobil's Philippine subsidiary, "from an atmosphere of hostility to one of genuine hospitality." "The most encouraging aspect of President Marcos's assertion of one man rule," a correspondent for the *New York Times* reported, "has been the disappearance of the anti-foreign feeling that had been mounting in the press and the Constitutional Convention in the year preceding the proclamation of martial law." Executives noted too that they no longer had demonstrations or strikes hampering their activities.[100] In this heady atmosphere, foreign firms, including American firms, dramatically increased their investments in the Philippines. Foreign banks extended new loans to the Philippine government and helped roll over old debts.[101]

What remains to be examined is the U.S. role in martial law. Any final discussion of this matter must await the opening of the relevant archives. Nevertheless, some general observations can be made.

Two alternative hypotheses seem inconsistent with the available evidence. One hypothesis is that the initiative for martial law came from the United States. This view, however, ignores the reservations that American policymakers must surely have had about martial law, for despite the fact that in private U.S. officials had little regard for Philippine democratic institutions, and despite the fact that they found the situation prevailing prior to September 1972 to be desperate, martial law did not provide the ideal solution from Washington's point of view. In the quarter century since 1946, the United States had publicly invested much rhetoric in its Philippine "showcase of democracy." Martial law meant the abandonment of this investment. More important, Marcos was not a very reliable instrument of U.S. policy. His first loyalty was not to the United States (or to the Philippines) but to himself, and this meant that U.S. officials always had to worry about higher bidders for his favor, Filipino or foreign.[102] A related problem was that regimes with a single dictatorial ruler inevitably face the uncertainty of what will happen in the event of the dictator's death. And finally, martial law had the potential to turn even those Filipinos who were friendly toward the United States to an increasingly oppositionist stance—the Catholic church being the most dramatic example. To some U.S. officials the specter of converting a bad situation into a catastrophe must have been frightening. So although most U.S. officials supported martial law, there was always underlying concern. And although Washington was publicly uncritical of what occurred in the Philippines (while vaguely criticizing, for example, the dictatorial developments in South Korea), martial law was not extolled as Philippine "democracy" had been on countless earlier fourths of July.[103]

A second hypothesis that even more clearly cannot be supported by the evidence is the contention that martial law represents a break with the United States and an espousal of Philippine nationalism. Advocates of this view commonly point to Marcos's expanding ties with China and the Soviet Union and his militant statements regarding the U.S. bases.

Philippine moves to open diplomatic relations with China and the Soviet Union, however, began before rather than after martial law.[104] And far from indicating a split with the United States, these Philippine moves were fully consistent with U.S. policies with respect to the Communist powers. The United States had, of course, established relations with the Soviet Union four decades earlier, and Marcos's trip to China followed Nixon's by three years. Revealing in this regard was a 1949 exchange of telegrams between the U.S. ambassador to the Philippines, Myron M. Cowen, and Secretary of State Dean Acheson at a time when the United States was considering recognition of the Peking government. Cowen urged Acheson that if the United States decided to recognize China the Philippines be told beforehand.

> We feel Philippine Government in preserving common front with U.S. by postponement recognition has earned right expect this courtesy from U.S. which would enable it announce its decision regarding recognition in advance of U.S. should it wish to do so. If Philippine Government finds itself in position where it feels impelled accord recognition at same time as U.S. or immediately thereafter it would be put in position suggesting absence true independence and it might be less likely cooperate with us when we next feel need Philippine support.

Acheson cabled back his agreement: "Dept sympathetic Phil Govt desire avoid appearance fol[low] U.S. lead in this matter."[105]

With the U.S. defeat in Indochina and the shifting balance of power in the western Pacific, it was no longer useful to the United States for the Philippines to engage in such theatrics as denying entrance visas to a Yugoslav basketball team.[106] This kind of thing discredited the Philippines in Asian and world opinion as a puppet of the United States—a situation advantageous neither to Washington nor to Manila. To the United States, what is important is not subservience to the point of caricature but cooperation on such fundamentals as investments and military bases.

On the question of the bases, nationalist sentiments had always poured out of Malacañang (the Philippine presidential palace), but, as U.S. policymakers realized, Philippine officials had no intention of getting rid of the American installations. The bases provided the Philippines with employment and foreign exchange, factors that could not lightly be ignored by a government unwilling to undertake fundamental social reform. The militant rhetoric was aimed at most at getting a better price for the bases.[107] Rather than viewing martial law as an impediment to U.S. strategic interests in the Philippines, Washington considered the absence of a Congress in which speakers tried to outbid one another in nationalist rhetoric as a real advantage to the United States in any negotiations that might take place regarding the bases.[108]

And sure enough, when the bases agreement was amended in January 1979—by an exchange of notes not requiring the approval of the U.S. Senate—the United States recognized Philippine sovereignty over the bases, the Philippines assured the United States "unhampered military operations involving its Forces in the Philippines," and President Carter concurrently pledged to make his best effort to obtain $500 million in military and security-supporting aid over the following five years. United States State Department and Pentagon officials were "fully satisfied that U.S. operations will not be impaired" by the terms of the amendment.[109]

If the United States had really viewed martial law as opposed to its interests, it only had to refuse to give Marcos military and economic aid to render martial law untenable. This the United States clearly did not do. On the contrary, aid was stepped up. Despite its reservations, the United States decided to back Marcos and his martial law regime to the hilt.

United States military assistance to the Philippines went from $80.8 million in the four fiscal years 1969–1972 to $166.3 million in the succeeding four fiscal years, 1973–1976—a huge leap even if one takes inflation into account. Military grant aid increased about 12 percent in this period, but excess defense articles more than tripled, ship transfers (especially useful for combating the Muslims in the Sulu Archipelago) increased more than tenfold, and foreign military sales credits went from zero to $39.6 million.[110] Moreover, during the first year of martial law, U.S. military aid already in the pipeline (i.e., authorized but not yet delivered) was speeded up.[111] JUSMAG has continued to provide advice to the Philippine Armed Forces, and the United States still trains Philippine military personnel.[112]

United States officials, in testimony subsequently made public, stated that the purpose of the military aid was to promote internal security, to protect the U.S. bases by preserving stability, to help maintain the U.S.-Philippine military partnership in Southeast Asia, to give the Philippines the capability of deploying limited forces within the SEATO area, and "deleted." There was general agreement in Washington that the Philippines did not face a credible external threat. The Departments of State and Defense asserted that economic aid could not be substituted for the military aid because, among other things, this would reduce the Philippine government's ability to maintain law and order. And a study of the weapons and weapons systems delivered to the Philippines since the imposition of martial law has concluded that they have been especially suited for counterinsurgency operations.[113]

In 1975 a State Department official testified that since the U.S. military assistance program to the Philippines had been in existence for three decades, he could not understand how a continuation of this long-standing program "now constitutes 'intervening in the domestic affairs of the Philippines.' "[114] This point is well taken. United States military aid has *always* been a mechanism for intervening in the internal affairs of the Philippines.

In 1973 William H. Sullivan, one of the principal architects of the U.S. air war in North Vietnam and Laos, was appointed American ambassador to the Philippines. Sullivan had shown himself capable of ordering counterinsurgency operations of considerable brutality and of lying to hide the truth about these operations.[115] His assignment to Manila was indicative of the importance Washington attached to the Philippine situation and of the skills Washington felt useful for its chief envoy to the martial law regime. Behind Sullivan was a U.S. embassy staff of which four of the ten political officers had served in postescalation Vietnam; another had served in Laos, and another was a "public safety" adviser for AID.[116]

A new AID program in the Philippines, the Provincial Development Assistance Project, was instituted, under which U.S. civilian advisers were attached to Philippine provincial chiefs in areas of insurgency. Sixteen U.S. officials were initially involved, of whom eight, including the two in charge, had been rural pacification operatives in Vietnam.[117]

A number of sources have reported the presence of U.S. military personnel directing antidissident operations. This has been denied by U.S. and Philippine officials.[118] Green Berets conducted ten civic action exercises in the Philippines between late 1970 and mid-1974, six of them since martial law. United States officials claim that these were not fully qualified Green Berets, that the operations were training exercises, and that areas of insurgency were avoided. It is known that at least the last of these claims is untrue.[119] It further seems that Philippine aircraft which attacked NPA positions in Isabela province were based at Clark Air Field.[120]

United States economic aid to the Philippines also rose sharply the year following the imposition of martial law.[121] As before, much of the economic assistance was suspiciously military in character. For example, some planes provided to the Philippines as part of the U.S. economic aid program were outfitted with machine guns, and others were used to ferry troops to fight Muslim rebels. But a Philippine official explained that it was all a matter of semantics, since the Philippine government considered "peace and order" part of its development program.[122] The public safety program provided advice and equipment to the police forces of the martial law regime in its first year. Six of the eight advisers were veterans of post-1965 Vietnam or Laos, where one can be sure they were not just helping to direct traffic.[123]

The labor programs established with AID money demonstrated their commitment to free and democratic trade unionism by their post–martial law activities. The Asian Labor Education Center sponsored training sessions and forums designed to teach "labor union executives" their new role in the "New Society," where strikes were prohibited. And the Asian-American Free Labor Institute sent two experts to Manila to train arbitrators, now that Philippine labor relations were confined to compulsory arbitration. In the meantime, Marcos was arresting militant trade union leaders.[124]

Postscript

In January 1981, as this book goes to press, Ferdinand Marcos proclaimed that he was lifting martial law.[125] The goals of martial law, he declared, had been accomplished, and it was now time to return to normality.

In fact, however, the New Society has been a failure in terms of virtually every one of its announced objectives. Corruption is rampant,[126] living standards have declined, 60 percent of children remain malnourished,[127] tax reform has been stillborn, the country's foreign debt has grown five-fold since 1971,[128] flagrant abuses by the military add to the continuing abuse of the poor by the rich,[129] the fighting in the south has claimed some 60,000 lives with no end yet in sight,[130] and the New People's Army is gaining in influence.[131]

Not accomplishment but a deteriorating social base accounts for Marcos's January 1981 proclamation. Church leaders were becoming increasingly critical of martial law and its excesses, and some moderate opponents were turning to bombings.[132] Externally, there was heightening alarm in the international financial community about the future stability of the country,[133] and the U.S. government in particular had visions of a growing radicalization and a collapse like that in Iran.[134] There was thus considerable pressure on Marcos to broaden the base of his regime and restore foreign confidence. The lifting of martial law was an effort by Marcos to do this, though without fundamentally lessening his power.

In the present situation of no martial law, all of the more than 1,000 decrees issued by Marcos remain in force unless modified by him or by the National Assembly.[135] (The current interim National Assembly was chosen in rigged elections in 1978 and contains but a handful of oppositionists.[136]) Marcos retains the right to order arrests without charge, legislate by decree, overrule or dissolve the Assembly, and ratify treaties. Strikes are still banned.[137] Marcos has promised to hold a presidential election, but it would be astonishing if this were any less dishonest than the others held under martial law.[138] In any event, Marcos has used the martial law period to so weaken the power of his elite opponents that it is doubtful that they could muster the resources necessary to mount an effective challenge.[139]

The U.S. attitude was suggested by two incidents in the closing days of the Carter administration. A State Department official advised the Philippine opposition to accept Marcos's lifting of martial law as a "generous offer" and to forswear violence, and President-Elect Ronald Reagan made the single exception to his rule of receiving no foreign leaders before his inauguration for Imelda Marcos.[140]

So, despite the formal end of martial law, authoritarian rule seems likely to continue in the Philippines—and with the backing of the United States.

Neocolonialism and the Philippines

On July 4, 1946, formal U.S. sovereignty over the Philippines came to an end. But although the American flag was pulled down, the Philippines remained subordinate to U.S. domination. More accurately, the great majority of Filipinos remained subordinate to a neocolonial alliance between the Philippine elite and Washington.

To say that colonialism was replaced by neocolonialism is not to suggest that the two relationships are equivalent. The latter gives the Philippines more freedom to maneuver; it can play great powers off against one another, it can join regional pacts, it can garner support in international organizations. Neocolonialism also places greater constraints upon the actions of the United States. American personnel may be stationed in the Philippines only with Manila's consent, U.S. intervention in Philippine affairs cannot be too overt, and U.S. officials must take pains not to offend Philippine sovereignty and nationalism. In short, even if the only difference between the colonial and the neocolonial relationships was a legal one—the specific locus of sovereignty—this difference can have a significant effect on the behavior of nation-states.

But the discontinuities occasioned by the achieving of formal independence can be exaggerated, and in this study I have tried to draw attention to the considerable similarities between colonial and neocolonial rule. The similarities are all the more striking, in fact, when it is realized that many of the options and constraints of the neocolonial period were present before independence as well.

In the 1930s Manila leaders tried to steer a course between the

United States and Japan—they did not wait until independence.[1] The U.S. share of foreign investment in the Philippines was actually lower before World War II than in 1970.[2] American officials had to be as sensitive to Philippine national pride before 1946 as after, as the diaries of colonial administrators attest.[3] And the use of covert funds to manipulate Philippine opinion was not a tactic unique to the postindependence period.[4]

While the United States had a military position in the prewar Philippines shared by no other power, it had similarly exclusive military rights after the war—and almost as many U.S. troops were stationed in the Philippines in 1969 (26,000) as U.S. troops (20,575) plus Philippine Scouts (12,000) a week before Pearl Harbor.[5] To take another example, Washington's support for Marcos in 1972 after he abolished formal democratic procedures was but a repetition of the decision by U.S. officials to support Quezon before World War II, even though they considered him a dictator.[6]

There have certainly been changes in the relationship between the United States and the Philippines, but it is difficult to attribute these to the fact of Philippine independence. There had been incremental U.S. concessions to Philippine nationalism before 1946, and there have been incremental concessions since then. Most government functions were under Philippine control by 1935; the peso remained tied to the value of the dollar until 1955. The distribution of Manila's foreign trade shifted in the mid-1950s from its exclusive dependence on the United States, and the source of the Philippines' new foreign investment did not begin to shift until the 1970s. It was the changing relative strength of the Japanese and American economies, not independence, that accounted for the latter shifts.

Even the first stages of industrialization that took place in the 1950s in the Philippines cannot be ascribed to the fact of independence. The growth of Philippine industry, economists generally agree, occurred as a consequence of the import and exchange controls imposed by Manila. But these were imposed with the approval of the U.S. president, as required by the Bell Trade Act. Washington was willing to permit the introduction of controls in order to prevent the total collapse of the Philippine economy. There is no reason to suspect that the U.S. government would not have had the same concern and allowed the same controls had the Philippines still been a colony.

The United States did not abandon formal sovereignty over the Philippines because it considered neocolonialism the equivalent of colonialism. Rather, it did so because colonialism was not a live option for U.S. policy. The United States could not pressure other nations to dismantle their extensive empires if Washington retained the Philippines. And Filipinos—who had fought the first guerrilla war in Asia against Western imperialism half a century before— would not long submit to the continued denial of their most basic rights. In 1946 neocolonialism had a deceptive attraction to colonial peoples. In the villages of Indochina, reported the U.S. Office of Strategic Services, the peasants wanted nothing more than to have independence like the Philippines.[7] Ho Chi Minh himself asked the United States to support Annamese independence according to the Philippine example.[8] In the postwar era of nationalism, neocolonialism was the one viable form of imperial domination.

Although I have argued throughout this book that the alliance between the U.S. elite and the Philippine elite has been a fundamental aspect of the neocolonial relationship, nowhere have I implied that the interests of the two elites have been identical. On the contrary, Washington had many serious qualms about its Philippine partners—the collaborationist background of the Roxas supporters, the unparalleled corruption of the Quirino administration, the inability or unwillingness of any Philippine president to blunt the rapacity of the wealthy minority, and the abrogation of democratic forms by Marcos in 1972. But more significant than Washington's qualms has been the fact that the United States has invariably chosen to support the Philippine elite despite the qualms, because only by so doing could the United States guarantee its own economic and strategic interests.

To be sure, everything else being equal, U.S. officials would have preferred that those Filipinos who backed American interests were also humane, enlightened, and incorruptible—not because U.S. officials were necessarily at a higher moral level than Philippine leaders, but because the corruption and social backwardness of the latter were of no advantage to Washington. In any case, given the reality of the situation, Washington has always been forced to make a choice between those who would defend both U.S. interests and elite privilege and those who would challenge the status quo in all its aspects. It has not been coincidental that those who cared most about the welfare of the Philippine people were not powerful advocates of "parity," foreign investment, or military bases; Philippine leaders who both supported U.S. interests and favored fundamental social change simply did not exist. So the United States backed the elite after the war—despite misgivings regarding collaboration—for fear of leaving an opening for the Democratic Alliance. For all of Washington's low regard for Quirino, the

United States salvaged his regime to forestall a Huk victory. And despite the embarrassment that martial law has created for the United States on the issue of human rights, the United States clearly decided to back Marcos.

Even the American support for Magsaysay was no exception. Preserving the old political system and placing Magsaysay at the head of it was not a strategy likely to reduce the wide disparities of wealth and power in Philippine society. Magsaysay was a new *style* political leader, but his programs did nothing to reduce the power and privilege of the few. From Washington's point of view, it was better to have cosmetic reforms under an indisputably pro-American regime than real reforms under a government less favorably disposed to U.S. interests.

Misgivings have operated in the opposite direction as well. The Philippine elite would clearly prefer not to be the junior partners in the neocolonial relationship, not to have to share control of the Philippine economy with U.S. corporations or control over the instruments of coercion with the officers of JUSMAG. But the elite's desire for autonomy has always been exceeded by its need for Washington's assistance: military aid to suppress insurrection and economic aid to pacify the poor.

So the U.S. elite and the Philippine elite do not by any means have identical interests. But the reciprocal benefits to each of them from the neocolonial relationship have been substantial enough to maintain that relationship for over thirty years.

Studies of modern imperialism often focus on the social and economic impact of the multinational corporation, covering such issues as balance of payments effects, employment, and transfer of technology. But aside from being quite difficult to measure, these kinds of consequences of U.S.-based multinationals are only of secondary importance in the Philippines. Far more important than, for example, the relative capital intensity of U.S. versus local firms is the fact that U.S. capital has sought a business environment in which the opportunities for profit-making are maximized. To this end, U.S. investors wanted "parity" rights in 1946 and responded enthusiastically to martial law in 1972. And the U.S. government gave powerful support to American business interests, tying rehabilitation funds to Philippine acceptance of "parity" and sharply increasing its aid to Marcos after he imposed martial law. In general, in order to maintain in the Philippines a climate as conducive as possible to foreign investment, the U.S. government has strongly backed the status quo and opposed movements directed toward fundamental social change. And by preserving the status quo, Washington has consigned the majority of Filipinos to continuing poverty and oppression.

Advocates of the multinational corporation like to point out that a more equitable income distribution in developing nations is not contrary to the interests of foreign firms, for there would then be a larger market for the goods these firms produce. But public policies which might reduce inequality tend to be precisely those policies that restrict the freedom of corporations to do as they choose: high taxes, antitrust legislation, controls on foreign exchange, promotion of strong unions, and so on. Accordingly, when the U.S. government pressures Manila to eliminate exchange controls, initiates labor programs aimed at taming Philippine trade unions, or provides Marcos with the military supplies that make possible his continued dictatorial rule, there are no complaints from the business community, no charges of a "foreign-aid giveaway."

The indictment against U.S. corporations in the Philipines, then, is not based primarily on the particular way in which they conduct their operations—although there is much that can be said on this score.[9] Rather, the major charge against the corporations is their eagerness for a sound business climate, for stability, for the status quo, for martial law. And by aiding in the preservation of this favorable business environment, the U.S. government shares responsibility for the consequences—the poverty, the malnutrition, and the absence of freedom.

Nothing in the writing of this book has given me the ability to predict the future. There are too many imponderables—the strength of Marcos's opposition, the mood of the American Congress, even the health of Marcos—to allow any serious projection of what will happen in the Philippines. But this much can be said: as long as the neocolonial relationship continues, as long as the United States, out of concern for its own economic and strategic interests, backs the Philippine elite, the future for the great mass of the Philippine people will not be very bright.

═NOTES═

Abbreviations for manuscript collections are listed in Section I-A of the Bibliography. Other abbreviations used in the notes are listed below. All government documents cited are U.S. government documents unless otherwise specified.

ADB	Asian Development Bank, Manila
AFP	Armed Forces of the Philippines
AFPAC	Army Forces, Pacific (U.S.)
AFWESPAC	Army Forces in the Western Pacific (U.S.)
AID	Agency for International Development (U.S.)
BCS	Bureau of the Census and Statistics (Philippines)
CFA	U.S. House Committee on Foreign Affairs
CFR	U.S. Senate Committee on Foreign Relations
CIA	Central Intelligence Agency (U.S.)
CIC	Counter Intelligence Corps (U.S. Army)
CIR	U.S. House Committee on International Relations
Cong.	U.S. Congress
CWM	U.S. House Committee on Ways and Means
Doc.	Document
DSB	U.S. *Department of State Bulletin*
FAA	Foreign Assistance Act (U.S.)
FARAA	Foreign Assistance and Related Agencies Appropriations (U.S.)
FARPA	Foreign Assistance and Related Programs Appropriations (U.S.)
FR	*Foreign Relations of the United States*
GAO	General Accounting Office (U.S.)
HCAp	U.S. House Committee on Appropriations
HCAS	U.S. House Committee on Armed Services
HR or H.	House of Representatives
ICA	International Cooperation Administration (U.S.)
ILO	International Labour Office, Geneva
JCS	Joint Chiefs of Staff (U.S.)
JUSMAG	Joint U.S. Military Advisory Group
MSA	Mutual Security Act (U.S.)

NEDA	National Economic and Development Authority (Philippines)
NSC	National Security Council (U.S.)
NYT	*New York Times*
OPS	Office of Public Safety, Agency for International Development (U.S.)
OSS	Office of Strategic Services (U.S.)
PFP	*Philippines Free Press*
Phil. *Cong. Rec.*	Philippine *Congressional Record*
PPP	*Public Papers of the Presidents of the United States*
RG	Record Group
RP	Republic of the Philippines
SCAp	U.S. Senate Committee on Appropriations
Sen.	Senate
sess.	session
TIAS	*Treaties and Other International Agreements Series*
U.S. *Cong. Rec.*	U.S. *Congressional Record*
U.S. Stat.	*United States Statutes at Large*

Introduction

1. *PPP*, Nixon, 1969, p. 546.

2. *NYT,* 26 July 1969, pp. 1, 8; *Washington Post,* 26 July 1969, pp. A1, A14. Reporters were not permitted to quote Nixon's words directly, but there is no reason they could not have asked him to clarify his remarks.

3. *The Times* (London), 21 March 1964, cited in Jack Woddis, *Introduction to Neo-Colonialism* (New York: International Publishers, 1967), p. 11.

4. Woddis, *Introduction,* p. 23.

5. I discuss the colonial period at greater length in my "U.S.-Philippine Relations: A Study of Neo-Colonialism" (Ph.D. dissertation, Boston University, 1976), chap. 2.

6. See, e.g., W. Cameron Forbes to William H. Taft, 13 November 1909, and W. Cameron Forbes to Frank W. Carpenter, 2 March 1910, both in WCF Papers, fms am 1366.1, vol. 1; Henry L. Stimson and McGeorge Bundy, *On Active Service in Peace and War* (New York: Harper & Bros., 1948), p. 128.

7. *Fifth Annual Report of the United States High Commissioner to the Philippine Islands, Covering the Fiscal Year Ending 30 June 1941,* 31 July 1942 (Washington, D.C.: Government Printing Office, 1943), p. 34.

8. William J. Pomeroy, *American Neo-Colonialism: Its Emergence in the Philippines and Asia* (New York: International Publishers, 1970), pp. 198, 203; Daniel B. Schirmer, "The Conception and Gestation of a Neo-Colony," Paper read at the Conference of Asian Studies on the Pacific Coast, San Diego, 14–16 June 1974, p. 5.

9. See Grayson L. Kirk, *Philippine Independence: Motives, Problems, and Prospects* (New York: Farrar & Rinehart, 1936); Theodore Friend, *Between*

Two Empires: The Ordeal of the Philippines, 1929–1946 (New Haven: Yale University Press, 1965), chaps. 5–7.

Chapter One: The Restoration, 1944–1946

1. Laurence E. Salisbury, "Brief Biographical Sketches of the 24 Nominees for Senator of the Nationalist Party," Enclosure no. 7 to dispatch of 25 August 1941 by Salisbury entitled "Convention of the Nationalist Party," FBS Papers, box 9, Philippines, Personnel File; OSS, Research and Analysis Branch, R & A no. 2634, *Philippine Collaborators,* 15 February 1945, DSNA; Charles Parsons to Manuel Quezon, 27 September 1943, pp. 14ff., CW Papers, box 16, folder 63.

2. For example, Aurello Alvero, who was charged after the war with founding or drafting articles of association for a number of pro-Japanese organizations during the occupation, with sending a letter to President Laurel praising the declaration of war against the United States, with donating money and offering his services to the Japanese, with trying to persuade guerrillas to surrender, and with setting up a buy-and-sell firm, claimed that he had sympathized with and given positive assistance to the guerrillas (*Manila Times,* 3 December 1945, p. 10).

3. David J. Steinberg, *Philippine Collaboration in World War II* (Ann Arbor: University of Michigan Press, 1967), p. 63; David J. Steinberg, "Jose P. Laurel: A Collaborator Misunderstood," *Journal of Asian Studies,* 24, no. 4 (August 1965), pp. 652, 652 n.7.

4. Steinberg, "Laurel," p. 659; OSS, Research and Analysis Branch, R & A no. 2330, "Law Enforcement in the Philippine Islands," 25 September 1944, in *The Philippines: Section 14, Public Safety,* Army Civil Affairs Handbook, p. 65, DSNA; A. H. Peterson, G. C. Reinhardt, and E. E. Conger, eds., *Symposium on the Role of Airpower in Counter-insurgency and Unconventional Warfare: Allied Resistance to the Japanese on Luzon, World War II,* RM-3655-PR (Santa Monica: Rand Corporation, July 1963), p. 29. See also Joyce C. Lebra, *Japanese-Trained Armies in Southeast Asia* (New York: Columbia University Press, 1977), pp. 140–45. The Japanese did conscript 14,000 Japanese nationals living in the Philippines in September 1944, and they organized a force of some 3,000 to 5,000 Filipino volunteers, few of whom saw combat.

5. D. Clayton James, *The Years of MacArthur,* vol. 1, *1880–1941* (Boston: Houghton Mifflin, 1970), p. 544; Rōyama Masamichi and Takéuchi Tatsuji, *The Philippine Polity: A Japanese View,* ed. Theodore Friend, Southeast Asia Studies, Monograph Series no. 12 (New Haven: Yale University, 1967), p. 277.

6. Renze L. Hoeksema, "Communism in the Philippines: A Historical and Analytical Study of Communism and the Communist Party in the Philippines and Its Relations to Communist Movements Abroad" (Ph.D. dissertation, Harvard University, 1956), p. 250.

7. Benedict J. Kerkvliet, "Peasant Rebellion in the Philippines: The Origins and Growth of the HMB" (Ph.D. dissertation, University of Wisconsin, 1972), pp. 94–203; Charles O. Houston, Jr., "The Philippine Sugar Industry, 1934–1950," *Journal of East Asiatic Studies* (University of Manila), 3, no. 4 (July–October 1954), p. 394; Military Police Command, AFWESPAC, G-2, "Military Organization of the Hukbalahaps," 20 December 1945, p. 6, RG 319, box 663; OSS, Research and Analysis Branch, R & A no. 760, *Survey of the Philippine Islands*, 10 July 1942 (2d ed., 1 November 1943), DSNA, p. 73.

8. Kerkvliet, "Peasant," pp. 247–48; Benedict J. Kerkvliet, *The Huk Rebellion: A Study of Peasant Revolt in the Philippines* (Berkeley: University of California Press, 1977), pp. 99, 102.

9. Boyd T. Bashore, "Dual Strategy for Limited War," in Franklin Mark Osanka, ed., *Modern Guerrilla Warfare* (New York: Free Press of Glencoe, 1962), p. 191; A. H. Peterson, G. C. Reinhardt, and E. E. Conger, eds., *Symposium on the Role of Airpower in Counter-insurgency and Unconventional Warfare: the Philippine Huk Campaign*, RM-3652-PR (Santa Monica: Rand Corporation, June 1963), pp. 2, 4.

10. Kerkvliet, *Huk Rebellion*, p. 87; Edward G. Lansdale, *In the Midst of Wars: An American's Mission to Southeast Asia* (New York: Harper & Row, 1972), p. 7.

11. Kerkvliet, "Peasant," pp. 318–19.

12. F. L. Worcester, Report No. 45, 16 May 1946, transmitted with Paul Steintorf to Secretary of State, 23 May 1946, DSNA 811B.00/5-2346. (Worcester was a special assistant with the office of the high commissioner; all his reports were transmitted with Steintorf's dispatches to the secretary of state on the date indicated after the slash of the DSNA number [month, dash, day, year]. Hereafter Worcester's reports will be cited without reference to the Steintorf dispatches.) Richard M. Leighton, Ralph Sanders, and Jose N. Tinio, *The Huk Rebellion: A Case Study in the Social Dynamics of Insurrection*, Pub. No. R-231 (Washington, D.C: Industrial College of the Armed Forces, March 1964), pp. 43, 51–52 (section written by Tinio, a Philippine military attaché). See also the account of a violently anti-Huk American priest who proudly acknowledges USAFFE-Japanese collaboration against the Huks: Forbes J. Monaghan, *Under the Red Sun: A Letter from Manila* (New York: Declan X. McMullen Co., 1946), p. 144.

13. Kerkvliet, "Peasant," p. 259; Kerkvliet, *Huk Rebellion*, pp. 105–6; Robert Ross Smith, "The Hukbalahap Insurgency: Economic, Political, and Military Factors," photocopied (Washington, D.C.: Office of the Chief of Military History, Department of the Army, 1963), p. 57; *Manila Times*, 26 August 1945, p. 8; Violet E. Wurfel, "American Implementation of Philippine Independence" (Ph.D. dissertation, University of Virginia, 1951), pp. 455–56; 441st CIC, AFPAC, "Monthly Information Report," October 1945, Appendix V, p. A-40, RG 407 (quote).

14. Quoted in Charles Willoughby and John Chamberlain, *MacArthur, 1941–1951* (New York: McGraw-Hill, 1954), p. 239.

15. Teodoro A. Agoncillo, *A Short History of the Philippines* (New York: Mentor Books, 1969), p. 199; James, *Years of MacArthur*, vol. 1, p. 482.

16. James, *Years of MacArthur*, vol. 1, pp. 296–97, 333, 555, 563, 573; Quezon to MacArthur, 18 April 1944, DAM Papers, RG 4, box 2, Correspondence, Philippine Government nos. 100–199; Douglas MacArthur, *Reminiscences* (New York: McGraw-Hill, 1964), p. 140; James K. Eyre, Jr., *The Roosevelt-MacArthur Conflict* (Chambersburg, Pa.: Craft Press, 1950), p. 172; Theodore Friend, *Between Two Empires: The Ordeal of the Philippines, 1929–1946* (New Haven: Yale University Press, 1965), p. 78.

17. Hotel: James, *Years of MacArthur*, vol. 1, p. 560. Soriano firms: Hernando J. Abaya, *Betrayal in the Philippines* (New York: A. A. Wyn Co., 1946), p. 172 n.5. D. Clayton James has found no evidence either way regarding investments in Soriano's firms (*The Years of MacArthur*, vol. 2, *1941–1945* [Boston: Houghton Mifflin, 1975], p. 892 n.13), but the following facts lend support to Abaya's claim: (1) MacArthur acknowledged that he owned "some shares of [Philippine] mining stock bought on the stock exchange as investment many years before the war" (*Manila Times*, 3 April 1946, p. 5). (2) If MacArthur had owned Soriano stock, it is unlikely that he would have left behind evidence of this, given that a supporter had warned him that a left-wing newspaper was hunting for derogatory information on him, especially on his financial ties to Soriano (L. Lehrbas to MacArthur, 4 January 1946, DAM Papers, RG 5, box 1A, file 1, 28 July 1945 to 28 June 1946). See also Eyre, *Roosevelt-MacArthur Conflict*, p. 110; Clark Lee and Richard Henschel, *Douglas MacArthur* (New York: Henry Holt & Co., 1952), p. 82.

18. "Memorandum on Andres Soriano," 17 July 1943, 27 July 1943, and Report of the Intelligence Division, headquarters, Philippine Department, enclosed with J. Weldon Jones to Secretary of State, 10 August 1939, all in RG 126, box 52, File: Soriano, Commonwealth, 1942–45.

19. Friend, *Between Two Empires*, pp. 115, 117, 118 n.36; Sumner Welles to Woodring, 27 July 1937, copy to McNutt, RG 126, box 52, File: Soriano, Commonwealth, 1942–45.

20. Sidney Reitman to Harold Ickes, 13 November 1945, RG 126, box 770, file no. 9-7-30, Politics-General (Reitman, Sidney—Correspondence); Friend, *Between Two Empires*, pp. 229–30; Quezon to MacArthur, 8 October 1943, and MacArthur to R. K. Sutherland, 29 October 1943, DAM Papers, RG 4, box 2, Correspondence, Philippine Government nos. 1–99; "Memorandum for Record, 1 October 1944, Subject: Request That Col. Andres Soriano not be placed on duty in the Philippines," RG 165, OPD 210.1 (28 September 1944); Paul Steintorf to Secretary of State, 13 August 1945, DSNA 811B.00/8-1345; Abaya, *Betrayal*, p. 166.,

21. William Manchester, *American Caesar: Douglas MacArthur, 1880–1964* (New York: Dell, 1978), p. 203 (Sutherland); James, *Years of MacArthur*, vol. 2, p. 668; Willoughby to Walter Bedell Smith, 15 January 1951, WBS Papers, 1951 Personal Correspondence, "W" file.

22. Manchester, *American Caesar*, pp. 439, 442; Quezon to MacArthur, 28 September 1943, DAM Papers, RG 4, Correspondence, Philippine Government nos. 1–99. See also Carlos Quirino, *Quezon: Paladin of Philippine Freedom* (Manila: Filipiniana Book Guild, 1971), pp. 364, 382 n.373.

23. Carol M. Petillo, "Douglas MacArthur and Manuel Quezon: A Note on an Imperial Bond," *Pacific Historical Review*, 48, no. 1 (February 1979): passim, but esp. pp. 107–9, 110 (Roxas), 114–15 (Washington's knowledge).

24. *DSB*, 2 July 1944, p. 17.

25. *FR* 1942, vol. 1, pp. 883–84.

26. *Seventh and Final Report of the High Commissioner to the Philippines*, 14 September 1945 to 4 July 1946, printed as H. Doc. 389, 80th Cong., 1st sess., 8 July 1947, p. 5 (hereafter cited as *7th and Final Report*); *FR* 1945, vol. 6, pp. 1195–96; *Manila Free Philippines*, 23 August 1945, p. 1.

27. Text in U.S. *Cong. Rec.*, 27 November 1944, p. A4515.

28. Quoted in Abaya, *Betrayal*, pp. 217–18, who states that the officer had been a mining broker in Manila before the war.

29. Intelligence Report, Headquarters, 6th Service Command, ASF, 29 December 1945, Subject: Hukbalahap, Source: Walter Humboldt, p. 2, RG 226, XL 34731; Kenneth M. Hammer, "Huks in the Philippines," in Osanka, *Modern Guerrilla Warfare*, p. 179; U.S. *Cong. Rec.*, 1 August 1946, p. A4721 (statement of American Veterans of the Philippine Campaign); R. R. Smith, "Hukbalahap Insurgency," p. 52.

30. Kerkvliet, "Peasant," p. 377. For the intelligence warnings, see B. Cabangbang to MacArthur, NR 86, 29 October 1944, CW Papers, box 20, Cabangbang—Central Luzon file; General Headquarters, AFPAC, Military Intelligence Section, General Staff, *The Guerrilla Resistance Movement in the Philippines*, prepared during the campaign, initially issued 31 March 1945, corrections made from data available since first issue 1948, vol. 1, p. 12, but cf. p. 13 (unpublished document available at Fort McNair, Washington, D.C.). Cabangbang's reports merely repeated USAFFE anti-Huk propaganda and were largely incorrect. *Guerrilla Resistance* relies heavily on Cabangbang, and although it was supposedly brought up-to-date in 1948, it still states that the Huks would probably be a problem during the reoccupation (future tense).

31. F. L. Worcester, Report No. 15, 28 January 1946, DSNA 811B.00/1-3146; R. R. Smith, "Hukbalahap Insurgency," pp. 54–55; Kerkvliet, "Peasant," pp. 356–57, 366.

32. Kerkvliet, "Peasant," pp. 703–5.

33. 441st CIC, "Monthly Activities Report," February 1945, p. 44, exhibit III, pp. A-22-23, RG 407; 441st CIC, "Monthly Information Report," October 1945, p. 84, RG 407; Headquarters, 1135th CIC, AFWESPAC, "Hukbalahap," 24 October 1946, appendix 6, RG 319; Intelligence Report, Headquarters, 6th Service Command, ASF, 29 December 1945, Subject: Hukbalahap, Source: Walter Humboldt, p. 5, RG 226, XL 34731; R. R.

Smith, "Hukbalahap Insurgency," p. 54; "Military Organization of the Huk-balahap," p. 8; Eduardo Lachica, *The Huks: Philippine Agrarian Society in Revolt* (New York: Praeger, 1971), p. 116; Kerkvliet, "Peasant," pp. 379–83; Kerk-vliet, *Huk Rebellion*, pp. 111–13; *Manila Times*, 30 May 1946, pp. 1, 8.

34. MacArthur's handwritten comments on Courtney Whitney to Mac-Arthur, 20 February 1945, CW Papers, box 13, SWPA, AIB [Southwest Pacific Area, Allied Intelligence Bureau], Philippine Guerrilla, Hukbalahaps file. The document does not make explicit which guerrillas are being re-ferred to, the Huks or all irregular units. See also Manchester, *American Caesar*, pp. 488–89.

35. *Manila Times*, 15 July 1945, p. 2.

36. R. R. Smith, "Hukbalahap Insurgency," pp. 55–56; Ismael D. La-pus, "The Communist Huk Enemy," in Department of Defense, *Counter-Guerrilla Operations in the Philippines, 1946–1953: A Seminar on the Huk Cam-paign Held at Ft. Bragg, N.C., 15 June 1961* (n.p., n.d.), p. 15.

37. Houston, "Sugar Industry," pp. 387–88.

38. *Manila Times*, 5 August 1945, p. 1; F. L. Worcester, Report No. 1, 7 January 1946, DSNA 811B.00/1-1546. In September, Montelibano was also made secretary of the interior (*Manila Times*, 27 September 1945, p. 1).

39. Teodoro A. Agoncillo, *The Fateful Years: Japan's Adventure in the Philippines, 1941–1945* (Quezon City: Garcia, 1965), opp. p. 862; *NYT*, 31 December 1944, p. 14.

40. CIA, "Possible Developments Resulting from the Granting of Am-nesty to Accused Collaborators in the Philippines," ORE 11-48, 28 April 1948, p. 5, RG 319 MMR, P & O 350.05, case 302; George E. Taylor, *The Philippines and the United States: Problems of Partnership* (New York: Praeger, 1964), p. 118; Agaton Pal, "The Philippines," in Richard D. Lambert and Bert F. Hoselitz, eds., *The Role of Savings and Wealth in Southern Asia and the West* (Paris: UNESCO, 1963), p. 327; Courtney Whitney, *MacArthur: His Rendezvous with History* (New York: Knopf, 1956), pp. 179–80. The "contem-porary" cited is Walter Wilgus, "MacArthur Campaign Promises Early Inde-pendence for Filipinos," *Foreign Policy Bulletin*, 24, no. 14 (19 January 1945), p. 3.

41. *Manila Free Philippines*, 18 April 1945, p. 1.

42. Abaya, *Betrayal*, pp. 167, 170; David Bernstein, *The Philippine Story* (New York: Farrar, Straus & Co., 1947), p. 240.

43. Steinberg, *Collaboration*, p. 183 n.40; Dale Pontius, "MacArthur and the Filipinos," part 1, *Asia and the Americas*, 46, no. 10 (October 1946), p. 438; Friend, *Between Two Empires*, pp. 238–41; Claro Recto's comment in A. V. H. Hartendorp, *Short History of Industry and Trade of the Philippines* (Ma-nila: American Chamber of Commerce of the Philippines, 1953), p. 97; *7th and Final Report*, p. 7; Agoncillo, *Fateful Years*, pp. 559–60; Garel A. Grunder and William E. Livezey, *The Philippines and the United States* (Nor-man: University of Oklahoma Press, 1951), p. 255; Abaya, *Betrayal*, p. 65; OSS, Research and Analysis Branch, R & A no. 1752.1 *Personnel of the Philippine Puppet Government*, 1 November 1944, DSNA, p. 2.

44. Minutes of the meeting of the Cabinet and the Council of State that approved declaration of war on the United States and Britain, "The Puppet Declaration of War," *Philippine Press*, 15 July 1945, enclosure no. 1 to dispatch no. 205, 17 July 1945, RG 126, Roxas, Manuel, 1945–47, part A file.

45. General Staff, Supreme Commander for the Allied Powers, *Reports of General MacArthur*, vol. 1, *The Campaigns of MacArthur in the Pacific*, prepared by MacArthur's Tokyo headquarters in 1950 (Washington, D.C.: U.S. Government Printing Office, 1966), p. 266 n.77; General Headquarters, AFPAC, Military Intelligence Section, General Staff, *Intelligence Activities in the Philippines During the Japanese Occupation* (Intelligence Series, G-2, USAFFE-SWPA-AFPAC-FEC-SCA, vol. 11), 1948 edition, expansion and revision by Major General Courtney A. Whitney, et al., vol. 1, pp. 89–90, in RG 407, boxes 679–80 (hereafter cited as *Intelligence Activities*). The out-of-the-blue mention of Roxas in these sources prepared by MacArthur's staff gives one the strong feeling that they exaggerate Roxas's intelligence activities because of postwar political considerations.

46. *Intelligence Activities*, vol. 1, pp. 78 n.1, 89–90; *Manila Times*, 27 February 1946, p. 1; Marcial P. Lichauco, *Roxas* (Manila: Kiho Printing Press, 1952), pp. 185, 192; F. Mangahas, "The Story of Roxas: The War Years," pp. 5, 11, JWJ Papers, box 14, Government of the Philippine Islands, 1941–47 file; Abaya, *Betrayal*, pp. 66–67; Bernstein, *Philippine Story*, p. 165.

47. M. P. Lichauco, *Roxas*, p. 175; Rōyama and Takéuchi, *Philippine Polity*, p. 257.

48. Friend, *Between Two Empires*, p. 249; Paul Steintorf to Secretary of State, 2 May 1945, DSNA 811B.00/5-245; Abaya, *Betrayal*, p. 99; M. P. Lichauco, *Roxas*, p. 195.

49. Steinberg, *Collaboration*, p. 115.

50. Roxas: OSS, Research and Analysis Branch, R & A no. 1752.2, *Status of the Philippine Puppet Government as of 14 October 1944*, 14 October 1944, DSNA, pp. 4–5; Other arrestees: e.g., *Intelligence Activities*, vol. 1, p. 24.

51. Petillo, "MacArthur and Quezon," pp. 110, 116; Paul Steintorf to Secretary of State, 23 May 1945, DSNA 811B.00/5-2345; Paul Steintorf to Secretary of State, 16 June 1945, DSNA 811B.00/6-1645; Bonner Fellers and Andres Soriano, "Report on Activities Related to Manuel Roxas," Memorandum for the Commander-in-Chief, 29 March 1945, DAM Papers, RG 3, box 8, Military Secretary File 1.

52. Paul Steintorf to Secretary of State, 25 April 1945, DSNA 811B.00/4-2545; Friend, *Between Two Empires*, pp. 248, 250–51; Bernard Seeman and Laurence Salisbury, *Crosscurrents in the Philippines* (New York: Institute of Pacific Relations, 1946), p. 43.

53. Bernstein, *Philippine Story*, pp. 206–7; Steinberg, *Collaboration*, pp. 115–16; Walter R. Hutchinson to Attorney General Tom C. Clark, "Preliminary Report on the Progress of the Investigation and Trial of Collabora-

tionists by the Commonwealth Government of the Philippines and Recommendations for Immediate Action by the United States Government," 28 January 1946 (Department of Justice, unpublished), p. 19 (hereafter cited as Hutchinson Report).

54. Harry S. Truman, *Memoirs*, vol. 1, *Years of Decision* (Garden City, N.Y.: Doubleday & Co., 1955), p. 276; *U.S. Stat.*, vol. 58, pt. 1, pp. 625–26; U.S. *Cong. Rec.*, 20 September 1944, pp. A4167–68; 27 November 1944, pp. A4523–24; 20 April 1945, p. A1871.

55. Henry L. Stimson, Memorandum of a meeting at the White House, 19 April 1945, HLS Papers, box 172; *Manila Times*, 13 June 1945, p. 12.

56. *Manila Times*, 20 September 1945; Department of State, Interim Research and Intelligence Service, Research and Analysis Branch, R & A no. 3269, *Recent Developments in Philippine-American Relations*, 5 October 1945, DSNA, p. 2, citing the *Washington Post;* OSS, Research and Analysis Branch, *Situation Report: the Far East, Philippines, China, and NEI*, 2 April 1945, in Committee Print, *The Amerasia Papers: A Clue to the Catastrophe of China*, Senate Judiciary Committee subcommittee, 91st Cong., 1st sess., 26 January 1970, p. 1582 (OSS report hereafter cited as OSS, *Situation Report*); A. L. Moffat to Acheson, 27 December 1945, DSNA 811B.01/12-2645. On 17 January 1946, Acheson cabled the U.S. Embassy in Moscow asking to be kept informed of Soviet press comment on the Philippines—indicating U.S. concern with avoiding charges of imperialism (DSNA 811B.00/1-1746).

57. Truman, *Memoirs*, vol. 1, p. 275; OSS, *Situation Report*, pp. 1579–81; *Manila Free Philippines*, 26 March 1945, p. 1; W. Willoughby to Clayton, 26 September 1945, DSNA 611.11B31/9-2645.

58. U.S. *Cong. Rec.*, 20 April 1945, p. A1871; *Manila Times*, 10 June 1945, p. 2. Re MacArthur, see Bernstein, *Philippine Story*, p. 209; Steinberg, *Collaboration*, pp. 118–19.

59. Paul McNutt and Abe Fortas, Memorandum for the President, 29 September 1945, RG 126, Atty Gen. Mission (Collaboration) file. Other sources state that there were fifteen senators.

60. *Manila Times*, 10 June 1945, p. 12.

61. *Manila Times*, 10 June 1945, p. 12; 24 June 1945, p. 2; *Daily News* (Manila), 6 September 1945, enclosed with Paul Steintorf to Secretary of State, 6 September 1945, DSNA 811B.00/9-645.

62. *Manila Times*, 11 September 1945, pp. 1, 4; Paul Steintorf to Secretary of State, 24 August 1945, RG 226, XL-17117; *FR* 1945, vol. 6, pp. 1231–32; Department of State, Interim Research and Intelligence Service, Research and Analysis Branch, *Recent Developments* (as cited in note 56, above), p. 6; Steinberg, *Collaboration*, p. 124.

63. *Manila Times*, 6 October 1945, pp. 1, 8; 7 October 1945, p. 1; 9 October 1945, p. 1; 10 October 1945, p. 1; 5 December 1945, p. 1; F. L. Worcester, Report No. 34, 22 March 1946, DSNA 811B.00/3-2746; V. E. Wurfel, "American Implementation," p. 179 n.55; Steinberg, *Collaboration*, p. 141; Abaya, *Betrayal*, pp. 226–27.

64. *Manila Times,* 14 October 1945, p. 1.

65. Phil. *Cong. Rec.,* HR, 20 August 1945, pp. 648–49; 22 August 1945, pp. 687–88.

66. F. L. Worcester, Report No. 51, 7 June 1946, DSNA 811B.00/6-1746; Bernstein, *Philippine Story,* p. 248.

67. *7th and Final Report,* p. 47; Paul Steintorf to Secretary of State, 16 June 1945, DSNA 811B.00/6-1645; Paul Steintorf to Secretary of State, 30 June 1945, DSNA 811B.00/6-3045; F. L. Worcester, Report No. 24, 28 February 1946, DSNA 811B.00/3-1846; *Manila Times,* 15 July 1945, p. 1.

68. Abaya, *Betrayal,* p. 75. His candidacy was not publicly announced until December 1945 (*Manila Times,* 8 December 1945, p. 1; 22 December 1945, p. 3).

69. Abaya, *Betrayal,* pp. 81, 83.

70. Quoted in *Manila Free Philippines,* 19 April 1945, p. 4.

71. *Manila Times,* 6 January 1946, p. 8; F. L. Worcester, Report No. 16, 6 February 1946, DSNA 811B.00/2-1546.

72. F. L. Worcester, Report No. 24, 28 February 1946, DSNA 811B.00/3-1846; F. L. Worcester, Report No. 25, 2 March 1946, DSNA 811B.00/3-546. See also F. L. Worcester, Report No. 21, 14 February 1946, DSNA 811B.00/2-2646. Some of the governors were retained from their prewar election, but Osmeña still had to reappoint them.

73. *7th and Final Report,* p. 75.

74. F. L. Worcester, Report No. 31, 14 March 1946, DSNA 811B.00/3-2746.

75. *Manila Times,* 7 September 1945, p. 4; 11 September 1945, p. 1; 14 September 1945, p. 1; Steinberg, *Collaboration,* pp. 124–27; A. V. H. Hartendorp, *A History of Industry and Trade of the Philippines: From Pre-Spanish Times to the End of the Quirino Administration* (Manila: American Chamber of Commerce of the Philippines, 1958), p. 214; Hutchinson Report, pp. 3, 18. For text of Ickes telegram, see *7th and Final Report,* pp. 141–42.

76. *Manila Times,* 24 September 1945, p. 4; 29 September 1945, p. 1; 30 September 1945, p. 15; Phil. *Cong. Rec.,* HR, 25 September 1945, pp. 1374–75.

77. *Manila Free Philippines,* 20 March 1945, p. 1; 7 May 1945, p. 3; *Manila Times,* 26 August 1945, p. 1; Paul Steintorf to Secretary of State, 11 July 1945, DSNA 811B.00/7-1145; Paul Steintorf to Secretary of State, 13 July 1945, DSNA 811B.221/7-1345; Hutchinson Report, p. 15; Abaya, *Betrayal,* pp. 152–59.

78. F. L. Worcester, Report No. 48, 1 June 1946, DSNA 811B.00/6-746.

79. Phil. *Cong. Rec.,* HR, 20 June 1945, pp. 3–4; 20 December 1945, pp. 1727–28; Selden Menefee, *Christian Science Monitor,* 23 February 1946, in U.S. *Cong. Rec.,* 26 February 1946, p. A976; *Manila Times,* 15 December 1945, pp. 1, 12; 19 January 1946, p. 1. Hartendorp, *History* (1958), pp. 78, 163–64; Friend, *Between Two Empires,* p. 256; Francisco Ortigas, Jr., "Aftermath of Japanese Currency in the Philippines," *Commercial and Financial Chronicle,* 13 March 1947, in CW Papers, box 16, folder 63.

80. Ortigas, "Aftermath" (as cited in note 79, above), p. 6; *Manila Times*, 16 September 1945, p. 1; M. Jesus Cuenco in *Daily News* (Manila), 12 October 1945, RG 126, Osmeña, Pres. Sergio 1945, part A file. On other politicians, see Friend, *Between Two Empires*, p. 256 n.31; Menefee (as cited in note 79, above), p. A976.

81. *Manila Times*, 20 January 1946, p. 1; *PPP*, Truman, 1946, pp. 113–14; Richard R. Ely to Paul McNutt, 27 December 1945, RG 126, Correspondence with Manila file.

82. Paul Steintorf to Secretary of State, 26 January 1946, DSNA 811B.51/1-2646.

83. Frank P. Lockhart to Mr. Vincent, 29 April 1946, DSNA 896.00/4-2946.

84. Support: OSS, Research and Analysis Branch, R & A No. 3220, *Personalities in the Philippine Political Scene*, 30 July 1945, DSNA p. 3; A. V. H. Hartendorp to author, 24 October 1968; *Manila Times*, 30 April 1946, p. 1; John A. O'Donnell to Charles Ross, 20 October 1949, HST Papers, OF 1055 (1949); Friend, *Between Two Empires*, pp. 250–51; Paul Steintorf to Secretary of State, 23 May 1945, DSNA 811B.00/5-2345; interview with Julius C. C. Edelstein, 23 June 1978; Ronald K. Edgerton, "The Politics of Reconstruction in the Philippines, 1945–1948" (Ph.D. dissertation, University of Michigan, 1975), pp. 305–6; James, *Years of MacArthur*, vol. 2, pp. 691–701. Authority: W. Willoughby to Clayton, 26 September 1945, DSNA 611.11B31/9-2645.

85. E. D. Hester to McNutt, 15 March 1946, and 4 April 1946, RG 126, Radio Messages Outgoing-Incoming, 1946 file; E. D. Hester to McNutt, 12 April 1946, RG 126, Roxas, Manuel, 1945–47, part A file; *7th and Final Report*, p. 82.

86. Steinberg, *Collaboration*, p. 125.

87. *FR* 1945, vol. 6, p. 1233.

88. *7th and Final Report*, p. 17; Warner W. Gardner to Secretary of Interior, 16 November 1945, WWG Papers, Philippines Puerto Rico file (quote).

89. *Manila Times*, 27 February 1946, p. 1; 18 March 1946, p. 1; *PPP*, Truman, 1946, pp. 160–61; Hutchinson Report, pp. 3, 20; Paul Steintorf to Secretary of State, 24 August 1945, RG 226, XL-17117; F. L. Worcester, Report No. 32, 20 March 1946, DSNA 811B.00/3-2746.

90. J. Weldon Jones to Sergio Osmeña, 19 June 1945, JWJ Papers, box 16, Osmeña, Sergio, 1943–45 file; Bonner F. Fellers, Memorandum for the Commander-in-Chief, 31 March 1945, DAM Papers, RG 3, box 8, Military Secretary File 1; interview with Julius C. C. Edelstein, 23 June 1978.

91. J. Weldon Jones to Sergio Osmeña, 19 June 1945, JWJ Papers, box 16, Osmeña, Sergio, 1943–45 file; J. Weldon Jones to Manuel Roxas, 21 June 1945, JWJ Papers, box 14, Government of the Philippine Islands, 1941–47 file; Harold Ickes to Truman, 17 July 1945, HST Papers, OF 400 (1945).

92. E.g., F. L. Worcester, Report No. 15, 28 January 1946, DSNA 811B.00/1-3146.

93. Taylor, *Philippines and the U.S.*, p. 119.

94. *7th and Final Report*, p. 47.

95. Interview with Julius C. C. Edelstein, 23 June 1978.

96. MacArthur to Adjutant General, Department of War, 3 March 1946, DAM Papers, RG 9, War Crimes: September 1945–May 1950; Paul Steintorf to Secretary of State, 16 October 1945, DSNA 811B.00/10-1645; J. Weldon Jones, Memorandum for "The Files," of telephone conversation with Richard R. Ely, 11 December 1945, JWJ Papers, box 14, Government of the Philippine Islands, 1941–47 file; McNutt to Attorney General Tom Clark, 9 February 1946, RG 126, Atty Gen. Mission (Collaboration) file; *PPP*, Truman, 1946, p. 161.

97. J. R. Hayden to MacArthur, 8 May 1944, p. 4, DAM Papers, RG 4, box 2, Correspondence, Philippine Government nos. 100–199; F. L. Worcester, Report No. 10, 16 January 1946, DSNA 811B.00/1-2446.

98. McNutt and Abe Fortas, Memorandum for the President, 29 September 1945, RG 126, Atty Gen. Mission (Collaboration) file.

99. F. L. Worcester, Report No. 45, 16 May 1946, DSNA 811B.00/5-2346; R. R. Smith, "Hukbalahap Insurgency," p. 64; Hoeksema, "Communism in the Philippines," p. 272.

100. G-2 Liaison Office, Cabanatuan, Nueva Ecija, Headquarters, Military Police Command, AFWESPAC, "Survey of Hukbalahap Activities, Nueva Ecija," 13 November 1945, pp. 3, 4, 11, RG 319, box 663. no. 285993.

101. Intelligence Division, War Department General Staff, "Problems Facing the New Republic of the Philippines," 20 July 1946, pp. 62–63, RG 319 MMR, P & O 350.05, case 94. See also Kerkvliet, *Huk Rebellion*, p. 76.

102. See, e.g., the First Report of the Government's Agrarian Commission, 29 June 1946, in Phil. *Cong. Rec.*, Sen., 12 August 1946, pp. 329–30, for the landlord complaint that peasant union activities were depriving them of their proprietary rights; or the complaint of a landowner that Huks among his employees were refusing to work (*Manila Times*, 4 May 1946, p. 1). For the conflict over crop division, see F. L. Worcester, Report No. 15, 28 January 1946, DSNA 811B.00/1-3146.

103. R. R. Smith, "Hukbalahap Insurgency," p. 57; certified true copies of Concepcion Municipal Ordinances, sent by Sidney Reitman to Harold Ickes, 19 November 1945, RG 126, box 770, file 9-7-30, Politics—General (Reitman, Sidney—Correspondence); *Manila Times*, 11 December 1945, p. 5.

104. Quoted in Robert Lovett to Truman, 3 November 1945, HST Papers, OF 1055 (1945). See also WCF Journal, p. 554; Nathaniel P. Davis to Secretary of State, 28 June 1947, DSNA 896.105/6-2847.

105. Bonner F. Fellers, Memorandum for the Commander-in-Chief, 29 July 1945, DAM Papers, RG 3, box 8, Military Secretary File 1.

106. Robert Lovett to Truman, 3 November 1945; Truman to Robert Patterson, 13 November 1945, both in HST Papers, OF 1055 (1945); Joint Staff Planners, "United States Military Assistance to the Philippines," JPS

756/6, 17 January 1946, appendix B, RG 218, File: CCS 686.9, Philippine Islands (11-7-43), sec. 2.

107. Robert Lovett to Truman, 3 November 1945, HST Papers, OF 1055 (1945); "Ten Months of President Osmeña's Administration: A Review of Work Done Under Unprecedented Conditions" (no date), pp. 28–29, RG 126, File: Osmeña, Pres. Sergio, 1945, part D; R. W. Bunch to R. R. Ely, 5 February 1946, RG 126, File: Rehabilitation–General 1945, part B; *Manila Times,* 16 December 1945, p. 1; 3 January 1946, p. 1; 1 March 1946, p. 1; 28 March 1946, p. 1.

108. F. L. Worcester, Report No. 45, 16 May 1946, DSNA 811B.00/5-2346; *Manila Times,* 5 May 1946, p. 1.

109. F. L. Worcester, Report No. 1, 7 January 1946, DSNA 811B.00/1-1546; F. L. Worcester, Report No. 9, 15 January 1946, DSNA 811B.00/1-1846. On the submachine guns, see Barbara Entenberg, "Agrarian Reform and the Hukbalahap," *Far Eastern Survey,* 15, no.16 (14 August 1946), p. 247.

110. F. L. Worcester, Report No. 21, 14 February 1946, DSNA 811B.00/2-2646. For charges by the Democratic Alliance and others of MP terror, see *Manila Times,* 13 January 1946, pp. 1, 8; 5 February 1946, p. 4; 9 February 1946, p. 2. For a further directive to restore peace and order "at any cost," see *Manila Times,* 16 January 1946, p. 1.

111. F. L. Worcester, Report No. 45, 16 May 1946, DSNA 811B.00/5-2346; Kerkvliet, "Peasant," pp. 485–87; *Manila Times,* 16 May 1946, p. 7; Headquarters 1135th CIC, AFWESPAC, "Hukbalahap," 24 October 1946, p. 11, RG 319.

112. WCF Journal, pp. 554–55. See also F. L. Worcester, Report No. 15, 28 January 1946, DSNA 811B.00/1-3146.

113, *Manila Times,* 7 January 1946, p. 10; 8 January 1946, p. 1; 9 January 1946, p. 1; 10 January 1946, p. 1.

114. U.S. *Cong. Rec.,* 17 January 1946, p. A94.

115. WCF Journal, pp. 585–86.

116. *Manila Times,* 6 January 1946, pp. 1, 8; 18 January 1946, p. 12; 1 May 1946, p. 1; Abaya, *Betrayal,* p. 134; *7th and Final Report,* p. 79.

117. McNutt and Abe Fortas, Memorandum for the President, 29 September 1945, RG 126, Atty Gen. Mission (Collaboration) file; Warner W. Gardner to Harold Ickes, 16 November 1945, WWG Papers, Philippine–Puerto Rico file; *7th and Final Report,* pp. 74–76; *Manila Times,* 22 December 1945, p. 3; 20 January 1946, p. 1; 22 January 1946, p. 1.

118. Draft, for Central Directive, "Philippine Elections," 23 January 1946, p. 1, attached to E. D. Hester to McNutt, 12 April 1946, RG 126, Elections, Commonwealth 1945–46 file; interview with Julius C. C. Edelstein, 23 June 1978; *7th and Final Report,* p. 76; Friend, *Between Two Empires,* p. 251.

119. "Philippine Elections" (as cited in note 118, above), p. 3; Paul Steintorf to Secretary of State, 23 May 1945, DSNA 811B.00/5-2345; Paul Steintorf to Secretary of State, 13 July 1945, DSNA 811B.01/7-1345; F. L.

Worcester, Report No. 11, 19 January 1946, DSNA 811B.00/1-2446; J. H. Baumann to General Hull, 2 June 1945, RG 165, OPD 381, case 64; Hugh Bain Snow, Jr., "United States Policy and the 1953 Philippine Presidential Election" (Master's thesis, American University, 1968), p. 15, citing interview with W. Y. Elliott, 1967.

120. *7th and Final Report,* pp. 76–78; *Manila Times,* 19 September 1945, p. 8; 5 February 1946, p. 1; "Philippine Elections" (as cited in note 118, above), pp. 1–2; Hutchinson Report, p. 19; F. L. Worcester, Report No. 20, 12 February 1946, DSNA 811B.00/2-1546; F. L. Worcester, Report No. 4, 11 January 1946, DSNA 811B.00/1-1546; Steinberg, *Collaboration,* pp. 129–32.

121. F. L. Worcester, Report No. 19, 12 February 1946, DSNA 811B.00/2-1546; F. L. Worcester, Report No. 35, 27 March 1946, DSNA 811B.00/4-446.

122. Abaya, *Betrayal,* pp. 121–22.

123. *Manila Times,* 5 February 1946, p. 1; 22 February 1946, pp. 1, 4; 17 April 1946, p. 2; 4 May 1946, p. 1; Roxas quoted in Shirley Jenkins, *American Economic Policy Towards the Philippines* (Stanford: Stanford University Press, 1954), p. 82, citing *Manila Post,* 10 April 1946.

124. *Manila Times,* 13 April 1946, p. 1; *7th and Final Report,* pp. 81, 154–55.

125. On MP terrorism, see note 110, above. Registration: F. L. Worcester, Report No. 42, 24 April 1946, DSNA 811B.00/4-3046; *Manila Times,* 4 April 1946, p. 1.

126. I. George Blake, *Paul V. McNutt: Portrait of a Hoosier Statesman* (Indianapolis: Central Publishing Co., 1966), pp. 240, 161–62, 230.

127. *7th and Final Report,* p. 18; *Manila Times,* 30 January 1946, pp. 1, 14; J. Weldon Jones, Memorandum for "The Files," of phone conversation with Richard R. Ely, 11 December 1945, JWJ Papers, box 14, Government in the Philippine Islands, 1941–47 file.

128. E. D. Hester to McNutt, 12 April 1946, RG 126, Elections, Commonwealth 1945–46 file; WCF Journal, pp. 511–12; Julius Edelstein to Secretary of State, 17 February 1947, DSNA 896.00/2-1747; *Manila Times,* 3 December 1945, p. 1; *7th and Final Report,* p. 75.

129. Paul Steintorf to Secretary of State, 16 June 1945, DSNA 811B.00/6-1645; F. L. Worcester, Report No. 1, 7 January 1946, DSNA 811B.00/1-1546; Intelligence Division, War Department General Staff, "Problems Facing the New Republic" (as cited in note 101, above), p. 29 (these last two sources mention Osmeña's financial backers as well); WCF Journal, pp. 549–50, 562; Friend, *Between Two Empires,* p. 255.

130. Dapen Liang, *Philippine Political Parties,* rev. ed. (San Francisco: Gladstone Co., 1970), p. 332 n.67; *7th and Final Report,* p. 80.

131. Bernstein, *Philippine Story,* pp. 247–48; Steinberg, *Collaboration,* passim.

132. Colonel R. F. Treacy, Memorandum to General Lincoln, 12 April 1946, RG 319 MMR, P & O 350.05 case 58; J. E. Hull, Memorandum for the Secretary of War, 29 April 1946, RG 319 MMR, ABC 686 Phil (8 Nov 43)

sec. 1-B; S. M. Mellnik, "Report on Roxas U.S. Visit," May 1946(?), p. 3, RG 319 MMR, P & O 091.711 PI sec. IV, case 25; Intelligence Division, War Department General Staff, "Problems Facing the New Republic" (as cited in note 101, above), p. 103.

133. *Manila Times*, 28 April 1946, p. 1; Mellnik, "Report on Roxas U.S. Visit," (as cited in note 132, above), p. 2.

134. Phil. *Cong. Rec.*, Sen., 14 August 1946, p. 370; Steinberg, *Collaboration*, pp. 149, 157–58; Hutchinson Report, p. 3; *NYT*, 29 December 1946, p. 15 (AP); David J. Steinberg, "The Philippines: Survival of an Oligarchy," in Josef Silverstein, ed., *Southeast Asia in World War II: Four Essays*, Southeast Asia Monograph Series No. 7 (New Haven: Yale University, 1966), p. 85 n.55.

135. Steinberg, "Survival," p. 80 n.13; V. E. Wurfel, "American Implementation," pp. 174–75; *NYT*, 29 January 1948, p. 20 (Ford Wilkins); 14 February 1948, p. 6 (AP).

136. Taylor, *Philippines and the U.S.*, p. 110; Robert Aura Smith, *Philippine Freedom, 1946–1958* (New York: Columbia University Press, 1958), p. 126.

137. *Manila Times*, 7 May 1946, p. 1; 25 May 1946, p. 1; *Manila Daily Bulletin*, 4 July 1946, p. 2; F. L. Worcester, Report No. 45, 16 May 1946, DSNA 811B.00/5-2346. See also *Manila Times*, 30 April–18 May 1946, passim.

138. McNutt to Office of High Commissioner in Manila, 14 May 1946, RG 126, Radio Messages, Outgoing, 1946, part A; *7th and Final Report*, pp. 104–5.

139. Frank P. Lockhart to Acheson, 22 July 1946, DSNA 811B.00/7-2246; Phil. *Cong. Rec.*, Sen., 2 September 1946, p. 605; Kerkvliet, "Peasant," pp. 517–18; Leighton, Sanders, and Tinio, *Huk Rebellion*, pp. 29, 57–58.

140. Phil. *Cong. Rec.*, HR, 29 August 1946, p. 1343.

141. *7th and Final Report*, pp. 97–98; Julius Edelstein to Secretary of State, 11 September 1946, DSNA 896.00/9-1146. For Edelstein's service as Roxas's adviser, McNutt to James Forrestal, 19 June 1946, RG 126, Radio Messages Incoming, 1946, part B; interview with Julius C. C. Edelstein, 23 June 1978.

142. Phil. *Cong. Rec.*, Sen., 12 August 1946, p. 326; *7th and Final Report*, p. 99. Cf. previous crop division, Phil. *Cong. Rec.*, Sen., 12 August 1946, pp. 328–29.

143. Quoted in Margaret Parton, "Philippine Farmers Fight for Reform," *New York Herald Tribune*, 17 July 1946, attached to Frank P. Lockhart to Acheson, 22 July 1946, DSNA 896.50/7-2246. Lockhart noted that the article presented an "objective and accurate account of the situation as it exists today."

144. Headquarters, 1135th CIC, AFWESPAC, "Staff Study on Communism in the Philippines," 24 October 1946, pp. 6–7, RG 332, stack 1/50, box 11104 2/39.

145. Walter Millis, ed., *The Forrestal Diaries* (New York: Viking Press, 1951), p. 180 (14 July 1946).

Chapter Two: Independence Legislation

1. *Remarks of Senator Millard E. Tydings: The Philippine Islands,* printed as Sen. Doc. 53, 79th Cong., 1st sess., 1945.

2. *DSB,* 14 August 1943, p. 91; 2 July 1944, p. 17; 6 May 1945, p. 867; Hearings, *To Amend the Philippine Rehabilitation Act of 1946,* CFA, 81st Cong., 1st and 2nd sess., 1949–50, pp. 72–76 (hereafter cited as Hearings, *Amend Rehabilitation*); U.S. *Cong. Rec.,* 7 February 1946, pp. A591–92; Harry S. Truman, *Memoirs,* vol. 1, *Years of Decision* (Garden City, N.Y.: Doubleday & Co., 1955), pp. 65–66, 276.

3. *NYT,* 29 December 1945, p. 12 (editorial); U.S. *Cong. Rec.,* 10 April 1946, p. 3442; *Seventh and Final Report of the High Commissioner to the Philippines,* printed as H. Doc. 389, 80th Cong., 1st sess., 8 July 1947, p. 20 (quote) (hereafter cited as *7th and Final Report*).

4. *Washington Evening Star,* 5 September 1945, printed in U.S. *Cong. Rec.,* 11 September 1945, p. A3835.

5. R. C. Kramer, Memorandum to Deputy Chief of Staff, 20 July 1945, DAM Papers, RG 3, box 8, Military Secretary File 1.

6. OSS XL-8540 in RG 226; *FR* 1946, vol. 8, p. 936; P.I. to Mr. Meader, 24 September 1947, p. 3, DSNA 711.96/9-2447; E. Mill to Butterworth, 24 November 1947, DSNA 896.00/11-2447.

7. Frank P. Lockhart to Acheson, 22 July 1946, DSNA 896.50/7-2246.

8. Robert P. Patterson to William L. Clayton, 4 June 1945, in Department of State, Executive Committee on Economic Foreign Policy records, ECEFP D-84/85, 12 June 1945, lot 122, box 19, new box number (hereafter these records will be cited as ECEFP, number, and date; all are in the same lot and box).

9. Sen. Report 755, 79th Cong., 1st sess., November 1945, p. 2.

10. Hearings, *To Provide for the Rehabilitation of the Philippine Islands,* HR, Committee on Insular Affairs, 79th Cong., 2nd sess., 1946, pp. 193–94 (hereafter cited as Hearings, *Rehabilitation*).

11. Ibid., p. 200. McNutt, however, felt that the United States might "have to support experiments by government which we would call socialistic if they were proposed in this country." But the result, he hoped, would be the perpetuation of the "existence in the Orient of a miniature version of our own way of life." U.S. *Cong. Rec.,* 3 July 1946, p. A3921.

12. *U.S. Stat.,* vol. 60, part 1, pp. 134–35; U.S. *Cong. Rec.,* 27 November 1945, pp. 11036–37.

13. Frank H. Golay, "Economic Consequences of the Philippine Trade Act," *Pacific Affairs,* 28, no. 1 (March 1955), p. 67.

14. Frank A. Waring to Ahern, 9 April 1949, JWJ Papers, box 16, Philippine War Damage Commission, 1948–49 file; U.S. Philippine War Damage Commission, *Final and Ninth Semiannual Report,* 31 March 1951, p. 40, in FAW Papers, box 4, Final and Semiannual Report file.

15. Hernando J. Abaya, *Betrayal in the Philippines* (New York: A. A. Wyn, 1946), pp. 197–200; *7th and Final Report,* p. 23.

16. Sen. Doc. 53 (as cited in note 1, above), p. 6; Violet E. Wurfel, "American Implementation of Philippine Independence" (Ph.D. dissertation, University of Virginia, 1951), p. 221.

17. *Report and Recommendations of the Joint Philippine-American Finance Commission,* Manila, 7 June 1947, pp. 106–7, printed as H. Doc. 390, 80th Cong., 1st sess., 8 July 1947; Charles O. Houston, Jr., "Rice in the Philippine Economy, 1934–1950," *Journal of East Asiatic Studies* (Manila), 3, no. 1 (October 1953), pp. 64, 67, 83; Benedict J. Kerkvliet, "Peasant Rebellion in the Philippines: The Origins and Growth of the HMB" (Ph.D. dissertation, University of Wisconsin, 1972), p. 434; *Manila Times,* 17 February 1946, p. 1.

18. *U.S. Stat.,* vol. 60, part 1, p. 131, sec. 106a; p. 128, sec. 101; Hearings, *Rehabilitation,* p. 176.

19. *DSB,* 16 April 1951, pp. 618–19.

20. U.S. *Cong. Rec.,* 3 July 1946, pp. A3921–22; Hearings, *Philippine Trade Act of 1945,* CWM, 79th Cong., 2nd sess., 1946, pp. 12–14 (hereafter cited as Hearings, *Trade Act, 1945;* the act was passed as the Trade Act of 1946).

21. WCF Journal, p. 581; *U.S. Stat.,* vol. 60, part 1, p. 140; Hearings, *Rehabilitation,* p. 119.

22. HST Papers, White House Bill File, S1610, 30 April 1946; *PPP,* Truman, 1946, p. 217. On State Department concern about charges of imperialism, see DSNA 811B.00/1-1746.

23. U.S. *Cong. Rec.,* 7 May 1946, pp. A2511–12; McNutt to Ely, 18 June 1946, and Richmond B. Keech to Truman, 21 June 1946, HST Papers, OF 1055 (February–June 1946).

24. Hearings, *Post-War Economic Policy and Planning,* HR, Special subcommittee on Post-War Economic Policy and Planning, 78th Cong., 2nd sess., 1944, cited in William Appleman Williams, *The Tragedy of American Diplomacy,* rev. ed. (New York: Delta, 1962), pp. 235–37.

25. ECEFP D-39/45, 12 March 1945, "United States–Philippine Trade Preferences in Relation to General Commercial Policy," p. 6 of text, p. 1 of summary. See also Dean Acheson, Memorandum for the President, 1 October 1945, DSNA 611.11B31/10-145; W. Willoughby to Clayton, 26 September 1945, DSNA 611.11B31/9-2645.

26. This was one of the arguments advanced by the Department of the Interior in favor of trade preferences. See Richard R. Ely to Woodbury Willoughby, 4 June 1945, in ECEFP D-83/45, 12 June 1945.

27. ECEFP D-39/45, p. 6 of text. It would be wrong to overemphasize the consistency of the State Department's position. E. D. Hester of the Interior Department tried to reconcile trade preferences with the most-favored-nation treaties being negotiated with other countries. He suggested that the United States give to any country the same preferences that he wanted the United States to give to the Philippines (i.e., free trade) if the country grants the United States, as the Philippines would, free entry in trade, naval and air bases, and equal investment rights. A Tariff Commission official replied that Washington had abandoned conditional application of the most-favored-

nation treaties as being discriminatory. When Hester then inquired about Cuba, he was told: "That arrangement is what we call exclusive concessions based on the principle of reciprocity. It is the granting of exclusive concessions in return for exclusive concessions and is still in a third category." (Report on Proceedings before the Committee on Trade Relations of the Filipino Rehabilitation Commission, executive session, 11 April 1945, session 2, pp. 70–72, DSNA 611.11B31/4-1145.)

28. Hearings, *Trade Act, 1945*, p. 231.

29. Vernon E. Moore, "More Funds for Philippine War Damage Claims," 9 May 1949, pp. 5–6, HST Papers, OF 521; "Some Leading Americans in Philippine Islands," FBS Papers, box 9, Philippine Personnel file; J. Weldon Jones to McNutt, 2 August 1939, JWJ Papers, box 8, McNutt, Paul V., 1939–40 file

30. U.S. *Cong. Rec.*, 12 April 1946, p. 3537.

31. Hearings, *Trade Act, 1945*, p. 221. For additional comments on Congress's opposition to the foreign economic policy of the State Department, see Joyce and Gabriel Kolko, *The Limits of Power* (New York: Harper & Row, 1972), pp. 87–89, 377.

32. John B. Gordon to chairperson, Subcommittee on Trade Relations, Filipino Rehabilitation Commission, 25 April 1945, RG 126, box 47, File: Rehabilitation Copra, 1944–46; *Manila Free Philippines,* 7 April 1945, p. 2; 2 March 1945, p. 2; Jaime Hernandez to Millard Tydings, 13 February 1945, in Report of the Proceedings of the Filipino Rehabilitation Commission, executive session, 1 March 1945, session 1, pp. 15–16, DSNA 611.11B31/4-1145; *Manila Times*, 19 September 1945, p. 1; U.S. *Cong. Rec.*, 24 September 1945, p. 8924; 31 October 1945, p. A4605.

33. Department of State, Interim Research and Intelligence Service, Research and Analysis Branch, R & A No. 3269, *Recent Developments in Philippine–American Relations,* 5 October 1945, DSNA, p. 5. On Interior Department role, see W. Willoughby to Clayton, 26 September 1945, DSNA 611.11B31/9-2645.

34. *FR* 1945, vol. 6, pp. 1216, 1218 n.74, 1218–19; James F. Byrnes, Memorandum for the President, 5 November 1945, DSNA 611.11B31/11-545; ECEFP D-39/45, 12 March 1945, p. 8 of text; U.S. *Cong. Rec.*, 12 April 1946, p. 3534.

35. Urbano A. Zafra and J. A. Barreto to E. D. Hester, "Memorandum on Agricultural Rehabilitation of the Philippines," 5 April 1943, exhibit D, RG 126, Rehabilitation-Agriculture-Zafra-1944 file; ECEFP D-39/45, 12 March 1945, p. 7 of text; ECEFP M-25/45, 26 June 1945, p. 5, in RG 165, 093.5 P.I., FW 18/8; OSS, Research and Analysis Branch, R & A no. 400, "Prospects of Cotton Production in the Philippines" (no date), DSNA; XL-23716, enclosure 3, RG 226; XL-23717, enclosure 1, RG 226; XL-40438, pp. 1–2, RG 226; *Manila Times*, 18 November 1945, p. 7; 11 December 1945, p. 1; Phil. *Cong. Rec.*, HR, 23 August 1946, pp. 1202, 1204.

36. ECEFP D-39/45, 12 March 1945, p. 2 of summary; ECEFP D-82/45, "Proposed Report and Recommendations to the Chairman of the

Filipino Rehabilitation Commission in Regard to Trade Relations with the Philippines," 12 June 1945, p. 10.

37. *Complete Presidential Press Conferences of Franklin D. Roosevelt* (New York: Da Capo Press, 1972), vol. 25, sec. 115; *FR* 1945, vol. 6, pp. 1197, 1199–1200, 1204, 1204 n.39; E. R. Stettinius, Memorandum for the President, 22 April 1945, DSNA 811.24511B/4-2245; U.S. *Cong. Rec.*, 21 August 1944, p. A3656; 21 September 1944, p. 8124.

38. *FR* 1945, vol. 6, p. 1204.

39. U.S. *Cong. Rec.*, 29 March 1946, p. 2832.

40. Cited in RP, Department of Labor, Labor Statistics Division, "Wages and Working Conditions in Our Sugar Cane Haciendas in Negros Occidental," *Philippine Labor*, May 1962, p. 14.

41. Robert P. Patterson to William L. Clayton, 4 June 1945, ECEFP D-84/85, 12 June 1945. This point was supported by the Navy and Interior Departments; see ECEFP M-25/45, 26 June 1945, pp. 2, 3, in RG 165, 093.5 P.I., FW 18/8; Richard R. Ely to Woodbury Willoughby, 4 June 1945, ECEFP D-83/45, 12 June 1945.

42. James F. Byrnes to C. Jasper Bell, 26 November 1945, DSNA 611.11B31/11-1445; *FR* 1945, vol. 6, p. 1219; *7th and Final Report*, p. 33.

43. ECEFP D-82/45, 12 June 1945, pp. 12–13; U.S. *Cong. Rec.*, 28 March 1946, p. 2761; 29 March 1946, p. 2828; 10 April 1946, p. 3438; 7 February 1946, p. A586. For analysis, see Sen. Report 1145, 79th Cong., 2nd sess., April 1946. The text of the "Philippine Trade Act of 1946" is in *U.S. Stat.*, vol. 60, part 1, pp. 141–59.

44. Hearings, *Trade Act, 1945*, pp. 318, 34, 36, 247.

45. *7th and Final Report*, pp. 147, 34.

46. Hearings, *Philippine Trade Act of 1946*, Sen., Committee on Finance, 79th Cong., 2nd sess., 1946, pp. 50–51 (hereafter cited as Hearings, *Trade Act, 1946*). London dispatch: John G. Winant to Secretary of State, 20 February 1946, DSNA 611.11B31/2-2046. See also Hearings, *Trade Act, 1946*, pp. 75–79; Hearings, *Trade Act, 1945*, pp. 288–89; William L. Clayton to Robert L. Doughton, 19 November 1945, JWJ Papers, box 13, Economic aspects of preparing Philippines for Defense, 1941–45 file.

47. U.S. *Cong. Rec.*, 28 March 1946, p. 2763; 29 March 1946, p. 2840.

48. Sen. Report 1145, 79th Cong., 2nd sess., April 1946, p. 13; U.S. *Cong. Rec.*, 28 March 1946, p. 2770.

49. Harold Ickes to Truman, 24 January 1946, HST Papers, OF 1055 (February–June 1946); U.S. *Cong. Rec.*, 3 July 1946, p. A3921; Hearings, *Trade Act, 1946*, p. 128.

50. Hearings, *Trade Act, 1946*, p. 99. On the discouragement of diversification caused by this provision, see Norman W. Schul, "Problems in Land Tenure as Viewed from a Study of the Visayan Sugar Industry," in *Proceedings of the First National Colloquium on the Philippines*, held 1966, ed. Charles O. Houston, Jr. (Kalamazoo, Mich.: Western Michigan University, 1969), p. 54.

51. Hearings, *Trade Act, 1945*, pp. 140–41.

52. Golay, "Economic Consequences," p. 67.

53. Bankers Trust Company, N.Y., "The Philippines, January 1948: Notes Prepared by One of Our Representatives Who Recently Visited That Country," p. 6, in MMC Papers, box 3, correspondence, Bankers Trust Co. (J. Morden Murphy) file. See also Schul, "Problems," pp. 52, 66 n.4.

54. Hearings, *Trade Act, 1946*, pp. 76–78; Hearings, *Trade Act, 1945*, pp. 288–89; Brown, Memorandum of conversation with John D. Dingell, 8 March 1946, DSNA 611.11B31/3-846. See also U.S. *Cong. Rec.*, 28 March 1946, p. 2770; 29 March 1946, p. 2829.

55. G. Luthringer to E. C. Collado, 27 November 1945, DSNA 811.51/11-2745.

56. Hearings, *Trade Act, 1945*, pp. 12–14, 32, 226; U.S. *Cong. Rec.*, 3 July 1946, p. A3921; 28 March 1946, p. 2773 (Dingell).

57. *7th and Final Report*, p. 150.

58. *NYT*, 17 November 1948, p. 41; Theodore Friend, *Between Two Empires: The Ordeal of the Philippines, 1929–1946* (New Haven: Yale University Press, 1965), p. 259 n.43; *American Chamber of Commerce Journal* (Phil.), April 1955, p. 128; Hernando J. Abaya, *The Untold Philippine Story* (Quezon City: Malaya Books, 1967), p. 255; I. George Blake, *Paul V. McNutt: Portrait of a Hoosier Statesman* (Indianapolis: Central Publishing Co., 1966), p. 375; Hearings, *Amend Rehabilitation*, p. 173.

59. *FR* 1946, vol. 8, pp. 873–75.

60. ECEFP D-82/45, 12 June 1945, p. 14; *FR* 1945, vol. 6, p. 1226.

61. Hearings, *Trade Act, 1945*, p. 138. For State and Commerce Department objections, see Hearings, *Trade Act, 1946*, pp. 58, 76, 78; Hearings, *Trade Act, 1945*, pp. 288–89. Laws of various U.S. states which discriminate against Filipinos are listed in Hearings, *Trade Act, 1946*, pp. 27–31.

62. William L. Clayton to Robert L. Doughton, 19 November 1945, enclosing memorandum on "Proposed Changes in HR 4676," in JWJ Papers, box 13, Economic aspects of preparing Philippines for defense, 1941–45 file.

63. E. C. Carlson, "Policy Recommendations with Respect to Paragraph 4, Article X of the United States–Philippine Agreement on Trade, Signed July 4, 1946; Approved by the Country Committee," 25 March 1947, DSNA 611.9631/4-447; *FR* 1947, vol. 6, pp. 1113–14.

64. Center for Strategic and International Studies, *U.S.-Philippines Economic Relations*, Special Report Series No. 12 (Washington, D.C.: Georgetown University, 1971), pp. 100–101.

65. J. F. Shaw to CTW and E. C. Carlson, 2 August 1948, DSNA 711.962/8-248; George Marshall to U.S. Embassy, Manila, 22 July 1948, DSNA 711.962/7-848.

66. U.S. *Cong. Rec.*, 28 March 1946, p. 2759; Shirley Jenkins, "Great Expectations in the Philippines," *Far Eastern Survey*, 16, no. 15 (13 August 1947), p. 171.

67. U.S. *Cong. Rec.*, 28 March 1946, pp. 2771, 2768.

68. HST Papers, White House Bill File, HR 5856, 30 April 1946; *FR* 1946, vol. 8, pp. 873–75; *PPP*, Truman, 1946, p. 217.

69. *FR* 1946, vol. 8, pp. 889–91, 893–94, 937–38; Phil. *Cong. Rec.*, HR, 29 June 1946, pp. 511, 527.

70. Phil. *Cong. Rec.*, HR, 29 June 1946, pp. 530 and passim; *Manila Daily Bulletin*, 3 July 1946, p. 8.

71. McNutt to Richard Ely for John Snyder, 14 June 1946, JWS Papers, Philippine Islands—loans, 1945–46 alphabetical file.

72. F. L. Worcester, Report No. 45, 16 May 1946, DSNA 811B.00/5-2346 (see note 12, Chapter One).

73. *Manila Times*, 22 May 1946, p. 1; 23 May 1946, p. 1; 24 May 1946, p. 1; 26 May 1946, p. 1; F. L. Worcester, Report No. 46, 21 May 1946, DSNA 811B.00/5-2446 (Roy).

74. Phil. *Cong. Rec.*, HR, 25 May 1946, p. 12.

75. F. L. Worcester, Report No. 48, 1 June 1946, DSNA 811B.00/6-746.

76. Phil. *Cong. Rec.*, HR, 29 May 1946, pp. 73–74; *Manila Times*, 27 May 1946, p. 10; 30 May 1946, p. 1.

77. Phil. *Cong. Rec.*, HR, 13 June 1946, p. 257; 25 May 1946, p. 32; *Manila Times*, 26 May 1946, p. 12; F. L. Worcester, Report No. 48, 1 June 1946, DSNA 811B.00/6-746.

78. Phil. *Cong. Rec.*, HR, 25 May 1946, pp. 34–38; Ramon Diokno, "Roxas Violates the Constitution," *Amerasia*, 10, no. 6 (December 1946), p. 176; F. L. Worcester, Report No. 48, 1 June 1946, DSNA 811B.00/6-746; Philippine Constitution (1935), art. 6, sec. 11.

79. Phil. *Cong. Rec.*, HR, 13 June 1946, p. 250; 29 June 1946, p. 510; 2 July 1946, p. 670; "Alejo Mabanag et al. v. Jose Lopez Vito et al.," *Philippine Reports*, vol. 78, March 5 to July 31, 1947 (Manila: Bureau of Printing, 1954), case no. L-1123, 5 March 1947, p. 33 (Nacionalistas).

80. *Manila Times*, 26 May 1946, p. 12; R. Diokno, "Roxas," pp. 176–77; F. L. Worcester, Report No. 48, 1 June 1946, DSNA 811B.00/6-746.

81. G-2 Liaison Office, Cabanatuan, Nueva Ecija, Headquarters, Military Police Command, AFWESPAC, "Survey of Hukbalahap Activities, Nueva Ecija," 13 November 1945, p. 2, RG 319, box 663, no. 285993; Ronald K. Edgerton, "General Douglas MacArthur and the American Military Impact in the Philippines," *Philippine Studies*, 25 (4th quarter 1977), p. 437; Phil. *Cong. Rec.*, Sen., 12 August 1946, p. 328.

82. Quoted in Ronald K. Edgerton, "The Politics of Reconstruction in the Philippines, 1945–1948" (Ph.D. dissertation, University of Michigan, 1975), p. 229.

83. I have not seen the text of the report of the Commission on Elections, but excerpts are given in the resolutions calling for the unseating of the opposition senators and representatives. Presumably, these are the excerpts containing the most damning evidence against the Democratic Alliance. The resolutions are printed in Phil. *Cong. Rec.*, HR, 6 June 1946, p. 136; and "Jose O. Vera et al. v. Jose A. Avelino et al.," *Philippine Reports*, vol. 77, August 5, 1946 to February 28, 1947 (Manila: Bureau of Printing, 1953), case no. L-543, 31 August 1946, pp. 305–8. On appointment of Election Commission, see Phil. *Cong. Rec.*, HR, 29 May 1946, p. 89.

84. F. L. Worcester, Report No. 43, 30 April 1946, DSNA 811B.00/5-1446.

85. *Manila Times*, 25 April 1946, p. 8.

86. Ibid., p. 1; 12 May 1946, p. 12; Luis Taruc, *He Who Rides the Tiger* (New York: Praeger, 1967), p. 26; Edgerton, "Reconstruction," pp. 310–11; S. Walter Washington to Secretary of State, transmitting memorandum of conversation, 14 August 1948, DSNA 896.00/8-1448; Robert Ross Smith, "The Hukbalahap Insurgency: Economic, Political, and Military Factors," photocopied (Washington, D.C.: Office of the Chief of Military History, Department of the Army, 1963), pp. 66–67.

87. McNutt: *FR* 1946, vol. 8, p. 917; pork-barrel: Edgerton, "Reconstruction," pp. 358–59; collaborator: McNutt to Secretary of State, 2 February 1947, DSNA 896.00/2-247.

88. Quoted in Milton Meyer, *A Diplomatic History of the Philippine Republic* (Honolulu: University of Hawaii Press, 1965), pp. 50–51.

89. "Mabanag v. Lopez Vito," pp. 3, 31, and passim; Phil. *Cong. Rec.*, HR, 2 July 1946, pp. 677–78. See also R. Diokno, "Roxas," p. 177.

90. *DSB*, 29 June 1947, p. 1275 (Edward W. Mill); Julius Edelstein to Secretary of State, 31 December 1946, DSNA 896.00/12-3146. See also Manuel Roxas, *Important Speeches, Messages and Other Pronouncements of President Manuel Roxas* (Manila: Bureau of Printing, 1947), pp. 198–226, 381–422.

91. Phil. *Cong. Rec.*, Sen., 25 September 1946, p. 4; Abaya, *Untold Philippine Story*, p. 25; Edgerton, "Reconstruction," p. 367; Julius Edelstein to Secretary of State, 24 February 1947, DSNA 896.00/2-2447.

92. U.S. *Cong. Rec.*, 21 March 1947, pp. A1192–93; 18 March 1947, pp. A1158–59.

93. Creed F. Cox, Memorandum for the Secretary of War, 2 February 1934; Creed F. Cox, Memorandum for the Secretary of War, 20 December 1935; and "Notes on the Far Eastern Situation (from the Viewpoint of the State Department)," 16 December 1936, all in RG 126, file 9-7-2, Administration—General; Claude A. Swanson to Franklin D. Roosevelt, 22 April 1935, FDR Papers, PSF: Navy; Roosevelt to Swanson, 3 May 1935, in Edgar B. Nixon, ed., *Franklin D. Roosevelt and Foreign Affairs* (Cambridge, Mass.: Belknap Press of Harvard University Press, 1969), vol. 2, pp. 495–96; *FR* 1937, vol. 3, p. 958; H. R. Stark to Francis B. Sayre, 25 August 1939, enclosing Memorandum by Admiral Meyers, "Philippine Independence and Naval Bases," August 1939, pp. 2–3, FBS Papers, box 9, Philippines, Defense—Collaboration; Francis B. Sayre, Memorandum of Interview with Admiral Yarnell, 5 September 1939, FBS Papers, box 6, Special Correspondence, "W–Z."

94. Lloyd C. Gardner, *Economic Aspects of New Deal Diplomacy* (Madison: University of Wisconsin Press, 1964), pp. 180–81; Manuel Quezon to Douglas MacArthur, 10 October 1943, DAM Papers, RG 4, box 2, AFFE, SWPA [Army Forces in the Far East, Southwest Pacific Area], AFPAC, Correspondence, Philippine Government nos. 1–99. For Quezon's prewar views, see Friend, *Between Two Empires*, pp. 88, 101; Manuel Quezon, *The Good Fight* (New York: D. Appleton-Century, 1946), p. 151.

95. *U.S. Stat.*, vol. 58, pt. 1, pp. 625–26; telephone conversation between Henry Stimson and James W. Wadsworth, 13 June 1944, HLS Papers, box 172. On Quezon and Osmeña: U.S. *Cong. Rec.*, 21 August 1944, p. A3656; 21 September 1944, p. 8124; *FR* 1945, vol. 6, p. 1204; *The Public Papers and Addresses of Franklin D. Roosevelt*, 1944–45 volume, *Victory and the Threshold of Peace*, compiled by Samuel I. Rosenman (New York: Harper Bros., 1950), p. 186.

96. U.S. *Cong. Rec.*, 7 June 1945, p. 5697.

97. OSS, "Problems and Objectives of United States Policy," 2 April 1945, HST Papers, OSS Memoranda for the President, OSS April–May 1945, Donovan Chronological File, box 15.

98. Strategy Section, Operations Division, War Department General Staff, "Post War Base Requirements in the Philippines," 23 April 1945, appendix to tab E, RG 319 MMR, ABC 686 Phil (8 Nov 43), sec. 1-A.

99. JCS 1027/5, 20 September 1945, "Negotiations for the Retention of American Bases in the Philippines After Independence," annex A to appendix A: "Special Instructions Regarding Selection of U.S. Military Bases in the Philippines," RG 218, File: CCS 686.9 Philippine Islands, (11-7-43) sec. 1.

100. Strategy Section, Operations Division, War Department General Staff, "Post War Base Requirements" (as cited in note 98, above), p. 4.

101. U.S. *Cong. Rec.*, 3 July 1946, p. A3922.

102. Ibid.; George F. Kennan, *Memoirs* (New York: Bantam Books, 1967), p. 402.

103. E. R. Stettinius, Memorandum for the President, 22 April 1945, DSNA 811.24511B/4-2245; *FR* 1945, vol. 6, pp. 1208–9.

104. *Manila Times*, 15 July 1945, p. 2; 12 January 1946, p. 1; "Acceptance Speech of President Osmeña Before the Nacionalista Convention, 24 January 1946," p. 7, RG 126, U.S. High Commissioner to the Philippine Islands, Osmeña, President Sergio, 1945, part C file; R. B. W[arren, U.S. Army], Memorandum for the Record, 12 May 1946, RG 319 MMR, ABC 686 Phil (8 Nov 43), sec. 1-C.

105. Interview with Julius C. C. Edelstein, 23 June 1978; U.S. *Cong. Rec.*, 24 September 1945, pp. 8925–26.

106. *FR* 1946, vol. 8, pp. 880–81. On jurisdiction under NATO bases agreements, see Hearings, *United States Security Agreements and Commitments Abroad, Part 1: The Republic of the Philippines*, CFR subcommittee, 91st Cong., 1st sess., 1969, pp. 33–34 (hereafter cited as Hearings, *Security Agreements*).

107. "Military Bases: Agreement Between the United States and the Republic of the Philippines, March 14, 1947," in *A Decade of American Foreign Policy, Basic Documents, 1941–1949*, printed as Sen. Doc. 123, 81st Cong., 1st sess., 1950, pp. 869–81.

108. George Gray to Fahy, 5 March 1947, DSNA 811.24596/3-547; Acheson to U.S. Embassy, Manila, 12 March 1947, DSNA 811.24596/3-1247; McNutt to Secretary of State, 13 March 1947, DSNA 811.24596/3-1347.

109. *FR* 1946, vol. 8, p. 920; R. B. W[arren, U.S. Army], Memorandum for the record, 15 May 1946, RG 319 MMR, ABC 686 Phil (8 Nov 43) sec. 1-C; Edgerton, "Reconstruction", p. 391 n.21, quoting interview with Charles Parsons, 15 July 1971. See V. E. Wurfel, "American Implementation," pp. 245–48, on frictions between U.S. military personnel and Filipinos, 1946–47.

110. *FR* 1946, vol. 8, p. 934.

111. Ibid., pp. 934 n.17, 935, 935 n.19, 939–41; A. C. Wedemeyer, Memorandum for Chief of Staff, 11 May 1948, RG 319 MMR, P & O 091 PI, sec. II-B, case 12/63.

112. *Time*, 20 July 1959, p. 34; Douglas F. Loveday, *The Role of U.S. Military Bases in the Philippine Economy*, RM-5801-ISA (Santa Monica: Rand Corporation, April 1971), p. 34.

113. Kenneth C. Royall to Secretary of Defense, 4 March 1948, JCS, 1027/10, 9 April 1948, RG 218, CCS 686.9 Phil Is. (11-7-43), sec. 7; William D. Leahy, for JCS, Memorandum for Secretary of Defense, 13 July 1948, JSPC 822/2/D, RG 218, CCS 686.9 Phil Is. (11-7-43), sec. 8; C.V.R.S., Memorandum to General Wedemeyer, 14 April 1948, and A. C. Wedemeyer, Memorandum for Chief of Staff, 11 May 1948, both in RG 319 MMR, P & O 091 PI, sec. II-B, case 12/63. See also Butterworth to Secretary of State, 3 December 1948, DSNA 811.24596/12-348.

114. William D. Leahy, for JCS, Memorandum for Secretary of Defense, 13 July 1948, JSPC 822/2/D, RG 218, CCS 686.9 Phil Is. (11-7-43), sec. 8; C.V.R.S., Memorandum to General Wedemeyer, 14 April 1948, p. 2, RG 319 MMR, P & O 091 PI, sec. II-B, case 12/63. See also Joint War Plans Committee, Memorandum for Colonel Twitchel, 26 April 1946, RG 319 MMR, ABC 686 Phil (8 Nov 43), sec. 1-B; Intelligence Division, War Department General Staff, "Problems Facing the New Republic of the Philippines," 20 July 1946, p. 2, RG 319 MMR, P & O 350.05, case 94; Butterworth to Secretary of State, 3 December 1948, DSNA 811.24596/12-348.

115. William D. Leahy, for JCS, Memorandum for Secretary of Defense, 13 July 1948, JSPC 822/2/D, RG 218, CCS 686.9 Phil Is. (11-7-43), sec. 8; C.V.R.S., Memorandum to General Wedemeyer, 14 April 1948, RG 319 MMR, P & O 091 PI, sec. II-B, case 12/63; Butterworth to Secretary of State, 3 December 1948, DSNA 811.24596/12-348.

116. William D. Leahy, for JCS, Memorandum for Secretary of Defense, 13 July 1948, JSPC 822/2/D, RG 218, CCS 686.9 Phil Is. (11-7-43), sec. 8.

117. "Military Assistance to the Philippines: Agreement Between the United States and the Republic of the Philippines, March 21, 1947," pp. 881–85, in Sen. Doc. 123 (as cited in note 107, above); Joint Staff Planners, JPS 822/1, 31 January 1947, appendix B, p. 9, RG 319 MMR, ABC 686 Phil (8 Nov 43), sec. 1-D; McNutt to Secretary of State, 14 March 1947, DSNA 811.24596/3-1447. On denials, see Hearings, *Security Agreements*, pp. 243–44.

118. Joint Staff Planners, JPS 756/6, 17 January 1946, "United States Military Assistance to the Philippines," appendix B, RG 218, CCS 686.9 Phil

Is. (11-7-43), sec. 2; U.S. *Cong. Rec.*, 14 June 1946, p. 6967; JCS 1519/6, 2 October 1947, p. 69, RG 218, CCS 686.9 Phil Is. (11-7-43), sec. 6.

119. E.g., MacArthur to Manuel Roxas, 29 October 1946, DAM Papers, RG 10, VIP Correspondence, Manuel Roxas; Chief JUSMAG Philippines to Commander-in-Chief Far East, NR: GX 5174 JUSMAG, 17 November 1948, DAM Papers, RG 9, Messages Phil. Is.; JCS 1519/44, 19 July 1950, p. 418, RG 218, CCS 686.9 Phil Is. (11-7-43), sec. 12.

120. Joint Strategic Plans Committee, JSPC 822/9, 23 February 1949, enclosure B, p. 8, RG 218, CCS 686.9 Phil Is. (11-7-43), sec. 9.

121. Adjutant General, War Department, to Commander-in-Chief, AFPAC, 9 October 1946, p. 2, enclosure 6 to U.S. Military Mission to the Philippines, *History of United States Military Advisory Group to Republic of the Philippines*, vol. 1, *1 July 1946 to 30 June 1947*, unpublished, available at Fort McNair, Washington, D.C.

122. U.S. Military Mission to the Philippines, vol. 1 (as cited in note 121 above), p. 8; Nathaniel P. Davis to Secretary of State, 28 June 1947, DSNA 896.105/6-2847; JUSMAG, *Weekly Summary of Activities*, 30 July 1947, RG 319 MMR, P & O 091.711 PI, sec. V-A, case 46; Chief JUSMAG to JCS, 9 September 1948, JCS 1519/15, 24 September 1948, p. 150, RG 218, CCS 686.9 Phil Is. (11-7-43), sec. 8; Chief JUSMAG to MacArthur, NR: GX 5188, 13 December 1948, NR: GX 5199, 22 December 1948, DAM Papers, RG 9, messages: Philippine Islands.

123. *FR* 1947, vol. 6, pp. 130, 130 n.48; *Washington Post*, 11 January 1946, printed in U.S. *Cong. Rec.*, 7 February 1946, p. A584; *NYT*, 12 October 1946, p. 5; J. K. Penfield to Colonel Bastion, 16 October 1946, RG 319 MMR, P & O 091 PI, case 2.

Chapter Three: The Crisis of the Early 1950s

1. Benedict J. Kerkvliet, *The Huk Rebellion: A Study of Peasant Revolt in the Philippines* (Berkeley: University of California Press, 1977), pp. 168–72. On the Huks' not intending at this time to overthrow the government, see also Benedict J. Kerkvliet, "Peasant Rebellion in the Philippines: The Origins and Growth of the HMB" (Ph.D. dissertation, University of Wisconsin, 1972), p. 578; Renze L. Hoeksema, "Communism in the Philippines: A Historical and Analytical Study of Communism and the Communist Party in the Philippines and Its Relations to Communist Movements Abroad" (Ph.D. dissertation, Harvard University, 1956), pp. 344, 375.

2. *NYT*, 7 March 1948, p. 25 (Ford Wilkins); Teodoro A. Agoncillo, *A Short History of the Philippines* (New York: Mentor, 1969), pp. 268–69; Richard M. Leighton, Ralph Sanders, and Jose N. Tinio, *The Huk Rebellion: A Case Study in the Social Dynamics of Insurrection*, Pub. No. R-231 (Washington, D.C.: Industrial College of the Armed Forces, March 1964), p. 29; Alvin H. Scaff, *The Philippine Answer to Communism* (Stanford, Calif.: Stanford University Press, 1955), pp. 28, 35.

3. Robert Ross Smith, "The Hukbalahap Insurgency: Economic, Political, and Military Factors," photocopied (Washington, D.C.: Office of the Chief of Military History, Department of the Army, 1963), p. 81; Lockett to Secretary of State, 18 August 1948, DSNA 896.00/8-1848; Uldarico S. Baclagon, *Lessons from the Huk Campaign in the Philippines* (Manila: M. Colcol & Co., 1960), pp. 179–80; Lockett to Secretary of State, 15 August 1948, DSNA 896.00/8-1548.

4. Hester to Secretary of State, 17 November 1949, DSNA 896.00/11-1749; Lockett to Secretary of State, 25 March 1949, DSNA 896.00(W)/3-2549; Gabriel, AC of S [Assistant Chief of Staff], G-2, AFP, Intelligence Summary no. 142, week ending 12 September 1948, transmitted with Manila Embassy to Secretary of State, 17 September 1948, DSNA 896.00/9-1748; *FR* 1950, vol. 6, pp. 1435–36; Lockett to Secretary of State, 15 April 1949, DSNA 896.00(W)/4-1549.

5. *Report and Recommendations of the Joint Philippine-American Finance Commission*, Manila, 7 June 1947, H. Doc. 390, 80th Cong., 1st sess., 8 July 1947, pp. 35–37 (hereafter cited as JPAFC); U.S. *Cong. Rec.*, 9 April 1947, p. 3247; 22 April 1947, p. A1807; 26 September 1949, p. 13237.

6. JPAFC, pp. 3–5; William McC. Martin, Jr., Memorandum for John W. Snyder, 1 February 1950, JWS Papers, Philippine Islands—General, 1946–51, alphabetical file; Hearings, held in executive session, *Reviews of the World Situation: 1949–1950*, CFR, 81st Cong., 1st and 2nd sess., 1949–50, made public June 1974, Historical Series, p. 156 (hereafter cited as Hearings, *World Situation*); Dean Acheson, *Present at the Creation: My Years in the State Department* (New York: Signet, 1969), p. 341. On business interests: Bankers Trust Company, N.Y., "The Philippines, Jan. 1948: Notes Prepared by One of Our Representatives Who Recently Visited That Country," p. 10, in MMC Papers, box 3, correspondence, Bankers Trust Co. (J. Morden Murphy) file; *FR* 1950, vol. 6, p. 1519.

7. Jean Grossholtz, *Politics in the Philippines* (Boston: Little, Brown & Co., 1964), p. 167 n.12, citing Elpidio Quirino, "Memoirs," *Manila Sunday Times Magazine*, 27 January 1957.

8. Jose V. Abueva, *Ramon Magsaysay: A Political Biography* (Manila: Solidaridad Publishing House, 1971), p. 142. For background on the Quirino-Avelino feud, see Dapen Liang, *Philippine Political Parties and Politics*, rev. ed. (San Francisco: Gladstone Co., 1970), pp. 304–5, 335 n.116.

9. Lockett to Secretary of State, 6 July 1949, DSNA 896.00/7-649; Cowen to Secretary of State, 27 September 1949, DSNA 896.00/9-2749; Edward W. Mill, Memorandum of Conversation, 21 April 1949, enclosure to Lockett to Secretary of State, 22 April 1949, DSNA 711.96/4-2249; CIA, "The Death of Philippine President Roxas," Special Evaluation No. 30, 6 April 1948, p. 2, RG 319 MMR, P & O 350.05, sec. XIII, case 316; Merle D. Thompson, "Memorandum Re—The Philippine Islands" (April or May 1949?), in MMC Papers, box 4, correspondence, National Foreign Trade Council file; Ely to Acting Secretary of State, 26 May 1949, DSNA 896.00/5-2649; James E. Webb, 3 June 1949, DSNA 896.00/8-349. Contribu-

tions: U.S. *Cong. Rec.*, 20 May 1953, p. 5201, citing interview with Jose P. Laurel by Homer Bigart in *Manila Herald,* 13 March 1953. Laurel's comments are likely to be reliable because they were made at a time when he was supporting the pro-American Magsaysay.

10. A. V. H. Hartendorp, *A History of Industry and Trade of the Philippines: From Pre-Spanish Times to the End of the Quirino Administration* (Manila: American Chamber of Commerce of the Philippines, 1958), p. 280; James K. Dalton, "The Ins and Outs in the Philippines," *Far Eastern Survey,* 21, no. 12 (30 July 1952), p. 121.

11. Dalton, "Ins and Outs," p. 121; *NYT,* 9 November 1949, p. 19 (Ford Wilkins); Blake Clark, "Are the Philippines Going the Way of China?" *Reader's Digest,* June 1950, p. 33.

12. *NYT,* 24 November 1949, p. 20 (AP); 30 November 1949, p. 19 (UP); Department of State, Office of Public Affairs, *The Philippines Today,* Far Eastern Series 51, Department of State Publication 4415, (Washington, D.C., November, 1951), pp. 9–10; Hoeksema, "Communism," pp. 344, 372, 375; Carlos P. Romulo and Marvin Gray, *The Magsaysay Story* (New York: John Day Co., 1956), p. 104; *FR* 1950, vol. 6, pp. 1441–42. Estimates of Huk strength vary widely; the figures in the text are those most commonly cited.

13. *FR* 1946, vol. 8, p. 911 n.79; JPAFC, pp. 1–5 and passim.

14. William McC. Martin, Jr., Memorandum for John W. Snyder, 1 February 1950, JWS Papers, Philippine Islands—General, 1946–51, alphabetical file. See also Melby to Jessup, 31 August 1949, DSNA 896.00/8-3149.

15. Hearings, *Nomination of Philip C. Jessup to Be United States Representative to the 6th General Assembly of the United Nations,* CFR, 82nd Cong., 1st sess., 1951, p. 603 (assumption); Department of Defense, *United States–Vietnam Relations, 1945–1967,* printed for the use of the HCAS, 1971, vol. 8, pp. 257, 271 (on NSC) (hereafter cited as Pentagon Papers, DoD).

16. Acheson, Memorandum of Conversation with the President, 25 April 1949, DSNA 896.00/5-1949; *FR* 1950, vol. 6, p. 1410; Hearings, *To Amend the Philippine Rehabilitation Act of 1946,* CFA, 81st Cong., 1st and 2nd sess., 1949–50, p. 62 (hereafter cited as Hearings, *Amend Rehabilitation*); U.S. *Cong. Rec.,* 30 June 1950, p. A4899; Hearings, *World Situation,* p. 156.

17. Pentagon Papers, DoD, vol. 8, pp. 247–49, 253; Egbert White, "How to Make Friends in Asia," 25 November 1952, pp. 7, 10, attached to Egbert White to Dwight D. Eisenhower, 5 December 1952, DDE Papers, OF 116-I, Far East. See also Hearings, *World Situation,* p. 87; Acheson, *Present at Creation,* p. 856.

18. Amry Vandenbosch and Richard A. Butwell, *Southeast Asia Among the World Powers* (Lexington, Ky.: University of Kentucky Press, 1957), p. 94 n.11.

19. *FR* 1947, vol. 5, p. 700; Jacobs, Memorandum of Conversation, 1 November 1948, DSNA 896.00/11-148; *DSB,* 28 September 1947, p. 646; Manuel Roxas, *Papers, Addresses and Other Writings of Manuel Roxas* (Manila: Bureau of Printing, 1954), vol. 1, pp. 146–47; R. A. Burman, 4 May 1948, DSNA 896.20/5-448.

20. NSC 51, 1 July 1949, p. 21, in MMR Records (hereafter cited as NSC 51).

21. Hearings, *Amend Rehabilitation*, pp. 59–60.

22. Ibid., p. 98; Edgar G. Crossman to Truman, 19 August 1947, JWS Papers, Philippine Islands—General, 1946–51, alphabetical file. See also *PPP*, Truman, 1950, p. 448; NSC 51, p. 16; *FR* 1950, vol. 6, pp. 171–72, 1443; *FR* 1951, vol. 6, p. 24.

23. Hearings, *Amend Rehabilitation*, pp. 94–95; Cheryl Payer, "Exchange Controls and National Capitalism: The Philippine Experience," *Journal of Contemporary Asia*, 3, no. 1 (1973), pp. 58–59. See also *DSB*, 19 June 1950, p. 1019.

24. William McC. Martin, Jr., Memorandum for John W. Snyder, 1 February 1950, JWS Papers, Philippine Islands—General, 1946–51, alphabetical file; Dean Acheson to Truman, 1 June 1950, Truman to Quirino, 1 June 1950, Quirino to Truman, 8 June 1950, all in HST Papers, OF 1055-G, American Economic Survey Mission to Manila file; Myron M. Cowen to James A. Jacobson, 10 August 1950, MMC Papers, box 3, correspondence, Chase National Bank file; *PPP*, Truman, 1950, pp. 506–7.

25. *FR* 1947, vol. 6, pp. 1117–20; *FR* 1948, vol. 6, pp. 630–31; Joint Strategic Plans Committee, JSPC 822/11, 2 May 1949, enclosure B, p. 7, RG 218, CCS 686.9 Phil Is. (11-7-43), sec. 9.

26. Hearings, *To Amend the Mutual Defense Assistance Act of 1949*, CFA, 81st Cong., 2nd sess., 1950, p. 43; *Communication from the President of the U.S. Transmitting a Supplemental Estimate of Appropriations for the Fiscal Year 1951 of $4,000,000,000 to Provide Military Assistance to Foreign Nations*, H. Doc. 670, 81st Cong., 2nd sess., August 1950, p. 2; Minutes of Briefing for Erskine Mission, 18 September 1950, p. 17, attached to JUSMAG, *Weekly Summary of Activities*, for week ending 23 September 1950, issued 29 September 1950, RG 334, 319.1; JCS 1519/44, 19 July 1950, pp. 421, 423, RG 218, CCS 686.9 Phil Is. (11-7-43), sec. 12.

The JUSMAG records in RG 334 do not contain the entire account of JUSMAG activities, even for the years covered. The collection consists largely of reports prepared by JUSMAG for the information of U.S. officials in other agencies and departments. Excluded are "items of intelligence affecting the security of the U.S. and matters pertaining to the AFP," "complete staff studies and reports prepared for the exclusive use of JUSMAG or the AFP," and "items of information, the release of which might adversely affect the accomplishment of our mission or our relationship with the AFP." See JUSMAG internal memorandum no. 4, 7 May 1952, RG 334, 300.6.

Hereafter the reports in RG 334, 319.1 shall be referred to as follows: (1) Semi-Annual Appraisals and Semi-Annual Reports will be cited as JUSMAG, Semi, with the date of issuance; (2) *Weekly Summary of Activities* will be cited as JUSMAG, Weekly, with the date of issuance.

27. Outside aid: JUSMAG, Semi, 1 February 1953, annex 2, p. 8; Hearings, *To Amend the Mutual Defense Assistance Act of 1949*, CFA, 81st Cong., 2nd sess., 1950, pp. 61–62; Hoeksema, "Communism," p. 466; Max

Beloff, *Soviet Policy in the Far East, 1944–1951* (London: Oxford University Press, 1953), pp. 243 n.4, 245; Department of Defense, *Counter-Guerrilla Operations in the Philippines, 1946–1953: A Seminar on the Huk Campaign Held at Ft. Bragg, N.C., 15 June 1961* (n.p., n.d.), p. 24 (Edward G. Lansdale) (hereafter cited as Fort Bragg Seminar); A. H. Peterson, G. C. Reinhardt, and E. E. Conger, eds., *Symposium on the Role of Airpower in Counter-Insurgency and Unconventional Warfare: The Philippine Huk Campaign*, RM-3652-PR (Santa Monica: Rand Corporation, June 1963), p. 22; RP, HR, Special Committee on Un-Filipino Activities, *Report on 1. The Illegality of the Communist Party of the Philippines, 2. The Functions of the Special Committee on Un-Filipino Activities* (Manila, 1951), p. 97; Luis Taruc, *He Who Rides the Tiger* (New York: Praeger, 1967), p. 33; Lockett to Secretary of State, 8 April 1949, DSNA 896.00(W)/4-849. State Department: *FR* 1951, vol. 6, p. 6. Internal subversion: *FR* 1951, vol. 6, p. 242; *FR* 1950, vol. 6, pp. 172, 1516.

28. *Report of the MDAP Survey Team to the Philippines*, FMACC D-32, 8 February 1950, unpublished, available at Department of State, Washington, D.C., 64 A867, box 353, 2/44/29-4, folder Philippines, January–June 1950, pp. 1, 3; Chief JUSMAG, 4th Semi-Annual Report, 20 September 1949, in JCS 1519/33, 4 October 1949, pp. 309, 316, RG 218, CCS 686.9 Phil Is. (11-7-43), sec. 11; JUSMAG, Semi, 25 March 1950, p. 1; Semi, 18 January 1951, p. 2; Weekly, 8 December 1949, p. 1; Leland S. Hobbs to Quirino, 10 August 1950, Hobbs to MacArthur, 11 August 1950, Hobbs to MacArthur, 25 September 1950, all in DAM Papers, RG 10, VIP Correspondence, Leland S. Hobbs file; Hearings, *U.S. Security Agreements and Commitments Abroad, Part 1: The Republic of the Philippines*, CFR subcommittee, 91st Cong., 1st sess., 1969, p. 36 (hereafter cited as Hearings, *Security Agreements*); *FR* 1951, vol. 6, p. 233. On Japanese Peace Treaty, see Frederick S. Dunn et al., *Peace-Making and the Settlement with Japan* (Princeton: Princeton University Press, 1963).

29. JUSMAG, Semi, 25 March 1950, pp. 4, 5; Semi, 18 January 1951, p. 28; Weekly, 8 December 1949, p. 1; Weekly, 8 June 1950, p. 5; Weekly, 20 April 1950, p. 1. "Insisted": *FR* 1951, vol. 6, p. 1544.

30. JUSMAG, Semi, 25 March 1950, pp. 9–10; Weekly, 2 February 1950, p. 1; Weekly, 9 February 1950, p. 1.

31. Edward G. Lansdale, *In the Midst of Wars: An American's Mission to Southeast Asia* (New York: Harper & Row, 1972), pp. 14–15.

32. Abueva, *Magsaysay*, p. 153 n.13; H. Bradford Westerfield, *The Instruments of America's Foreign Policy* (New York: Thomas Y. Crowell Co., 1963), p. 410; Romulo and Gray, *Magsaysay Story*, p. 106; William O. Douglas, *North from Malaya: Adventure on Five Fronts* (Garden City, N.Y.: Doubleday, 1953), p. 110; Carlos Quirino, *Magsaysay of the Philippines* (Rizal: Carmelo & Bauermann, 1964), pp. 44–45; Carlos P. Romulo, *Crusade in Asia* (New York: John Day Co., 1955), p. 123; Frances L. Starner, *Magsaysay and the Philippine Peasantry: The Agrarian Impact on Philippine Politics, 1953–1956* (Berkeley: University of California Press, 1961), pp. 52, 245 n.39, 250 n.104; William E. Daugherty, "Magsaysay and the Philippine Huks," in Wil-

liam E. Daugherty, ed., in collaboration with Morris Janowitz, *Psychological Warfare Casebook* (Baltimore: Operations Research Office, Johns Hopkins University, 1958), p. 370. Cowen quotation from Myron M. Cowen to Macario Peralta, Jr., 6 July 1950, MMC Papers, box 3, correspondence, Congress—Philippines file.

33. Abueva, *Magsaysay*, pp. 1–33, 48–51, 60, 62–64. Wage in 1939 is from Commonwealth of the Philippines, Commission of the Census, *Census of the Philippines, 1939* (Manila: Bureau of Printing, 1941), vol. 2, p. 676.

34. Abueva, *Magsaysay*, pp. 133 (Galahad), 143, 146 (JUSMAG), 145 (speech). Contacts during trips: Lansdale, *In the Midst*, pp. 13–14; Westerfield, *Instruments*, p. 410; Abueva, *Magsaysay*, p. 146; Hugh Bain Snow, Jr., "United States Policy and the 1953 Philippine Presidential Election" (Master's thesis, American University, 1968), p. 43; A. C. Wedemeyer, Memorandum for Chief of Staff Bradley, 22 August 1948, RG 319 MMR, P & O 091 Phil, case 19/1.

35. C. Quirino, *Magsaysay*, p. 53.

36. Abueva, *Magsaysay*, pp. 172, 172 n. 31; Leland S. Hobbs to Eisenhower, 6 April 1954, DDE Papers, President's Personal File, PPF 248 Hobbs, Maj.-Gen. Leland S. file; JUSMAG, Semi, 18 January 1951, p. 3, *FR 1951*, vol. 6, p. 11.

37. Lansdale, *In the Midst*, pp. 4–5, 36–37, 68; *Time*, 23 November 1953, p. 37; *FR 1951*, vol. 6, p. 1567. Lansdale's early friendship with Magsaysay is mentioned in Edward G. Lansdale, "Lessons Learned: The Philippines, 1946–1956," *Alert*, no. 6A (Washington, D.C.: Department of Defense, 11 December 1962), p. 4.

38. Abueva, *Magsaysay*, p. 159 n.4.

39. Romulo and Gray, *Magsaysay Story*, pp. 133–34; *NYT*, 30 August 1951, p. 3 (Henry R. Lieberman); Westerfield, *Instruments*, p. 411; Romulo, *Crusade*, p. 130; Abueva, *Magsaysay*, p. 180 n.6. On removal of corrupt officers, see R. R. Smith, "Hukbalahap Insurgency," p. 102. A leaflet offering rewards is printed in Fort Bragg Seminar. C. Quirino, *Magsaysay*, p. 63, claims some rewards were as high as 250,000 pesos. Average income figure is from *Report to the President of the United States by the Economic Survey Mission to the Philippines*, Far Eastern Series 38, Department of State Publication No. 4010 (Washington, D.C.: 9 October 1950), p. 16 (daily wage multiplied by 300) (hereafter cited as Bell Report).

40. Hearings, *MSA of 1959*, CFA, 86th Cong., 1st sess., 1959, p. 1476; top secret letter to Myron M. Cowen, from internal evidence from Edward G. Lansdale, 15 April 1952, MMC Papers, box 12, Philippine file (general correspondence). (This file contains top secret letters to Cowen, all unsigned. One has pencilled in "CIA Manila." One is undated and another has the date 15 April 1951 pencilled in. From internal evidence, the latter date should almost certainly be 1952, and the undated one is probably late February 1952. Also from internal evidence, all are from Lansdale. Hereafter these letters will be referred to as Lansdale to Cowen letters no. 1 and no. 2, for the presumed February and 15 April 1952 letters respectively.) Donn V.

Hart, "Magsaysay: Philippine Candidate," *Far Eastern Survey*, 22, no. 6 (May 1953), p. 68, citing Jose M. Crisol, "Psychological Warfare in the Philippines," *Philippine Armed Forces Journal*, November 1952, pp. 18–21; Daugherty, "Magsaysay and the Huks," pp. 371–72; JUSMAG, Semi, 1 August 1952, annex 4, p. 21; Weekly, 24 January 1951, p. 1.

41. Lansdale to Cowen letters, no. 1 and no. 2; JUSMAG, Semi, 1 August 1952, annex 4, pp. 20–21; Semi, 1 February 1953, annex 2, p. 16; Abueva, *Magsaysay*, pp. 183–84, 226 n.13; Lansdale, *In the Midst*, pp. 92–93; Napoleon D. Valeriano and Charles T. R. Bohannan, *Counter-Guerrilla Operations: The Philippine Experience* (New York: Praeger, 1962), p. 226.

42. Jorge R. Coquia, *The Philippine Presidential Election of 1953* (Manila: University Publishing Co., 1955), pp. 309–10; Bureau of Social Science Research, The American University, *Communications and Public Opinion in the Philippines: A Survey of Selected Sources* (Washington, D.C.), Draft prepared for the Office of Research and Intelligence, U.S. Information Agency, BSSR no. 674, January 1955, pp. 53, 68–69, 87–89; Violet E. Wurfel, "American Implementation of Philippine Independence" (Ph.D. dissertation, University of Virginia, 1951), pp. 555–56. See also F. Siolin Jose, "Commentary," *Comment* (Manila), no. 15 (3rd quarter 1962), p. 175.

43. Lansdale, *In the Midst*, pp. 72–73; Lansdale to Cowen letter, no. 1. See also JUSMAG, Weekly, 6 March 1952, p. 1.

44. JUSMAG, Semi, 1 August 1952, annex 4, p. 21.

45. Lansdale, *In the Midst*, p. 376.

46. Frate Bull, *Land Reform in the Philippines, 1950–1958* (N.p.: International Cooperation Administration, 1958[?]), pp. 18–19, citing Ray E. Davis, final report, February 1957; Scaff, *Philippine Answer*, p. 128. Huk views are indicated in Hearings, *MSA Extension*, CFA, 82nd Cong., 2nd sess., 1952, p. 924 (cf. William J. Pomeroy, "Lessons of the Philippine Guerrilla War," *Monthly Review*, 15, no. 5 (September 1963), p. 247; Scaff, *Philippine Answer*, p. 112. EDCOR figures are from Frank H. Golay, *The Philippines: Public Policy and National Economic Development* (Ithaca: Cornell University Paperbacks, 1968), p. 284. Number of tenant families (actually the number of farms cultivated by tenants) is the 1948 figure from Golay, *The Philippines*, p. 271.

47. Roger Hilsman, interview transcript, 14 August 1970, p. 22, KOHP.

48. R. R. Smith, "Hukbalahap Insurgency," p. 105; JUSMAG, Semi, 18 July 1951, p. 17; FR 1951, vol. 6, p. 1493.

49. JUSMAG, Semi, 18 January 1951, pp. 13, 28; Minutes of Briefing for Erskine Mission, 18 September 1950, pp. 13–14, attached to JUSMAG, Weekly, 29 September 1950; R. R. Smith, "Hukbalahap Insurgency," p. 122. For some sample treatment of prisoners, see Scaff, *Philippine Answer*, pp. 55, 57, 60, 126–28.

50. Minutes of Briefing for Erskine Mission, 18 September 1950, pp. 13–14, attached to JUSMAG, Weekly, 29 September 1950; JUSMAG, Semi, 14 February 1952, p. 2; Semi, 1 February 1953, annex 1.

51. *FR* 1951, vol. 6, p. 1555; JCS 1519/67, 6 April 1951, revised 23 April 1951, pp. 585–86, RG 218, CCS 686.9 Phil Is. (11-7-43), sec. 15.

52. JUSMAG, Semi, 18 January 1951, pp. 7, 28, 49; Semi, 18 July 1951, pp. 14–16, 21; Weekly, 4 January 1951, p. 1; Weekly, 1 February 1951, p. 1; Weekly, 21 February 1951, p. 1; Weekly, 14 March 1951, p. 1; Weekly, 26 April 1951, p. 2; Weekly, 7 May 1951, p. 2.

53. JUSMAG, Weekly, 3 August 1950, p. 2; Minutes of Briefing for Erskine Mission, 18 September 1950, pp. 13–14, attached to JUSMAG, Weekly, 29 September 1950; JUSMAG, Semi, 18 July 1951, pp. 27–28.

54. JUSMAG, Semi, 18 January 1951, p. 26; Semi, 18 July 1951, p. 49; Weekly, 7 February 1951, pp. 1–2; Semi, 1 August 1952, annex 4, p. 22; Lansdale to Cowen letter, no. 1; *FR* 1951, vol. 6, pp. 1520–21 (quote), 1538, 1549; JCS 1519/44, 19 July 1950, pp. 421–22, 427, RG 218, CCS 686.9 Phil Is. (11-7-43), sec. 12; JCS 1519/46, 1 September 1950, pp. 435–42, RG 218, CCS 686.9 Phil Is. (11-7-43), sec. 13.

55. JUSMAG, Semi, 18 January 1951, p. 16; Semi, 18 July 1951, p. 60; Semi, 14 February 1952, p. 4, annex F, pp. 4–5; Semi, 1 August 1952, p. 5, annex 6, p. 7.

56. JUSMAG, Weekly, 17 November 1949, pp. 2–3; Weekly, 13 December 1950, p. 2; Weekly, 22 December 1950, pp. 3–4; Weekly, 11 January 1952, p. 7; Semi, 14 February 1952, annex F, p. 5; Hester to Secretary of State, 17 November 1949, DSNA 896.00/11-1749; *FR* 1951, vol. 6, pp. 1549–53, 1572–73, 1577, 1579–80, 1588–89, 1593.

57. Peterson, Reinhardt, and Conger, eds., *Symposium: Huk Campaign,* p. 36.

58. Lansdale to Cowen letter, no.1.

59. *FR* 1950, vol. 6, pp. 1515, 1520; JCS 1519/44, 19 July 1950, p. 421, RG 218, CCS 686.9 Phil Is. (11-7-43), sec. 12; *FR* 1950, vol. 6, p. 170.

60. Bell Report, pp. 1 (quote), 3–5, 59, 81, 95, 101, 105. The high-level acceptance of the Bell Mission's recommendations is reflected in NSC 84/2, printed in *FR* 1950, vol. 6, pp. 1514–20.

61. Bell Report, p. 5; David Wurfel, "Foreign Aid and Social Reform in Political Development: A Philippine Case Study," *American Political Science Review,* 53, no. 2 (1959), p. 463; *FR* 1950, vol. 6, p. 1432; Department of State, *Transcript of Round Table Discussion on American Policy Toward China Held in the Department of State, October 6, 7, and 8, 1949* (available at Department of State, Washington, D.C.), p. 127; *FR* 1950, vol. 6, p. 1483.

62. RP, Department of Foreign Affairs, *Treaty Series,* vol. 2, no. 1 (January 1953), pp. 11–12; *FR* 1951, vol. 6, pp. 1495–97; Hearings, *World Situation,* p. 386.

63. U.S. *Cong. Rec.,* 23 August 1951, pp. A5369–70; D. Wurfel, "Foreign Aid," p. 466; *NYT,* 3 January 1952, p. 81; Louis F. Felder, *Socioeconomic Aspects of Counterinsurgency, A Case History: The Philippines* (Washington, D.C: Industrial College of the Armed Forces, 1963), p. 37.

64. Bell Report, p. 55; David Wurfel, "Philippine Agrarian Reform Under Magsaysay (II)," *Far Eastern Survey,* 37, no. 2 (February 1958), p. 28;

Conrado F. Estrella, *The Democratic Answer to the Philippine Agrarian Problem* (Manila: Solidaridad Publishing House, 1969), p. 37; *FR* 1950, vol. 6, p. 1449 n.4. Concerning not being included in Quirino-Foster agreement, *FR* 1951, vol. 6, p. 1529.

65. Theodore Tannenwald, Jr., to Norman Paul, 10 November 1952, TT Papers, box 3, chronological file, 1952. On aid, see Westerfield, *Instruments,* p. 409.

66. Mutual Security Administration (Robert S. Hardie), *Philippine Land Tenure Reform: Analysis and Recommendations* (Manila, 1952), pp. 21, 32–33, 25 (principle), 8 (communism).

67. Starner, *Magsaysay,* p. 137; Bull, *Land Reform,* p. 72; Hernando J. Abaya, *The Untold Philippine Story* (Quezon City: Malaya Books, 1967), pp. 75–78.

68. Harry S. Truman, 6 April 1951, HST Papers, OF 1055 (1950–53); George W. Humphrey, Memorandum for the President, 29 June 1953, DDE Papers, OF 212, Philippines, Republic of the (1); *NYT,* 15 April 1951, p. 46 (UP); Dun and Bradstreet's *International Markets,* December 1953, p. 42.

69. Bell Report, pp. 70, 67; also pp. 53, 68.

70. Golay, *The Philippines,* pp. 79–80, 84.

Chapter Four: "America's Boy"

1. Joseph Burkholder Smith, *Portrait of a Cold Warrior* (New York: G. P. Putnam's Sons, 1976), pp. 107–8. See also Jose A. Lansang, "The Philippine-American Experiment: A Filipino View," *Pacific Affairs,* 25, no. 3 (September 1952), p. 228; Russell H. Fifield, "The Challenge to Magsaysay," *Foreign Affairs,* 33, no. 1 (October 1954), p. 152; Willard H. Elsbree, "The Philippines," in Rupert Emerson, ed., *Representative Government in Southeast Asia* (Cambridge, Mass.: Harvard University Press, 1955), p. 107.

2. *FR* 1951, vol. 6, p. 1570; Carlos Quirino, *Magsaysay of the Philippines* (Rizal: Carmelo & Bauermann, 1964), pp. 76–77; Edward G. Lansdale, "Lessons Learned: The Philippines, 1946–1956," *Alert,* no. 6A (Washington, D.C.: Department of Defense, 11 December 1962), p. 7.

3. Dapen Liang, *Philippine Parties and Politics,* rev. ed. (San Francisco: Gladstone Co., 1970), p. 339 n.179; *NYT,* 11 November 1951, p. 3. "Election-related deaths" is, of course, a subjective term, so estimates vary widely.

4. *FR* 1951, vol. 6, p. 247; Butterworth to Lovett, 16 April 1948, DSNA 711.96/4-1648; Acheson, Memorandum for President, 26 July 1949, DSNA 896.001 Quirino/7-2649; *FR* 1950, vol. 6, pp. 1442–44; *FR* 1951, vol. 6, p. 8; *FR* 1950, vol. 6, p. 1405.

5. *FR* 1950, vol. 6, pp. 1442, 1447, 1455–56.

6. C. Quirino, *Magsaysay,* p. 69; A. V. H. Hartendorp, *A History of Industry and Trade of the Philippines: The Magsaysay Administration* (Manila: Philippine Education Co., 1961), p. 1. Articles are listed in Jorge R. Coquia, *The Philippine Presidential Election of 1953* (Manila: University Publishing Co.,

1955), p. 236 n.47; Harold F. Gosnell, "An Interpretation of the Philippine Election of 1953," *American Political Science Review,* 48, no. 4 (December 1954), pp. 1132–33 n.13. CIA: interview with Ralph B. Lovett by Thomas B. Buell, p. 6 of transcript, TBB Papers.

7. Quoted in Coquia, *Election of 1953,* p. 237.

8. Jose V. Abueva, "Bridging the Gap Between the Elite and the People in the Philippines," *Philippine Journal of Public Administration,* 8, no. 4 (October 1964), pp. 333–34.

9. CIA: interviews by Thomas B. Buell with Ralph B. Lovett, p. 5 of transcript; with Edward G. Lansdale, p. 2; Robert Cannon, p. 7, all in TBB Papers. AFP: Jose V. Abueva, *Ramon Magsaysay: A Political Biography* (Manila: Solidaridad Publishing House, 1971), p. 210 n.15; L. Fletcher Prouty, *The Secret Team: The CIA and Its Allies in Control of the World* (New York: Ballantine Books, 1973), pp. 38–39, 93.

10. Carlos P. Romulo and Marvin Gray, *The Magsaysay Story* (New York: John Day Co., 1956), pp. 162–66, 168; H. Bradford Westerfield, *The Instruments of America's Foreign Policy* (New York: Thomas Y. Crowell Co., 1963), pp. 413–14; C. Quirino, *Magsaysay,* pp. 85–90; Abueva, *Magsaysay,* pp. 212 n.19, 213. On Gonzalez, see Isidro L. Retizos and D. H. Soriano, *Philippine Who's Who* (Quezon City: Capitol Publishing House, Inc., 1957), pp. 117–18; Hartendorp, *History,* 1961, pp. 26–27.

11. Romulo and Gray, *Magsaysay Story,* p. 167; Westerfield, *Instruments,* p. 414; Abueva, *Magsaysay,* pp. 190–91; JUSMAG, Semi, 18 January 1951, pp. 46–47 (see Chapter Three, note 26).

12. On fund: Westerfield, *Instruments,* p. 411; Lansdale, "Lessons," p. 5. On Mexico City, Romulo and Gray, *Magsaysay Story,* pp. 168–69.

13. Abueva, *Magsaysay,* pp. 226, 229–30, 232; Thomas B. Buell, *The Quiet Warrior: A Biography of Admiral Raymond A. Spruance* (Boston: Little, Brown & Co., 1974), pp. 407–8; interview with Edward G. Lansdale by Thomas B. Buell, pp. 6–7 of transcript, TBB Papers. The quote is from C. Quirino, *Magsaysay,* p. 94.

14. *NYT,* 30 March 1953, pp. 1, 3; Coquia, *Election of 1953,* p. 126; *Manila Chronicle,* 31 March 1953, reprinted in U.S. *Cong. Rec.,* 18 June 1953, p. 6795; *Christian Science Monitor,* 11 April 1953, reprinted in U.S. *Cong. Rec.,* 20 May 1953, p. 5201; *NYT,* 31 March 1953, p. 3.

15. *Manila Chronicle,* 31 March 1953, reprinted in U.S. *Cong. Rec.,* 18 June 1953, p. 6795; *Seventh and Final Report of the High Commissioner to the Philippines,* Sen. Doc. 389, 80th Cong., 1st sess., 1947, pp. 78, 154; Milton Meyer, *A Diplomatic History of the Philippine Republic* (Honolulu: University of Hawaii Press, 1965), p. 108.

16. Abueva, *Magsaysay,* p. 264; Coquia, *Election of 1953,* pp. 307–10, 237 (Howard), 126–27 (Alsop); Carlos P. Romulo to Myron M. Cowen, 10 March 1953, MMC Papers, box 7, correspondence, Carlos Romulo file.

17. Romulo and Gray, *Magsaysay Story,* p. 197; Hartendorp, *History,* 1961, p. 26; Russell H. Fifield, *Southeast Asia in United States Policy* (New York: Praeger, 1963), p. 306; Abueva, *Magsaysay,* pp. 260, 358.

18. Romulo: *FR* 1951, vol. 6, p. 1527; blackmail: J. B. Smith, *Portrait,* pp. 109–10.

19. Abueva, *Magsaysay,* pp. 256–59; Carlos P. Romulo to Myron M. Cowen, 9 July 1953, MMC Papers, box 7, correspondence, Carlos Romulo file; Hugh Bain Snow, Jr., "United States Policy and the 1953 Philippine Presidential Election" (Master's thesis, American University, 1968), p. 68; Westerfield, *Instruments,* pp. 415–16; Coquia, *Election of 1953,* p. 269; Carlos P. Romulo, *Crusade in Asia* (New York: John Day Co., 1955), p. 198.

20. Coquia, *Election of 1953,* pp. 219, 246, 262; David Wurfel, "The Philippines," *Journal of Politics,* 25, no. 4 (1963), pp. 758, 758 n.3; Frances L. Starner, *Magsaysay and the Philippine Peasantry: The Agrarian Impact on Philippine Politics, 1953–1956* (Berkeley: University of California Press, 1961), p. 53; Edward G. Lansdale to Myron M. Cowen, 11 June 1953, secret, MMC Papers, box 6, correspondence, Edward Lansdale file. Almost every businessperson: interview with Robert Cannon by Thomas B. Buell, p. 7 of transcript, TBB Papers.

21. Lansdale to author, 20 May 1975; *Time,* 23 November 1953, p. 37; Carl H. Landé, "Politics in the Philippines" (Ph.D. dissertation, Harvard University, 1958), p. 230. Other references to private U.S. funds backing Magsaysay are in Westerfield, *Instruments,* p. 416; David Wurfel, "The Philippines," in George McT. Kahin, ed., *The Governments and Politics of Southeast Asia* (Ithaca, N.Y.: Cornell University Press, 1964), p. 703; and Edward R. Kiunisala, "What Elections Mean to Me," *PFP,* 11 November 1967, p. 6. Lansdale says Americans contributed "small amounts" (Lansdale to author, 20 May 1975).

22. Interviews by Thomas B. Buell with Edward G. Lansdale (p. 3 of transcript) and with Ralph B. Lovett (pp. 2–4), TBB Papers.

23. Buell, *Quiet Warrior,* p. 416; *DSB,* 19 October 1953, p. 524; 16 November 1953, pp. 676–77; Theodore Tannenwald to Norman Paul, 10 November 1952, TT Papers, box 3, chronological file, 1952; Spruance to Nimitz, 19 October 1953, TBB Papers, box 2, correspondence 1942–73; Spruance to Secretary of State, 6 March 1953, 796.00/3-653 in TBB Papers; Snow, "U.S. Policy," p. 90.

24. Interviews by Thomas B. Buell with Edward G. Lansdale, p. 5 of transcript; with Ralph B. Lovett, pp. 4, 6; with Robert Cannon, p. 19, all in TBB Papers.

25. Abueva, *Magsaysay,* pp. 253, 269.

26. *NYT,* 5 November 1953, p. 6; Liang, *Philippine Parties,* p. 341 n.208.

27. *NYT,* 11 November 1953, pp. 1, 4 (Tillman Durdin); Liang, *Philippine Parties,* pp. 328, 342 n.214. On JUSMAG, see Westerfield, *Instruments,* p. 418; Coquia, *Election of 1953,* pp. 134–35; *Time,* 23 November 1953, p. 37; *NYT,* 19 November 1953, p. 10 (Ford Wilkins).

28. J. B. Smith, *Portrait,* p. 113; *Time,* 23 November 1953, p. 37; State of the Union message quoted in Hartendorp, *History,* 1961, p. 34.

29. Department of Commerce, Bureau of Foreign Commerce, *Investment in the Philippines: Conditions and Outlook for United States Investors* (Washington, D.C., 1955), p. 4.

30. Ramon Magsaysay, "Roots of Philippine Policy," *Foreign Affairs*, 35, no. 1 (October 1956), p. 33.

31. Meyer, *Diplomatic History*, p. 167; Sung Yong Kim, *United States–Philippine Relations, 1946–1956* (Washington, D.C.: Public Affairs Press, 1968), p. 37. Recto's views are in Kim, *Relations*, pp. 42, 44, 63, 153 n.11, 153 n.12; and Abueva, *Magsaysay*, p. 387.

32. J. B. Smith, *Portrait*, pp. 254–55.

33. Carlos P. Garcia, interview transcript, 18 September 1964, p. 14, DOHC; Abueva, *Magsaysay*, p. 449; Raul S. Manglapus, "The Philippine Stand on the Recognition of South Vietnam," *Department of Foreign Affairs Review* (Phil.), 2, no. 2 (January 1956), pp. 31–35.

34. Department of Defense, *History of United States Decisionmaking on Vietnam* (Boston: Beacon Press, 1971), vol. 1, p. 473; vol. 2, pp. 647–48; J. B. Smith, *Portrait*, pp. 251–52.

35. *Report to the President of the United States by the Economic Survey Mission to the Philippines*, Far Eastern Series 38, Department of State Publication No. 4010 (Washington, D.C., 9 October 1950), pp. 85, 88 (hereafter cited as Bell Report).

36. Ibid., p. 85, also pp. 87–88; RP, Department of Foreign Affairs, *Treaty Series*, vol. 2, no. 1 (January 1953), p. 11.

37. *DSB*, 7 September 1953, p. 317 n.2; 19 October 1953, p. 524; *Philippine Newsletter Supplement*, 18 September 1953, in MMC Papers, box 6, Correspondence, Philippines—General.

38. H. Report 1887, 83rd Cong., 2nd sess., 17 June 1954; Sen. Report 1700, 83rd Cong., 2nd sess., 1 July 1954; U.S. *Cong. Rec.*, 23 June 1954, pp. 8766–67.

39. U.S. *Cong. Rec.*, 22 June 1954, pp. 8656–57; 23 June 1954, pp. 8766–68; 2 July 1954, p. 9604; *TIAS* 3039, 7 July 1954, pp. 1629–37; Walter K. Scott, Memorandum for A. J. Goodpaster, 26 April 1955, DDE Papers, OF 212, Philippines, Republic of (2).

40. Cheryl Payer, "Martial Law and the Economic Crisis," in *The Philippines: End of an Illusion* (London: Association for Radical East Asian Studies, 1973), p. 94; Amry Vandenbosch and Richard A. Butwell, *Southeast Asia Among the World Powers* (Lexington, Ky.: University of Kentucky Press, 1957), p. 104. See also Hartendorp, *History*, 1961, pp. 137–38.

41. U.S. *Cong. Rec.*, 10 May 1955, pp. 5993–94; Hearings, *Philippine Trade Revision Act of 1955*, CWM, 84th Cong., 1st sess., 1955, p. 44. The text of the act is in U.S. *Stat.*, vol. 69, pp. 413–27.

42. RP, Department of Labor, Labor Statistics Division, "Wages and Working Conditions in Our Sugar Cane Haciendas in Negros Occidental," *Philippine Labor*, May 1962, pp. 14, 17.

43. U.S. *Cong. Rec.*, 10 May 1955, pp. 5993–94; Frank H. Golay, *The Revised United States Philippine Trade Agreement of 1955*, Southeast Asia

Program, Department of Far Eastern Studies, Data Paper No. 23 (Ithaca, N.Y.: Cornell University, November 1956), p. 26; *DSB,* 19 September 1955, p. 466.

44. Frank H. Golay, "The Philippine Monetary Policy Debate," *Pacific Affairs,* 29, no. 3 (September 1956), pp. 260–64.

45. Golay, *Revised Trade Agreement of 1955,* p. 12; U.S. *Cong. Rec.,* 10 May 1955, p. 5994; Vincent P. Rock, Memorandum for Arthur S. Fleming, 27 October 1954, and Carl D. Corse, Memorandum for McPhee (no date, 1955), both in DDE Papers, OF 149-B-2, Cordage (1).

46. U.S. *Cong. Rec.,* 10 May 1955, p. 5994.

47. Ibid., p. 5995; 18 July 1955, p. 10662; Hearings, *Philippine Trade Revision Act of 1955,* CWM, 84th Cong., 1st sess., 1955, pp. 41–42.

48. U.S. *Cong. Rec.,* 7 July 1955, p. 10079; 18 July 1955, pp. 10661–62; 7 July 1955, pp. 10078, 10082; H. Report 934, 84th Cong., 1st sess., 27 June 1955, pp. 9–10.

49. *Survey of Current Business,* annual issues 1958–72, for book value and earnings. Center for Strategic and International Studies, *U.S.-Philippines Economic Relations,* Special Report Series No. 12 (Washington, D.C.: Georgetown University, 1971), p. 17; *Business Week,* 4 November 1972, p. 42; *Wall Street Journal,* 21 August 1972, p. 12; and *NYT,* 26 September 1972, p. 13 (Gerd Wilcke) for market value. The 10 percent tax figure and overall profitability from Thomas E. Weisskopf, "United States Foreign Private Investment: An Empirical Study," in *The Capitalist System,* written and edited by Richard C. Edwards, Michael Reich, and Thomas E. Weisskopf (Englewood Cliffs, N.J.: Prentice-Hall, 1972), pp. 428 n.3, 429.

50. RP, Inter-Agency Working Group on Foreign Investments, "Study of Private Foreign Investments in the Philippines," part 2, *Philippine Progress,* 6 (3rd quarter 1972), p. 5; RP, National Economic Council, Office of Statistical Coordination and Standards, "American Investments in the Philippines," *Philippine Progress,* 2, no. 7 (March 1969), p. 5; Felipe Suva Martin, "U.S. Direct Investment in the Philippines" (Ph.D. dissertation, MIT, 1971), pp. 379–82, 384, 425; Kunio Yoshihara, "A Study of Philippine Manufacturing Corporations," *Developing Economies,* 9, no. 3 (September 1971), p. 279.

51. Cesar Virata et al., *Restrictions on Exports in Foreign Collaboration Agreements in the Republic of the Philippines,* TD/B/388, (New York: U.N. Conference on Trade and Development, 1972), pp. 10, 18, 20. See also Yoshihara, "Manufacturing Corporations," pp. 282–83; Alejandro Lichauco, "Imperialism in the Philippines," *Monthly Review,* 25, no. 3 (July–August 1973), p. 30.

52. One-third: International Labour Office, *Sharing in Development: A Programme of Employment, Equity and Growth for the Philippines* (Geneva, 1974), p. 284; Amado Castro quoted in Philippine Association, *Weekly Economic Review,* 20, no. 22 (9 June 1972), p. 218. Eighty percent: Inter-Agency Working Group on Foreign Investments, "Study of Private For-

eign Investments in the Philippines," part 1, *Philippine Progress*, 6 (2nd quarter 1972), p. 7.

53. Westerfield, *Instruments*, p. 446; David Wise and Thomas B. Ross, *The Invisible Government* (New York: Bantam Books, 1964), p. 147; Claude A. Buss, *Arc of Crisis* (Garden City, N.Y.: Doubleday & Co., 1961), pp. 165–66; Roger Hilsman, *To Move a Nation* (Garden City, N.Y.: Doubleday & Co., 1967), p. 369; Fred Greene, *United States Policy and the Security of Asia* (New York: McGraw-Hill, 1968), p. 148.

54. Hearings, *FAA of 1962*, CFA, 87th Cong., 2nd sess., 1962, pp. 237–38; Hearings, *FAA of 1964*, CFA, 88th Cong., 2nd sess., 1964, p. 500; *DSB*, 21 March 1966, p. 446; Hearings, *FAA of 1967*, CFA, 90th Cong., 1st sess., 1967, p. 113.

55. Greene, *U.S. Policy*, pp. 147, 325; *NYT*, 21 November 1965, p. 8 (Seymour Topping); 27 December 1968, p. 14; Comptroller General, *Report to the Congress: Military Assistance and Commitments in the Philippines*, 12 April 1973, B-133359, pp. 37–38; Hearings, *U.S. Security Agreements and Commitments Abroad, Part 1: The Republic of the Philippines*, CFR subcommittee, 91st Cong., 1st sess., 1969, p. 91 (hereafter cited as Hearings, *Security Agreements*); *NYT*, 21 January 1973, sec. 4, p. 17 (Tom Wicker on nuclear weapons).

56. Hearings, *MSA of 1959*, CFR, 86th Cong., 1st sess., 1959, p. 12; Hearings, *Security Agreements*, pp. 60–61; Hearings, *To Amend the FAA of 1961*, CFA, 91st Cong., 2nd sess., 1970, p. 110; Hearings, *FARPA, FY73*, SCAp subcommittee, 92nd Cong., 2nd sess., 1972, p. 938.

57. William E. Stevenson, interview transcript, 4–5 May 1969, pp. 46, 65, KOHP; Department of State, *Transcript of Round Table Discussion on American Policy Toward China Held in the Department of State, October 6, 7, and 8, 1949* (available at Department of State, Washington, D.C.), p. 402 (Marshall); *PFP*, 28 June 1969, pp. 8ff. (Edward R. Kiunisala).

58. Department of State, Historical Division, *American Foreign Policy: Current Documents, 1956* (Washington, D.C., 1959), pp. 858–59; U.S. *Cong. Rec.*, 17 July 1956, p. 13193. On the U.S. Attorney General, see Teodoro A. Agoncillo, *A Short History of the Philippines* (New York: Mentor, 1969), p. 290.

59. *TIAS* 4388 (1959); Hearings, *Security Agreements*, pp. 12, 352, 27, 38.

60. *DSB*, 30 August 1965, p. 358; Hearings, *Status of Forces Agreements*, CFA, 84th Cong., 1st sess., 1955, pt. 1, pp. 41, 16; *TIAS* 6084 (1966).

61. Relinquishment: *TIAS* 5289 (1963), 5924 (1965), 6180 (1966), 6506 (1968), 7204 (1971); *PFP*, 8 January 1966, p. 64. Resources: *TIAS* 4008 (1958), 6335 (1967). Employment: *TIAS* 5452 (1963), 6542 (1968).

62. Committee Print, *Korea and the Philippines: November 1972*, Staff report for CFR, 93rd Cong., 1st sess., 18 February 1973, p. 41.

63. Frank H. Golay, *The Philippines: Public Policy and National Economic Development* (Ithaca, N.Y.: Cornell University Paperbacks, 1968), p. 89. See also *NYT*, 15 March 1955, p. 4 (Robert Alden).

Chapter Five: The Instruments of Neocolonialism

1. Department of Defense, *United States–Vietnam Relations, 1945–1967*, printed for the use of the HCAS, 1971, vol. 10, p. 734 (hereafter cited as Pentagon Papers, DoD).

2. Interview by Thomas B. Buell with Ralph B. Lovett, p. 3 of transcript, TBB Papers.

3. Joseph Burkholder Smith, *Portrait of a Cold Warrior* (New York: G. P. Putnam's Sons, 1976), p. 280, chap. 17, esp. pp. 315–17; William E. Stevenson, interview transcript, 4–5 May 1969, p. 108, KOHP.

4. J. B. Smith, *Portrait*, pp. 421, 278; John M. Crewdson and Joseph B. Treaster, *NYT*, 25 December 1977, pp. 1, 12; 26 December 1977, pp. 1, 37.

5. Department of Defense, *History of United States Decisionmaking on Vietnam* (Boston: Beacon Press, 1971), vol. 2, p. 648 (hereafter cited as Pentagon Papers, Gravel).

6. J. B. Smith, *Portrait*, pp. 252, 258–59 (COMPADRE); Jose V. Abueva, *Focus on the Barrio* (Manila: Institute of Public Administration, University of the Philippines, 1959), pp. 127, 149 n.2 (PRRM), 103–8 (NAMFREL). On CFA: John M. Crewdson and Joseph B. Treaster, *NYT*, 26 December 1977, pp. 1, 37; Steve Weissman and John Shoch, "CIAsia Foundation," *Pacific Research and World Empire Telegram*, 3, no. 6 (September–October 1972), pp. 3–4; Victor Marchetti and John D. Marks, *The CIA and the Cult of Intelligence* (New York: Dell, 1974), p. 46.

7. J. L. Vellut, *The Asian Policy of the Philippines, 1954–61*, Working Paper No. 6 (Canberra: Australian National University, Department of International Relations, 1965), p. 5, citing *Manila Chronicle*, 6 and 7 October 1959; Milton Meyer, *A Diplomatic History of the Philippine Republic* (Honolulu: University of Hawaii Press, 1965), p. 42, citing Phil. *Cong. Rec.*, Sen., 15 August 1946.

8. Hearings, *FAA of 1964*, CFA, 88th Cong., 2nd sess., 1964, p. 713; Michael Dueñas, "The U.S. and Our Army," *PFP*, 6 July 1968, pp. 7, 66; Edward R. Kiunisala, "Another Roces Report," *PFP*, 4 January 1969, pp. 5ff.; Hearings, *U.S. Security Agreements and Commitments Abroad, Part 1: The Republic of the Philippines*, CFR subcommittee, 91st Cong., 1st sess., 1969, p. 318 (hereafter cited as Hearings, *Security Agreements*).

9. Boyd T. Bashore, "Dual Strategy for Limited War," in Franklin Mark Osanka, ed., *Modern Guerrilla Warfare* (New York: Free Press of Glencoe, 1962), pp. 200–201 (mid-1950s); John Duffy, "Signpost: Success in the Philippines," *Army*, 13, no. 12 (July 1963), p. 60 (four functions); Willard F. Barber and C. Neale Ronning, *Internal Security and Military Power: Counterinsurgency and Civic Action in Latin America* (Columbus, Ohio: Ohio State University Press, 1966), pp. 181–82. On the origins of the term, see Harry F. Walterhouse, *A Time to Build: Military Civic Action—Medium for Economic Development and Social Reform* (Columbia, S.C.: University of South Carolina Press, 1964), p. 9.

10. Hearings, *FAA of 1962*, CFA, 87th Cong., 2nd sess., 1962, p. 77 (McNamara); Duffy, "Signpost," pp. 61–62 (encouragement); Hearings, *Security Agreements*, pp. 105, 321–22; Committee Print, *Korea and the Philippines: November 1972*, Staff report for CFR, 93rd Cong., 1st sess., 18 February 1973, p. 41 (hereafter cited as *Korea and the Philippines*).

11. *NYT*, 25 January 1970, p. 27 (Robert M. Smith).

12. Wilbur M. Brucker to William H. Draper, Jr., 22 January 1959, JMD Files, box 3, President's Commission to Study the U.S. Military Assistance Program—Information for Members, January 28–30, 1959; Hearings, *FAA of 1962*, CFA, 87th Cong., 2nd sess., 1962, p. 69; Hearings, *FAA of 1965*, CFR, 89th Cong., 1st sess., 1965, p. 453.

13. Hearings, *FAA of 1963*, CFR, 88th Cong., 1st sess., 1963, pp. 177, 180.

14. Hearings, *FAA of 1963*, CFA, 88th Cong., 1st sess., 1963, p. 308.

15. Hearings, *MSA of 1959*, CFR, 86th Cong., 1st sess., 1959, pp. 216–17 (JFK); Gen. Richard G. Stilwell, "Training Under the Mutual Security Program," 15 May 1959, printed in L. Fletcher Prouty, *The Secret Team: The CIA and Its Allies in Control of the World* (New York: Ballantine Books, 1973), p. 512; Committee Print, Conlon Associates Ltd., *United States Foreign Policy: Asia*, Studies prepared at the request of the CFR, no. 5, 86th Cong., 1st sess., November 1959, p. 9; Hearings, *FAA of 1966*, CFA, 89th Cong., 2nd sess., 1966, p. 250 (Pentagon official).

16. Philippine Desk to Mr. Meader, 24 September 1947, DSNA 711.96/9-2447.

17. Digest of Discussion, Council on Foreign Relations Study Group Reports, U.S. Relations with the Philippines, 4th meeting, 21 November 1957, p. 5, in MMC Papers, box 5, correspondence, Council on Foreign Relations Philippine Study Group file (Lansdale); Committee Print, *Military Assistance Training in East and Southeast Asia*, Staff report for CFA subcommittee, 91st Cong., 2nd sess., 16 February 1971, p. 28 (data); Eduardo Lachica, *The Huks: Philippine Agrarian Society in Revolt* (New York: Praeger, 1971), p. 247 (Asia Foundation funds).

18. The objectives of U.S. military aid to the Philippines are stated in the annual congressional hearings, with some deletions. See, e.g., Hearings, *MSA of 1953*, CFR, 83rd Cong., 1st sess., 1953, p. 306; Hearings, *MSA of 1958*, CFA, 85th Cong., 2nd sess., 1958, p. 528; Hearings, *FAA of 1963*, CFA, 88th Cong., 1st sess., 1963, p. 761; Hearings, *FAA of 1964*, CFA, 88th Cong., 2nd sess., 1964, p. 92; Hearings, *FAA of 1966*, CFA, 89th Cong., 2nd sess., 1966, pp. 236, 268; Hearings, *FAA of 1968*, CFA, 90th Cong., 2nd sess., 1968, p. 715; Hearings, *Security Agreements*, p. 242; Hearings, *FARAA for 1970*, HCAp subcommittee, 91st Cong., 1st sess., 1969, pt. 1, p. 744; Hearings, *FAA of 1971*, CFA, 92nd Cong., 1st sess., 1971, p. 463.

19. Hearings, *Security Agreements*, p. 309; Hearings, *FARAA for 1973*, HCAp subcommittee, 92nd Cong., 2nd sess., 1972, pt. 1, p. 864; Hearings, *FARPA, FY73*, SCAp subcommittee, 92nd Cong., 2nd sess., 1972, p. 939.

20. Hearings, *Security Agreements*, pp. 246, 261, 299.

21. Hearings, *FAA of 1967*, CFA, 90th Cong., 1st sess., 1967, pp. 200–201, 283; Hearings, *Security Agreements*, p. 358; Comptroller General, *Report to the Congress: Military Assistance and Commitments in the Philippines*, 12 April 1973, B-133359, pp. 26, 31–32 (hereafter cited as GAO, *Philippines*); Elmer B. Staats to Stuart Symington, 21 March 1970, printed in U.S. *Cong. Rec.*, 25 March 1970, p. 9260.

22. CIA, "Certain Problems Created by the U.S. Military Assistance Program," 30 January 1959, pp. 3, 7, in JMD Files, box 3, President's Committee to Study the U.S. Military Assistance Program—Information for Members, January 28–30, 1959; " 'More Officers Than Privates,' " *PFP*, 6 March 1965, pp. 2ff., reprinted from *PFP*, 28 May 1960; Hearings, *FAA of 1971*, CFA, 92nd Cong., 1st sess., 1971, p. 350.

23. *Korea and the Philippines*, p. 42; AID, *U.S. Overseas Loans and Grants and Assistance from International Organizations, July 1, 1945–June 30, 1972* (Washington, D.C., May 1973), pp. 3, 77 (hereafter cited as AID, *Loans and Grants*); Comptroller General, *Report to the Committee on Foreign Relations, U.S. Senate: Use of Excess Defense Articles and Other Resources to Supplement the Military Assistance Program*, 21 March 1973, B-163742, p. 14; GAO, *Philippines*, p. 25.

24. GAO, *Philippines*, p. 23; Hearings, *Security Agreements*, pp. 161–62.

25. Hearings, held in executive session, *Reviews of the World Situation: 1949–1950*, CFR, 81st Cong., 1st and 2nd sess., 1949–50, made public June 1974, Historical Series, p. 303.

26. Hearings, *MSA of 1955*, CFR, 84th Cong., 1st sess., 1955, p. 19; "Survey No. 5: Korea, Japan, Taiwan (Formosa), and the Philippines," (John A. Hannah) in *Foreign Aid Programs: Compilation of Studies and Surveys Prepared Under the Direction of the Special Committee to Study the Foreign Aid Program*, Sen. Doc. 52, 85th Cong., 1st sess., July 1957, p. 1366; Charles Wolf, Jr., *Foreign Aid: Theory and Practice in Southern Asia* (Princeton: Princeton University Press, 1960), pp. 283–84; Hearings, *FARAA for 1963*, SCAp, 87th Cong., 2nd sess., 1962, p. 82.

27. Pentagon Papers, DoD, vol. 12, pp. 455–56 (JFK); Michael Klare, *War Without End* (New York: Alfred A. Knopf, 1972), pp. 245–46; Hearings, *FARAA for 1965*, SCAp, 88th Cong., 2nd sess., 1964, pp. 72–73 (rationale); Nancy Stein and Michael Klare, "Police Aid for Tyrants," in Steve Weissman et al., *The Trojan Horse: A Radical Look at Foreign Aid* (San Francisco: Ramparts Press, 1974), p. 223 (Taylor).

28. Hearings, *FARAA for 1965*, SCAp, 88th Cong., 2nd sess., 1964, pp. 72, 74; Roger Hilsman, *To Move a Nation* (Garden City, N.Y.: Doubleday & Co., 1967), p. 401. On South Vietnam, see among many sources Noam Chomsky and Edward S. Herman, *Counter-Revolutionary Violence: Bloodbaths in Fact and Propaganda*, Module 57 (Andover, Mass.: Warner Modular Publications, 1973), pp. 29–32; and Klare, *War*, pp. 261–68.

29. AID, *Assistance to the Philippines, 1946–1970* (Manila: U.S. AID Philippines, Program Office, September 1970), pp. 18–20 (hereafter cited as AID, *Assistance, 1946–70*); Hearings, *MSA of 1959*, CFA, 86th Cong., 1st sess., 1959, pp. 1551–55.

30. Holmes Brown and Don Luce, *Hostages of War: Saigon's Political Prisoners* (Washington, D.C.: Indochina Mobile Education Project, 1973), pp. 36, iii.

31. Clinton F. Wheeler, Director, Office of Public Affairs, AID, to author, 1 November 1973.

32. Office of Public Safety, AID, *Survey of Philippine Law Enforcement*, 15 December 1966, pp. 1, 36, 38, and passim (hereafter cited as OPS, *Survey*).

33. Ibid., pp. 229–30, 233; (A Correspondent), "Among Friends," *Far Eastern Economic Review*, 5 August 1972, p. 13 (utilize STC).

34. OPS, *Survey*, recommendation no. 109, pp. 227–28.

35. Filemon V. Tutay, "Long-Awaited Christmas Gift," *PFP*, 17 December 1966, p. 2; Michael Klare, "The Police Apparatus: Courtesy of USAID," *Philippines Information Bulletin*, 1, no. 1 (January 1973), p. 19; *Washington Post*, 31 January 1970.

36. RP, National Economic Council, Office of Foreign Aid Coordination, *Annual Report on the Foreign Aid Programs in the Philippines*, fiscal year 1968 (Manila, 1969), p. 50 (hereafter cited as NEC, *Annual Report*, fiscal year [year]); Klare, "Police Apparatus," p. 19; Stein and Klare, "Police Aid," pp. 232–33; AID, *Operations Report, Data as of June 30, 1972* (Washington, D.C., 1972), pp. 30–34.

37. U.S. *Cong. Rec.*, 12 April 1973, p. S7312; AID, *Assistance, 1946–70*, pp. 18–20; U.S. *Cong. Rec.*, 2 October 1974, pp. S18047–49.

38. Quoted in Jack Anderson, "Who Gets U.S. Food Aid—And Why," *Parade*, 2 February 1975, p. 9.

39. George McGovern, "Food for Peace," *AID Digest*, 1 February 1962, p. 21; *Washington Post*, 30 June 1974, p. A12 (Dan Morgan).

40. Israel Yost, "The Food for Peace Arsenal," in Steve Weissman et al., *The Trojan Horse*, pp. 159–67; Hearings, *FARAA for 1972*, HCAp subcommittee, 92nd Cong., 1st sess., 1971, pt. 1, pp. 15, 18 (common defense).

41. Yost, "Arsenal," pp. 160–61, 167; *NYT*, 17 November 1974, p. 14 (Clyde H. Farnsworth) (humanitarian side).

42. Yost, "Arsenal," pp. 160–62.

43. Ibid., p. 159; figures calculated from ibid., p. 160; Humphrey quoted in Harry Cleaver, "Will the Green Revolution Turn Red?" in Steve Weissman et al., *The Trojan Horse*, p. 174; Joseph M. Dodge to Tracy S. Voorhees, 10 April 1959, JMD Files, box 1, correspondence-Draper-Voorhees.

44. Yost, "Arsenal," p. 159; figures calculated from Yost, p. 160; *NYT*, 15 September 1974, sec. 4, p. 3.

45. AID, *Loans and Grants*, p. 77; AID, *Assistance, 1946–70*, p. 39; Hearings, *Security Agreements*, p. 249.

46. AID, *Loans and Grants*, p. 77; AID, *Assistance, 1946–70*, p. 26 (cotton and tobacco); *NYT*, 4 October 1970, p. 11 (malnutrition).

47. A. Willis Robertson to John Foster Dulles, 24 May 1955, DDE Papers, OF 149-B-2, Tobacco.

48. Department of State, *Land Reform: A World Challenge, with Related Papers,* Economic Cooperation Series 29, Department of State Publication 4445, February 1952 (Washington, D.C., 1952), pp. 4, 58; Hearings, *MSA Extension,* CFA, 82nd Cong., 2nd sess., 1952, p. 936.

49. Hearings, *FAA of 1968,* CFA, 90th Cong., 2nd sess., 1968, p. 539; Hearings, *FARPA, FY73,* SCAp subcommittee, 92nd Cong., 2nd sess., 1972, pp. 641–42.

50. On conspicuous consumption and the prestige value of land, see Charles Wolf, Jr., "Public Policy and Economic Development in the Philippines," *Asian Survey,* 1, no. 10 (December 1961), p. 38; Frank H. Golay, *The Philippines: Public Policy and National Economic Development* (Ithaca, N.Y.: Cornell University Paperbacks, 1968), pp. 15, 186, 423–24. See also Agaton Pal, "The Philippines," in Richard D. Lambert and Bert F. Hoselitz, eds., *The Role of Savings and Wealth in Southern Asia and the West* (Paris: UNESCO, 1963).

51. Al McCoy, "Land Reform as Counter-Revolution," *Bulletin of Concerned Asian Scholars,* 3, no. 1 (Winter–Spring 1971), p. 29; Frances L. Starner, *Magsaysay and the Philippine Peasantry: The Agrarian Impact on Philippine Politics, 1953–1956* (Berkeley: University of California Press, 1961), p. 263 n.6.

52. Frate Bull, *Land Reform in the Philippines, 1950–1958* (N.p.: International Cooperation Administration, 1958 [?]), pp. 20–22.

53. Harold D. Koone and Lewis E. Gleeck, "Land Reform in the Philippines," in AID, *Spring Review of Land Reform,* 2nd edition, vol. 4, Country Papers (Washington, D.C., June 1970), p. 41; U.S. AID Mission, Philippines, "USAID Reports: AID Support for Land Reform," in AID, *Spring Review of Land Reform,* 2nd edition, vol. 12, Background Papers (Washington, D.C., June 1970), p. D-1 (hereafter cited as AID, "Support for Land Reform"); Jose V. Abueva, *Ramon Magsaysay: A Political Biography* (Manila: Solidaridad Publishing House, 1971), p. 437.

54. International Labour Conference, *Agrarian Reform with Particular Reference to Employment and Social Aspects,* 49th sess., Geneva, 1965, report no. 6 (Geneva: ILO, 1964), p. 50; Hugh L. Cook, "Land Reform and Development in the Philippines," in Walter Froehlich, ed., *Land Tenure, Industrialization and Social Stability: Experience and Prospects in Asia* (Milwaukee: Marquette University Press, 1961), p. 178; David Wurfel, "Philippine Agrarian Reform Under Magsaysay (II)," *Far Eastern Survey,* 37, no. 2 (February 1958), p. 27.

55. D. Wurfel, "Agrarian Reform," p. 25; Cook, "Land Reform," pp. 172–73; Koone and Gleeck, "Land Reform," pp. 39–42; RP, Department of Commerce and Industry, BCS, *Yearbook of Philippine Statistics, 1966* (Manila, 1966), p. 193.

56. George Taylor, *The Philippines and the United States: Problems of Partnership* (New York: Praeger, 1964), p. 206; Bull, *Land Reform,* p. 51.

57. AID, "Support for Land Reform," p. D-1. The text of the 1963 Code (Republic Act 3844) is in Conrado F. Estrella, *The Democratic Answer to*

the Philippine Agrarian Problem (Manila: Solidaridad Publishing House, 1969); see pp. 102, 109 (secs. 4, 35). Exclusion figure is from Benedict J. Kerkvliet, "Land Reform in the Philippines Since the Marcos Coup," *Pacific Affairs*, 47, no. 3 (Fall 1974), pp. 295–96, who estimates 84 percent of tenants would be excluded if plots larger than 25 hectares were covered.

58. Estrella, *Democratic Answer*, p. 70.

59. Frederick L. Wernstedt and J. E. Spencer, *The Philippine Island World: A Physical, Cultural, and Regional Geography* (Berkeley: University of California Press, 1967), p. 179; Taylor, *Philippines and the U.S.*, pp. 222–23; Vernon W. Ruttan, "Equity and Productivity Issues in Modern Agrarian Reform Legislation," *Philippine Studies* (Phil.), 14, no. 1 (January 1966), p. 61 (quote); Estrella, *Democratic Answer*, pp. 107, 109, secs. 29(3), 36(4).

60. Estrella, *Democratic Answer*, pp. 101, 114, 117–22, secs. 2(1), 56, 71, 75(6), 76, 80, 85; pp. 21, 67–68, 45; Lyle P. Schertz, "Factors in Carrying Out Land Reform: Finance," in AID, *Spring Review of Land Reform*, 2nd edition, vol. 11, Analytical Papers (Washington, D.C., June 1970), pp. 5, 8; Perfecto V. Fernandez, "The Constitutionality of the Compensation Provisions of the Agricultural Land Reform Code," *Philippine Law Journal*, 38 (October 1963), pp. 566–68.

61. Estrella, *Democratic Answer*, p. 115, sec. 60; Marshall S. McLennan, "Land and Tenancy in the Central Luzon Plain," *Philippine Studies* (Phil.), 17, no. 4 (October 1969), p. 681; Koone and Gleeck, "Land Reform," p. 78; Jose W. Diokno, "Legal Aspects of Land Reform: The Central Luzon Experience," *Solidarity* (Phil.), 2, no. 8 (July–August 1967), pp. 9–10.

62. Hearings, *FARAA for 1972*, HCAp, 92nd Cong., 1st sess., 1971, pt. 2, pp. 342–43; Koone and Gleeck, "Land Reform," pp. 47, 13, 87. See also International Labour Office, *Sharing in Development: A Programme of Employment, Equity and Growth for the Philippines* (Geneva: ILO, 1974), pp. 474–76.

63. AID, "Support for Land Reform," p. D-2; AID, Mission to the Philippines, *A Survey of Foreign Economic and Technical Assistance Programs in the Philippines*, 1965–66 edition (Washington, D.C., 1966), p. 47 (hereafter cited as AID, *Survey, 1965–66*).

64. Among the voluminous literature, see Zubeida Manzoor Ahmad, "The Social and Economic Implications of the Green Revolution in Asia," *International Labour Review*, 105, no. 1 (January 1972), pp. 11, 14, 21; Marvin Harris, "How Green the Revolution," *Natural History*, June–July 1972, p. 30; Clifton R. Wharton, Jr., "The Green Revolution: Cornucopia or Pandora's Box?" *Foreign Affairs*, 47, no. 3 (April 1969), p. 467; Asian Development Bank, *Southeast Asia's Economy in the 1970's* (London: Longman Group Ltd., 1971), pp. 155, 158 (Harry Walters and Joseph Willett) (hereafter cited as ADB, *Southeast*); *Business Week*, 21 November 1970, p. 84; Michael Perelman, "Second Thoughts on the Green Revolution," *New Republic*, 17 July 1971, p. 21; Proceedings, *Symposium on Science and Foreign Policy: The Green Revolution*, CFA subcommittee, 91st Cong., 1st sess., 1969, pp. 48–49 (hereafter cited as Proceedings, *Green Revolution*); Cleaver, "Will the Green Revolution Turn Red?" p. 193.

65. Ahmad, "Social and Economic Implications," pp. 19–20, citing H. Voelkner, "The Philippines Rice Revolution: A Case Study of Title IX Implementation," December 1969, mimeographed.

66. Special Release no. 104, Series of 1970, BCS Manila, cited in Erich H. Jacoby, in collaboration with Charlotte F. Jacoby, *Man and Land: The Essential Revolution* (New York: Alfred A. Knopf, 1971), p. 70 n.

67. Koone and Gleeck, "Land Reform," pp. 90–91; Ahmad, "Social and Economic Implications," p. 20; Schertz, "Factors," p. 22. See also T. M. Burley, *The Philippines: An Economic and Social Geography* (London: G. Bell & Sons, 1973), p. 314 n.14.

68. Hearings, *Rural Development in Asia*, CFA subcommittee, 89th Cong., 2nd sess., 1966, pt. 2, pp. 397, 373.

69. Ibid., pp. 373, 371 (U.S. aid); Orlando Sacay, "Small Farmer Credit in the Philippines," in AID, *Spring Review of Small Farmer Credit*, vol. 13, Country Papers (Washington, D.C., February 1973), pp. 2, 4–6; E. B. Rice, "History of AID Programs in Agricultural Credit, 1950–1972," in AID, *Spring Review of Small Farmer Credit*, vol. 18, Evaluation Paper 6 (Washington, D.C., June 1973), pp. 12–13. On cash costs, see Wharton, "Green Revolution," p. 470.

70. Dana G. Dalrymple, "Technological Change in Agriculture: Effects and Implications for Developing Nations," *Foreign Agricultural Service*, U.S. Department of Agriculture in cooperation with AID, April 1969, reprinted in Proceedings, *Green Revolution*, p. 169. Figures from ADB, *Southeast*, p. 120 (Walters and Willett).

71. Wharton, "Green Revolution," p. 468; Lester R. Brown, *Seeds of Change: The Green Revolution and Development in the 1970's* (New York: Praeger, 1970), pp. 91–92; Perelman, "Second Thoughts," p. 21; H. Garrison Wilkes and Susan Wilkes, "The Green Revolution," *Environment*, 14, no. 8 (October 1972), pp. 33, 35, 38.

72. Marvin Harris, "The Withering Green Revolution," *Natural History*, March 1973, p. 21; RP, Central Bank, *Twenty-fourth Annual Report, 1972* (Manila, 1973[?]), p. 18; Edward R. Kiunisala, "A Political Gimmick?" *PFP*, 9 October 1971, p. 6.

73. Harry Bayard Price, ed., *Rural Reconstruction and Development: A Manual for Field Workers* (New York: Praeger, 1967), pp. 19–20, 34–35; AID, *Survey*, 1965–66, pp. 162–63; Abueva, *Focus*, pp. 127, 149 n.2.

74. Price, ed., *Rural Reconstruction*, pp. 26, 55, 105–12.

75. Ibid., pp. 70–72, 336; E. H. Valsan, *Community Development Programs and Rural Local Development* (New York: Praeger, 1970), pp. 337–38.

76. Valsan, *Community Development*, p. 336; Walterhouse, *Time to Build*, pp. 10–11.

77. Valsan, *Community Development*, pp. 339 (hacienda), 355 (limited), 319 (marginal); Orlando Sacay, "Small Farmer Savings Behavior," in AID, *Spring Review of Small Farmer Credit*, vol. 13, Country Papers (Washington, D.C., February 1973), pp. 9–12 (48 credit unions); AID, *Survey*, 1965–66, p. 162 (civic action).

78. Abueva, *Focus*, pp. 303–4; Abueva, *Magsaysay*, pp. 362–63; AID, Mission to the Philippines, Community Development Division, *Community Development in the Philippines: A Joint Project of the Republic of the Philippines and the United States of America* (Manila, 8 February 1965), pp. 3, 11 (hereafter cited as AID, *Community Development*).

79. Remigio E. Aglapo, *The Political Elite and the People: A Study of Politics in Occidental Mindoro* (Manila: College of Public Administration, University of the Philippines, 1972), p. 348; Abueva, *Focus*, pp. 303–4; International Labour Office, *Employment Problems and Policies in the Philippines* (Geneva: ILO, 1969), p. 82.

80. AID, *Community Development*, p. 2 (U.S. role); John H. Romani and M. Ladd Thomas, *A Survey of Local Government in the Philippines* (Manila: Institute of Public Administration, University of the Philippines, 1954), p. 9. For comments comparing the Huk local governments and the barrio governments, see Benedict J. Kerkvliet, "Agrarian Conditions Since the Huk Rebellion: A Barrio in Central Luzon," in Benedict J. Kerkvliet, ed., *Political Change in the Philippines: Studies of Local Politics Preceding Martial Law*, Asian Studies at Hawaii no. 14 (Honolulu: University Press of Hawaii, 1974), pp. 58–60.

81. Jose M. Aruego, *Barrio Government Law and Administration in the Philippines* (Manila: Metropolitan Publishing Co., 1968), pp. 212–16, 220, 222, 225–26 (Republic Act 3590, secs. 13(a) and (b), 17, 20, 23); RP, Joint Legislative-Executive Tax Commission, *Local Government Finance* (Manila, 1962), pp. 19–20; Valsan, *Community Development*, pp. 217–18. Russell J. Cheetham and Edward K. Hawkins, *The Philippines: Priorities and Prospects for Development*, Report of a study mission sent to the Philippines by the World Bank (Washington, D.C.: World Bank, 1976), p. 119.

82. Valsan, *Community Development*, pp. 221–22, 216; David Hapgood, ed., *The Role of Popular Participation in Development*, Report of a Conference on the Implementation of Title IX of the Foreign Assistance Act, June 24 to August 2, 1968, MIT Report No. 17 (Cambridge, Mass.: MIT Press, 1969), pp. 105, 108.

83. Hapgood, *Role*, pp. v, 1, 14.

84. Ibid., p. 55.

85. AID, *Increasing Participation in Development: Primer on Title IX of the United States Foreign Assistance Act* (Washington, D.C., 1970), p. 45 (private sector); Hapgood, *Role*, pp. 28, 161, 56.

86. Hapgood, *Role*, pp. 156, 173–74.

87. Ibid., p. 1; Hearings, *FAA of 1969*, CFA, 91st Cong., 1st sess., 1969, p. 292; Hearings, *FARAA for 1971*, HCAp subcommittee, 91st Cong., 2nd sess., 1970, pt. 2, p. 164.

88. *PPP*, Kennedy, 1962, p. 483; Sorensen quoted in Richard J. Walton, *Cold War and Counter-Revolution: The Foreign Policy of John F. Kennedy* (Baltimore: Penguin, 1972), p. 60; AID, *Loans and Grants*, p. 6.

89. Hearings, *FARAA for 1964*, SCAp subcommittee, 88th Cong., 1st sess., 1963, p. 529; Marshall Windmiller, *The Peace Corps and Pax Americana*

(Washington, D.C.: Public Affairs Press, 1970), pp. 58–59, 61, 173 n.11; Brent K. Ashabranner, *A Moment in History: The First Ten Years of the Peace Corps* (Garden City, N.Y.: Doubleday & Co., 1971), pp. 316–17.

90. Gerald D. Berreman, "The Peace Corps: A Dream Betrayed," *The Nation*, 26 February 1968, pp. 264–66; "The Peace Corps: A Dream Betrayed," *PFP*, 12 October 1968, p. 12.

91. Windmiller, *Peace Corps*, p. 57; Hearings, *Peace Corps Act Amendments of 1970*, CFR, 91st Cong., 2nd sess., 1970, p. 66, reprint of article by Paul Grimes, *Philadelphia Bulletin*, 26 February 1970.

92. Ashabranner, *Moment in History*, pp. 295–99.

93. *PPP*, Kennedy, 1962, p. 609; Hearings, *FARAA for 1968*, SCAp, 90th Cong., 1st sess., 1967, p. 100; Hearings, *FAA of 1969*, CFA, 91st Cong., 1st sess., 1969, pp. 336–37; Hearings, *FARAA for 1970*, HCAp subcommittee, 91st Cong., 1st sess., 1969, pt. 2, pp. 595–96; Windmiller, *Peace Corps*, p. 141.

94. Hearings, *FARPA FY72*, SCAp subcommittee, 92nd Cong., 1st sess., 1971, pp. 247–50; Hearings, *The Peace Corps*, CFR, 87th Cong., 1st sess., 1961, p. 74, also pp. 83, 107–8; Ray Hoopes, *The Complete Peace Corps Guide* (New York: Dial Press, 1961), p. 91 (quote).

95. Hearings, *MSA of 1958*, CFR, 85th Cong., 2nd sess., 1958, pp. 127–28.

96. Hearings, *Foreign Economic Policy*, CFA subcommittee, 83rd Cong., 1st sess., 1953, p. 97; Hearings, *Foreign Policy and Mutual Security*, CFA, 84th Cong., 2nd sess., 1956, pp. 17, 20; Hearings, *FAA of 1963*, CFA, 88th Cong., 1st sess., 1963, p. 1223; Hearings, *FAA of 1964*, CFA, 88th Cong., 2nd sess., 1964, p. 1029; Hearings, *FAA of 1967*, CFR, 90th Cong., 1st sess., 1967, p. 90; Report of the Advisory Committee on Private Enterprise in Foreign Aid, *Foreign Aid Through Private Initiative* (Washington, D.C.: AID, July 1965), pp. 16–19.

97. Hearings, *International Development and Security*, CFR, 87th Cong., 1st sess., 1961, pp. 263, 269–70; Hearings, *FAA of 1964*, CFR, 88th Cong., 2nd sess., 1964, p. 10 (fraud).

98. Hearings, *FAA of 1964*, CFR, 88th Cong., 2nd sess., 1964, pp. 30–31.

99. Hearings, *FARPA FY70*, SCAp subcommittee, 91st Cong., 1st sess., 1969, pp. 117–18; Hearings, *Multinational Corporations and United States Foreign Policy*, CFR subcommittee, 93rd Cong., 1st sess., 1973, pt. 3, p. 23 (hereafter cited as Hearings, *MNCs*, pt. [no.]).

100. Hearings, *MSA of 1957*, CFA, 85th Cong., 1st sess., 1957, p. 1261; Hearings, *FARAA for 1971*, HCAp subcommittee, 91st Cong., 2nd sess., 1970, pt. 2, pp. 462–64; Hearings, *MNCs*, pt. 3, p. 549.

101. *U.S. Stat.*, vol. 73, p. 252; vol. 77, pp. 386–87; *PPP*, Nixon, 1972, p. 33.

102. Thomas E. Weisskopf, "Dependence and Imperialism in India," in Mark Selden, ed., *Remaking Asia: Essays on the American Uses of Power* (New York: Pantheon, 1974), p. 220.

103. Center for Strategic and International Studies, *U.S.-Philippines Economic Relations*, Special Report Series No. 12 (Washington, D.C.: Georgetown University, 1971), pp. 8, 103 (hereafter cited as CSIS, *Relations*) (cf. Hearings, *Security Agreements*, pp. 214–15); Morton quoted in *Business Week*, 30 October 1965, cited by Carlos F. Díaz Alejandro, "Direct Foreign Investment in Latin America," in Charles P. Kindleberger, ed., *The International Corporation: A Symposium* (Cambridge, Mass.: MIT Press, 1970), p. 330 n.13; Corporate Information Center of the National Council of Churches of Christ in the U.S.A., "The Philippines: American Corporations, Martial Law, and Underdevelopment," *IDOC*, International/North American edition, no. 57, November 1973, p. 80 (hereafter cited as CIC, "The Philippines"); U.S. *Cong. Rec.*, 2 April 1969, p. 8440 (sugar mills).

104. See, e.g., John J. Carroll, "Philippine Labor Unions," *Philippine Studies* (Phil.), 9, no. 2 (April 1961), p. 226; Grant K. Goodman, "Japan's Support for Anti-Communism in the Philippines," *Philippine Historical Review* (Phil.), 3, no. 1 (1970), pp. 229–30, 232–37.

105. Richard Deverall, "Labor in the Philippines," *American Federationist*, 61, no. 1 (January 1954), p. 25; Carroll, "Unions," pp. 239–40; David Wurfel, "Trade Union Development and Labor Relations Policy in the Philippines," *Industrial and Labor Relations Review*, 12, no. 4 (July 1959), pp. 590–91. See in general C. D. Calderon, "From Compulsory Arbitration to Collective Bargaining in the Philippines," *International Labour Review*, 81, no. 1 (January 1960); G. I. Levinson, *The Workers' Movement in the Philippines* (Moscow, 1957), JPRS/DC-434, CSO DS-2309, Scholarly Book Translation Series, Research and Microfilm Publications, Inc., Annapolis, Md.

106. D. Wurfel, "Union," pp. 594, 599–600; J. S. Peterson to Myron M. Cowen, 4 June 1949, in MMC Papers, box 3, correspondence, Benguet Consolidated Mining Co. file; Perfecto Fernandez, "Philippine Labor Law— A Survey," *Washington Law Review*, 40, no. 2 (June 1965), p. 246.

107. D. Wurfel, "Union," pp. 594–95, 598; Calderon, "From Compulsory Arbitration," p. 12; Carroll, "Unions," p. 246; International Labour Office, *Report to the Government of the Philippines on Labour-Management Relations*, ILO/TAP/Philippines/R.3, confidential (declassified) (Geneva, 1958), p. 35; Laurence D. Stifel, *The Textile Industry: A Case Study of Industrial Development in the Philippines*, Southeast Asia Program, Data Paper No. 49 (Ithaca, N.Y.: Cornell University, 1963), p. 137 (contract).

108. D. Wurfel, "Union," pp. 599–600; U.S. *Cong. Rec.*, 24 May 1962, p. 9164; RP, Central Bank, *Statistical Bulletin*, 24 (December 1972), p. 378; Department of Commerce, Bureau of International Commerce, *Foreign Economic Trends and Their Implications for the United States*, ET 72-100 (Manila: U.S. Embassy, September 1972), pp. 5–6.

109. Asian Labor Education Center (ALEC), University of the Philippines, *ALEC Annual Report, 1961–62*, p. 4; *ALEC Annual Report, 1960–61*, pp. 24, 34 (on advisers) (hereafter cited as *ALEC*, [date]); Hearings, *FAA of 1964*, CFR, 88th Cong., 2nd sess., 1964, pp. 141–42; AID, *Assistance, 1946– 70*, pp. 31–32.

110. NEC, *Annual Report*, fiscal year 1965, p. 105; NEC, *Annual Report*, fiscal year 1964, p. 61; *ALEC*, 1956–57, annex C, annex D; *ALEC*, 1957–58, p. 19.

111. Arnold Zack, *Labor Training in Developing Countries* (New York: Praeger, 1964), pp. 137–38.

112. *ALEC*, 1956–57, annex F, pp. 1–3. For other references to management enthusiasm, see D. Wurfel, "Union," p. 606; NEC *Annual Report*, fiscal year 1966, p. 96; Hearings, *MSA of 1957*, CFA, 85th Cong., 1st sess., 1957, p. 972.

113. Zack, *Labor Training*, p. 140.

114. Department of Commerce, *Factors Limiting U.S. Investment Abroad* (Washington, D.C., 1953), p. 122.

115. NEC, *Annual Report*, fiscal year 1967, p. 105.

116. Hearings, *FAA of 1964*, CFR, 88th Cong., 2nd sess., 1964, pp. 141–42 (said AID); Hearings, *MSA of 1959*, CFA, 86th Cong., 1st sess., 1959, p. 1547 (ICA); AID, *Assistance, 1946–70*, pp. 131–32 (Asian). Number of trainees from appendix A of the relevant *ALEC Annual Reports*.

117. Vern McCarty, "Philippine Copper," *Pacific Research and World Empire Telegram*, 3, no. 3 (March-April-May 1972), p. 20 (ALU); Hearings, *FAA of 1962*, CFA, 87th Cong., 2nd sess., 1962, pp. 754–56; AID, *Proposed Foreign Aid Program FY 1968, Summary Presentation to Congress* (Washington, D.C., 1967), p. 185; AID, *Assistance, 1946–70*, pp. 32, 29; Rolando E. Garcia, "Tools, Not Masters," *Graphic* (Manila), 19 April 1972, pp. 10–11, 39 (AIM).

118. Sonya Diane Cater, "The Philippine Federation of Free Farmers (A Case Study in Mass Agrarian Organizations)," in Socorro C. Espiritu and Chester L. Hunt, eds., *Social Foundations of Community Development* (Manila: R. M. Garcia Publishing House, 1964).

119. CIA: Lenny Siegel, "Asian Labor: The American Connection," *Pacific Research and World Empire Telegram*, 6, no. 5 (July–August 1975), pp. 3–4; quote: Committee Print (Robert H. Dockery), *Survey of the Alliance for Progress: Labor Policies and Programs*, Study prepared for subcommittee on American Republics Affairs, CFR (together with a report by the Comptroller General, 15 July 1968), 90th Cong., 2nd sess., 1968, p. 6. For background on U.S. labor's international role, see Ronald Radosh, *American Labor and United States Foreign Policy* (New York: Random House, 1969).

120. Suffridge: James A. Suffridge, "The Urgent Needs of Asian Workers," *American Federationist*, 68, no. 7 (July 1961), p. 11; Phil. program: *Afro-Asian Labour Bulletin* (Singapore), 6, no. 3 (March 1971), p. 9; TUC: *Afro-Asian Labour Bulletin* (Singapore), 5, no. 6 (June 1970), p. 7.

121. Comptroller General, *Report to the Congress: Improvements Needed in System for Managing U.S. Participation in the Asian Development Bank*, B-173240, 8 May 1973, p. 5 (hereafter cited as GAO, *Bank*); Report to the President of the U.S. from the [Peterson] Task Force on International Development, *U.S. Foreign Assistance in the 1970's: A New Approach* (Washington, D.C., 4 March 1970), pp. 3–4; AID, *Foreign Assistance for the Seventies: President Nixon's Message to the Congress, September 15, 1970* (Washington, D.C., 1970), p. 2.

122. Steve Weissman, "Foreign Aid: Who Needs It?" in Steve Weissman et al., *The Trojan Horse*, p. 24; Africa Research Group, *International Dependency in the 1970's* (Cambridge, Mass.: ARG, 1970), pp. 23, 14 (quote).

123. Africa Research Group, *International Dependency*, p. 22; Weissman, "Foreign Aid," p. 24; Hearings, *Asian Development Bank Act*, HR, Committee on Banking and Currency subcommittee, 89th Cong., 2nd sess., 1966, p. 99 (hereafter cited as Hearings, *Bank*); Bruce Nissen, "Building the World Bank," in Steve Weissman et al., *The Trojan Horse*, pp. 50 (McCloy), 52.

124. Africa Research Group, *International Dependency*, p. 32; GAO, *Bank*, pp. 43, 11–12; Richard De Camp, "The Asian Development Bank: An Imperial Thrust into the Pacific," in Mark Selden, ed., *Remaking Asia*, pp. 78–79. For more data on voting power of the United States and developing nations in the international banks, see Hearings, *Bank*, p. 40.

125. Edward S. Mason and Robert E. Asher, *The World Bank Since Bretton Woods* (Washington, D.C.: Brookings Institution, 1973), pp. 68, 335–37; Nissen, "Building the World Bank," p. 46; GAO, *Bank*, p. 12; Hearings, *MNCs*, pt. 1, pp. 323–24.

126. GAO, *Bank*, p. 19.

127. Teresa Hayter, *Aid as Imperialism* (Harmondsworth, Middlesex, Eng.: Penguin, 1971), pp. 19–20 n.10, 54; De Camp, "Asian Development Bank," p. 83.

128. Hayter, *Aid*, pp. 15, 87, 55; De Camp, "Asian Development Bank," p. 78.

129. GAO, *Bank*, p. 17; *PPP*, Nixon, 1972, p. 33; Hearings, *MNCs*, pt. 1, p. 324. See also Mason and Asher, *World Bank*, pp. 30, 40, 91.

130. Hayter, *Aid*, pp. 64, 31 n.5; De Camp, "Asian Development Bank," p. 83; Harry Magdoff, *The Age of Imperialism* (New York: Monthly Review Press, 1969), pp. 142–49; Cheryl Payer, "The IMF and the Third World," in Steve Weissman et al., *The Trojan Horse*, p. 63 and passim. Also Mason and Asher, *World Bank*, pp. 161, 233, 338.

131. AID, *Loans and Grants*, p. 186. The rest of this section draws heavily on two articles by Cheryl Payer: "Martial Law and the Economic Crisis," in *The Philippines: End of an Illusion* (London: Association for Radical East Asian Studies, 1973); and "Exchange Controls and National Capitalism: The Philippine Experience," *Journal of Contemporary Asia*, 3, no. 1 (1973).

132. Robert F. Emery, "The Successful Philippine Decontrol and Devaluation," *Asian Survey*, 3, no. 6 (June 1963), p. 280; Diosdado Macapagal, *A Stone for the Edifice: Memoirs of a President* (Quezon City: MAC Publishing Co., 1968), pp. 62–63.

133. Hearings, *FAA of 1962*, CFA, 87th Cong., 2nd sess., 1962, p. 666; Hearings, *FAA of 1963*, CFA, 88th Cong., 1st sess., 1963, p. 752; John H. Power and Gerardo P. Sicat, "The Philippines: Industrialization and Trade Policies," in *The Philippines and Taiwan* (London: Oxford University Press, for the Development Centre of the Organization for Economic Co-operation and Development, Paris, 1971), pp. 46–47 (burden).

134. Alejandro Lichauco, "Imperialism in the Philippines," *Monthly Review*, 25, no. 3 (July–August 1973), pp. 35–36; CIC, "The Philippines," p. 18.

135. Payer, "Martial Law," p. 95.

136. CSIS, *Relations*, p. 52; Payer, "Martial Law," pp. 98–99; Power and Sicat, "Philippines," p. 50 (election); Economist Intelligence Unit, *Quarterly Economic Review: Philippines, Taiwan*, no. 1—1970, pp. 4 (election), 7 (1969 debt); no. 2—1970, pp. 2, 3, 5; no. 1—1972, p. 9 (1971 debt); RP, Central Bank, *Statistical Bulletin*, 24 (December 1972), p. 378 (wage).

137. Committee Print, *United States Development Assistance Programs in Pakistan, the Philippines, and Indonesia*, Staff reports to the subcommittee on Foreign Assistance of CFR, 95th Cong., 1st sess., February 1977, p. 19.

138. Hearings, *FARPA, FY72*, SCAp subcommittee, 92nd Cong., 1st sess., 1971, p. 808.

Chapter Six: The Human Costs of Neocolonialism

1. International Labour Office, *Sharing in Development: A Programme of Employment, Equity and Growth for the Philippines* (Geneva: ILO, 1974), p. 3 (hereafter cited as ILO, *Sharing*).

2. Mahar Mangahas, "A Broad View of the Philippine Employment Problem," *Philippine Economic Journal* 23, vol. 12, nos. 1 and 2 (1973), p. 12.

3. E. M. Bernstein, Address before the Far East-America Council, N.Y., 20 October 1950, p. 5, in MMC Papers, box 3, Far Eastern Council folder (correspondence). See also *Report to the President of the United States by the Economic Survey Mission to the Philippines*, Far Eastern Series 38, Department of State Publication No. 4010 (Washington, D.C., 9 October 1950), p. 2 (hereafter cited as Bell Report); Hearings, *The Mutual Security Program*, CFA, 82nd Cong., 1st sess., 1951, p. 900; Bureau of Social Science Research, The American University, *Communications and Public Opinion in the Philippines: A Survey of Selected Sources* (Washington, D.C.), Draft prepared for the Office of Research and Intelligence, U.S. Information Agency, BSSR no. 674, January 1955, p. 25.

4. Hearings, *Rural Development in Asia*, CFA subcommittee, 90th Cong., 1st sess., 1967, pt. 2, p. 369 (hereafter cited as Hearings, *Rural Development*); RP, Committee Report no. 2513, *Compilation of Statistics on the Philippine Economy*, Sen., Committee on Economic Affairs, 6th Cong., 4th sess., 15 May 1969, p. 5.

5. First, various official sources give different figures for the same item. The table on page 239 lists the percentage of total income going to the bottom fifth of families in selected years according to various sources.

Second, within particular sources the figures are inconsistent. Both BCS no. 34 (table 63) and NEDA, *Statistical Yearbook, 1975* (table 13.2), give figures for the total income of the lowest fifth of the families in 1956–57

	1956–57	1961	1971
(1) BCS no. 34	4.5%	4.2%	3.7%
(2) BCS no. 14	4.5%	4.2%	—
(3) NEDA, 1975	4.5%	4.2%	3.6%
(4) Mijares and Belarmino	—	4.6%	3.8%
(5) International Labour Office	4.5%	4.2%	3.8%
(6) Reyes and Chan	4.7%	4.6%	—

Full citations: (1) RP, Department of Commerce and Industry, Bureau of the Census and Statistics, *BCS Survey of Households Bulletin, Family Income and Expenditures, 1971,* Series no. 34, Manila (hereafter referred to as BCS no. 34), table 63, p. 158. (2) RP, Bureau of the Census and Statistics, *Philippine Statistical Survey of Households Bulletin, Family Income and Expenditures, 1961,* Series no. 14, Manila (hereafter referred to as BCS no. 14), table C, p. xiii. (3) RP, National Economic and Development Authority, *Statistical Yearbook of the Philippines, 1975* (Manila, 1975), Table 13.2, p. 410. (4) Tito A. Mijares and I. C. Belarmino, "Some Notes on the Sources of Income Disparities Among Philippine Families," *Journal of Philippine Statistics,* 24, no. 4 (4th quarter 1973), p. xv (authors are, respectively, Director of and Consultant for the Bureau of Census and Statistics). (5) ILO, *Sharing,* table 3, p. 10 (based on independent analysis of BCS raw data). (6) Peregrino S. Reyes and Teresita L. Chan, "Family Income Distribution in the Philippines," *Statistical Reporter,* 9, no. 2 (April–June 1965), table 2, p. 31 (authors were, respectively, Acting Assistant Director of and Senior Staff member of the Office of Statistical Coordination and Standards, National Economic Council; data based on BCS Household Surveys, Series nos. 4 and 14).

and 1961 which, when divided by one-fifth of the number of families, results in average figures different from the ones in the same tables.

The tables presented in my text are based on (a) the share of total family income (not the percentages) given in the NEDA, *Statistical Yearbook, 1975,* table 13.2 (which concurs with BCS no. 34, table 63); and (b) the percentages of rural and urban income shares given in ILO, *Sharing,* table 3, p. 10, which is the only source to give complete urban-rural figures on income distribution.

Third, the reference period of the "1971" data is inconsistently reported. The survey was taken in May 1971, supposedly covering the previous twelve months "more or less." (BCS no. 34, p. ix) Yet in BCS no. 34, table 63, the period is given as the calendar year 1971. NEDA, *Statistical Yearbook, 1975,* reports the data as covering May 1970–April 1971 but uses the consumer price index for calendar year 1971 to calculate real incomes (table 13.1). This is a serious matter, because there was considerable price inflation in 1970 and 1971 and real incomes are thus significantly influenced by which months the data includes.

In the tables in my text that present information on real incomes, the May 1970–April 1971 time period has been used and a composite consumer price index has been constructed for these twelve months. To the extent that respondents to the survey gave their twelve-month earnings as twelve times the most recent income (which they were not supposed to do), the figures given in my text for real income in 1970–71 are significantly overstated. The World Bank suggests using reported *expenditure* figures instead of reported *income* (Russell J. Cheetham and Edward K. Hawkins, *The Philippines: Priorities and Prospects for Development* [Washington, D.C.: The World Bank, 1976], pp. 94–95), but as Khan has shown (Azizur Rahman Khan, "Growth and Inequality in the Rural Philipines," in International Labour Office, *Poverty and Landlessness in Rural Asia* [Geneva: ILO, 1977], pp. 235–42), in the Philippine case income figures are likely to be more accurate.

6. RP, Department of Commerce and Industry, Bureau of the Census and Statistics, *BCS Survey of Households Bulletin, Family Income and Expenditures, 1965*, Series no. 22, Manila (hereafter referred to as BCS no. 22), p. x. See also BCS no. 34, p. x; Gerry Rodgers, Mike Hopkins, and René Wéry, *Population, Employment and Inequality: BACHUE—Philippines* (Farnborough, Eng.: Saxon House, for the ILO, 1978), p. 177; Khan, "Growth and Inequality," p. 240.

7. Robert F. Emery, *The Financial Institutions of Southeast Asia: A Country by Country Study* (New York: Praeger, 1970), p. 434; Hugh L. Cook, "Land Reform and Development in the Philippines," in Walter Froehlich, ed., *Land Tenure, Industrialization and Social Stability: Experience and Prospects in Asia* (Milwaukee: Marquette University Press, 1961), p. 161; Robert E. Huke, *Shadows on the Land: An Economic Geography of the Philippines* (Manila: Bookmark, 1963), p. 208 (chapter by Domingo C. Salita).

8. Frank H. Golay, *The Philippines: Public Policy and National Economic Development* (Ithaca, N.Y.: Cornell University Paperbacks, 1968), pp. 192, 191 n.6, 192 n.10.

9. RP, Joint Legislative-Executive Tax Commission, *4th Annual Report, 1962* (Manila, 1963), p. 31; *7th Annual Report, 1965* (Manila, 1966), p. 30; Angel Q. Yoingco, "The Philippine Tax System: Progressive or Regressive," *The Tax Monthly* (Manila), 11, no. 6 (December 1970), p. 6.

10. ILO, *Sharing*, p. 9. There is general agreement that the 1971 BCS study is of lower quality than that of 1965. See Rodgers, Hopkins, and Wéry, *Population*, p. 176.

11. This follows from the fact that the average income of squatters and slum dwellers in Metropolitan Manila is less than the average income of all residents in the adjacent provinces. See (Special Committee, Office of the President), "A Comprehensive Report on Squatting and Slum Dwelling in Metropolitan Manila," April 1968, printed in Aprodicio A. Laquian, *Slums Are for People* (Honolulu: East-West Center Press, 1969), p. 220 (report hereafter cited as "Comprehensive Report"); NEDA, *Statistical Yearbook, 1975*, p. 412 (Central Luzon is region IV, Southern Luzon is region V). Statisticians: Mijares and Belarmino, "Some Notes," p. xvii.

12. Calculated from NEDA, *Statistical Yearbook, 1975*, pp. 412–13 (Manila is region I).

13. The reported urban gini ratio went from 0.53 to 0.45 from 1965 to 1970–71 (see ILO, *Sharing*, p. 10). This is an 18 percent decrease. Mijares and Belarmino (p. xvi) note that removing the bottom 20 percent of the urban population in 1971 lowers the gini ratio from 0.446 to 0.378—or about 18 percent.

14. "Comprehensive Report," p. 228; Maria Victoria Valenzuela, "Philippine Policy in Housing the Urban Poor" (MCP thesis, MIT, 1974), p. 46; Leandro A. Viloria, "Manila," in Aprodicio A. Laquian, ed., *Rural-Urban Migrants and Metropolitan Development* (Toronto: INTERMET Metropolitan Studies Series, 1971), p. 147.

15. Number of squatters and slum dwellers interpolated from 1963 figure in Laquian, *Slums*, p. 19 (divided by 6 to convert to families), and 1968 figure in "Comprehensive Report," p. 216 (with 7 suburbs eliminated to make definitions of Metropolitan Manila consistent with NEDA, *Statistical Yearbook*, 1975, p. 407). Squatters and slum dwellers income from Laquian, *Slums*, p. 86, with variable incomes eliminated. Though this is a report from just one community, the slum and squatter studies show "an amazing comparability of findings" with respect to social characteristics ("Comprehensive Report," p. 220). Household survey data is in NEDA, *Statistical Yearbook, 1975*, p. 414.

16. ILO, *Sharing*, p. 9.

17. The household surveys include as income the value of income-in-kind. The BCS has stated that, because the imputed value of crops and goods consumed by those who grew or made them was based on prevailing prices in the locality and not on the usually higher prices in trading centers, the income of lower-income families has been understated (Jean Grossholtz, *Politics in the Philippines* [Boston: Little, Brown & Co., 1964], p. 83 n.2; see also BCS no. 22, p. x). But the local prices are what these families would actually have had to pay had they not grown the crops or made the goods themselves, so it is hard to see why there should be any understatement. The 1971 BCS report (BCS no. 34, p. x) states its belief that in many cases wholesale farm prices rather than retail prices were used to calculate the value of income-in-kind. This may well indicate understatement. Note three points, however. First, while it makes some sense to include the crops a farm family eats as part of income (since the crops really are the same quality product as what the family would otherwise have had to purchase at retail prices), does one really want to include as income the retail value minus costs of every article of clothing or piece of furniture made by a member of the family? (This the BCS does; see BCS no. 34, p. 171.) If a family member sews clothing for resale and keeps some for family use, this is one thing; but the household survey does not ask whether this is the case. Respondents are merely asked to list the value of all items they made for their own use. Second, using retail prices to determine the imputed value of income-in-kind ignores a crucial advantage

that cash has over such income-in-kind; namely, that cash allows a family to choose what it will consume, presumably in such a way as to maximize its welfare. Third, observe that upper-class income-in-kind is not included in the household surveys at either wholesale or retail prices (e.g. a doctor treating a member of his or her own family, or a manufacturer purchasing some of his or her own products at cost).

18. RP, Joint Legislative-Executive Tax Commission, *5th Annual Report, 1963* (Manila, 1964), p. 15; Ruben F. Trinidad, "Tax Policies and Their Influence on Income Distribution: The Philippine Experience," *The Tax Monthly* (Manila), 13, no. 10 (October 1973), p. 5; RP, National Tax Research Center, "Initial Report on Taxation and Income Redistribution: A Study of Tax Burden by Income Class, 1971," *The Tax Monthly* (Manila), 15, no. 1 (January 1974), p. 1.

19. Yoingco, "Philippine Tax System," p. 6.

20. Golay, *The Philippines*, p. 191.

21. Calculated from RP, Central Bank, *Statistical Bulletin*, 24 (December 1972), p. 372. Gerardo P. Sicat has stated that the same consumer price index should not be used for different income classes, because the effects of inflation are not uniform across income levels. In particular, he has asserted that since (1) the lower the family income, the greater the fraction of income spent on food and other necessities, and (2) the prices of food and other necessities have grown more slowly than those of other goods, therefore (3) a conversion factor should be added to the consumer price index so that the lower the income the lower the inflation rate (Gerardo P. Sicat, *Economic Policy and Philippine Development* [Quezon City: University of the Philippines Press, 1972], pp. 302–7). At least for the time period that I have been considering, however, premise (2) seems to be incorrect, and thus the conclusion does not follow. The price of food rose about 10 percent *faster* than the consumer price index for 1955 or 1957 to 1970, whether one uses the old or the new data series and whether one looks at Manila, regions outside Manila, or at the Philippines as a whole. Moreover, the price of "miscellaneous"—items other than food, clothing, housing and repairs, and fuel, light, and water—rose more slowly than the price of all items (*Statistical Reporter*, 15, no. 2 [April–June 1971], pp. 63–64; RP, Central Bank, *Statistical Bulletin* 24 [December 1972], pp. 353, 371–72).

Two series of data give a consumer price index for low-income families in Manila covering some but not all of the relevant years. The earlier series shows low-income families (constituting the bottom two-thirds of families) undergoing slightly greater price inflation than the average Manila family from 1961 to 1970 (*Statistical Reporter*, 15, no. 2 [April–June 1971], p. 64, 66). The second series shows low-income Manila families experiencing less inflation than middle-income families, but both less than the Manila average from 1966 to October 1971 (*Journal of Philippine Statistics*, 23, no. 1 [1st quarter 1972], p. 53; RP, Central Bank, *Statistical Bulletin* 24 [December 1972], p. 353).

In all my tables on real income, I have used the consumer price index unadjusted for income level. If anything, this overstates the real income of the poor.

22. Hearings, *Rural Development*, pt. 2, p. 369.

23. *Journal of Philippine Statistics*, 19, no. 3 (July–September 1968), p. xii.

24. Gelia Tagumpay-Castillo, "Toward Understanding the Filipino Farmer" (May 1965), in Raymond E. Borton, ed., *Selected Readings to Accompany "Getting Agriculture Moving,"* (New York: Agricultural Development Council, 1966), vol. 1, p. 59.

25. NEDA, *Statistical Yearbook, 1975*, pp. 489–91; *Statistical Reporter*, 12, no. 4 (October–December 1968), p. 20; 14, no. 4 (October–December 1970), p. 31 (vitamin-C-rich); 13, no. 4 (October–December 1969), p. 21 (all recommended allowances).

26. Calculated from Cheetham and Hawkins, *Philippines*, p. 266. Surveys in 1970 and 1972 showed similar results.

27. Ibid., p. 95.

28. Ibid., p. 279; Albert Ravenholt, "Rising Expectations—Crisis for the Philippines," *AUFS Fieldstaff Perspectives* (Hanover, N.H., 1971), p. 3; Albert Ravenholt, "So Many Makes for Malnutrition," *AUFS Fieldstaff Reports*, Southeast Asia Series, 22, no. 5, AR-1-'74 (Phil.) (August 1974), p. 2; biochemical data calculated from Conrado R. Pascual, "Nutrition Problems and Programs in the Philippines," *Journal of Vitaminology* (Osaka), 14 (Suppl.) (1968), pp. 24–25.

29. Hearings, *FARPA, FY73*, SCAp subcommittee, 92nd Cong., 2nd sess., 1972, p. 365; International Labour Office, U.N. Development Programme, Technical Assistance Sector, *Report to the Government of the Philippines on a National Vocational Preparation Programme for Out-of-School Youth*, ILO/TAP/Phil/R.14 (Geneva, 1972), confidential (declassified), pp. 8–9, 20. See also Carl H. Landé, "The Philippines," in James S. Coleman, ed., *Education and Political Development* (Princeton: Princeton University Press, 1965), p. 315.

30. Bell Report, p. 16. Only "apparently," because a consumer price index existed only for Manila.

31. RP, Department of Labor, Labor Statistics Division, "Wages and Working Conditions in Our Sugar Cane Haciendas in Negros Occidental," *Philippine Labor* (Manila), May 1962, p. 16; Liwayway M. Calalang, "A Survey of Selected Conditions of Employment in the Sugar Industry in Mainland Luzon," *Philippine Labor* (Manila), June 1962, p. 17.

32. *NYT*, 8 March 1970, p. 14.

33. Church: Bell Report, p. 91; money median income: NEDA, *Statistical Yearbook, 1975*, p. 410; median income in 1950 pesos computed from RP, Central Bank, *Statistical Bulletin*, 24, (December 1972), p. 353, and (for 1970 months May–December only) *Statistical Reporter*, 15, no. 2 (April–June 1971), p. 64.

34. RP, Central Bank, *22nd Annual Report, 1970* (Manila, 1970), pp. 129–30; Mangahas, "Broad View," p. 14. See also John H. Power and

Gerardo P. Sicat, "The Philippines: Industrialization and Trade Policies," in *The Philippines and Taiwan* (London: Oxford University Press, for the Development Centre of the Organization for Economic Co-operation and Development, Paris, 1971), pp. 100–101; Edward R. Kiunisala, "Labor Pains," *PFP*, 20 January 1968, p. 4.

35. *Statistical Reporter*, 16, no. 3 (July–September 1972), p. 60.

36. AID, Office of Public Safety, *Survey of Philippine Law Enforcement* (Washington, D.C., 15 December 1966), p. 47; Napoleon G. Rama, "The Cruel City," *PFP*, 7 September 1968, p. 4.

37. Calculated from Food and Nutrition Research Center, National Institute of Science and Technology, National Science Development Board, "Nutrition Re-Survey of Metropolitan Manila," *Statistical Reporter*, 6, no. 3 (July 1962), p. 17.

38. Francis C. Madigan, *Birth and Death in Cagayan de Oro: Population Dynamics in a Medium-Sized Philippine City* (Quezon City: Ateneo University Press, 1972), pp. 178–80.

39. "Comprehensive Report," pp. 220, 215; Laquian, *Slums*, p. 89; Cheetham and Hawkins, *Philippines*, p. 271 (children); F. Landa Jocano, *Slum as a Way of Life* (Quezon City: University of the Philippines Press, 1975), pp. 15–16, 25; T. M. Burley, *The Philippines: An Economic and Social Geography* (London: G. Bell & Sons, 1973), p. 18 (fire).

40. Business International Asia/Pacific Ltd., *The Philippines: Operating for Profit in the New Society* (Hong Kong, 1974), p. 134; Renato S. Esguerra, "The Philippines," in S. Watson Dunn, *International Handbook of Advertising* (New York: McGraw-Hill, 1964), p. 612.

41. *Marketing Horizons* (Manila), September 1966.

42. Ibid., November–December 1969, p. 33.

43. ILO, *Report . . . Out-of-School Youth*, p. 9.

44. Jocano, *Slum*, p. 31. "Most hostesses, according to . . . informants, 'are part-time prostitutes.' " Ibid., p. 137.

Chapter Seven: Martial Law

1. Center for Strategic and International Studies, *U.S.-Philippines Economic Relations*, Special Report Series No. 12 (Washington, D.C.: Georgetown University, 1971), p. 72 (hereafter cited as CSIS, *Relations*); Kunio Yoshihara, "A Study of Philippine Manufacturing Corporations," *Developing Economies*, 9, no. 3 (September 1971), p. 284; John H. Power and Gerardo P. Sicat, "The Philippines: Industrialization and Trade Policies," in *The Philippines and Taiwan* (London: Oxford University Press, for the Development Centre of the Organization for Economic Co-operation and Development, Paris, 1971), p. 67.

2. See, e.g., U.S. *Cong. Rec.*, 29 July 1959, p. 14649.

3. *Boston Evening Globe*, 11 November 1969, p. 8 (UPI); "In the News," *PFP*, 18 December 1971, p. 14. Figures on election-related killings

often vary because of the ambiguity in defining "election-related." See Albert Ravenholt, "Tony Diaz Runs for Congress," *AUFS Fieldstaff Reports*, Southeast Asia Series, 9, no. 5, AR-6-'61 (November 1961), pp. 18–20.

4. Filemon V. Tutay, " 'Private Armies' Legalized!" *PFP*, 23 January 1971, pp. 8ff. See also Filemon V. Tutay, " 'Private Armies,' " *PFP*, 27 June 1970, pp. 8ff.

5. Pat Duffy Hutcheon, "Power in the Philippines: How Democratic Is Asia's 'First Democracy'?" *Journal of Asian and African Studies* (Leiden), 6, nos. 3/4 (July/October 1971), p. 208 (married); Edward R. Kiunisala, "The President's Income Tax," *PFP*, 8 March 1969, p. 6 (1963–64); *PFP*, 11 January 1969, p. 64 (1968); *Business Week*, 4 November 1972, p. 42 (1972).

6. *Business Week*, 4 November 1972, p. 42.

7. Jose F. Lacaba, "All This, and Meralco, Too!" *PFP*, 20 January 1968, pp. 7, 61; *Baltimore Sun*, 23 January 1968 (Peter J. Kumpa), quoted in *I.F. Stone's Weekly*, 22 January 1968, p. 3.

8. *NYT*, 16 January 1971, p. 4; W. Scott Thompson, *Unequal Partners: Philippine and Thai Relations with the United States, 1965–75* (Lexington, Mass.: Lexington Books, 1975), pp. 138–39.

9. *PFP*, 9 October 1971, pp. 50–51 (text of "ban-Marcos" clause); Economist Intelligence Unit, *Quarterly Economic Review: Philippines, Taiwan*, no. 4—1972, p. 3 (money and patronage). See also Thompson, *Unequal Partners*, p. 140. For sample bribery charges, see *PFP*, 3 June 1972, pp. 2–3, 4ff., and 17 June 1972, pp. 4ff.

10. George Taylor, confidential remarks, in Digest of Discussion, Council on Foreign Relations Study Group Reports, U.S. Relations with the Philippines, 5th meeting, 17 December 1957, p. 1, in MMC Papers, box 5, correspondence, Council on Foreign Relations Philippine Study Group file; Jean Grossholtz, *Politics in the Philippines* (Boston: Little, Brown & Co., 1964), pp. 136–37, 239; Arthur Alan Shantz, "Political Parties: The Changing Foundations of Philippine Democracy" (Ph.D. dissertation, University of Michigan, 1972), p. 109 n.5; Hirofumi Ando, "Elections in the Philippines: Mass-Elite Interaction Through the Electoral Process, 1946–1969" (Ph.D. dissertation, University of Michigan, 1971), p. 174; Carl H. Landé, *Leaders, Factions, and Parties: The Structure of Philippine Politics*, Southeast Asia Studies, Monograph Series No. 6 (New Haven: Yale University, 1965), passim; *NYT*, 27 July 1969, p. 29 (Charles Mohr); *Washington Post*, 6 November 1969, p. A24 (Antonio Escoda).

11. Landé, *Leaders*, p. 49; Steve Frantzich, "Party Switching in the Philippine Context," *Philippine Studies* (Phil.), 16, no. 4 (October 1968), pp. 750–68; Dante C. Simbulan, "A Study of the Socio-Economic Elite in Philippine Politics and Government" (Ph.D. dissertation, Research School of Social Science, Australian National University, 1965), pp. 250, 378–79.

12. "Marcos on Vietnam," *PFP*, 5 February 1966, p. 3, reprinted from *PFP*, 5 June 1965.

13. Eduardo Lachica, *The Huks: Philippine Agrarian Society in Revolt* (New York: Praeger, 1971), p. 29; Peter R. Kann, "The Philippines Without

Democracy," *Foreign Affairs*, 52, no. 3 (April 1974), p. 614. See also Edward R. Kiunisala, "The Coming Elections—Who Cares?" *PFP*, 10 June 1967, p. 16.

14. Ando, "Elections," p. 155 (quote), 159, 113.

15. Gunnar Myrdal, *Asian Drama: An Inquiry into the Poverty of Nations* (New York: Pantheon, 1968), vol. 3, pp. 1778, 1772.

16. Robert O. Tilman, "The Impact of American Education on the Philippines," *Asia*, no. 21 (Spring 1971), p. 74; Heather Low Ruth, "The Philippines," in The Committee on the International Migration of Talent, *The International Migration of High-Level Manpower: Its Impact on the Development Process* (New York: Praeger, in cooperation with Education and World Affairs, 1970), p. 55.

17. Justus M. van der Kroef, "Communist Fronts in the Philippines," *Problems of Communism*, 16, no. 2 (March–April 1967), pp. 71–72.

18. See Amado Guerrero, *Philippine Society and Revolution* (Hong Kong: Ta Kung Pao, 1971); Lachica, *Huks*.

19. *Washington Post*, 9 March 1970, p. A6 (Antonio Escoda).

20. E.g., *Washington Post*, 31 January 1970, p. A3 (Mario Roxas); 9 March 1970, p. A6 (Antonio Escoda); *NYT*, 18 March 1970, p. 14.

21. 1947–55: David Wurfel, "Trade Union Development and Labor Relations Policy in the Philippines," *Industrial and Labor Relations Review*, 12, no. 4 (July 1959), p. 602; 1957–61 and 1964–68: William J. Pomeroy, *An American-Made Tragedy: Neo-Colonialism and Dictatorship in the Philippines* (New York: International Publishers, 1974), p. 87.

22. Kay A. Snyder and Thomas C. Nowak, "Philippine Labor Before Martial Law: Threat or Nonthreat?" unpublished (Indiana University of Pennsylvania, 1978), pp. 21–24; *NYT*, 25 May 1970, p. 12 (AP); 27 February 1970, p. 8 (Philip Shabecoff); 4 March 1970, p. 3 (Philip Shabecoff); 19 February 1970, p. 3.

23. Hearings, *U.S. Security Agreements and Commitments Abroad, Part 1: The Republic of the Philippines*, CFR subcommittee, 91st Cong., 1st sess., 1969, p. 353; Lachica, *Huks*, p. 14.

24. Municipalities: Committee Print, *Korea and the Philippines: November 1972*, Staff report for CFR, 93rd Cong., 1st sess., 18 February 1973, pp. 1–2 (hereafter cited as *Korea and the Philippines*); air strikes: *Washington Post*, 12 July 1972, p. A20; Bart Lubow, "Philippines: Next Vietnam?" *Real Paper* (Cambridge, Mass.), 29 November 1972, p. 11.

25. For background, see Felix Razon, "Filipino Muslims and the Revolution," *Philippines Information Bulletin* (Cambridge, Mass.) 1, no. 2 (March–April 1973); Ernst Utrecht, "The War in the Southern Philippines," in *The Philippines: End of an Illusion* (London: Association for Radical East Asian Studies, 1973); Alunan Glang, *Muslim Secession or Integration* (Manila: Cardinal Bookstore, 1971).

26. AID, Office of Public Safety, *Survey of Philippine Law Enforcement* (Washington, D.C., 15 December 1966), pp. 150, 155; *NYT*, 27 June 1971, sec. 4, p. 4; Manuel H. Ces, "Kill!" *PFP*, 3 July 1971, p. 7; RP, Department of Public Information, National Media Production Center, *Vital Documents on*

the Declaration of Martial Law in the Philippines (Manila, October 1972), p. 10 (hereafter cited as *Vital Documents*).

27. Nicholas O. Berry, "Representation and Decisionmaking: A Case Study of Philippine-American War Claims" (Ph.D. dissertation, University of Pittsburgh, 1967), p. 125.

28. E.g., Thompson, *Unequal Partners*, pp. 138–39.

29. Lachica, *Huks*, pp. 222–24, 151. Shantz ("Political Parties," pp. 53–54) claims that the Sumulong Huks were hired by Marcos's political opponents in Pampanga and that the formation of the Monkees was the government's response.

30. *DSB*, 3 May 1965, p. 664; 21 March 1966, p. 448; 10 October 1966, p. 533.

31. See CSIS, *Relations*, p. 127; Magdangal B. Elma, "The Scope and Effects of the Quasha Decision on Private Agricultural Lands Acquired by Americans Under the Parity Amendment," in *Philippine Supreme Court Reports, Annotated*, vol. 46, July–August 31, 1972 (Quezon City: Central Lawbook Publishing Co., 1972), p. 190.

32. *DSB*, 29 January 1968, p. 150, par. 26.

33. Quijano de Manila, "Fore! on '74," *PFP*, 25 May 1968, pp. 2, 70.

34. *DSB*, 29 January 1968, pp. 147–48, pars. 7, 13–15, 17. See also Richard E. Usher, "Philippine-American Economic Relations," *Asia*, no. 23 (Autumn 1971), p. 85.

35. *DSB*, 29 January 1968, pp. 151, 154, pars. 31, 32, appendix IV. See also Usher, "Philippine-American Economic Relations," pp. 82–83.

36. *DSB*, 29 January 1968, pp. 150–51, par. 28.

37. Felipe Suva Martin, "U.S. Direct Investment in the Philippines" (Ph.D. dissertation, MIT, 1972), pp. 109–126; "The Nation," *PFP*, 31 December 1966, pp. 59–60; 14 January 1967, pp. 59–61; 5 August 1967, pp. 68–69. See also Remigio E. Aglapo, *The Political Process and the Nationalization of the Retail Trade in the Philippines* (Quezon City: University of the Philippines, 1962).

38. Quoted in *Business Asia*, 27 August 1971, p. 277. On strikes, see Snyder and Nowak, "Philippine Labor," pp. 24–26 and table 15.

39. CSIS, *Relations*, p. 13.

40. Bankers Trust Company, N.Y., "The Philippines, January 1948: Notes Prepared by One of Our Representatives Who Recently Visited That Country," p. 6, in MMC Papers, box 3, correspondence, Bankers Trust Co. (J. Morden Murphy) file; *Survey of Current Business*, annual issues, sum of "net capital outflow" and sum of "income." For documentation regarding royalties and transfer-pricing, see the sources cited in note 51 of Chapter Four, above.

41. National Industrial Conference Board, *Obstacles and Incentives to Private Foreign Investment, 1967–1968*, vol. 1, *Obstacles*, Studies in Business Policy No. 130 (New York, 1969), p. 102; *Pacific Imperialism Notebook* (San Francisco), 4, no. 2 (February 1973), pp. 27–28; *Business Day* (Phil.), 9 May 1972, p. 3 (survey).

42. Interview, Richard E. Usher, U.S. Department of State, Desk Officer for the Philippines, Washington, D.C., 23 November 1973; Department of Commerce, Bureau of International Commerce, *Foreign Economic Trends and Their Implications for the United States*, ET 72-100 (Manila: U.S. Embassy, September 1972), p. 7 (hereafter cited as *Foreign Economic Trends*, [number] and [date]).

43. *Foreign Economic Trends*, ET 72-100, September 1972, p. 10. See also *Business Asia*, 14 July 1972, pp. 221, 224; 21 December 1973, p. 403.

44. RP, Inter-Agency Working Group on Foreign Investments, "Study of Private Foreign Investments in the Philippines," part 2, *Philippine Progress*, 6 (3rd quarter 1972), p. 7; *Foreign Investment in Asia*, cited in Corporate Information Center of the National Council of Churches of Christ in the U.S.A., "The Philippines: American Corporations, Martial Law, and Underdevelopment," *IDOC*, International/North American edition, no. 57 (November 1973), p. 20 (hereafter cited as CIC, "The Philippines"); Bernardino Ronquillo, "Cloudy Climate," *Far Eastern Economic Review*, 19 August 1972, p. 60; *Business Asia*, 12 May 1972, p. 148. See also *Foreign Economic Trends*, ET 72-021, March 1972, pp. 4, 9; ET 72-100, September 1972, p. 8.

45. Economist Intelligence Unit, *Quarterly Economic Review: Philippines, Taiwan*, no. 4—1971, p. 12; "In the News," *PFP*, 11 March 1972, p. 16. For background on the oil situation, see Malcolm Caldwell, "ASEANisation," in *The Philippines: End of an Illusion;* First National City Bank (Jesus M. Villegas), *Investment Guide to Oil Exploration in the Philippines* (Philippines: First National City Bank, 1973[?]).

46. Edward R. Kiunisala, "The Outrage," *PFP*, 4 September 1971, p. 2; Filemon V. Tutay, "Who Did It?" *PFP*, 4 September 1971, pp. 6ff.; text of suspension in *PFP*, 4 September 1971, pp. 4ff.; "Lansang v. Garcia," *Philippine Supreme Court Reports, Annotated*, vol. 42, October 22–December 31, 1971, pp. 454–55, 461–62.

47. Norman Lorimer, "The Philippine Left: An Historical Survey," in *The Philippines: End of an Illusion.*

48. Text of suspension, *PFP*, 4 September 1971, pp. 4ff.; Filemon V. Tutay, "Well, Who Did It?" *PFP*, 9 October 1971, p. 4; Filemon V. Tutay, "But Who Is the Mastermind?" *PFP*, 4 March 1972, pp. 6ff.

49. *Business Asia*, 27 August 1971, p. 277.

50. Napoleon G. Rama, "A Question of Parity Rights," *PFP*, 22 March 1969, pp. 10ff. (lower court); CSIS, *Relations*, p. 15 (expectation).

51. "Republic of the Philippines and/or the Solicitor General v. William H. Quasha," *Philippine Supreme Court Reports, Annotated*, vol. 46, July–August 31, 1972.

52. *Business Day* (Phil.), 22 August 1972, p. 11.

53. "Luzon Stevedoring Corporation v. Anti-Dummy Board," *Philippine Supreme Court Reports, Annotated*, vol. 46, July–August 31, 1972; *Foreign Economic Trends*, ET 72-100, September 1972, p. 8.

54. *Business Asia*, 1 September 1972, p. 280; Radio News and Editorial Service, Office of Public Information, Malacanang, RP (news summary), 22 August 1972 (seen at Philippine Embassy, Washington, D.C.).

55. See discussion in National Committee for the Restoration of Civil Liberties in the Philippines, "Martial Law *Is* Dictatorship," *Philippines Information Bulletin*, 1, no. 2 (March–April 1973), pp. 5, 29 (hereafter cited as NCRCLP, "Martial Law").

56. Robert E. Klitgaard, *Martial Law in the Philippines*, P-4964 (Santa Monica: Rand Corporation, November 1972), p. 13; Kann, "Philippines Without Democracy," p. 618; NCRCLP, "Martial Law," pp. 5, 29.

57. Klitgaard, *Martial Law*, p. 13; Kann, "Philippines Without Democracy," p. 618; *Wall Street Journal*, 11 October 1972, p. 23 (Peter R. Kann); *Korea and the Philippines*, p. 4; Thompson, *Unequal Partners*, p. 140.

58. *NYT*, 24 September 1972, p. 1 (UPI) (re Romulo); Hearings, *Human Rights in South Korea and the Philippines: Implications for U.S. Policy*, CIR subcommittee, 94th Cong., 1st sess., May–June 1975, pp. 286–87 (hereafter cited as Hearings, *Human Rights, SK and Phil); Hearings, Human Rights in the Philippines: Report by Amnesty International*, CIR subcommittee, 94th Cong., 2nd sess., 15 September 1976, pp. 3, 28 (hereafter cited as Hearings, *Amnesty*).

59. Hearings, *Amnesty*, pp. 4, 21, 25, 28. See also testimony of Benedict J. Kerkvliet, U.S. *Cong. Rec.*, 4 June 1974, pp. S9565–66; Documentation Committee for Philippine Political Prisoners, *Political Prisoners in the Philippines*, 762 N. Virgil Ave., Los Angeles, CA 90029, May 1975; *Philippines Information Bulletin*, 3, no. 1 (March 1975); the following articles from *Pahayag* (Honolulu): "Morphine Used to Break Political Prisoners," no. 20 (August 1974); "FFF Leader Killed by Military" and "What About Santiago Arce?" no. 24 (December 1974); "Labor Leader Murdered," no. 31 (July 1975); and *NYT*, 8 January 1975, p. 5; 19 January 1975, p. 7; 16 March 1975, p. 9.

60. See David A. Rosenberg, "The End of the Freest Press in the World," *Bulletin of Concerned Asian Scholars*, 5, no. 1 (July 1973); David A. Rosenberg, "Liberty versus Loyalty: The Transformation of Philippine News Media under Martial Law," in David A. Rosenberg, ed., *Marcos and Martial Law in the Philippines* (Ithaca, N.Y.: Cornell University Press, 1979); Committee Print, *Human Rights and U.S. Policy: Argentina, Haiti, Indonesia, Iran, Peru, and the Philippines:* Reports submitted to the CIR by the Department of State, 94th Cong., 2nd sess., 31 December 1976, p. 31 (Department of State) (hereafter cited as *Argentina . . . and the Philippines*).

61. See Kerkvliet testimony, U.S. *Cong. Rec.*, 4 June 1974, pp. S9565, S9568; F. D. Pinpin, comp. and ed., *The First 107 Presidential Decrees*, Handbook Series No. 7, (Rizal: Cacho Hermanos Inc., 1973), pp. 346 (General Order no. 5, 22 September 1972), 289 (Presidential Decree no. 90, 6 January 1973).

62. The staff report to the U.S. Senate Foreign Relations Committee has this formulation: "The Congress had not been dissolved, although it had no role to play under martial law." *Korea and the Philippines*, p. 29.

63. *Argentina . . . and the Philippines*, p. 28.

64. Hearings, *Human Rights, SK and Phil*, p. 517; *Argentina . . . and the Philippines*, p. 28; Hearings, *Amnesty*, p. 3.

65. Frank R. Valeo, Senate Secretary, Report on Philippine trip, November 1972, in U.S. *Cong. Rec.*, 21 February 1973, p. S3016; Harvey Stockwin, "In Marcos Style," *Far Eastern Economic Review*, 9 December 1972, p. 11.

66. Kann, "Philippines Without Democracy," p. 623; *Kansas City Times*, 15 June 1974 (Robin Osborne); Bernard Wideman, "The New Society at Home," *Far Eastern Economic Review*, 31 December 1973, p. 18; Association of Major Religious Superiors, "National Survey of Public Opinion on Martial Law, October 1973" unpublished, (Manila[?], 1974[?]), p. 20 (hereafter cited as Superiors, "Survey"); *NYT*, 13 January 1973, p. 3 (Tillman Durdin); 18 January 1973, p. 9 (Tillman Durdin); 21 January 1973, sec. 4, p. 3 (Tillman Durdin); 5 August 1973, sec. 4, p. 4; Primitivo Mijares, "Statement of Defection," *Philippine News* (Calif.), 20–27 February 1975; Hearings, *Human Rights, SK and Phil*, pp. 281, 304–6, 474 (defector); *Philippine News* (Calif.), 9–15 August 1973, p. 9 (prisoners).

67. Hearings, *Human Rights, SK and Phil*, p. 517.

68. Economist Intelligence Unit, *Quarterly Economic Review: Philippines, Taiwan*, no. 4—1972, p. 2. For Marcos explanation, see Proclamation no. 1081 printed in *Vital Documents*.

69. Marcos citations in *Vital Documents*, pp. 19–20; conclusion quoted in NCRCLP, "Martial Law," p. 4.

70. *Wall Street Journal*, 11 October 1972, p. 23 (Peter R. Kann).

71. *Korea and the Philippines*, pp. 30–31.

72. T. J. S. George, "Rainy Day Guns," *Far Eastern Economic Review*, 1 July 1972, p. 14.

73. Relocation: *NYT*, 20 October 1972, pp. 1, 9 (Henry Kamm); William Overholt, "Martial Law, Revolution and Democracy in the Philippines," *Southeast Asia*, 2, no. 2 (Spring 1973), p. 177. Activity: *NYT*, 8 May 1973, p. 8; 13 January 1974, p. 18; 22 September 1974, p. 19; *Washington Star News*, 2 December 1974, p. A-10 (Henry Bradsher); Economist Intelligence Unit, *Quarterly Economic Review: Philippines, Taiwan*, no. 1—1975, p. 2.

74. See "The Jolo Massacre: A Neo-Colonial Story in Six Parts," *Philippines Information Bulletin*, 2, no. 2 (April 1974); *Washington Post*, 3 March 1974, p. A24 (Harvey Stockwin); *Christian Science Monitor*, 26 March 1974, p. F1 (Richard Critchfield); *NYT*, 17 February 1974, p. 5 (Reuters); 26 March 1974, p. 3 (Sydney H. Schanberg) (on Enrile).

75. *NYT*, 25 September 1973, p. 8. A lower figure for 1971–72 deaths is given in *NYT*, 24 August 1972, p. 17 (UPI). "It was Marcos's declaration of martial law that triggered the outbreak of open warfare" (Lela Noble, "Rebellion in the Philippines," *Inquiry*, 2 April 1979, p. 17.

76. Claude A. Buss, *The United States and the Philippines: Background for Policy* (Washington, D.C.: American Enterprise Institute for Public Policy Research; and Stanford: Stanford University, Hoover Institution on War, Revolution and Peace, 1977), p. 58; *NYT*, 22 April 1975, p. 2 (Joseph Lelyveld); Lloyd Shearer, "Extortion in High Places," *Parade*, 2 March 1975; Tillman Durdin, "The Philippines: Martial Law, Marcos-Style," *Asian Affairs*, 3, no. 2 (November–December 1975), p. 77 (quote).

77. Klitgaard, *Martial Law*, p. 11, citing *Economist*, 6 October 1972; *Far Eastern Economic Review*, 7 October 1972, pp. 14–15. See also Filemon V. Tutay, "Change of Command," *PFP*, 8 June 1968, pp. 6, 72–73.

78. Kerkvliet testimony, U.S. *Cong. Rec.*, 4 June 1974, p. S9567; Committee Print, *United States–Philippine Base Negotiations*, Staff report to CFR subcommittee, 95th Cong., 1st sess., 7 April 1977, p. 10 (hereafter cited as *Base Negotiations*); Ela Silang, "The New Society's Military Establishment," *Pahayag* (Honolulu), no. 23 (November 1974), p. 7; Buss, *U.S.-Phil.*, pp. 67–68; *NYT*, 13 May 1973, p. 7 (draft).

79. Kann, "Philippines Without Democracy," p. 620; Francisco F. Claver, "Church and State Under Martial Law: A Biased View," *Pahayag* (Honolulu), no. 15 (February 1974), p. 6. Press: *NYT*, 20 October 1973, p. 3 (Joseph Lelyveld); David Wurfel, "Martial Law in the Philippines: Methods of Regime Survival," *Pacific Affairs*, 50, no. 1 (Spring 1977), p. 10.

80. Marcos appointees: *Honolulu Star Bulletin*, 13 November 1975, p. B-3 (Arnold Zeitlin), excerpted in *Pahayag* (Honolulu), no. 35 (November 1975), pp. 6–7. Observers: *Philadelphia Bulletin*, 21 January 1974, p. 4 (Charles F. Thomson); Superiors, "Survey," pp. 21–22; Hearings, *Amnesty*, p. 12; *Base Negotiations*, p. 6. On executive-legislative agreement, see Gregorio A. Francisco, Jr., and Raul P. de Guzman, "The 50-50 Agreement," in Raul P. de Guzman, ed., *Patterns in Decision-Making: Case Studies in Philippine Public Administration* (Manila: University of the Philippines Press, Graduate School of Public Administration, 1963).

81. International Labour Office, *Sharing in Development: A Programme of Employment, Equity and Growth for the Philippines* (Geneva: ILO, 1974), p. 93; Benedict J. Kerkvliet, "Land Reform in the Philippines Since the Marcos Coup," Paper presented at the annual meeting of the Association of Asian Studies, 1–3 April 1974, pp. 29–30 (hereafter cited as Kerkvliet, "Land," AAS).

82. Benedict J. Kerkvliet, "Land Reform: Emancipation or Counterinsurgency?" in Rosenberg, ed., *Marcos and Martial Law in the Philippines*, pp. 129–32; ILO, *Sharing*, pp. 93, 480; Duncan A. Harkin, *Philippine Agrarian Reform in the Perspective of Three Years of Martial Law*, Research Paper no. 68 (Madison: University of Wisconsin, Land Tenure Center, April 1976), p. 8.

83. Harkin, *Philippine Agrarian Reform*, p. 18.

84. Bernard Wideman, "The New Society at Home," *Far Eastern Economic Review*, 31 December 1973, p. 18; Kerkvliet, "Emancipation or Counterinsurgency," pp. 124–27; Superiors, "Survey," pp. 4–7; *NYT*, 14 March 1975, p. 2 (Joseph Lelyveld); Duncan A. Harkin, "The Philippine Land Reform," *Land Tenure Center Newsletter* (Madison), no. 48 (April–June 1975), pp. 3–4.

85. Superiors, "Survey," pp. 8–9; Brewster Grace, "The Politics of Income Distribution in the Philippines," *AUFS Fieldstaff Reports*, Southeast Asia Series, vol. 25, no. 8, BG-3-'77 (Phil.) (August 1977), p. 12; ILO, *Sharing*, p. 94; Kerkvliet, "Emancipation or Counterinsurgency," pp. 127–28.

86. Harkin, *Philippine Agrarian Reform*, pp. 27 (200,000), 1, 1 n.2 (not received); Russell J. Cheetham and Edward K. Hawkins, *The Philippines:*

Priorities and Prospects for Development (Washington, D.C.: World Bank, 1976), pp. 483 (not received), 478 (not title).

87. Gerald C. Hickey and John L. Wilkinson, *Agrarian Reform in the Philippines: Report of a Seminar, December 16–17, 1977 at The Rand Corporation, Washington, D.C.*, P-6194 (Santa Monica[?]: Rand Corporation, August 1978), pp. 2, 38, v (quote).

88. Christopher Araullo, "Dissent's Repercussions," *Far Eastern Economic Review*, 4 March 1974, p. 20.

89. Committee Print, *United States Development Assistance Programs in Pakistan, the Philippines, and India,* Staff reports to CFR subcommittee, 95th Cong., 1st sess., February 1977, p. 19; *NYT*, 8 November 1974, p. 4 (Joseph Lelyveld); Bernard Wideman, "Banana Boom: Fruits for Only a Few," *Far Eastern Economic Review*, 21 January 1974, pp. 52–53; *Philippine Times* (Chicago), 16–31 October 1975, p. 7 (Priscila Donato). For documentation on the continuing destitution of sugar workers, see Antonio J. Ledesma, "Socioeconomic Aspects of Filipino Sugar Farm Workers: Three Views from the Cane Fields," *Philippine Studies*, 27 (2nd quarter 1979), pp. 231–39.

90. Figures from RP, Central Bank, *Statistical Bulletin,* 26 (December 1974), p. 398. Reports: Superiors, "Survey," pp. 11–16.

91. Cheetham and Hawkins, *Philippines,* pp. 264–65. See also Keith Dalton, "The Undernourished Philippines," *Far Eastern Economic Review*, 1 September 1978, p. 35.

92. Calculated from *Business Day's 1000 Top Corporations [for 1972]* (Quezon City: Enterprise Publications, n.d. [1973?]), pp. 6–7; *Business Day's Top 1000 Corporations [for 1974]* (Quezon City: Businessday Corporation, n.d. [1975?]), p. 7.

93. *Philippine Prospect,* no. 5 (August 1973), p. 7; no. 3 (June 1973), p. 1; Benedict J. Kerkvliet, "Marcos to Limit Wages," *Pahayag* (Honolulu), no. 14 (January 1974), p. 7. See also *Business Asia,* 16 February 1973, p. 50; 9 May 1975, p. 146.

94. Committee Print, *Winds of Change: Evolving Relations and Interests in Southeast Asia,* Report by Senator Mike Mansfield to CFR, 94th Cong., 1st sess., October 1975, p. 16; Economist Intelligence Unit, *Quarterly Economic Review: Philippines, Taiwan,* no. 4—1972, p. 4; *U.S. News and World Report,* 16 October 1972, p. 38; *Business Asia,* 6 October 1972, p. 314; 22 December 1972, pp. 404, 407; 14 June 1974, p. 192; 13 June 1975, p. 187.

95. RP, Central Bank, *24th Annual Report, 1972,* pp. 32–33 (Pres. Decree no. 8, 2 October 1972), 153–65 (Pres. Decree no. 87, 31 December 1972); *Philippine Prospect,* no. 1 (April 1973), p. 5 (Indonesian): First National City Bank, *Investment Guide to Oil,* p. 2; *Business Week,* 4 November 1972, p. 42 (Marcos). See also *NYT*, 21 January 1973, sec. 3, pt. 2, p. 52; Economist Intelligence Unit, *Quarterly Economic Review: Philippines, Taiwan,* no. 4—1972, p. 14.

96. RP, Securities and Exchange Commission, and Businessday Corporation, *1000 Top Corporations in the Philippines* (Quezon City, 1979), p. 113.

97. *Foreign Economic Trends,* ET 74-028, April 1974, pp. 7–8; CIC, "The Philippines," pp. 28, 46–47; *Philippine Prospect,* no. 1 (April 1973), p. 6; no. 2 (May 1973), p. 1; no. 4 (July 1973), p. 1; no. 7 (October 1973), p. 2; no. 10 (January 1974), pp. 6, 7; Bernardino Ronquillo, "Martial Law Reforms," *Far Eastern Economic Review,* 18 June 1973, p. 58; *Business Asia,* 15 June 1973, p. 185; 25 January 1974, p. 28; 29 March 1974, pp. 97–98; 27 December 1974, p. 411; 13 June 1975, pp. 186–87; RP, Central Bank, *24th Annual Report, 1972,* pp. 34 (Pres. Decree no. 10, 2 October 1972), 35 (Pres. Decree no. 16, 5 October 1972); Business International Asia/Pacific Ltd., *The Philippines: Operating for Profit in the New Society* (Hong Kong, 1974), pp. 84–86; "Liberalization of Foreign Investment Rules," *Philippine Progress,* 2nd quarter 1973, pp. 15–16. For a summary of investment legislation, see First National City Bank, *Investment Guide to the Philippines* (Makati, October 1973), pp. 12–25.

98. *NYT,* 20 November 1977, p. 66 (Fox Butterfield); 7 October 1976, p. 69; Bernard Wideman, *Far Eastern Economic Review,* 5 March 1976, p. 29; A. Lin Neumann, " 'Hospitality Girls' in the Philippines," *Southeast Asia Chronicle,* no. 66 (January–February 1979), p. 18.

99. Text of cable is in *Philippines Information Bulletin,* 1, no. 4 (September 1973), p. 11. See also *Time,* 9 October 1972, p. 27; CIC, "The Philippines," p. 32.

100. *Philippine Prospect,* no. 3 (June 1973), p. 6; *NYT,* 21 January 1973, sec. 3, pt. 2, p. 52; CIC, "The Philippines," p. 33; *Philadelphia Bulletin,* 22 January 1973, pp. 1, 3, 4 (Charles F. Thomson). See also *Journal of the American Chamber of Commerce of the Philippines,* April 1973, p. 6; U.S. *Cong. Rec.,* 21 February 1973, p. S3016; CIC, "The Philippines," pp. 32–33; PHILPROM Inc., *PHILPROM Report on Economic Trends* (Manila, 15 April 1973) (seen at Philippine Embassy, Washington, D.C.); *Foreign Economic Trends,* ET 73-030, March 1973, p. 6; ET 74-028, April 1974, p. 7; *Business Asia,* 27 October 1972, p. 339; 3 November 1972, p. 348; *Business Week,* 4 November 1972, p. 42; *U.S. News and World Report,* 4 December 1972, p. 71; *NYT,* 21 January 1973, sec. 3, pt. 2, p. 52; *Christian Science Monitor,* 21 September 1973, p. 3 (Daniel Sutherland).

101. *Philippine Prospect,* no. 1 (April 1973), p. 4; no. 3 (June 1973), pp. 2–3; no. 12 (March 1974), p. 1; *Business Asia,* 23 August 1974, p. 271; CIC, "The Philippines," pp. 29–30; *Business Week,* 4 November 1972, p. 42; Philippine Airlines, Press Service, *News from the Philippines,* P.O. Box 954, Manila, 09-73, 27 April 1973 (seen at the Philippine Embassy, Washington, D.C.).

102. *NYT,* 18 January 1973, p. 8 (Bernard Gwertzman).

103. Thompson, *Unequal Partners* p. 157 (enthusiastic); *Korea and the Philippines,* p. 45. See also the column by Paul M. Kattenburg, former State Department country director for the Philippines, *NYT,* 24 July 1974, p. 41.

104. *NYT,* 3 January 1969, p. 4 (Tillman Durdin); 25 January 1972, p. 8 (UPI); interview with an officer of the Philippine Embassy, Washington, D.C., 27 November 1973.

105. *FR* 1949, vol. 9, pp. 234–35, 247.

106. Diosdado Macapagal, *A Stone for the Edifice: Memoirs of a President* (Quezon City: MAC Publishing Co., 1968), p. 162.

107. Committee Print, *Winds of Change,* p. 1; Committee Print, *Outlook on the Far East, November 1976,* Report of a Fact-Finding Mission to the Far East, November 5–23, 1976, printed for the use of the CIR, 94th Cong., 2nd sess., December 1976, p. 12; Hearings, *Shifting Balance of Power in Asia: Implications for Future U.S. Policy,* CIR subcommittee, 94th Cong., 1st and 2nd sess., 1975–76, p. 184; Terry James O'Rear, "U.S. Bases in the Philippines: Are They Leaving or Is Their Rent Increasing?" *Pahayag* (Honolulu), no. 29, May 1975; interview with an officer of the Philippine Embassy, Washington, D.C., 27 November 1973; *NYT,* 19 April 1975, p. 13 (David A. Andelman); 4 May 1975, sec. 4, p. 4.

108. *Philadelphia Bulletin,* 22 January 1974, p. 1 (Charles F. Thomson).

109. U.S. Department of State, "Fact Sheet: Amendment of the 1947 U.S.-Philippines Military Bases Agreement," January 1979(?).

110. Walden Bello and Severina Rivera, eds., *The Logistics of Repression and Other Essays* (Washington, D.C.: Friends of the Filipino People, 1977), p. 8, based on U.S. government sources.

111. Interview with Richard E. Usher, U.S. Department of State, Philippine desk officer, Washington, D.C., 23 November 1973; Brian Phelan, "Spectre of Jihad," *Far Eastern Economic Review,* 14 May 1973, p. 29; Kerkvliet testimony, U.S. *Cong. Rec.,* 4 June 1974, pp. S9568–69, citing Hearings, *FY 1974 Authorization for Military Procurement, Research and Development Construction Authorization for the Safeguard ABM, and Active Duty and Selected Reserve Strengths,* Senate Armed Services Committee, 93rd Cong., 1st sess., 1973, pt. 1, p. 163.

112. Staff of the U.S. General Accounting Office, *Profiles of Military Assistance Groups in 15 Countries,* ID-78-51 (Washington, D.C.: General Accounting Office, 1 September 1978), pp. 79–87.

113. *Korea and the Philippines,* p. 42; Hearings, *Mutual Development and Cooperation Act of 1973,* CFA, 93rd Cong., 1st sess., 1973, p. 157; *Base Negotiations,* p. 11; Comptroller General, *Report to the Congress: Military Assistance and Commitments in the Philippines,* B-133359, 12 April 1973, pp. 16, 29; Bello and Rivera, *Logistics,* pp. 17–23.

114. Hearings, *Human Rights, SK and Phil,* p. 321.

115. Providence Chapter, Committee of Concerned Asian Scholars, "Sullivan: Ambassador to Martial Law," *Philippines Information Bulletin,* 1, no. 3 (June 1973), pp. 8–10; Benedict J. Kerkvliet, "The New U.S. Ambassador to the Philippines," *Pahayag* (Honolulu), no. 7 (June 1973), pp. 12–13; Noam Chomsky, *For Reasons of State* (New York: Vintage, 1973), pp. 172–87.

116. See my "U.S. Embassy Team in Manila," *Philippines Information Bulletin,* 2, no. 2 (April 1974), pp. 29–30. (The ten include the deputy chief of mission.)

117. Tad Szulc, "The Moveable War," *New Republic,* 12 May 1973, excerpted in *Philippines Information Bulletin,* 1, no. 4 (September 1973), pp. 17–18.

118. Superiors, "Survey," p. 24; Kerkvliet testimony, U.S. *Cong. Rec.,* 4 June 1974, p. S9569; Russell Johnson, "The U.S. Military in the Philippines," *Pahayag* (Honolulu), no. 18 (May/June 1974), pp. 6–8. Denials: interview with Richard E. Usher, U.S. Department of State, Philippine desk officer, Washington, D.C., 23 November 1973; interview with an officer of the Philippine Embassy, Washington, D.C., 27 November 1973.

119. Bello and Rivera, *Logistics,* pp. 25–28; Kerkvliet testimony, U.S. *Cong. Rec.,* 4 June 1974, p. S9569; *Bulletin Today* (Manila), 16 February 1973, pp. 1ff.; Robert Whymant, "Whitewash on the Green Berets," *The Guardian* (Britain), 11 September 1973, reprinted in *Pahayag* (Honolulu) no. 10 (September 1973). Official claims: interview with Richard E. Usher, U.S. Department of State, Philippine desk officer, Washington, D.C., 23 November 1973; *Boston Sunday Globe,* 28 October 1973, p. 56 (Crocker Snow, Jr.); Thompson, *Unequal Partners,* p. 148.

120. Bello and Rivera, *Logistics,* p. 24.

121. Hearings, *Human Rights, SK and Phil,* p. 321. See also Bello and Rivera, *Logistics,* pp. 49–52. In subsequent years, U.S. bilateral aid to Marcos faced some difficulties in a U.S. Congress roused by Manila's violations of human rights. But the slowdown in bilateral assistance to the Philippines has been more than offset by an astronomical increase in World Bank aid. For data and extensive discussion, see Bello and Rivera, *Logistics,* pp. 93–133.

122. *International Herald Tribune,* 6–7 October 1973, p. 5 (AP).

123. Bello and Rivera, *Logistics,* pp. 28–32; and my "U.S. AID Staff," *Philippines Information Bulletin,* 2, no. 4 (August 1974), p. 7.

124. Asian Labor Education Center, University of the Philippines, *Annual Report,* fiscal year 1972–73, pp. 1–2; *NYT,* 17 August 1975, p. 11. Arrests: *Afro-Asian Labor Bulletin* (Singapore), 8, no. 2 (February 1973), p. 7; 8, no. 8 (August 1973), p. 6; Committee Print, *The Status of Human Rights in Selected Countries and the U.S. Response,* Prepared by the Congressional Research Service, Library of Congress, for CIR, 95th Cong., 1st sess., 25 July 1977, p. 50.

125. *Los Angeles Times,* 18 January 1981, p. 11 (AP).

126. *Time,* 24 September 1979, pp. 28, 31; *Far Eastern Economic Review,* 27 April 1979, p. 32 (Sheilah Ocampo); 7 September 1979, p. 31 (Sheilah Ocampo); 11 January 1980, p. 37.

127. Ibid., 29 June 1979, p. 24 (Sheilah Ocampo); 22 August 1980, p. 69 (Sheilah Ocampo); *NYT,* 17 June 1980, p. A4 (UPI).

128. Jim Morrell, "Aid to the Philippines: Who Benefits?" *International Policy Report,* 5, no. 2 (October 1979), p. 7, citing IMF documents; *Far Eastern Economic Review,* 5 September 1980, p. 61.

129. *Time,* 24 September 1979, p. 28; *Far Eastern Economic Review,* 16 March 1979, p. 21 (Richard Vokey and Sheilah Ocampo), p. 28 (Richard Vokey); 23 March 1979, p. 24 (Richard Vokey); 18 May 1979, p. 18 (Sheilah Ocampo); 29 June 1979, pp. 24, 26 (Sheilah Ocampo); 11 April 1980, p. 21 (Sheilah Ocampo); 13 June 1980, p. 23 (Sheilah Ocampo); *NYT,* 29 January 1981, p. A3 (Henry Kamm).

130. *NYT*, 20 September 1980, p. 20.

131. *Far Eastern Economic Review*, 16 March 1979, p. 21 (Richard Vokey and Sheilah Ocampo); 29 June 1979, pp. 25–26 (Sheilah Ocampo); 11 January 1980, p. 37; 28 March 1980, p. 19 (Sheilah Ocampo); 11 April 1980, p. 20 (Sheilah Ocampo); 13 June 1980, p. 24 (Richard Vokey).

132. E.g., *NYT*, 30 November 1979, p. A10; 23 August 1980, p. 2; 13 September 1980, p. 4; 26 October 1980, p. E3.

133. *Far Eastern Economic Review*, 14 September 1979, p. 54 (Paul Wilson); 16 November 1979, p. 78 (Ho Kwon Ping); 17 October 1980, p. 25 (Rodney Tasker); Walden Bello and John Kelly, "The World Bank Writes Off Marcos & Co.," *Nation*, 31 January 1981, pp. 104–6.

134. *Time*, 24 September 1979, p. 28, citing a highly classified U.S. diplomatic cable.

135. *NYT*, 20 January 1981, p. A9 (Henry Kamm).

136. Rigged: e.g., *NYT*, 8 April 1978, p. 1 (Fox Butterfield); 19 March 1979, p. A4; 3 February 1980, p. E3 (Henry Kamm); *Time*, 24 September 1979, p. 31. Oppositionists: *NYT*, 20 January 1981, p. A9 (Henry Kamm).

137. *NYT*, 16 January 1981, p. A7 (Henry Kamm); 17 January 1981, p. 16 (AP); 20 January 1981, p. A9 (Henry Kamm); *Far Eastern Economic Review*, 17 October 1980, p. 26 (Rodney Tasker), p. 28 (Rodney Tasker interview with Marcos). Strikes: *NYT*, 6 January 1981, p. A4 (AP); *Los Angeles Times*, 18 January 1981, p. 11 (AP).

138. *NYT*, 30 January 1981, p. A3 (Pamela G. Hollie). On conduct of other elections, see notes 66 and 136 above and *NYT*, 30 January 1980, p. A10; 3 February 1980, p. 6; 3 February 1980, p. E3 (Henry Kamm); *Far Eastern Economic Review*, 11 May 1979, p. 18 (Rodney Tasker); 28 March 1980, p. 17 (Sheilah Ocampo).

139. *NYT*, 25 January 1981, p. E6 (Henry Kamm).

140. *NYT*, 21 January 1981, p. A11 (Henry Kamm); 18 January 1981, p. 10 (Henry Kamm).

Conclusion

1. See Theodore Friend, *Between Two Empires: The Ordeal of the Philippines, 1929–1946* (New Haven: Yale University Press, 1965), p. 183.

2. Prewar: Felipe Suva Martin, "U.S. Direct Investment in the Philippines" (Ph.D. dissertation, MIT, 1972), p. 283. 1970: RP, Inter-Agency Working Group on Foreign Investments, "Study of Foreign Private Investments in the Philippines," part 1, *Philippine Progress*, 6 (2nd quarter 1972), p. 7.

3. E.g., Henry L. Stimson and McGeorge Bundy, *On Active Service in Peace and War* (New York: Harper & Bros., 1948), p. 138.

4. W. Cameron Forbes to Jacob M. Dickinson, 11 October 1909, WCF Papers, fms am 1366.1, vol. 1.

5. 1969: Hearings, *United States Security Agreements and Commitments*

Abroad, Part 1: The Republic of the Philippines, CFR subcommittee, 91st Cong., 1st sess., 1969, p. 96. Prewar: Strategy Section, Operations Division, War Department General Staff, "Post War Base Requirements in the Philippines," 23 April 1945, tab "C" and tab "C" appendix V, in RG 319 MMR, ABC 686 Philippines (8 November 43), sec. 1-A.

6. I. George Blake, *Paul V. McNutt: Portrait of a Hoosier Statesman* (Indianapolis: Central Publishing Co., 1966), p. 197; Francis Sayre, *Glad Adventure* (New York: Macmillan, 1957), p. 189; (Lawrence Salisbury?), "The Political Situation" (no date, probably late 1941), FBS Papers, box 8, Phil Islands, Reports 1938–42 file.

7. Department of Defense, *United States–Vietnam Relations, 1945–1967,* printed for use of HCAS, 1971, vol. 8, p. 55 (hereafter cited as Pentagon Papers, DoD); A. L. Moffat to Acheson, 27 December 1945, DSNA 811B.01/12-2645.

8. Pentagon Papers, DoD, vol. 8, p. 61.

9. For an introduction to the literature on this subject, see Robert B. Stauffer, *TNCs and the Transnational Political Economy of Development: The Continuing Philippine Debate,* TNC Research Project Monograph (Sydney, Australia: University of Sydney, forthcoming).

== BIBLIOGRAPHY ==

This bibliography contains only sources appearing in the notes. All cited sources are listed here except (a) a few general secondary works cited only once in the notes; (b) articles from periodicals listed in Section VII, below; and (c) articles from newspapers.

I. Archives and Unpublished Documents

A. MANUSCRIPT COLLECTIONS

An asterisk (*) indicates that only a few selected items were examined.

CW Papers	Courtney Whitney Papers, MacArthur Memorial Library, Norfolk, Virginia
DAM Papers	Douglas A. MacArthur Papers, MacArthur Memorial Library, Norfolk, Virginia (Record Groups 3, 4, 5, 9, and 10)
DDE Papers	Dwight D. Eisenhower Papers, Eisenhower Library, Abilene, Kansas
DOHC	Dulles Oral History Collection, Princeton University, Princeton, New Jersey
DSNA	Department of State Records, Record Group 59, National Archives, Washington, D.C.
FAW Papers	Frank A. Waring Papers, Truman Library, Independence, Missouri
FBS Papers	Francis B. Sayre Papers, Library of Congress, Washington, D.C.
FDR Papers	Franklin D. Roosevelt Papers, Roosevelt Library, Hyde Park, New York*
HLS Papers	Henry L. Stimson Papers, Yale University, New Haven, Connecticut*
HST Papers	Harry S. Truman Papers, Truman Library, Independence, Missouri
JMD Files	Joseph M. Dodge Files, Eisenhower Library, Abilene, Kansas

JWJ Papers	J. Weldon Jones Papers, Truman Library, Independence, Missouri
JWS Papers	John W. Snyder Papers, Truman Library, Independence, Missouri
KOHP	Kennedy Oral History Program, Kennedy Library, Boston, Massachusetts
MMR	Modern Military Records Division, National Archives, Washington, D.C.
MMC Papers	Myron M. Cowen Papers, Truman Library, Independence, Missouri
RG 126	Records of the High Commissioner to the Philippine Islands, Record Group 126, National Archives, Washington, D.C.
RG 165	Records of the War Department General and Special Staff, Record Group 165, National Archives, Washington, D.C.
RG 218	Records of the U.S. Joint Chiefs of Staff, Record Group 218, National Archives, Washington, D.C.
RG 226	Records of the Office of Strategic Services, Record Group 226, National Archives, Washington, D.C.
RG 319	Records of the Army Staff, Record Group 319, Federal Records Center, Suitland, Maryland
RG 319 MMR	Records of the Army Staff, Record Group 319, Modern Military Records Division, National Archives, Washington, D.C.
RG 332	Records of U.S. Theaters of War, World War II, Record Group 332, Federal Records Center, Suitland, Maryland
RG 334	JUSMAG Records, Record Group 334, National Archives, Washington, D.C.
RG 407	Records of the Adjutant General's Office, 1917–, Record Group 407, Federal Records Center, Suitland, Maryland
TBB Papers	Thomas B. Buell Papers, Naval War College, Newport, Rhode Island
TT Papers	Theodore Tannenwald, Jr., Papers, Truman Library, Independence, Missouri
WBS Papers	Walter Bedell Smith Papers, Eisenhower Library, Abilene, Kansas
WCF Journal	Journal of W. Cameron Forbes, Houghton Library, Harvard University, Cambridge, Massachusetts*
WCF Papers	W. Cameron Forbes Papers, Houghton Library, Harvard University, Cambridge, Massachusetts*
WWG Papers	Walter W. Gardner Papers, Truman Library, Independence, Missouri

B. UNPUBLISHED DOCUMENTS FROM U.S. GOVERNMENT AGENCIES

1. Department of Defense
   Documents at Fort McNair, Washington, D.C.

   General Headquarters. U.S. Army Forces, Pacific. Military Intelligence Section. General Staff. *The Guerrilla Resistance Movement in the Philippines.* Prepared during the campaign; initially issued 31 March 1945. Corrections made from data available since first issue, 1948, 2 vols.

   U.S. Military Mission to the Philippines. *History of United States Military Advisory Group to Republic of the Philippines,* vol. 1, *1 July 1946 to 30 June 1947;* vol. 2, *1 July 1947 to 31 December 1947.*

2. Department of Justice
   Documents at Department of Justice, Washington, D.C.

   Walter R. Hutchinson to Tom C. Clark, "Preliminary Report on the Progress of the Investigation and Trial of Collaborationists by the Commonwealth Government of the Philippines and Recommendations for Immediate Action by the United States Government." 28 January 1946.

3. Department of State
   Documents at Department of State, Washington, D.C.

   Executive Committee on Economic Foreign Policy. Records. Lot 122, box 19 (new box number).

   Report of the MDAP Survey Team to the Philippines. FMACC D-32, 8 February 1950, 64A867 box 353, 2/44/29-4, folder Philippines, January–June 1950.

   Agency for International Development. Office of Public Safety. *Survey of Philippine Law Enforcement.* Washington, D.C., 1966.

   "Fact Sheet: Amendment of the 1947 U.S.-Philippines Military Bases Agreement." January 1979(?).

II. Published Government Documents

A. UNITED STATES

1. Executive Branch
   a. Department of Commerce

      Department of Commerce. *Factors Limiting U.S. Investment Abroad.* Washington, D.C., 1953.

      Department of Commerce. Bureau of Foreign Commerce. *Investment in the Philippines: Conditions and Outlook for United States Investors.* Washington, D.C., 1955.

Department of Commerce. Bureau of International Commerce. *Foreign Economic Trends and Their Implications for the United States.* U.S. Embassy, Manila, various dates.

b. Department of Defense

Counter-Guerrilla Operations in the Philippines, 1946–1953: A Seminar on the Huk Campaign Held at Ft. Bragg, N.C., 15 June 1961. N.p., n.d.

General Staff, Supreme Commander for the Allied Powers. *Reports of General MacArthur,* vol. 1, *The Campaigns of MacArthur in the Pacific.* Washington, D.C.: Government Printing Office, 1966. (As prepared by MacArthur's Tokyo headquarters in 1950.)

Department of Defense. *History of United States Decisionmaking on Vietnam.* Four volumes. Boston: Beacon Press, 1971.

Department of Defense. *United States–Vietnam Relations, 1945–1967.* Twelve volumes. Printed for the use of the House Committee on Armed Services, 1971.

c. Department of State

i. Agency for International Development (AID) and Predecessor Agencies

Mutual Security Administration (Robert S. Hardie). *Philippine Land Tenure Reform: Analysis and Recommendations.* Manila, 1952.

Community Development Division. U.S. Operations Mission to the Philippines. AID, Manila. *Community Development in the Philippines: A Joint Project of the Republic of the Philippines and the United States of America,* 8 February 1965.

Foreign Aid Through Private Initiative. Report of the Advisory Committee on Private Enterprise in Foreign Aid. Washington, D.C.: AID, July 1965.

AID. Mission to the Philippines. *A Survey of Foreign Economic and Technical Assistance Programs in the Philippines.* 1965–1966 edition. Washington, D.C., 1966.

AID. *Proposed Foreign Aid Program FY 1968, Summary Presentation to Congress.* Washington, D.C., 1967.

AID. *Increasing Participation in Development: Primer on Title IX of the United States Foreign Assistance Act.* Washington, D.C., 1970.

AID, "U.S. AID Reports: AID Support for Land Reform." In AID, *Spring Review of Land Reform.* 2nd ed. Vol. 12, Background Papers. Washington, D.C., 1970.

AID. *Assistance to the Philippines, 1946–1970.* Manila: U.S. AID Philippines, Program Office, September 1970.

AID. *Foreign Assistance for the Seventies: President Nixon's Message to Congress, September 15, 1970.* Washington, D.C., 1970.

AID. *Operations Report, Data as of June 30, 1972.* Washington, D.C., 1972.

AID. Statistics and Reports Division. Office of Financial Management. *U.S. Overseas Loans and Grants and Assistance from International Organizations, July 1, 1945–June 30, 1972,* Washington, D.C., May 1973.

ii. Other State Department

Department of State. *Transcript of Round Table Discussion on American Policy Toward China Held in the Department of State, October 6, 7, and 8, 1949.* (I used a copy of this document at the Department of State in Washington, D.C. It has been printed in Hearings, *Institute of Pacific Relations,* Sen., Judiciary Committee subcommittee, 82nd Cong., 1st and 2nd sess., 1951–52.)

Report to the President of the United States by the Economic Survey Mission to the Philippines. Far Eastern Series 38. Department of State Publication No. 4010. Washington, D.C., 9 October 1950 (Bell Report).

Department of State. Office of Public Affairs. *The Philippines Today.* Far Eastern Series 51. Department of State Publication No. 4415. Washington, D.C., November 1951.

Department of State. *Land Reform: A World Challenge, with Related Papers.* Economic Cooperation Series 29. Department of State Publication No. 4445. Washington, D.C., February 1952.

Department of State. Historical Division. *American Foreign Policy: Current Documents, 1956.* Washington, D.C., 1959.

Department of State. *Department of State Bulletin.* Washington, D.C. (various years).

Department of State. *Foreign Relations of the United States.* Washington, D.C.: Government Printing Office (various years).

Department of State. *United States Treaties and Other International Agreements.* Washington, D.C. (various years).

d. General Accounting Office

Comptroller General of the United States. *Report to the Committee on Foreign Relations, U.S. Senate: Use of Excess Defense Articles and Other Resources to Supplement the Military Assistance Program,* B-163742, 21 March 1973.

Comptroller General of the United States. *Report to the Congress: Military Assistance and Commitments in the Philippines,* B-133359, 12 April 1973.

Comptroller General of the United States. *Report to the Congress: Improvements Needed in System for Managing U.S. Participation in the Asian Development Bank,* B-173240, 8 May 1973.

Staff of the U.S. General Accounting Office. *Profiles of Military Assistance Groups in 15 Countries*, ID-78-51, 1 September 1978.

e. Other Executive Branch

Public Papers of the Presidents of the United States. Washington, D.C.: Government Printing Office, 1945–1973 (Truman to Nixon).

The Public Papers and Addresses of Franklin D. Roosevelt. Compiled with special material and explanatory notes by Samuel I. Rosenman. 1944–45 vol.: *Victory and the Threshold of Peace.* New York: Harper & Bros., 1950.

Edgar B. Nixon, ed. *Franklin D. Roosevelt and Foreign Affairs.* Cambridge, Mass.: Belknap Press of Harvard University Press, 1969.

U.S. Foreign Assistance in the 1970's: A New Approach. Report to the President of the United States from the [Peterson] Task Force on International Development. Washington, D.C., 4 March 1970.

Complete Presidential Press Conferences of Franklin D. Roosevelt. 25 volumes. New York: Da Capo Press, 1972.

2. Congress

Congressional Record
United States Statutes at Large

a. Senate

i. Hearings

Committee on Appropriations

Foreign Assistance and Related Agencies Appropriations (1963, 1964, 1965, 1968).

Foreign Assistance and Related Programs Appropriations (1970, 1972, 1973).

Committee on Finance

Philippine Trade Act of 1946. 79th Cong., 2nd sess., 1946.

Committee on Foreign Relations

Reviews of the World Situation: 1949–1950. Held in executive session. 81st Cong., 1st and 2nd sess., 1949–50. Made public June 1974, Historical Series.

Nomination of Philip C. Jessup to be United States Representative to the Sixth General Assembly of the United Nations. 82nd Cong., 1st sess., 1951.

Mutual Security Act (1953, 1955, 1958, 1959).

International Development and Security. 87th Cong., 1st sess., 1961.

The Peace Corps. 87th Cong., 1st sess., 1961.

Foreign Assistance Act (1963–65, 1967).

United States Security Agreements and Commitments Abroad, Part 1: The Republic of the Philippines. 91st Cong., 1st sess., 1969.

Peace Corps Act Amendments of 1970. 91st Cong., 2nd sess., 1970.

Multinational Corporations and United States Foreign Policy. 93rd Cong., 1st and 2nd sess., 1973–74, pts. 1 and 3.

ii. Documents

Remarks of Senator Millard E. Tydings: The Philippine Islands. Sen. Doc. 53, 79th Cong., 1st sess., 1945.

A Decade of American Foreign Policy: Basic Documents, 1941–49. Sen. Doc. 123, 81st Cong., 1st sess., 1950.

Foreign Aid Program: Compilation of Studies and Surveys Prepared Under the Direction of the Special Committee to Study the Foreign Aid Program. Sen. Doc. 52, 85th Cong., 1st sess., 1957.

iii. Committee Prints

United States Foreign Policy: Asia. Studies prepared at the request of the Committee on Foreign Relations by Conlon Associates Ltd. No. 5, 1 November 1959. 86th Cong., 1st sess., 1959.

Survey of the Alliance for Progress: Labor Policies and Programs. Study prepared at the request of the subcommittee on American Republics Affairs by the staff of the Committee on Foreign Relations (Robert H. Dockery), together with a report of the Comptroller General, 15 July 1968. 90th Cong., 2nd sess., 1968.

The Amerasia Papers: A Clue to the Catastrophe of China. Prepared by the subcommittee to Investigate the Administration of the Internal Security Act and other Internal Security Laws of the Committee on the Judiciary. 91st Cong., 1st sess., 26 January 1970.

Korea and the Philippines: November 1972. Staff report prepared for the use of the Committee on Foreign Relations. 93rd Cong., 1st sess., 18 February 1973.

Winds of Change: Evolving Relations and Interests in Southeast Asia. Report by Senator Mike Mansfield to the Committee on Foreign Relations. 94th Cong., 1st sess., October 1975.

United States Development Assistance Programs in Pakistan, the Philippines, and Indonesia. Staff reports to subcommittee of the Committee on Foreign Relations. 95th Cong., 1st sess., February 1977.

United States–Philippine Base Negotiations. Staff report to subcommittee of the Committee on Foreign Relations. 95th Cong., 1st sess., 7 April 1977.

iv. Reports

No. 755. 79th Cong., 1st sess., 1945.

No. 1145. 79th Cong., 2nd sess., 1946.

No. 1700. 83rd Cong., 2nd sess., 1954.

b. House of Representatives
  i. Hearings
    Committee on Appropriations
    Foreign Assistance and Related Agencies Appropriations (1970–73).
    Committee on Banking and Currency
    Asian Development Bank. 89th Cong., 2nd sess., 1966.
    Committee on Foreign Affairs
    To Amend the Philippine Rehabilitation Act of 1946. 81st Cong., 1st and 2nd sess., 1949–50.
    To Amend the Mutual Defense Assistance Act of 1949. 81st Cong., 2nd sess., 1950.
    Mutual Security Program. 82nd Cong., 1st sess., 1951.
    Mutual Security Act Extension. 82nd Cong., 2nd sess., 1952.
    Foreign Economic Policy. 83rd Cong., 1st sess., 1953.
    Status of Forces Agreements. 84th Cong., 1st and 2nd sess., 1955–56.
    Foreign Policy and Mutual Security. 84th Cong., 2nd sess., 1956.
    Mutual Security Act (1957–59).
    Foreign Assistance Act (1962–64, 1966–69, 1971).
    Rural Development in Asia. 90th Cong., 1st sess., 1967, pt. 2.
    (Proceedings) *Symposium on Science and Foreign Policy: The Green Revolution.* 91st Cong., 1st sess., 1969.
    To Amend the Foreign Assistance Act of 1961. 91st Cong., 2nd sess., 1970.
    Mutual Development and Cooperation Act of 1973. 93rd Cong., 1st sess., 1973.
    Committee on Insular Affairs
    To Provide for the Rehabilitation of the Philippine Islands. 79th Cong., 2nd sess., 1946.
    Committee on International Relations
    Human Rights in South Korea and the Philippines: Implications for U.S. Policy. 94th Cong., 1st sess., 1975.
    Shifting Balance of Power in Asia: Implications for Future U.S. Policy. 94th Cong., 1st and 2nd sess., 1975–76.
    Human Rights in the Philippines: Report by Amnesty International. 94th Cong., 2nd sess., 1976.
    Committee on Ways and Means
    Philippine Trade Act of 1945. 79th Cong., 2nd sess., 1946.
    Philippine Trade Revision Act of 1955. 84th Cong., 1st sess., 1955.
  ii. Documents
    Seventh and Final Report of the High Commissioner to the Philippine Islands. H. Doc. 389, 80th Cong., 1st sess., 8 July 1947.
    Report and Recommendations of the Joint Philippine-American Fi-

nance Commission, Manila, 7 June 1947. H. Doc. 390, 80th
Cong., 1st sess., 8 July 1947.

*Communication from the President of the U.S. Transmitting a Sup-
plemental Estimate of Appropriations for the Fiscal Year 1951 of
$4,000,000,000 to Provide Military Assistance to Foreign Na-
tions.* H. Doc. 670, 81st Cong., 2nd sess., August 1950.

iii. Committee Prints

Military Assistance Training in East and Southeast Asia. Staff report prepared for subcommittee of Committee on Foreign
Affairs. 91st Cong., 2nd sess., 16 February 1971.

Outlook on the Far East: November 1976. Report of a Fact-Finding Mission to the Far East, November 5–23, 1976. Prepared for use of the House Committee on International
Relations. 94th Cong., 2nd sess., December 1976.

*Human Rights and U.S. Policy: Argentina, Haiti, Indonesia, Iran,
Peru, and the Philippines.* Reports submitted to House Com-
mittee on International Relations by the Department of
State. 94th Cong., 2nd sess., 31 December 1976.

*The Status of Human Rights in Selected Countries and the U.S.
Response.* Prepared by the Congressional Research Service,
Library of Congress, for House Committee on Interna-
tional Relations. 95th Cong., 1st sess., 25 July 1977.

iv. Reports

No. 1887. 83rd Cong., 2nd sess., 1954.

No. 934. 84th Cong., 1st sess., 1955.

3. Philippine Islands (U.S. Colony)

Commonwealth of the Philippines. Commission of the Census. *Census of the Philippines, 1939.* Manila: Bureau of Printing, 1941.

*Fifth Annual Report of the United States High Commissioner to the
Philippine Islands, Covering the Fiscal Year Ending 30 June
1941,* 31 July 1942. Washington, D.C.: Government Printing Office, 1943.

B. REPUBLIC OF THE PHILIPPINES

1. Executive Branch

a. Central Bank

22nd Annual Report, 1970. Manila.

24th Annual Report, 1972. Manila.

Statistical Bulletin. Vol. 24, December 1972.

Statistical Bulletin. Vol. 26, December 1974.

b. Department of Commerce and Industry, Bureau of the Census and
Statistics

Bureau of the Census and Statistics. *Philippine Statistical
Survey of Households Bulletin, Family Income and Expenditures,
1961.* Series no. 14. Manila, n.d.

Bureau of the Census and Statistics. *BCS Survey of Households Bulletin, Family Income and Expenditures, 1965.* Series no. 22. Manila, n.d.

Bureau of the Census and Statistics. *Yearbook of Philippine Statistics, 1966.* Manila, 1966.

Bureau of the Census and Statistics. *BCS Survey of Households Bulletin, Family Income and Expenditures, 1971.* Series no. 34. Manila, 1971.

c. Department of Foreign Affairs

Department of Foreign Affairs. *Treaty Series.*

Raul S. Manglapus. "The Philippine Stand on the Recognition of South Vietnam." *Department of Foreign Affairs Review,* 2, no. 2 (January 1956).

d. Department of Labor

Department of Labor. Labor Statistics Division. "Wages and Working Conditions in Our Sugar Cane Haciendas in Negros Occidental." *Philippine Labor,* May 1962.

e. Presidential Documents

Manuel Roxas. *Important Speeches, Messages and Other Pronouncements of President Manuel Roxas.* Manila: Bureau of Printing, 1947.

Manuel Roxas. *Papers, Addresses and Other Writings of Manuel Roxas.* Manila: Bureau of Printing, 1954.

f. Other Executive Branch

National Economic Council. Office of Foreign Aid Coordination. *Annual Report on the Foreign Aid Programs in the Philippines.* Manila, various years.

National Economic Council. Office of Statistical Coordination and Standards. "American Investments in the Philippines." *Philippine Progress,* 2, no. 7 (March 1969).

Inter-Agency Working Group on Foreign Investments. "Study of Private Foreign Investments in the Philippines." Part 1, *Philippine Progress,* 6 (2nd quarter 1972); part 2, *Philippine Progress,* 6 (3rd quarter 1972).

Department of Public Information. National Media Production Center. *Vital Documents on the Declaration of Martial Law in the Philippines.* Manila, October 1972.

F. D. Pinpin, comp. and ed. *The First 107 Presidential Decrees.* Handbook Series No. 7. Rizal: Cacho Hermanos Inc., 1973.

National Economic and Development Authority. *Statistical Yearbook of the Philippines, 1975.* Manila, 1975.

Securities and Exchange Commission and Businessday. *1000 Top Corporations in the Philippines.* Quezon City, 1979.

2. Joint Legislative-Executive Tax Commission and Successor Agencies

Joint Legislative-Executive Tax Commission. *Local Government Finance.* Manila, 1962.

Joint Legislative-Executive Tax Commission. *4th Annual Report, 1962.* Manila, 1963.

Joint Legislative-Executive Tax Commission. *5th Annual Report, 1963.* Manila, 1964.

Joint Legislative-Executive Tax Commission. *7th Annual Report, 1965.* Manila, 1966.

National Tax Research Center. "Initial Report on Taxation and Income Redistribution: A Study of Tax Burden by Income Class, 1971." *The Tax Monthly,* 15, no. 1 (January 1974).

3. Congress

Congressional Record. (Examined Sen., 1946–52; HR, June 1945–September 1946.)

House of Representatives. Special Committee on Un-Filipino Activities. *Report on 1. The Illegality of the Communist Party of the Philippines, 2. The Functions of the Special Committee on Un-Filipino Activities.* Manila, 1951.

Senate. Committee on Economic Affairs. *Compilation of Statistics on the Philippine Economy.* Committee Report no. 2513. 6th Cong., 4th sess., 15 May 1969.

4. Supreme Court

"Jose O. Vera et al. v. Jose A. Avelino et al." *Philippine Reports,* vol. 77, August 5, 1946 to February 28, 1947. Manila: Bureau of Printing, 1953.

"Alejo Mabanag et al. v. Jose Lopez Vito et al." *Philippine Reports,* vol. 78, March 5 to July 31, 1947. Manila: Bureau of Printing, 1954.

"Lansang v. Garcia." *Philippine Supreme Court Reports, Annotated,* vol. 42, October 22 to December 31, 1971. Quezon City: Central Lawbook Publishing Co., 1972.

"Luzon Stevedoring v. Anti-Dummy Board." *Philippine Supreme Court Reports, Annotated.* vol. 46, July to August 31, 1972. Quezon City: Central Lawbook Publishing Co., 1972.

"Republic of the Philippines and/or the Solicitor General v. William H. Quasha." *Philippine Supreme Court Reports, Annotated.* vol. 46, July to August 31, 1972. Quezon City: Central Lawbook Publishing Co., 1972.

C. OTHER DOCUMENTS

International Labour Office. Expanded Programme of Technical Assistance. *Report to the Government of the Philippines on Labour-Management Relations.* ILO/TAP/Phil/R.3, confidential (declassified). Geneva, 1958.

International Labour Conference. *Agrarian Reform, with Particular Reference to Employment and Social Aspects.* Sixth item on the agenda, report 6, 49th sess., Geneva, 1965. Geneva: ILO, 1964.

International Labour Office. *Employment Problems and Policies in the Philippines.* Geneva, 1969.

Asian Development Bank. *Southeast Asia's Economy in the 1970's.* London: Longman Group Ltd., 1971.

International Labour Office. United Nations Development Programme. Technical Assistance Sector. *Report to the Government of the Philippines on a National Vocational Preparation Programme for Out-of-School Youth.* ILO/TAP/Phil/R.14, confidential (declassified). Geneva, 1972.

International Labour Office. *Sharing in Development: A Programme of Employment, Equity and Growth for the Philippines.* Report of an inter-agency team financed by the U.N. Development Programme and organized by the ILO. Geneva, 1974.

III. Published Secondary Sources, Including Memoirs

Abaya, Hernando J. *Betrayal in the Philippines.* New York: A. A. Wyn Co., 1946.

———. *The Untold Philippine Story.* Quezon City: Malaya Books, 1967.

Abueva, Jose V. "Bridging the Gap Between the Elite and the People in the Philippines." *Philippine Journal of Public Administration,* vol. 8, no. 4, October 1964.

———. *Focus on the Barrio.* Manila: Institute of Public Administration, University of the Philippines, 1959.

———. *Ramon Magsaysay: A Political Biography.* Manila: Solidaridad Publishing House, 1971.

Acheson, Dean. *Present at the Creation: My Years in the State Department.* New York: Signet, 1969.

Africa Research Group. *International Dependency in the 1970's.* P.O. Box 213, Cambridge, Mass.: 1970.

Aglapo, Remigio E. *The Political Elite and the People: A Study of Politics in Occidental Mindoro.* Manila: College of Public Administration, University of the Philippines, 1972.

———. *The Political Process and the Nationalization of the Retail Trade in the Philippines.* Quezon City: University of the Philippines, 1962.

Agoncillo, Teodoro A. *The Fateful Years: Japan's Adventure in the Philippines, 1941–1945.* Quezon City: Garcia, 1965.

———. *A Short History of the Philippines.* New York: Mentor Books, 1969.

Ahmad, Zubeida Manzoor. "The Social and Economic Implications of the Green Revolution in Asia." *International Labour Review,* vol. 105, no. 1, January 1972.

Aruego, Jose M. *Barrio Government Law and Administration in the Philippines.* Manila: Metropolitan Publishing Co., 1968.

Ashabranner, Brent K. *A Moment in History: The First Ten Years of the Peace Corps.* Garden City, N.Y.: Doubleday & Co., 1971.

Asian Labor Education Center, University of the Philippines. *ALEC Annual Report.* 1956–57 to 1972–73.

Baclagon, Uldarico S. *Lessons from the Huk Campaign in the Philippines.* Manila: M. Colcol & Co., 1960.

Barber, Willard F., and Ronning, C. Neale. *Internal Security and Military Power: Counterinsurgency and Civic Action in Latin America.* Columbus: Ohio State University Press, 1966.

Bashore, Boyd T. "Dual Strategy for Limited War." In Franklin Mark Osanka, ed., *Modern Guerrilla Warfare.* New York: Free Press of Glencoe, 1962.

Bello, Walden, and Rivera, Severina, eds. *The Logistics of Repression and Other Essays.* Washington, D.C.: Friends of the Filipino People, 1977.

Bernstein, David. *The Philippine Story.* New York: Farrar, Straus & Co., 1947.

Berreman, Gerald D. "The Peace Corps: A Dream Betrayed." *Nation,* 26 February 1968.

Blake, I. George. *Paul V. McNutt: Portrait of a Hoosier Statesman.* Indianapolis: Central Publishing Co., 1966.

Brown, Holmes, and Luce, Don. *Hostages of War: Saigon's Political Prisoners.* Washington, D.C.: Indochina Mobile Education Project, 1973.

Brown, Lester R. *Seeds of Change: The Green Revolution and Development in the 1970's.* New York: Praeger, for the Overseas Development Council, 1970.

Buell, Thomas B. *The Quiet Warrior: A Biography of Admiral Raymond A. Spruance.* Boston: Little, Brown & Co., 1974.

Bull, Frate. *Land Reform in the Philippines, 1950–1958.* N.p.: International Cooperation Administration, 1958?.

Bureau of Social Science Research, The American University. *Communications and Public Opinion in the Philippines: A Survey of Selected Sources.* (Washington, D.C.) Draft prepared for the Office of Research and Intelligence, U.S. Information Agency, BSSR no. 674, January 1955.

Burley, T. M. *The Philippines: An Economic and Social Geography.* London: G. Bell & Sons, 1973.

Business Day's 1000 Top Corporations [for 1972]. Quezon City: Enterprise Publications, n.d. [1973?].

Business Day's Top 1000 Corporations [for 1974]. Quezon City: Businessday Corporation, n.d. [1975?].

Business International Asia/Pacific Ltd. *The Philippines: Operating for Profit in the New Society.* Hong Kong, 1974.

Buss, Claude A. *Arc of Crisis.* Garden City, N.Y.: Doubleday & Co., 1961.

————. *The United States and the Philippines: Background for Policy.* Washington, D.C.: American Enterprise Institute for Public Policy Research; and Stanford: Hoover Institution on War, Revolution and Peace, 1977.

Calalang, Liwayway. "A Survey of Selected Conditions of Employment in the Sugar Industry in Mainland Luzon." *Philippine Labor,* June 1962.

Calderon, C. D. "From Compulsory Arbitration to Collective Bargaining in the Philippines." *International Labour Review,* vol. 81, no. 1, January 1960.

Caldwell, Malcolm. "ASEANisation," in *The Philippines: End of an Illusion.* London: Association for Radical East Asian Studies, 1973. (This volume was also published as vol. 2, no. 2, 1973, of *Journal of Contemporary Asia.)*

Carroll, John J. "Philippine Labor Unions." *Philippine Studies,* vol. 9, no. 2, April 1961.

Cater, Sonya Diane. "The Philippine Federation of Free Farmers (A Case Study in Mass Agrarian Organizations)." In Socorro C. Espiritu and Chester L. Hunt, eds., *Social Foundations of Community Development.* Manila: R. M. Garcia Publishing House, 1964.

Center for Strategic and International Studies. *U.S.-Philippines Economic Relations.* Special Report Series no. 12, Georgetown University. Washington, D.C., 1971.

Cheetham, Russell J., and Hawkins, Edward K. *The Philippines: Priorities and Prospects for Development.* Washington, D.C.: World Bank, 1976.

Clark, Blake. "Are the Philippines Going the Way of China?" *Reader's Digest,* June 1950.

Cleaver, Harry. "Will the Green Revolution Turn Red?" In Steve Weissman et al., *The Trojan Horse: A Radical Look at Foreign Aid.* San Francisco: Ramparts Press, 1974.

Cook, Hugh L. "Land Reform and Development in the Philippines." In Walter Froehlich, ed., *Land Tenure, Industrialization and Social Stability: Experience and Prospects in Asia.* Milwaukee: Marquette University Press, 1961.

Coquia, Jorge R. *The Philippine Presidential Election of 1953.* Manila: University Publishing Co., 1955.

Corporate Information Center, National Council of Churches of Christ in the U.S.A. "The Philippines: American Corporations, Martial Law, and Underdevelopment." *IDOC,* International/North American edition, no. 57, November 1973.

Dalton, James K. "The Ins and Outs in the Philippines." *Far Eastern Survey,* vol. 21, no. 12, 30 July 1952.

Daugherty, William E. "Magsaysay and the Philippine Huks." in *Psychological Warfare Casebook,* edited by William E. Daugherty in collaboration with Morris Janowitz. Baltimore: Operations Research Office, Johns Hopkins University, by Johns Hopkins Press, 1958.

De Camp, Richard. "The Asian Development Bank: An Imperial Thrust into the Pacific," in Mark Selden, ed., *Remaking Asia: Essays on the American Uses of Power.* New York: Pantheon, 1974.

Deverall, Richard. "Labor in the Philippines." *American Federationist,* vol. 61, no. 1, January 1954.

Diokno, Jose W. "Legal Aspects of Land Reform: The Central Luzon Experience." *Solidarity,* vol. 2, no. 8, July–August 1967.

Diokno, Ramon. "Roxas Violates the Constitution." *Amerasia*, vol. 10, no. 6, December 1946.

Documentation Committee for Philippine Political Prisoners. *Political Prisoners in the Philippines*. 762 N. Virgil Ave., Los Angeles, Calif. 90029, May 1975.

Duffy, John. "Signpost: Success in the Philippines." *Army*, vol. 13, no. 12, July 1963.

Durdin, Tillman. "The Philippines: Martial Law, Marcos-Style." *Asian Affairs*, vol. 3, no. 2, November–December 1975.

Edgerton, Ronald K. "General Douglas MacArthur and the American Military Impact in the Philippines." *Philippine Studies*, vol. 25, 4th quarter 1977.

Elma, Magdangal B. "The Scope and Effects of the Quasha Decision on Private Agricultural Lands Acquired by Americans Under the Parity Amendment." In *Philippine Supreme Court Reports, Annotated*, vol. 46, July–August 31, 1972. (Quezon City: Central Lawbook Publishing Co., 1972).

Elsbree, Willard H. "The Philippines." In Rupert Emerson, ed., *Representative Government in Southeast Asia*. Cambridge, Mass.: Harvard University Press, 1955.

Emery, Robert F. *The Financial Institutions of Southeast Asia: A Country-by-Country Study*. New York: Praeger Special Studies in International Economics and Development, 1970.

———. "The Successful Philippine Decontrol and Devaluation." *Asian Survey*, vol. 3, no. 6, June 1963.

Entenberg, Barbara. "Agrarian Reform and the Hukbalahap." *Far Eastern Survey*, vol. 15, no. 16, 14 August 1946.

Esguerra, Renato S. "The Philippines." In S. Watson Dunn, ed., *International Handbook of Advertising*. New York: McGraw-Hill, 1964.

Estrella, C. F. *The Democratic Answer to the Philippine Agrarian Problem*. Manila: Solidaridad Publishing House, 1969.

Eyre, James K., Jr. *The Roosevelt-MacArthur Conflict*. Chambersburg, Pa.: Craft Press, 1950.

Felder, Louis F. *Socioeconomic Aspects of Counterinsurgency, A Case History: The Philippines*. Washington, D.C.: Industrial College of the Armed Forces, 1963.

Fernandez, Perfecto V. "The Constitutionality of the Compensation Provisions of the Agricultural Land Reform Code," *Philippine Law Journal*, vol. 38, October 1963.

———. "Philippine Labor Law—A Survey." *Washington Law Review*, vol. 40, no. 2, June 1965 (part 1).

Fifield, Russell H. "The Challenge to Magsaysay." *Foreign Affairs*, vol. 33, no. 1, October 1954.

———. *Southeast Asia in United States Policy*. New York: Praeger, 1963.

First National City Bank (Jesus M. Villegas). *Investment Guide to Oil Exploration in the Philippines*. 1973?

————. *Investment Guide to the Philippines.* Makati, October 1973.

Francisco, Gregorio A., Jr., and de Guzman, Raul P. "The 50-50 Agreement." In Raul P. de Guzman, ed., *Patterns in Decision-Making: Case Studies in Philippine Public Administration.* Manila: Graduate School of Public Administration, University of the Philippines Press, 1963.

Frantzich, Steve. "Party Switching in the Philippine Context." *Philippine Studies,* vol. 16, no. 4, October 1968.

Friend, Theodore. *Between Two Empires: The Ordeal of the Philippines, 1929–1946.* New Haven: Yale University Press, 1965.

Glang, Alunan C. *Muslim Secession or Integration.* Manila: Cardinal Bookstore, 1971.

Golay, Frank H. "Economic Consequences of the Philippine Trade Act." *Pacific Affairs,* vol. 28, no. 1, March 1955.

————. "The Philippine Monetary Policy Debate." *Pacific Affairs,* vol. 29, no. 3, September 1956.

————. *The Philippines: Public Policy and National Economic Development.* Ithaca, N.Y.: Cornell University Paperbacks, 1968.

————. *The Revised United States Philippine Trade Agreement of 1955.* Southeast Asia Program, Department of Far Eastern Studies, Data Paper No. 23. Ithaca, N.Y.: Cornell University, November 1956.

Goodman, Grant K. "Japan's Support for Anti-Communism in the Philippines." *Philippine Historical Review,* vol. 3, no. 1, 1970.

Gosnell, Harold F. "An Interpretation of the Philippine Election of 1953." *American Political Science Review,* vol. 48, no. 4, December 1954.

Grace, Brewster. "The Politics of Income Distribution in the Philippines." *AUFS Fieldstaff Reports,* Southeast Asia Series, vol. 25, no. 8, BG-3-'77 (Phil.), August 1977.

Greene, Fred. *United States Policy and the Security of Asia.* New York: McGraw-Hill, 1968.

Grossholtz, Jean. *Politics in the Philippines.* Boston: Little, Brown & Co., 1964.

Grunder, Garel A., and Livezey, William E. *The Philippines and the United States.* Norman: University of Oklahoma Press, 1951.

Guerrero, Amado. *Philippine Society and Revolution.* Hong Kong: Ta Kung Pao, 1971.

Hammer, Kenneth M. "Huks in the Philippines." In Franklin Mark Osanka, ed., *Modern Guerrilla Warfare.* New York: Free Press of Glencoe, 1962.

Hapgood, David, ed. *The Role of Popular Participation in Development,* Report of a Conference on the Implementation of Title IX of the Foreign Assistance Act, June 24 to August 2, 1968. MIT Report No. 17. Cambridge, Mass.: MIT Press, 1969.

Harkin, Duncan A. *Philippine Agrarian Reform in the Perspective of Three Years of Martial Law.* Land Tenure Center, Research Paper No. 68. Madison: University of Wisconsin, April 1976.

————. "The Philippine Land Reform." *Land Tenure Center Newsletter* (Madison), no. 48, April–June 1975.

Hart, Donn V. "Magsaysay: Philippine Candidate." *Far Eastern Survey*, vol. 22, no. 6, May 1953.

Hartendorp, A. V. H. *A History of Industry and Trade of the Philippines: From Pre-Spanish Times to the End of the Quirino Administration*. Manila: American Chamber of Commerce of the Philippines, 1958.

———. *A History of Industry and Trade of the Philippines: The Magsaysay Administration*. Manila: Philippine Education Co., 1961.

———. *Short History of Industry and Trade of the Philippines*. Manila: American Chamber of Commerce of the Philippines, 1953.

Hayter, Teresa. *Aid as Imperialism*. Harmondsworth, Middlesex, Eng.: Penguin, 1971.

Hickey, Gerald C., and Wilkinson, John L. *Agrarian Reform in the Philippines: Report of a Seminar, December 16–17, 1977 at the Rand Corporation, Washington, D.C.* P-6194. Santa Monica(?): Rand Corporation, August 1978.

Hilsman, Roger. *To Move a Nation*. Garden City, N.Y.: Doubleday & Co., 1967.

Hoopes, Roy. *The Complete Peace Corps Guide*. New York: Dial Press, 1961.

Houston, Charles O., Jr. "The Philippine Sugar Industry, 1934–1950." *Journal of East Asiatic Studies* (University of Manila), vol. 3, no. 4, July–October 1954.

———. "Rice in the Philippine Economy 1934–1950." *Journal of East Asiatic Studies* (University of Manila), vol. 3, no. 1, October 1953.

Huke, Robert E. *Shadows on the Land: An Economic Geography of the Philippines*. Manila: Bookmark, 1963.

Hutcheon, Pat Duffy. "Power in the Philippines: How Democratic Is Asia's 'First Democracy'?" *Journal of Asian and African Studies* (Leiden), vol. 6, nos. 3/4, July/October 1971.

Jacoby, Erich H., in collaboration with Charlotte F. Jacoby. *Man and Land: The Essential Revolution*. New York: Alfred A. Knopf, 1971.

James, D. Clayton. *The Years of MacArthur*. Vol. 1: *1880–1941;* vol. 2: *1941–1945*. Boston: Houghton Mifflin, 1970, 1975.

Jenkins, Shirley. *American Economic Policy Toward the Philippines*. Stanford: Stanford University Press, 1954.

———. "Great Expectations in the Philippines." *Far Eastern Survey*, vol. 16, no. 15, 13 August 1947.

Jocano, F. Landa. *Slum as a Way of Life*. Quezon City: University of the Philippines Press, 1975.

Kann, Peter R. "The Philippines Without Democracy." *Foreign Affairs*, vol. 52, no. 3, April 1974.

Kennan, George F. *Memoirs*. New York: Bantam Books, 1967.

Kerkvliet, Benedict J. "Agrarian Conditions Since the Huk Rebellion: A Barrio in Central Luzon." In Benedict J. Kerkvliet, ed., *Political Change in the Philippines: Studies of Local Politics Preceding Martial Law*. Asian Studies at Hawaii no. 14, Asian Studies Program, University of Hawaii. Honolulu: University of Hawaii Press, 1974.

———. *The Huk Rebellion: A Study of Peasant Revolt in the Philippines.* Berkeley: University of California Press, 1977.

———. "Land Reform: Emancipation or Counterinsurgency?" In David A. Rosenberg, ed., *Marcos and Martial Law in the Philippines.* Ithaca, N.Y.: Cornell University Press, 1979.

———. "Land Reform in the Philippines Since the Marcos Coup." *Pacific Affairs*, vol. 47, no. 3, Fall 1974.

Khan, Azizur Rahman. "Growth and Inequality in the Rural Philippines." In *Poverty and Landlessness in Rural Asia.* Geneva: International Labour Office, 1977.

Kim, Sung Yong. *United States Philippine Relations, 1946–1956.* Washington, D.C.: Public Affairs Press, 1968.

Kirk, Grayson L. *Philippine Independence: Motives, Problems, and Prospects.* New York: Farrar & Rinehart, 1936.

Klare, Michael. "The Police Apparatus, Courtesy of USAID." *Philippines Information Bulletin*, vol. 1, no. 1, January 1973.

———. *War Without End.* New York: Alfred A. Knopf, 1972.

Klitgaard, Robert E. *Martial Law in the Philippines.* P-4964. Santa Monica: Rand Corporation, November 1972.

Koone, Harold D., and Gleeck, Lewis E. "Land Reform in the Philippines." In AID, *Spring Review of Land Reform.* 2nd ed. Vol. 4, Country Papers. Washington, D.C., June 1970.

Lachica, Eduardo. *The Huks: Philippine Agrarian Society in Revolt.* New York: Praeger, 1971.

Landé, Carl H. *Leaders, Factions, and Parties: The Structure of Philippine Politics.* Monograph Series No. 6, Southeast Asia Studies, Yale University. New Haven: Yale University, 1965.

———. "The Philippines." In James S. Coleman, ed., *Education and Political Development.* Princeton: Princeton University Press, 1965.

Lansang, Jose A. "The Philippine-American Experiment: A Filipino View." *Pacific Affairs*, vol. 25, no. 3, September 1952.

Lansdale, Edward G. "Lessons Learned: The Philippines, 1946–1956." *Alert*, no. 6A (Washington, D.C.: Department of Defense), 11 December 1962.

———. *In the Midst of Wars: An American's Mission to Southeast Asia.* New York: Harper & Row, 1972.

Laquian, Aprodicio A. *Slums Are for People.* Honolulu: East-West Center Press, 1969.

Ledesma, Antonio J. "Socioeconomic Aspects of Filipino Sugar Farm Workers: Three Views from the Cane Fields." *Philippine Studies*, vol. 27, 2nd quarter 1979.

Lee, Clark, and Henschel, Richard. *Douglas MacArthur.* New York: Henry Holt & Co., 1952.

Leighton, Richard M.; Sanders, Ralph; and Tinio, Jose N. *The Huk Rebellion: A Case Study in the Social Dynamics of Insurrection.* Pub. No. R-231. Washington, D.C.: Industrial College of the Armed Forces, March 1964.

Levinson, G. I. *The Workers' Movement in the Philippines*. Moscow, 1957. (JPRS/DC-434, CSO DS-2309, Scholarly Book Translation Series, Research and Microfilm Publications, Inc., P.O. Box 267, Annapolis, Md.)

Liang, Dapen. *Philippine Parties and Politics*. Rev. ed. San Francisco: Gladstone Co., 1970.

Lichauco, Alejandro. "Imperialism in the Philippines." *Monthly Review*, vol. 25, no. 3, July–August 1973.

Lichauco, Marcial P. *Roxas*. Manila: Kiho Printing Press, 1952.

Lorimer, Norman. "The Philippine Left: An Historical Survey." In *The Philippines: End of an Illusion*. London: Association for Radical East Asian Studies, 1973. (This volume was also published as vol. 2, no. 2, 1973, of *Journal of Contemporary Asia*.)

Loveday, Douglas F. *The Role of U.S. Military Bases in the Philippine Economy*. RM-5801-ISA. Santa Monica: Rand Corporation, April 1971.

Macapagal, Diosdado. *A Stone for the Edifice: Memoirs of a President*. Quezon City: MAC Publishing Co., 1968.

MacArthur, Douglas. *Reminiscences*. New York: McGraw-Hill, 1964.

Madigan, Francis C. *Birth and Death in Cagayan de Oro: Population Dynamics in a Medium-Sized Philippine City*. Quezon City: Ateneo University Press, 1972.

Magsaysay, Ramon. "Roots of Philippine Policy." *Foreign Affairs*, vol. 35, no. 1, October 1956.

Manchester, William. *American Caesar: Douglas MacArthur, 1880–1964*. New York: Dell, 1978.

Mangahas, Mahar. "A Broad View of the Philippine Employment Problem." *Philippine Economic Journal* 23, vol. 12, nos. 1 and 2, 1973.

Marchetti, Victor, and Marks, John D. *The CIA and the Cult of Intelligence*. New York: Dell, 1974.

Mason, Edward S., and Asher, Robert E. *The World Bank Since Bretton Woods*. Washington, D.C.: The Brookings Institution, 1973.

McCarty, Vern. "Philippine Copper." *Pacific Research and World Empire Telegram*, vol. 3, no. 3, March-April-May 1972.

McCoy, Al. "Land Reform as Counter-Revolution." *Bulletin of Concerned Asian Scholars*, vol. 3, no. 1, Winter–Spring 1971.

McGovern, George. "Food for Peace." *AID Digest*, 1 February 1962.

McLennan, Marshall S. "Land and Tenancy in the Central Luzon Plain." *Philippine Studies*, vol. 17, no. 4, October 1969.

Meyer, Milton. *A Diplomatic History of the Philippine Republic*. Honolulu: University of Hawaii Press, 1965.

Mijares, Tito A., and Belarmino, I. C. "Some Notes on the Sources of Income Disparities Among Philippine Families." *Journal of Philippine Statistics*, vol. 24, no. 4, 4th quarter 1973.

Millis, Walter, ed. *The Forrestal Diaries*. New York: Viking Press, 1951.

Monaghan, Forbes J. *Under the Red Sun: A Letter from Manila*. New York: Declan X. McMullen Co., 1946.

Morrell, Jim. "Aid to the Philippines: Who Benefits?" *International Policy Report*, vol. 5, no. 2, October 1979.

National Committee for the Restoration of Civil Liberties in the Philippines. "Martial Law *Is* Dictatorship." *Philippines Information Bulletin,* vol. 1, no. 2, March–April 1973.

Neumann, A. Lin. " 'Hospitality Girls' in the Philippines." *Southeast Asia Chronicle,* no. 66, January–February 1979.

Nissen, Bruce. "Building the World Bank." In Steve Weissman et al., *The Trojan Horse: A Radical Look at Foreign Aid.* San Francisco: Ramparts Press, 1974.

Noble, Lela. "Rebellion in the Philippines." *Inquiry,* 2 April 1979.

Overholt, William. "Martial Law, Revolution and Democracy in the Philippines." *Southeast Asia,* vol. 2, no. 2, Spring 1973.

Pal, Agaton. "The Philippines." In Richard D. Lambert and Bert F. Hoselitz eds., *The Role of Savings and Wealth in Southern Asia and the West.* Paris: UNESCO, 1963.

Pascual, Conrado R. "Nutrition Problems and Programs in the Philippines." *Journal of Vitaminology* (Osaka), vol. 14 (Suppl.), 1968.

Payer, Cheryl. "Exchange Controls and National Capitalism: The Philippine Experience." *Journal of Contemporary Asia,* vol. 3, no. 1, 1973.

———. "The IMF and the Third World." In Steve Weissman et al., *The Trojan Horse: A Radical Look at Foreign Aid.* San Francisco: Ramparts Press, 1974.

———. "Martial Law and the Economic Crisis." In *The Philippines: End of an Illusion.* London: Association for Radical East Asian Studies, 1973. (This volume was also published as vol. 2, no. 2, 1973, of *Journal of Contemporary Asia.*)

Perelman, Michael. "Second Thoughts on the Green Revolution." *New Republic,* 17 July 1971.

Peterson, A. H.; Reinhardt, G. C.; and Conger, E. E., eds. *Symposium on the Role of Airpower in Counter-insurgency and Unconventional Warfare: Allied Resistance to the Japanese on Luzon, World War II.* RM-3655-PR. Santa Monica: Rand Corporation, July 1963.

———. *Symposium on the Role of Airpower in Counter-insurgency and Unconventional Warfare: The Philippine Huk Campaign.* RM-3652-PR. Santa Monica: Rand Corporation, June 1963.

Petillo, Carol M. "Douglas MacArthur and Manuel Quezon: A Note on an Imperial Bond." *Pacific Historical Review,* vol. 48, no. 1, February 1979.

Pomeroy, William J. *An American-Made Tragedy: Neo-Colonialism and Dictatorship in the Philippines.* New York: International Publishers, 1974.

———. *American Neo-Colonialism: Its Emergence in the Philippines and Asia.* New York: International Publishers, 1970.

———. "Lessons of the Philippine Guerrilla War." *Monthly Review,* vol. 15, no. 5, September 1963.

Pontius, Dale. "MacArthur and the Filipinos." Part 1. *Asia and the Americas,* vol. 46, no. 10, October 1946.

Power, John H., and Sicat, Gerardo P. "The Philippines: Industrialization and Trade Policies." In *The Philippines and Taiwan.* London: Oxford

University Press for the Development Centre of the Organization for Economic Co-operation and Development, Paris, 1971.

Price, Harry Bayard, ed. *Rural Reconstruction and Development: A Manual for Field Workers.* New York: Praeger Special Studies in International Economics and Development, 1967.

Prouty, L. Fletcher. *The Secret Team: The CIA and Its Allies in Control of the World.* New York: Ballantine Books, 1973.

Quezon, Manuel. *The Good Fight.* New York: D. Appleton-Century, 1946.

Quirino, Carlos. *Magsaysay of the Philippines.* Rizal: Carmelo & Bauermann, 1964.

Ravenholt, Albert. "Rising Expectations—Crisis for the Philippines." *AUFS Fieldstaff Perspectives.* Hanover, N.H., 1971.

———. "So Many Makes for Malnutrition." *AUFS Fieldstaff Reports,* Southeast Asia Series, vol. 22, no. 5, AR-1-'74 (Phil.), August 1974.

———. "Tony Diaz Runs for Congress," *AUFS Fieldstaff Reports,* Southeast Asia Series, vol. 9, no. 5, AR-6-'61, November 1961.

Razon, Felix. "Filipino Muslims and the Revolution." *Philippines Information Bulletin,* vol. 1, no. 2, March–April 1973.

Retizos, Isidro L., and Soriano, D. H. *Philippine Who's Who.* Quezon City: Capitol Publishing House, 1957.

Reyes, Peregrino S., and Chan, Teresita L. "Family Income Distribution in the Philippines." *Statistical Reporter,* vol. 9, no. 2, April–June 1965.

Rice, E. B. "History of AID Programs in Agricultural Credit, 1950–1972." In AID, *Spring Review of Small Farmer Credit.* Vol. 18, Evaluation Paper No. 6. Washington, D.C., June 1973.

Rodgers, Gerry; Hopkins, Mike; and Wéry, René. *Population, Employment and Inequality: BACHUE—Philippines.* Farnborough, England: Saxon House, for the International Labour Office, 1978.

Romani, John H., and Thomas, M. Ladd. *A Survey of Local Government in the Philippines.* Manila: Institute of Public Administration, University of the Philippines, 1954.

Romulo, Carlos P. *Crusade in Asia.* New York: John Day Co., 1955.

Romulo, Carlos P., and Gray, John. *The Magsaysay Story.* New York: John Day Co., 1956.

Rosenberg, David. "The End of the Freest Press in the World." *Bulletin of Concerned Asian Scholars,* vol. 5, no. 1, July 1973.

———. "Liberty versus Loyalty: The Transformation of Philippine News Media under Martial Law." In David A. Rosenberg, ed., *Marcos and Martial Law in the Philippines.* Ithaca, N.Y.: Cornell University Press, 1979.

Rōyama Masamichi and Takéuchi Tatsuji. *The Philippine Polity: A Japanese View.* Edited by Theodore Friend. Monograph Series no. 12, Southeast Asia Studies, Yale University. New Haven: Yale University, 1967.

Ruth, Heather Low. "The Philippines." In The Committee on the International Migration of Talent, *The International Migration of High-Level Manpower: Its Impact on the Development Process.* New York: Praeger Special

Studies in International Economics and Development, in cooperation with Education and World Affairs, 1970.

Ruttan, Vernon W. "Equity and Productivity Issues in Modern Agrarian Reform Legislation." *Philippine Studies,* vol. 14, no. 1, January 1966.

Sacay, Orlando. "Small Farmer Credit in the Philippines." In AID, *Spring Review of Small Farmer Credit.* Vol. 13, Country Papers. Washington, D.C., February 1973.

———. "Small Farmer Savings Behavior," in AID, *Spring Review of Small Farmer Credit.* Vol. 13, Country Papers, Washington, D.C., February 1973.

Sayre, Francis B. *Glad Adventure.* New York: Macmillan, 1957.

Scaff, Alvin H. *The Philippine Answer to Communism.* Stanford: Stanford University Press, 1955.

Schertz, Lyle P. "Factors in Carrying Out Land Reform: Finance." in AID, *Spring Review of Land Reform.* 2nd ed., vol. 11, Analytical Papers. Washington, D.C., June 1970.

Schul, Norman W. "Problems in Land Tenure as Viewed from a Study of the Visayan Sugar Industry." In Charles O. Houston, Jr., ed., *Proceedings of the First National Colloquium on the Philippines,* held in 1966. Kalamazoo: Western Michigan University, 1969.

Seeman, Bernard, and Salisbury, Laurence. *Crosscurrents in the Philippines.* New York: Institute of Pacific Relations, 1946.

Sicat, Gerardo P. *Economic Policy and Philippine Development.* Quezon City: University of the Philippines Press, 1972.

Siegel, Lenny. "Asian Labor: The American Connection." *Pacific Research and World Empire Telegram,* vol. 6, no. 5, July–August 1975.

Smith, Joseph Burkholder. *Portrait of a Cold Warrior.* New York: G. P. Putnam's Sons, 1976.

Smith, Robert Aura. *Philippine Freedom, 1946–1958.* New York: Columbia University Press, 1958.

Smith, Robert Ross. "The Hukbalahap Insurgency: Economic, Political, and Military Factors." Photocopied. Washington, D.C.: Office of the Chief of Military History, Department of the Army, 1963.

Starner, Frances L. *Magsaysay and the Philippine Peasantry: The Agrarian Impact on Philippine Politics, 1953–1956.* Berkeley: University of California Press, 1961.

Stauffer, Robert B. *TNCs and the Transnational Political Economy of Development: The Continuing Philippine Debate.* TNC Research Project Monograph. Sydney, Australia: University of Sydney, forthcoming.

Stein, Nancy, and Klare, Mike. "Police Aid for Tyrants." In Steve Weissman et al., *The Trojan Horse: A Radical Look at Foreign Aid.* San Francisco: Ramparts Press, 1974.

Steinberg, David J. "Jose P. Laurel: A Collaborator Misunderstood." *Journal of Asian Studies,* vol. 24, no. 4, August 1965.

———. *Philippine Collaboration in World War II.* Ann Arbor: University of Michigan Press, 1967.

———. "The Philippines: Survival of an Oligarchy." In Josef Silverstein, ed., *Southeast Asia in World War II: Four Essays*. Monograph Series No. 7, Southeast Asia Studies, Yale University. New Haven: Yale University, 1966.

Stifel, Laurence David. *The Textile Industry: A Case Study of Industrial Development in the Philippines*. Data Paper No. 49, Southeast Asia Program, Cornell University. Ithaca, N.Y.: Cornell University, 1963.

Stimson, Henry L., and Bundy, McGeorge. *On Active Service in Peace and War*. New York: Harper & Bros., 1948.

Suffridge, James A. "The Urgent Needs of Asian Workers." *American Federationist*, vol. 68, no. 7, July 1961.

Szulc, Tad. "The Moveable War." *New Republic*, 12 May 1973. Excerpted in *Philippines Information Bulletin*, vol. 1, no. 4, September 1973.

Tagumpay-Castillo, Gelia. "Toward Understanding the Filipino Farmer." In Raymond E. Borton, ed., *Selected Readings to Accompany 'Getting Agriculture Moving.'* vol. 1. New York: Agricultural Development Council, 1966.

Taruc, Luis. *He Who Rides the Tiger*. New York: Praeger, 1967.

Taylor, George E. *The Philippines and the United States: Problems of Partnership*. New York: Praeger, for the Council on Foreign Relations, 1964.

Thompson, W. Scott. *Unequal Partners: Philippine and Thai Relations with the United States, 1965–75*. Lexington, Mass.: Lexington Books, 1975.

Tilman, Robert O. "The Impact of American Education on the Philippines." *Asia*, no. 21, Spring 1971.

Trinidad, Ruben F. "Tax Policies and Their Influence on Income Distribution: The Philippine Experience." *The Tax Monthly* (Manila), vol. 13, no. 10, October 1973.

Truman, Harry S. *Memoirs*, vol. 1, *Years of Decision*. Garden City, N.Y.: Doubleday & Co., 1955.

Usher, Richard E. "Philippine-American Economic Relations." *Asia*, no. 23, Autumn 1971.

Utrecht, Ernst. "The War in the Southern Philippines." In *The Philippines: End of an Illusion*. London: Association for Radical East Asian Studies, 1973. (This volume was also published as vol. 2, no. 2, 1973, of *Journal of Contemporary Asia*.)

Valeriano, Napoleon D., and Bohannan, Charles T. R. *Counter-Guerrilla Operations: The Philippine Experience*. New York: Praeger, 1962.

Valsan, E. H. *Community Development Programs and Rural Local Development*. New York: Praeger Special Studies in International Economics and Development, 1970.

Vandenbosch, Amry, and Butwell, Richard A. *Southeast Asia Among the World Powers*. Lexington, Ky.: University of Kentucky Press, 1957.

van der Kroef, Justus M. "Communist Fronts in the Philippines." *Problems of Communism*, vol. 16, no. 2, March–April 1967.

Vellut, J. L. *The Asian Policy of the Philippines, 1954–61*. Working Paper No. 6. Canberra: Department of International Relations, Australian National University, 1965.

Viloria, Leandro A. "Manila." In Aprodicio A. Laquian, ed., *Rural-Urban Migrants and Metropolitan Development*. Toronto: INTERMET Metropolitan Studies Series, 1971.

Virata, Cesar, et al. *Restrictions on Exports in Foreign Collaboration Agreements in the Republic of the Philippines*. TD/B/388. New York and Geneva: U.N. Conference on Trade and Development, 1972.

Walterhouse, Harry F. *A Time to Build: Military Civic Action—Medium for Economic Development and Social Reform*. Columbia, S.C.: University of South Carolina Press, 1964.

Weissman, Steve. "Foreign Aid: Who Needs It?" In Steve Weissman et al. *The Trojan Horse: A Radical Look at Foreign Aid*. San Francisco: Ramparts Press, 1974.

Weissman, Steve, and Shoch, John. "CIAsia Foundation." *Pacific Research and World Empire Telegram*, vol. 3, no. 6, September–October 1972.

Wernstedt, Frederick L., and Spencer, J. E. *The Philippine Island World: A Physical, Cultural, and Regional Geography*. Berkeley: University of California Press, 1967.

Westerfield, H. Bradford. *The Instruments of America's Foreign Policy*. New York: Thomas Y. Crowell Co., 1963.

Wharton, Clifton R., Jr. "The Green Revolution: Cornucopia or Pandora's Box." *Foreign Affairs*, vol. 47, no. 3, April 1969.

Whitney, Courtney. *MacArthur: His Rendezvous with History*. New York: Knopf, 1956.

Wilgus, Walter. "MacArthur Campaign Promises Early Independence for Filipinos." *Foreign Policy Bulletin*, vol. 24, no. 14, 19 January 1945.

Willoughby, Charles, and Chamberlain, John. *MacArthur, 1941–1951*. New York: McGraw-Hill, 1954.

Windmiller, Marshall. *The Peace Corps and Pax Americana*. Washington, D.C.: Public Affairs Press, 1970.

Wise, David, and Ross, Thomas B. *The Invisible Government*. New York: Bantam Books, 1964.

Woddis, Jack. *Introduction to Neo-Colonialism*. New York: International Publishers, 1967.

Wolf, Charles, Jr. *Foreign Aid: Theory and Practice in Southern Asia*. Princeton: Princeton University Press, 1960.

———. "Public Policy and Economic Development in the Philippines." *Asian Survey*, vol. 1, no. 10, December 1961.

Wurfel, David. "Foreign Aid and Social Reform in Political Development: A Philippine Case Study." *American Political Science Review*, vol. 53, no. 2, June 1959.

———. "Martial Law in the Philippines: The Methods of Regime Survival." *Pacific Affairs*, vol. 50, no. 1, Spring 1977.

———. "Philippine Agrarian Reform Under Magsaysay (II)," *Far Eastern Survey*, vol. 37, no. 2, February 1958.

———. "The Philippines." In George McT. Kahin, ed., *Governments and Politics of Southeast Asia*. Ithaca, N.Y.: Cornell University Press, 1964.

────. "The Philippines." *Journal of Politics,* vol. 25, no. 4, 1963.

────. "Trade Union Development and Labor Relations Policy in the Philippines." *Industrial and Labor Relations Review,* vol. 12, no. 4, July 1959.

Yoingco, Angel Q. "The Philippine Tax System: Progressive or Regressive." *The Tax Monthly* (Manila), vol. 11, no. 6, December 1970.

Yoshihara, Kunio. "A Study of Philippine Manufacturing Corporations." *Developing Economies,* vol. 9, no. 3, September 1971.

Yost, Israel. "The Food for Peace Arsenal." In Steve Weissman et al. *The Trojan Horse: A Radical Look at Foreign Aid.* San Francisco: Ramparts Press, 1974.

Zack, Arnold. *Labor Training in Developing Countries.* New York: Praeger, 1964.

IV. Unpublished Secondary Sources

Ando, Hirofumi. "Elections in the Philippines: Mass-Elite Interaction Through the Electoral Process, 1946–1969." Ph.D. dissertation, University of Michigan, 1971.

Association of Major Religious Superiors of the Philippines. "National Survey of Public Opinion on Martial Law, October 1973." Manila(?), 1974(?).

Berry, Nicholas O. "Representation and Decision-Making: A Case Study of Philippine-American War Claims." Ph.D. dissertation, University of Pittsburgh, 1967.

Edgerton, Ronald K. "The Politics of Reconstruction in the Philippines, 1945–1948." Ph.D. dissertation, University of Michigan, 1975.

Hoeksema, Renze L. "Communism in the Philippines: A Historical and Analytical Study of Communism and the Communist Party in the Philippines and Its Relations to Communist Movements Abroad." Ph.D. dissertation, Harvard University, 1956.

Kerkvliet, Benedict J. "Land Reform in the Philippines Since the Marcos Coup." Paper read at the annual meeting of the Association of Asian Studies, 1–3 April 1974.

────. "Peasant Rebellion in the Philippines: The Origins and Growth of the HMB." Ph.D. dissertation, University of Wisconsin, 1972.

Landé, Carl H. "Politics in the Philippines." Ph.D. dissertation, Harvard University, 1958.

Schirmer, Daniel B. "The Conception and Gestation of a Neo-Colony." Paper read at the Conference of Asian Studies on the Pacific Coast, San Diego, 14–16 June 1974.

Shantz, Arthur Alan. "Political Parties: The Changing Foundations of Philippine Democracy." Ph.D. dissertation, University of Michigan, 1972.

Simbulan, Dante C. "A Study of the Socio-Economic Elite in Philippine Politics and Government." Ph.D. dissertation, Research School of Social Science, Australian National University, 1965.

Snow, Hugh Bain, Jr. "United States Policy and the 1953 Philippine Presidential Election." Master's thesis, The American University, 1968.

Snyder, Kay A., and Nowak, Thomas C. "Philippine Labor Before Martial Law: Threat or Nonthreat?" Indiana University of Pennsylvania, 1978.

Suva Martin, Felipe. "U.S. Direct Investment in the Philippines." Ph.D. dissertation, MIT, 1972.

Valenzuela, Maria Victoria. "Philippine Policy in Housing the Urban Poor." MCP thesis, MIT, 1974.

Wurfel, Violet E. "American Implementation of Philippine Independence." Ph.D. dissertation, University of Virginia, 1951.

V. Newspapers

This listing includes only those newspapers systematically examined. The period examined is indicated in parenthesis.

Manila Daily Bulletin (1–10 July 1946).
Manila Free Philippines (February 1945–August 1945).
Manila Times (June 1945–July 1946).
New York Times (1944–75).
Philippines Free Press (biweekly) (January 1965–June 1969; January 1970–August 1972).

VI. Miscellaneous

A. LETTERS

A. V. H. Hartendorp to author, 24 October 1968.
Edward G. Lansdale to author, 29 December 1968, 20 May 1975.
Clinton F. Wheeler (Director, Office of Public Affairs, AID) to author, 1 November 1973.

B. INTERVIEWS

Julius C. C. Edelstein, 23 June 1978.
Officer of the Philippine Embassy, Washington, D.C., 27 November 1973.
Richard E. Usher, Philippine Desk Officer, U.S. Department of State, Washington, D.C., 23 November 1973.

C. MISCELLANEOUS MATERIALS SEEN AT THE PHILIPPINE EMBASSY, WASHINGTON, D.C.

Philippine Air Lines. Press Service. *News from the Philippines*, P.O. Box 954, Manila, 09-73, 27 April 1973.

PHILPROM, Inc. *PHILPROM Report on Economic Trends.* Manila, 15 April 1973.

Radio News and Editorial Service. Office of Public Information, Malacañang, Republic of the Philippines (news summary). 22 August 1972.

VII. Unlisted Periodicals

Most articles from the following periodicals are not specifically listed in the bibliography. However, an asterisk indicates that some of the more important articles do appear in Sections II or III above.

Afro-Asian Labour Bulletin (Singapore)
American Chamber of Commerce Journal (Philippines), also called *Journal of the American Chamber of Commerce of the Philippines*
Business Asia
Business Week
Dun and Bradstreet's *International Markets*
Economist Intelligence Unit, *Quarterly Economic Review: Philippines, Taiwan*
Far Eastern Economic Review
I. F. Stone's Weekly
*Journal of Philippine Statistics**
Marketing Horizons (Phil.)
*Nation**
Pacific Imperialism Notebook (San Francisco)
Pahayag (Honolulu)
Parade
Philippine Association, *Weekly Economic Review*
*Philippine Progress**
Philippines Information Bulletin (Cambridge, Mass.)**
Philippine Prospect
Statistical Reporter (Phil.)
Survey of Current Business
Time
U.S. News and World Report

= INDEX =

1 2 3 4 5 6 7 8 9 10 11 12 13   90 89 88 87 86 85 84 83 82 81